A Woman's Guide

to

Coping with Disability

Resources for Rehabilitation
Winchester, Massachusetts

Resources for Rehabilitation
22 Bonad Road
Winchester, Massachusetts 01890
(781) 368-9094   FAX (781) 368-9096
e-mail: info@rfr.org   www.rfr.org

A Woman's Guide to Coping with Disability -- 4th edition

ISBN 0-929718-33-x

Resources for Rehabilitation is a nonprofit organization dedicated to providing training and information to professionals and the public about the needs of individuals with disabilities and the resources available to meet those needs.

Library of Congress Cataloging-in-Publication Data

A woman's guide to coping with disability -- 4th ed.
  p.   cm.
Includes bibliographical references and index.
ISBN 0-929718-33-x (pbk.: alk paper)
1. Women with disabilities--Health and hygiene 2. Women with disabilities--Social conditions
3. Adjustment (Psychology)   I. Resources for Rehabilitation (Organization)
RA778.W718   2003
362.4'082--dc21   2003006063
                                             CIP

This book is printed on acid-free paper.

For a complete listing of publications available from Resources for Rehabilitation, see pages 308 to 312.

TABLE OF CONTENTS

INTRODUCTION

Information can be empowering. For women with disabilities, information can mean the difference between independence and dependence. Having accurate information about programs that provide rehabilitation, training, and special equipment may enable women who would otherwise be institutionalized to live in the community, raise a family, and continue in a career. Knowledge of legal rights and opportunities is essential in our bureaucratic society.

A Woman's Guide to Coping with Disability provides essential information so that women may pursue their rights and obtain the services that enable them to be independent. In addition to providing information that is applicable to any woman with a disability or chronic condition, the book covers conditions that are most prevalent in women and those that are likely to affect women's special roles in society and unique physical functions, such as childbearing. Family members and service providers will also find the book to be extremely useful in their search for appropriate services. Because women have different lifestyles, needs, and degrees of impairment, the book is organized so that each woman may select the resources that are most appropriate to her own specific needs.

Each chapter includes an introductory narrative, information about national organizations that provide services to women with disabilities and chronic conditions, and information about relevant publications and tapes. Chapters 1, 2, and 3, "Women and Disability," "Coping with Daily Activities," and "Laws that Affect Women with Disabilities" provide information that is useful no matter what disability or condition interests the reader.

Beginning with Chapter 4, each chapter has introductory material describing causes and effects of a specific condition; effects of the condition on sexual functioning, pregnancy, and childrearing; psychological aspects; information on professional service providers and where to find services; major organizations serving women with the condition; and publications and tapes. Descriptions of organizations, publications and tapes, and assistive devices are alphabetical within sections. Although many of the publications described are available in libraries or bookstores, the addresses and phone numbers of publishers and distributors are included for those who wish to purchase the books by mail or phone. Only directories that have timely information and those that are updated regularly are included. Some books that are out of print are included; these may be located in libraries or bookstores that specialize in locating out of print books, as well as some online book services. Developments in computer technology, such as e-mail and the Internet, have greatly increased access to information for the general population as well as people with disabilities. E-mail and Internet addresses are given for many organizations listed in this book. Since changes and additions are frequent, readers should check the Internet regularly for updates.

All of the material is up-to-date, and prices were accurate at the time of publication. All prices are in U.S. dollars unless otherwise noted. It is always advisable to contact publishers and manufacturers to inquire about availability and current prices as well as shipping and handling charges.

Developments in computer technology, such as the Internet and e-mail, have greatly increased access to information for the general population as well as people with disabilities and chronic conditions. Internet and e-mail addresses are provided for organizations when available.

The use of "TTY" in the listings indicates a teletypewriter, a special telephone system for individuals who are deaf or have hearing impairments and those who have speech impairments (also known as a "TDD," telecommunication device for the deaf or "TT," text telephone). The use of "V/TTY" indicates that the same telephone number is used for both voice and TTY. Toll-free numbers may begin with "800," "888," "877," or "866."

The phrase "alternate formats" in the listings indicates that, in addition to standard print, publications may also be available in large print, audiocassette, braille, or disk.

Chapter 1

WOMEN AND DISABILITY

Over the years, little attention has bee n paid to the special needs of women with disabilities. Just as those who conduct research in the area of health have historically omitted women from major studies, both researchers and practitioners in the areas of disability and rehabilitation have failed to address the special needs of women with disabilities. A survey of the literature prior to 1985 reveals a dearth of information about women and disability. In the middle of the 1980s, several anthologies were produced addressing this topic and lamenting the lack of attention paid to women's needs (see, for example, Deegan and Brooks: 1985; Fine and Asch: 1988). Virtually all of these collections discussed women as having double disabilities or handicaps, since women's lower status in society was also viewed as a handicap.

Numerous writers have asserted that disabilities are more difficult for women than for men. Fine and Asch (1985) present this point of view, claiming that women are less likely to receive rehabilitation training for paid positions than men; have lower self-esteem than men with disabilities; are "roleless;" and have no role models to emulate. However, Bonwich's (1985) study of women with spinal cord injuries concludes that disability actually resulted in "role expansion;" that is, women were successful in carrying out extremely difficult roles and also had opportunities for education through the vocational rehabilitation system that they would not have had otherwise.

Despite the different interpretations made by these writers, it is apparent that women with disabilities have special needs. From both a statistical perspective and a substantive perspective, the needs of women with disabilities merit much greater attention than they have received. In 1997, women constituted 53.7% of the 52.6 million Americans with disabilities; 20.y7% of women have disabilities compared to 18.6% of men. Women 65 years or older have the highest rate of disability: 57.5% have disabilities, and 41.2% have severe disabilities. Just over half (50.4%) of men in this age range have disabilities. Thus, while women live longer than men, they are more likely to be disabled (McNeil: 2001).

Women play different roles in society than men and thus experience different consequences of disabilities. They are usually the nurturers in our society, providing most of the care for children, elders, and those who are sick. In addition to affecting their caregiving roles, disabilities and chronic conditions often affect the health of women during pregnancy and the health of the fetus. In recent years, most women have expanded their roles to include work outside the home, thus increasing their responsibilities. Balancing family and work can be challenging for any woman, but those with disabilities must seek out innovative solutions to the additional problems caused by their conditions.

WOMEN AND THE HEALTH CARE SYSTEM

The American health care system has always been dominated by men. Until recently, it was rare for a woman to be admitted to medical school, and the few who were admitted experienced the same type of sexism as women patients. Recent articles, some written by women medical students and physicians themselves, reveal how medical textbooks regularly omit the effects of common conditions on women, the disparagement of female medical students by faculty members, and the sexist and debasing language used by male physicians. Until recently, women were systematically excluded from most research studies sponsored by the National Institutes of Health (NIH). To remedy this situation, the NIH Revitalization Act of 1993 (P.L. 103-42) mandates inclusion of women and minorities in research projects sponsored by NIH.

It is common for physicians to assume that women's health complaints are psychosomatic, whereas men's health complaints are assumed to have a physiological basis. Such an assumption not only results in the prescription of unnecessary mood altering drugs for women (Correa: 1975; Howell: 1976), but also may result in missing the diagnoses of serious illness. Numerous studies have documented the differential treatment the health care system provides based on gender. One study of male physicians who treated men and women for five common complaints (back pain, headache, dizziness, chest pain, and fatigue) found that men received more extensive workups than women, suggesting that the physicians took the men's complaints more seriously and viewed the women as hypochondriacal (Armitage et al.: 1979).

Despite the documented findings of sexism practiced by many physicians, women have traditionally made more visits to physicians than men and continued to do so in 2000 (Cherry and Woodwell: 2002). Older women are the most frequent consumers of health services, yet physicians are often uninterested in their needs and overprescribe medications instead of seeking the physiological source of their problems. Raised in a generation that taught them to accept authority without question, older women are the most likely to be docile and accept physicians' prescriptions without question. Furthermore, the physical complaints of older women are often attributed to menopause, psychosomatic causes, or senility (Lewis: 1985; Porcino: 1983).

Since medical education emphasizes acute conditions, many physicians are unfamiliar with the impact of disabilities and the opportunities offered by rehabilitation agencies or have a negative attitude toward rehabilitation. Greenblatt (1989) found that ophthalmologists are themselves unaware of many of the services that exist to help people who are visually impaired or blind. Her study (1991) of people who had recently experienced vision loss found that these individuals are often given a diagnosis with no explanation of the available services or devices that would have enabled them to function independently and to continue working.

A small study by Beckmann and his colleagues (1989) found that most of the women with disabilities they studied had had pelvic examinations and pap smears within the prior 24 months, but their health care providers had not provided information about sexuality. Only one-third of the women felt that their health care providers had enough information about their disabilities to provide information related to sexuality. Nearly half of the women (45.5%) received information about contraception from their health care providers. A later study (Becker et al.: 1997) suggests that the situation has not improved with time. The subjects in this study complained about inaccessible facilities and equipment and some providers' insensitivity and lack of knowledge about disabilities. Providers were surprised to find that women with disabilities were sexually active and therefore did not ask about their need for information about contraception.

Women with disabilities, therefore, face not only the barriers imposed by sex discrimination in the health care system, but also their physicians' lack of knowledge about disabilities and rehabilitation. Compounding these factors are the physical aspects of visiting a physician, including inaccessible examination tables and bathrooms. In addition, women with disabilities are often subject to negative attitudes expressed by staff members who do not know how to accommodate them. According to Nosek (1992), such extreme situations often prevent women with disabilities from seeking out necessary medical care. She also notes that locating an obstetrician/gynecologist who is knowledgeable about the special needs of women with disabilities is extremely difficult.

Given physicians' lack of understanding of the needs and capabilities of women with disabilities, it is not surprising that many women have been advised to have hysterectomies in order to avoid pregnancy. The literature is replete with stories of women who either had medically unnecessary hysterectomies or were advised to have tubal ligations.

Furthermore, women who ask many questions are viewed as "difficult" and as questioning the professionals' competence. Kahan and Gaskill (1978) cite the case of a clinician bemoaning the fact that women have too much information about breast cancer and that "It just stirs them up." Such a statement invalidates a woman's ability to make her own decisions regarding her health care and subjects her to the sole authority of the physician.

Women with disabilities and chronic conditions face a lifetime of visits to physicians and other health care providers. In order to protect their health and obtain information about the best and most recent treatments and products, they must choose their doctors very carefully. Although health maintenance organizations may impose some restrictions on the choice of a physician, in most cases it is possible to "shop around" for a physician. Women should find a physician who takes the time to listen to their complaints, who understands their conditions, and who willingly discusses different treatment approaches and their concomitant risks and benefits. A willingness to respond to a woman's questions and fears, without making her feel that she is taking too much time or is neurotic, is a crucial element in a satisfactory patient-physician relationship.

A woman who feels that her physician does not meet her needs in relation to knowledge about her disability, treatment goals, or communication style should seek another physician. One way to start this process is by asking respected friends and colleagues, preferably those with similar conditions, for referrals. Members of self-help groups or other women's organizations may be good sources. In conducting this search, a woman should phone the prospective physician's office to learn about the physician's office practices, e.g., the physician's knowledge about the woman's condition, who fills in when the physician is not available, physical accessibility of the office and building, times when phone calls are taken, hours of practice, how long it takes to get an appointment, who conducts the examination - the physician or a nurse practitioner. During the first appointment the woman should express her individual needs and concerns in order to discover if the physician's style of practice is amenable. She should make clear what her informational needs are in order to learn if the physician is willing to accommodate them. She should also request copies of all medical reports, including test results, in order to maintain a file of her medical history.

Crewe (1993) refers to a model type of patient-physician relationship for people with disabilities as a consumer-consultant relationship, with greater equality between the participants. Because people who have lived with their disabilities for a period of time become experts not only on the condition itself, but also on their own bodies, they have valuable information to offer to health care providers.

In recent years, some physicians have begun private practices that specialize in women's health. Often these practices include internists, family physicians, and obstetrician/gynecologists with other specialists available for consultation. If these physicians are sensitive to women's needs, they will also have a library or resource center where women may read about their conditions and become knowledgeable about community resources that can help them.

In order to feel that she is obtaining the best possible medical care, a woman should ask questions about the condition, about her specific case, and about alternative treatments and outcomes. The physician may have copies of pertinent articles available to distribute to patients. If no literature is offered, it is a good idea to ask the physician for references on medical studies that support the prescribed treatment method. Physicians who respond that women are unable to understand medical literature feel threatened by questions; those who are confident in their judgment will not hesitate to provide these references. While it is true that not all readers will understand all aspects of every article, most will understand enough to help them with their decisions and to develop a list of additional questions to ask the physician.

Medical school and hospital libraries are often open to the public; if no medical library is available, the local public library or a university library may have medical journals in their collections. Reference librarians at public libraries may obtain copies of articles from other libraries. "Medline," an electronic database with references and abstracts from medical journals, enables users to do subject searches in order to review the pertinent literature on a given condition. "Medline" is available at medical and university libraries, as well as many public libraries. "Medline" is also available on the Internet at no charge (www.nlm.nih.gov).

PSYCHOSOCIAL RESPONSES

Not surprisingly, research has shown a significant relationship between disability and depression. A large community based study of individuals with chronic disabilities (Turner and Wood: 1985) found that over a third of the respondents (34.9%) had high scores on a scale that measured depression, indicating that they were clinically depressed. The proportion of individuals with disabilities who were depressed is higher than what would be expected in the general population. Higher proportions of women (40.1%) were depressed than men (28.9%). Higher proportions of respondents who were separated or divorced were depressed than those who were married, with 65% of separated or divorced women depressed compared to 40% of the men. The same study indicates that psychological adaptation to the disability occurs over time, with those whose disabilities had been present the longest least likely to be depressed. Thus, there is empirical evidence that individuals who become disabled go through different psychological stages, usually resulting in acceptance and adaptation.

An important issue for women with disabilities is the sense of lost control over their bodies and their lives. Bodies that do not function properly can disrupt all aspects of life. Planning medications, special diets, attendant care, special transportation, and inquiring about the accessibility of various facilities can all make a woman feel as though she lives in a different world. Brooks and Matson (1987) have described the broad array of coping mechanisms and skills that individuals with multiple sclerosis must develop in order to feel that they have a sense of control over their condition and their lives. They must make decisions about medications and treatment; search for information about their disease; adapt their environment to accommodate their current situation; and take measures to relieve anxiety, all while facing the uncertainty of flares that require different plans. All of these factors affect employment, family life, and relationships outside the family.

Disability and chronic conditions have different impacts depending upon the stage of life at which they occur. When disabilities are congenital, those affected have never experienced life as able-bodied. Nonetheless, their conditions may cause extreme stress within the family and may result in parents spending a great deal of time with the child who is disabled, to the neglect of other children and the parents' own relationship. In cases where the parents' relationship is not strong enough to withstand this stress and divorce results, the child may always feel guilty about the situation. As children with disabilities enter school and become adolescents, they are subject to rejection by both educational institutions and their peers. Obviously, such rejection can be devastating. When young girls begin dating, those with disabilities often find themselves left out, and counselors at schools are not usually trained to help them. The pattern of rejection continues as the girls mature, and women with disabilities are less likely to have romantic partners, whether they be heterosexual or homosexual. In fact, one of the major problems of women with disabilities is loneliness.

Girls learn at a very early age the importance of physical appearance, which becomes a major part of their self-image. Therefore, when a disability causes disfigurement or a change in bodily functioning, self-esteem may be shattered. Women in this situation often fear rejection by their mates, a fear that is not unrealistic. Even in situations where the mates do not reject women with disabilities, the changes that occur in the sexual and family relationships cause a great deal of additional stress. Women who become disabled or whose chronic conditions occur when they are married and have established families may experience strain within their marriages and families. When women are unable to carry out the roles that they played prior to becoming disabled, their partners or children must fill in the gap. In order to carry out these additional roles, family members must have an understanding of the condition; they must tread a fine line in learning not to do everything for the woman, which may make her feel devalued and guilty. Women whose partners and families become overprotective should draw the line and have frank discussions about their needs, both physical and emotional, and what they can and cannot do. Sexual relations may also be affected, sometimes by the physiological impact of the condition and sometimes due to depression (Rustad: 1984). In strong relationships, where the partner understands the condition and communicates with the woman about both of their needs, the woman benefits from the emotional and instrumental support she receives. As noted above, however, a large portion of women with disabilities live alone and therefore do not receive this support. In addition, women with disabilities are more likely than men to be single heads of families (LaPlante et al.: 1996) and must continue to fulfill this role following the onset of their disability or chronic condition. In cases where conditions flare and abate, emotions may be in constant upheaval, affecting all members of the family.

At midlife, women face a variety of changes that may cause anxiety and depression. Many middle-aged women are facing the "empty nest" syndrome, a situation which may be especially difficult for those who derived their primary identity from being mothers. Normal physical changes, such as aging skin and other symbols of decline in culturally defined physical beauty, contribute to a woman's decreased sense of self-worth. Adding a newly acquired disability to these other major changes in a woman's life may make coping seem an overwhelming task. Support from family, friends, and other women in similar situations may prove invaluable in helping middle-aged women to make the transition from healthy young women to this new stage of life. Williams, writing about women who have reached menopause, notes:

> Women whose self-esteem is intact, whose lives continue to be interesting and rewarding, and whose work, whatever its nature, helps them to feel that they are making a continuing contribution to the society, are the least likely to have negative reactions to the change of life. (1987, 490)

Those women who have acquired disabilities or chronic conditions and who find ways to be productive may also have an easier time adjusting to their new status.

In 1990, there were 31.1 million Americans age 65 or older; of these, 18.6 million were women, and 2.2 million women were age 85 or older. The growth in the older population is expected to continue through the middle of the twenty-first century, because of the aging of the baby boom generation. Women live longer than men, but they also experience higher rates of disabilities. Women 65 years or older are less likely than men to be employed, more likely to be poor, have lower pensions, and less likely to be married (Taeuber and Allen: 1993).

Older women with disabilities and chronic conditions face a different set of circumstances than younger women. Most elders live in the community and nearly a third (30.5%) live alone (U.S. Department of Health and Human Services: 1991). The older a woman gets, the more likely she is to live alone, with over half (54.0%) of all women 85 years or older living alone (U.S. Bureau of the Census: 1990). Older women are often coping with multiple disabilities, including osteoporosis, arthritis, and sensory impairments. For many women, living alone requires a great deal of adaptation, as they had spent many years living with a partner. Members of the oldest group of women have often outlived their friends and relatives, sometimes including their own children. Their support systems are composed of adult offspring, primarily daughters. In cases where daughters do not live in the same area as their mothers, mothers may feel extremely lonely and isolated. Other relatives and friends may be available, but offspring have traditionally been the caregivers for their mothers. Mothers with disabilities who do not have support systems available may have extreme difficulties in coping with their disabilities and experience psychological distress as well. In fact, when applied to a population of elders, the items on a widely used scale designed to measure depression were virtually all significantly associated with physical disability (Berkman et al.: 1986).

How an older woman adapts to recently acquired disabilities depends in part on the coping mechanisms she has developed over a lifetime. Kivnick's (1991) study of elders who ranged from their early 70s to their middle 90s found that those who had developed strong coping mechanisms prevented their disabilities from becoming major handicaps by encapsulating them into one specific area of life and compensating with other behaviors. Those who had more "fragile" personalities were more likely to respond to their disabilities with a sense of despair.

Accepting a disability takes time and the support of others, including family, friends, and women with similar conditions. Sherr Klein, a woman who experienced a severe stroke in mid-life, wrote about her experiences and ultimate acceptance of her new status. Her experience exemplifies how a disability becomes an overriding part of a woman's identity, outweighing her socioeconomic characteristics. However, Sherr Klein's gender and her identity as a feminist enabled her to accept her new status:

> I discover it is easier for me to be a disabled feminist than a disabled person.
> Feminism means loving myself as I am. After three long years, I am finally ready
> to accept myself as permanently, irrevocably disabled... (Sherr Klein: 1992, 73)

Accepting the limitations of a disability or chronic condition is not only psychologically liberating, but also makes daily living easier. Zola (1991) discovered that when he finally accepted the label "disabled," he was able to accept the types of assistance he needed in order to make living less of a challenge to his ego. Thus, when he went to airports, he no longer had to prove that he could walk long distances with his crutches but was willing to accept a wheelchair that made his travel easier and enabled him to use his energy for the purpose of his trip. For women with disabilities whose self-esteem is low, reaching this point may be difficult and take time. The willingness to accept assistance, without viewing it as a threat to independence, can help older individuals retain control over their own lives (Kivnick: 1991). The acceptance of realistic limitations and abilities may result in the restoration of self-esteem, the sense of control over life, and pride in achievements for women in all stages of life.

REHABILITATION FOR WOMEN

Rehabilitation services are available from both public and private providers. The federal government funds rehabilitation services by funneling money to the states. Each state must submit a plan to the federal government indicating how the designated state agency will provide the services required by law. Rehabilitation includes counseling, vocational assessment, job training and placement, provision of assistive technology, training in activities of daily living and homemaking, and transportation services. Women may locate their state's vocational rehabilitation agency by contacting the telephone information operator for the state government.

Originally designed primarily as vocational rehabilitation services, the goals of rehabilitation have been expanded to include the role of homemaker. While learning or re-learning the skills necessary to maintain a home is desirable in order to maintain independence, several studies suggest that women are more likely to receive rehabilitation that trains them to be homemakers, while men receive services that enable them to obtain paid employment (Altman: 1985; Thurber: 1991). Mudrick's study (1987) of recipients of vocational rehabilitation age 50 to 64 years found that women were as likely to receive rehabilitation services as men, but they were less likely to receive job oriented services and more likely to receive physical therapy. A 1993 report by the General Accounting Office cited 1980 data indicating that 29% of women with physical disabilities were rehabilitated as homemakers compared to 8% of men; 83% of men were rehabilitated for competitive employment compared to 67% of women.

Relegating women to the role of homemaker reveals a sexist attitude on the part of the service providers and forces women to remain dependent upon governmental assistance programs for their income. Women should be aware of their options in setting rehabilitation goals. Under federal law, an Individual Written Rehabilitation Program (IWRP) that specifies rehabilitation goals and the services to be provided by the vocational rehabilitation agency must be jointly developed and signed by both the client and the counselor. This means that the woman must agree to both the goals and the means of reaching these goals. Women should ask questions, express interests, and request to see the law when they feel that they are not receiving the services they are entitled to. The IWRP may be amended or modified with reasonable justification and agreement by both parties.

Women who do not know the type of position they are best qualified for should request a functional assessment and a vocational aptitude test. If the vocational rehabilitation agency delays or denies them the opportunity for job training, they should contact the Client Assistance Program. Established under an amendment to the federal Rehabilitation Act (P.L. 98-221), this program informs clients of their rights and all available benefits and assists them in obtaining all remedies due under the law. If this course of action does not result in satisfaction, attorneys who specialize in disability law can provide additional assistance (see Chapter 3, "Laws that Affect Women with Disabilities").

Women with severe disabilities often require assistance with personal care, transportation, and special equipment. Independent living programs enable people with disabilities to continue functioning within the community with assistance. A crucial element of the independent living movement is that consumers have control over the types of services provided. For some, this means living at home, with or without attendant care, and maintaining employment. Attendants assist people with disabilities in activities such as bathing, grooming, dressing, food preparation, and household tasks. Provisions of both Social Security and Medicaid laws have been used to finance the services of attendants. Women with disabilities or chronic conditions may opt to live in group residences, where individuals live under supervision but maintain a degree of responsibility for their own care and maintenance. Independent living programs or centers are sometimes administered by state vocational rehabilitation agencies and sometimes are free-standing organizations administered by individuals with disabilities themselves.

The Center for Women Veterans was established by the Department of Veterans Affairs (VA) to ensure that VA health care and benefits programs are responsive to the gender-specific needs of women veterans. The VA offers services such as counseling for sexual trauma, mammography, Pap smears, and general reproductive health care. There are full-time Women Veterans Coordinators at most VA Medical Centers. Women veterans are eligible for benefits such as disability compensation for service related disabilities; disability pensions for non-service related disabilities; vocational rehabilitation and counseling; education assistance; insurance; home loan benefits; and nursing home care.

(See chapters on specific conditions for information about how sexual functioning is affected by the condition.)

Women find that their disability becomes their primary identity to others, often resulting in rejection by potential sexual partners. The literature repeatedly quotes women with disabilities, whether their disabilities are congenital or acquired later in life, as being viewed by others as asexual. One woman with a mobility impairment noted:

> Once the other person perceives the disability, the switch on the sexual circuit breaker often pops off - the connection is broken. "Chemistry" is over. I have a lifetime of such experiences, and so does every other disabled woman I know.
> (King: 1993, 72)

Since women in our society are raised to place great value on physical attractiveness, women with disabilities may internalize the view that they are unattractive. Meeting people and seeking potential sexual partners are not only challenging, but may also be assaults on the woman's self-esteem. King notes that she never accepts a date with someone until the other person has seen her walking, to ensure that her disability is made known.

Women who experienced disabilities before adolescence report that their social and sexual encounters occur later and less frequently than those of their peers who were not disabled; they attribute these differences to physical barriers, lack of self-confidence, and negative stereotypes held by peers (Rousso: 1988). The possibility of spasticity during sexual encounters, incontinence, and the use of assistive devices all contribute to the difficulties women with disabilities have in approaching sexual relations with new partners. Parents often counsel their daughters with disabilities to focus on other sources of success, as they fear that they will not be successful in sexual relationships.

Some women with disabilities enter relationships that are less than satisfactory and possibly even abusive, because they fear that no one else will ever want them. Vash (1993) relates the story of how, after becoming paralyzed in her teens, she married a man who convinced her that he was the only one who would want her.

A study compared women with disabilities (most had mobility impairments) to women who did not have disabilities (Nosek et al.: 1996). Based on self-administered questionnaires, the study found significant differences between the two groups relative to sexual activity, sexual response, and sexual satisfaction; mean scores for these three variables were higher for the women who did not have disabilities. A fourth component of sexual function, sexual desire, did not appear to be significantly different for the two groups. Severity of disability was not significantly related to sexual activity. The strongest predictor of sexual activity was living with a significant other.

Women who experience disabilities while in an established relationship may avoid resuming sexual activity for fear of failure. Both the woman and her partner may have grave concerns over the new character of their relationship. Mobility impairment, loss of sensation, spasticity, and bowel and bladder incontinence may all seem insurmountable problems at first. Learning new positions for intercourse, additional means of stimulation, and ways to avoid embarrassing leakage problems due to incontinence will relieve the sexual partners of these fears. Sexual counseling, as a couple or in group sessions, can provide invaluable information on these topics. To a great extent, the couple's success at restructuring their sexual relationship depends upon the quality of their relationship prior to the disability; those who had good communications are more likely to be able to discuss their fears and needs openly (Lemon: 1993).

Lesbians with disabilities find that they are marginal to several different movements that are seeking equality for their members: the gay rights movement, the women's movement, and the disability rights movement. The view that heterosexuals have of people with disabilities as being asexual is evidently held for lesbians as well. For example, one lesbian with a disability noted the response she received from a colleague when she declared that she was a lesbian, "How can you be a lesbian if you have no sex?" (Boston Women's Health Book Collective: 1992). Health care providers often ignore the supportive role played by partners of women who are gay and eliminate them from the care of the woman with a disability or chronic condition (Lewis: 1985).

Birth control is another issue that presents special problems for women with disabilities. Women with mobility problems may have difficulty using barrier methods of contraception, such as the diaphragm. Some physical conditions are not amenable to the use of oral contraceptives, as the risks for side effects are increased. The elimination of these methods leaves few alternatives for women with disabilities. One relatively new contraceptive is Norplant, the implantation of a synthetic progesterone that prevents ovulation for as long as five years. Although side effects are minimal, women who take certain antiepileptic drugs are advised against using Norplant (Murphy: 1993). In addition, women have filed suit against the manufacturer of Norplant for pain and scarring associated with its removal.

It is common for both health care providers and rehabilitation professionals to ignore issues of sexuality for women with disabilities. Although the woman's condition itself may cause sexual dysfunction, it is rare to find programs that deal with sexuality, especially for women. Often the programs that do exist are oriented exclusively to the sexual dysfunctions of men. Rehabilitation counselors often ignore sexual orientation, assuming that clients are heterosexual and ignoring lesbian sexuality (Lonsdale: 1990).

Although not all sex therapists are familiar with the needs of women with disabilities, they may prove to be helpful if they are willing to learn about the functional effects of the disability from health care specialists (Cole: 1988) and from the women themselves. Once they are familiar with the woman's mobility limitations, the areas in which she feels stimulation, and other physical factors that affect sexual functioning, the therapist may use traditional history taking and counseling to learn about the woman's psychological attitudes toward sex. With this information, the therapist may help the woman and her partner to learn to feel comfortable with her body and to communicate effectively for a satisfactory sexual relationship.

PREGNANCY AND CHILDREARING

(See chapters on specific conditions for information about how pregnancy and childrearing are affected by the condition.)

Women with disabilities are often counseled by physicians to be sterilized; those already pregnant are advised to have abortions. This advice is often given by physicians who are unfamiliar with the impact of the disability on the woman's ability to live independently. With most of the disabilities and chronic conditions that are prevalent in women, fertility is unaffected and pregnancy runs a normal course, although extra precautions are sometimes necessary. With some conditions, such as rheumatoid arthritis, pregnancy may actually result in the remission of symptoms, while other conditions, such as epilepsy, may be exacerbated by pregnancy.

Women who are concerned about the possibility of passing their disability on to their children should seek out genetic counseling. Genetic counselors take detailed personal and family health histories to learn about hereditary and environmental causes of disease. They may perform tests to determine if the parents are carriers of genes that cause diseases. Counselors should present information concerning the probability of passing on a given condition but should not be directive in telling prospective parents whether to have children. Providing emotional and educational support for parents is an important function for the counselor, no matter what the couple's decision (Davis: 1978).

In making the decision whether or not to become pregnant, a number of factors should be considered. Among them are the effects of pregnancy on the mother's health; risks to the child; and ability to care for the child. Women who use medications to control symptoms or pain caused by their condition must learn whether these drugs will have deleterious effects on the fetus. Women who experience fatigue as a result of their condition may need to have assistance from a family member or a paid helper. The woman whose condition is exacerbated by fatigue must think about her daily schedule and how it will be affected by pregnancy. The logistics of child care should be discussed with the prospective father and planned in advance to avoid a crisis after the baby arrives. Financial aspects, such as the cost of paid help, should also be considered; some states that provide personal attendants to help the mother do not permit them to perform child care tasks. Mothers who delegate most of their child's care to others may feel left out and unable to bond with their child. Therefore, plans for child care should include the mother to the greatest extent possible.

Women with disabilities feel better about becoming mothers when their partner, family, and friends offer emotional support and help with child care. Roles for taking care of the new baby should be worked out in advance of the birth to avoid the possibility of conflict later. In some cases, fathers may resent the woman with a disability if the additional responsibilities they undertake during pregnancy must be continued after delivery, especially if a flare of the condition occurs. This possibility should be discussed and alternatives planned, so that the father is able to continue with his other activities as well as his share of child care.

Charlifue and colleagues (1992) found that having a child can be overwhelming for women who use wheelchairs. However, the decision to have a child must be a personal one. Campion (1990) suggests that women talk with other women with similar conditions who have children to learn about their experiences with pregnancy and with childrearing.

Once the decision has been made to have a child, finding an obstetrician who is sensitive to the needs of pregnant women with disabilities is the next step, and it may prove to be the most difficult part of the process. Obstetricians are not trained to work with women with disabilities and often have no specialized knowledge of the particular condition involved and its effects on pregnancy. For example, a list of specialists for women with spinal cord injuries included only three physicians in the entire country who specialized in treating pregnant women with this condition. Although it is unlikely that the obstetrician will be a specialist in disabilities, s/he should listen carefully to the woman's description of her condition, her limitations, and her abilities. S/he should also be willing to work with other medical specialists to provide multidisciplinary care.

The physical accessibility of the physician's office may become an issue if the woman needs to use a wheelchair or scooter. Since many obstetrical practices employ several physicians who fill in for each other, it is important that each physician be familiar with the woman's disability and the course of care that has been agreed upon. Other women with disabilities who have children may be the best source of referrals; talking with them may also alleviate the sense of isolation that many pregnant women with disabilities experience. Shaul and her colleagues (1985) discovered that pregnant women with disabilities found the usual informational systems available for pregnant women without disabilities to be very useful for them as well.

A case report (Wasser et al.: 1993) by a woman who has multiple sclerosis and who decided to have a baby illustrates the frustrations that many women with disabilities experience when they decide to have a child. The woman had developed her own methods of self-care to alleviate some of the symptoms of her multiple sclerosis over the course of her disease. When she decided to become pregnant and sought medical care, her physicians refused to acknowledge that her methods were effective and insisted that she first try traditional methods. Not only did her physicians fail to act jointly to coordinate her care, but they failed to provide her with the information she needed to make decisions. She responded by becoming her own de facto case manager, searching for information at medical libraries when her physicians failed to provide sufficient information. Taking this type of assertive action, however, requires a certain type of personality and the education necessary to locate medical literature. This information is becoming more accessible through the availability of "Medline," a medical database, at public libraries and over the Internet.

Pregnant women with disabilities may need to be monitored more closely than other women. They may require more frequent visits to the obstetrician, even in the first weeks of pregnancy. Women with diabetes may need to monitor their blood glucose more frequently than usual, as the metabolic changes caused by pregnancy alter glucose processing. Women with spinal cord injuries sometimes need to be hospitalized at the thirty-second week of gestation in order to prepare for labor. In some instances, a cesarean delivery may be necessary.

Teaching the new mother to diaper and bathe her infant may require devising adaptive techniques. Rehabilitation nurses and occupational therapists may work with the maternity nurse and mother to develop these techniques. Hospitals and health maintenance organizations offer classes in child care for prospective parents. Inquiring in advance about the accessibility of the facility and the instructor's knowledge about the effects of the woman's functional disabilities on child care can help the prospective parents find the best program for their specific needs. Since many new mothers with disabilities experience even greater fatigue than mothers without disabilities, it is important to consider labor saving methods.

Modifications to the environment and adaptations to regular equipment to care for babies may be necessary, especially for mothers with mobility impairments. Many women and their families are creative in designing their own baby carriers to attach to wheelchairs and modifying or making changing tables so that a wheelchair fits underneath. Babies learn very quickly to cooperate in ways that accommodate their mothers' needs, by turning their head to find their mother's breast, raising their body for diapering, and holding on for security. A nursing pillow that supports the baby while breastfeeding and a breastpump that is operated by foot enable mothers with mobility impairments to nurse more confidently

Couples may find it useful to consult with an occupational therapist, who can make suggestions for adaptive equipment and also suggest safety guidelines. It is important that parents "child proof" their homes while being careful to keep them accessible for the mother. Safety latches for cabinets may be difficult for women with joint disease to open; baby gates must be easy to open for mothers while keeping the toddler safe. Talking with experienced parents may allay many fears and provide a source for adaptive equipment.

Some mothers with disabilities worry about the effect that their disability will have on their children as they grow up. Children of women with disabilities learn at a very early age that they must respond to their mother's verbal admonitions regarding their behavior. In the case of women whose disabilities occur after they have established families, the children may take a long time to adjust to their mother's disabilities and altered lifestyles (Shaul et al.: 1985). Mothers have reported that their disabilities resulted in their children becoming independent, providing support for their mothers, and developing a sensitivity to people who have disabilities. Some mothers, however, are concerned that their children become too independent at an early age and give up some of their childhood in order to help the mothers. Mothers whose disabilities flare worry that their role in their children's lives is inconsistent; these mothers try to provide consistent emotional support as a balance (Thorne: 1990).

Perhaps the greatest barriers to childrearing for women with disabilities are the attitudes expressed by others. As the child begins to socialize with other children and attend school, s/he may be stigmatized by the mother's disability. Parents of other children may be reluctant to let them play at the home of a child whose mother has a disability. Being forthright and explaining the condition and the safety precautions taken for the child's welfare may alleviate some of the fears expressed by other parents. Some mothers deal with these concerns by meeting with teachers before their child starts school, in order to become comfortable with the teacher and vice versa. When parents with disabilities are familiar sights at school activities, everyone benefits. One way to educate children and parents about disabilities is having them participate in exercises where they simulate the conditions in order to learn the limitations imposed by the condition as well as the abilities maintained. Some schools now implement special curricula to teach children about disabilities.

COMPUTERS AND DISABILITIES

Personal computers (PCs) have opened up a wide variety of opportunities for people who have disabilities or chronic conditions. Used alone, adapted computers enable individuals to perform tasks that would otherwise be inaccessible to them; retaining a job is just one major opportunity that computers offer to people with disabilities. Using computers with the Internet or online subscription services, individuals are able to communicate with people all over the world. This instant communication provides up-to-the-minute information about new developments and the opportunity to "chat" with individuals in similar situations. Many of these services are free, with the exception of telephone charges or subscription fees for online services.

World wide web sites provide access to information from service agencies, educational institutions, the government, and commercial organizations. Most search engines provide information on health and disability.

World Wide Web pages provide access to information from service agencies, professional societies, educational institutions, and commercial organizations, as well as individuals who have established their own pages. Web sites listed throughout this book provide links to a wide variety of disability resources.

A variety of formats is available to receive and exchange information. When you join a usenet group, you may read messages and respond to them as well as submit your own information and questions. In order to join a usenet group, your host computer must provide access. When you subscribe to a usenet group, you will automatically receive all new messages whenever you log on. If you decide to exchange messages with just one member, you may send mail directly to that individual's e-mail address.

Listserv enables you to receive information by sending a message to an e-mail address stating you would like to subscribe. You may add your own messages which may in turn generate responses from other members of a group. Protocol requires that you then summarize your responses and mail them to all other members of the listserv group.

PubMed is a web site that provides access to MEDLINE, a medical database that enables the user to perform searches of the medical literature by topic and author. PubMed is available over the Internet at no charge, directly from the National Library of Medicine, as are several other online databases. MEDLINE performs searches of major medical journals and provides both citations and abstracts of articles. After searching MEDLINE and reading abstracts of the articles on the web site, it is possible to order the articles. You may also find the articles at local libraries. If your library

Rousso, Harilyn
1988   "Daughters with Disabilities: Defective Women or Minority Women?" pp. 139-171 in
          Michelle Fine and Adrienne Asch (eds.) Women with Disabilities: Essays in Psychology,
          Culture and Politics Philadelphia, PA: Temple University Press

Rustad, Lynne C.
1984   "Family Adjustment to Chronic Illness and Disability in Mid-Life" pp. 222-242 in Myron
          G. Eisenberg, LaFaye C. Sutkin, and Mary A. Jansen (eds.) Chronic Illness and Disability
          through the Life Span New York, NY: Springer Publishing Company

Shaul, Susan, Pamela J. Dowling, and Bernice F. Laden
1985   "Like Other Women: Perspectives of Mothers with Physical Disabilities" pp. 133-142 in
          Mary Jo Deegan and Nancy A. Brooks (eds.) Women and Disability: The Double Handicap
          New Brunswick, NJ: Transaction

Sherr Klein, Bonnie
1992   "We Are Who You Are" Ms. III(November/December):3:70-74

Taeuber, Cynthia M. and Jessie Allen
1993   "Women in Our Aging Society: The Demographic Outlook" pp. 11-45 in Jessie Allen and
          Allen Pifer (eds.) Women on the Front Lines: Meeting the Challenge of an Aging America
          Washington, DC: Urban Institute Press

Thorne, Sally E.
1990   "Mothers with Chronic Illness: A Predicament of Social Construction" Health Care for
          Women International 11:209-221

Thurber, Shari L.
1991   "Women and Rehabilitation" pp. 32-38 in Robert P. Marinelli and Arthur E. Dell Orto
          (eds.) The Psychological and Social Impact of Disability New York, NY: Springer
          Publishing Company

Turner, R. Jay and D. William Wood
1985   "Depression and Disability: The Stress Process in a Chronically Strained Population"
          Research in Community and Mental Health 5:77-109

U.S. Bureau of the Census
1990   "Marital Status and Living Arrangements March 1989" Current Population Reports, Series
          P-20 No. 445(June) cited in U.S. Senate Special Committee on Aging in America: Trends
          and Projections 1991 Edition

U.S. Department of Health and Human Services
1991   Aging in America: Trends and Projections Washington, DC: U.S. Department of Health
          and Human Services, DHHS Publication No. (FCoA) 91-28001

Vash, Carolyn L.
1993   "Sexuality Ascending" Sexuality and Disability 11:2:149-157

Wasser, Andrea M., Carrie L. Killoran, and Sarah S. Bansen
1993   "Pregnancy and Disability" AWHONN's Clinical Issues 4:2:328-337

Williams, Juanita
1987   Psychology of Women: Behavior in a Biosocial Context New York, NY: W. W. Norton

Zola, Irving Kenneth
1991   "Bringing Our Bodies and Ourselves Back In: Reflections on a Past, Present, 'Medical
          Sociology'" Journal of Health and Social Behavior 32(March):1-16

ORGANIZATIONS

<u>Agency for Healthcare Research and Quality</u> (AHRQ)
540 Gaither Road
Rockville, MD 20850
(301) 427-1200   e-mail: info@ahrq.gov   www.ahrq.gov

A federal agency that funds research studies on effectiveness of medical treatments, economic aspects of health care policy, and quality of care. In 1999, legislation reauthorizing the agency required that it study the needs of special populations, such as women and individuals with disabilities; this mandate is addressed by the Office of Priority Populations within AHRQ. Publishes monthly newsletter, "Research Activities." Free. Newsletter and reports also available on the web site.

<u>American Association of Sex Educators, Counselors and Therapists</u> (AASECT)
PO Box 5488
Richmond, VA 23220
e-mail: aasect@aasect.org   www.aasect.org

A membership organization for professionals who counsel individuals with sexual dysfunctions. Membership, individuals, $160.00; organizations, $360.00; includes monthly newsletter, "Contemporary Sexuality." Newsletter only, $42.00. AASECT will provide lists of its members in a local geographic area upon receipt of a self-addressed, stamped, business size envelope. Also available on the web site.

<u>American Disabled for Attendant Programs Today</u> (ADAPT)
201 South Cherokee
Denver, CO 80223
(303) 733-9324

or

<u>ADAPT\Incitement</u>
1339 Lamar SQ Drive, Suite 101
Austin, TX 78704
(512) 442-0252   FAX (512) 442-0522
e-mail: adapt@adapt.org   www.adapt.org

An organization dedicated to changing the structure of long term care and helping people with disabilities live in the community with supports instead of being sent to nursing homes and other institutions. Publishes "INCITEMENT," a newsletter describing ADAPT activities, three or four times a year (available in standard print and on audiocassette), free. ADAPT has supported federal legislation, the Medicaid Community-Based Attendant Services and Supports Act (MiCASSA), to provide personal attendants to individuals with disabilities. No membership fees, but a willingness to participate in ADAPT's activities is required.

American Medical Women's Association (AMWA)
801 North Fairfax Street, Suite 400
Alexandria, VA 22314-1757
(703) 838-0500   FAX (703) 549-3864
e-mail: info@amwa-doc.org   www.amwa-doc.org

A professional membership organization for women in the field of medicine. Addresses health issues specific to women and promotes equal status for women within the field of medicine. Publishes booklets to guide women who are contemplating a career in medicine and a directory of members. Some publications are available on the web site. Some branches offer referrals to local women physicians.

American Self-Help Clearinghouse
100 Hanover Avenue, Suite 202
Cedar Knolls, NJ 07927
(973) 326-6789   FAX (973) 326-9467   www.selfhelpgroups.org

Provides information and contacts for national self-help groups, information on model groups and individuals who are starting new networks, and state or local self-help clearinghouses.

Center for Research on Women with Disabilities (CROWD)
Baylor College of Medicine
3440 Richmond Avenue, Suite B
Houston, TX 77046
(800) 442-7693   (713) 960-0505 (V/TTY)   FAX (713) 961-3555
e-mail: crowd@bcm.tmc.edu   www.bcm.tmc.edu/crowd

A federally funded center that conducts research and develops and distributes information on the health and independence of women with disabilities. Research areas include sexuality, relationships, general health, reproductive health, and abuse. Executive Summary of a four year "National Study on Women with Disabilities" is available on the web site in English and Spanish. Entire report available on the web site in English. Free

Center for Women Veterans
Department of Veterans Affairs (VA)
Central Office (OOW)
810 Vermont Avenue, NW
Washington, DC 20420
(202) 273-6193   FAX (202) 273-7092
(800) 827-1000 (connects with regional offices)
www.va.gov/womenvet

Congress has mandated the establishment of several Comprehensive Women's Centers around the country to provide medical and mental health care; however, all VA Medical Centers have clinics for women veterans. Disability need not be service connected in order to receive services.

Combined Health Information Database (CHID)
Ovid Technologies, Attn: CHID Database
333 7th Avenue
New York, NY 10001
(800) 950-2035   (212) 563-3006
e-mail: chid@aerie.com   chid.nih.gov

A federally sponsored database that includes bibliographic citations and abstracts from journals, reports, books, and patient education brochures.

Commission on Accreditation of Rehabilitation Facilities (CARF)
4891 East Grant Road
Tucson, AZ 85712
(520) 325-1044 (V/TTY)   FAX (520) 318-1129
e-mail: webmaster@carf.org   www.carf.org

Conducts site evaluations and accredits organizations that provide rehabilitation, pain management, adult day services; and assisted living. Provides a free list of accredited organizations in a specific state.

Commission on Rehabilitation Counselor Certification
1835 Rohlwing Road, Suite E
Rolling Meadows, IL 60008
(847) 394-2104   www.crccertification.com

Provides certification to rehabilitation counselors.

Disabilityinfo.gov
www.disabilityinfo.gov

This web site, sponsored by the federal government, provides information about issues such as civil rights, employment, transportation, education, and housing as they relate to people with disabilities.

Genetic Alliance
4301 Connecticut Avenue, NW, Suite 404
Washington, DC 20008
(800) 336-4363   (202) 966-5557   FAX (202) 966-8553
e-mail: info@geneticalliance.org   www.geneticalliance.org

This coalition of individuals, professionals, and genetic support groups provides education and services to families and individuals affected by genetic disorders. The "Alliance Directory of National Genetic Support Organizations and Related Resources" is available as a searchable database on the web site.

Healthpages
www.thehealthpages.com

Provides articles on a wide variety of diseases and conditions. Also provides information on physicians and facilities that treat specific disorders in specified metropolitan areas.

Provides a single access point to the National Institutes of Health, including their individual clearinghouses, publications, and the Combined Health Information Database. Provides information on hotlines, PubMed, clinical trials and drug information.

National Library of Medicine (NLM)
8600 Rockville Pike
Building 38, Room 2S-10
Bethesda, MD 20894
(888) 346-3656   (301) 594-5983
www.nlm.nih.gov/PubMed

Operates PubMed, a web site which provides access to MEDLINE, a computerized database that provides access to articles in major medical journals from around the world. Users may search for a specific health related topic and receive citations and abstracts of articles. Available directly through NLM's web site and at most medical, public, and university libraries. Additional databases such as DIRLINE (Directory of Health Organizations), AIDSLINE, and AIDSDRUGS are also available. Also publishes clinical alerts online.

National Library Service for the Blind and Physically Handicapped (NLS)
1291 Taylor Street, NW
Washington, DC 20542
(800) 424-8567 or (800) 424-8572 (Reference Section)
(800) 424-9100 (to receive application)
(202) 707-5100   (202) 707-0744 (TTY)
FAX (202) 707-0712   e-mail: nls@loc.gov   www.loc.gov/nls

Provides services to all adults and children with print handicaps, including those who cannot hold a book or turn pages, through a network of regional libraries. Provides publications in braille, disc, and the machines to play them. Some NLS libraries also distribute large print books. A health professional must certify that the individual is unable to hold a book or turn pages; has blurred or double vision; extreme weakness or excessive fatigue; or other physical limitations which prevent her from reading standard print. All services from NLS are free.

National Organization for Rare Disorders (NORD)
55 Kenosia Avenue
PO Box 1968
Danbury, CT 06813-1968
(800) 999-6673 (voice mail only)   (203) 744-0100   (203) 797-9590 (TTY)
FAX (203) 798-2291   e-mail: orphan@rarediseases.org
www.rarediseases.org

Federation of voluntary health organizations that serve individuals with rare or "orphan" diseases. Rare disease, organization, and orphan drug databases may be searched online. Maintains a confidential patient networking program for individuals and family members who have been diagnosed with a rare disorder. Offers a Medication Assistance Program. Membership, $30.00, includes news-letter, "Orphan Disease Update," published three times a year. Reprints of articles on rare diseases available for $7.50 a copy; abstracts are free on the web site.

National Organization on Disability (NOD)
910 16th Street, NW, Suite 600
Washington, DC 20006
(202) 293-5960   (202) 293-5968 (TTY)
FAX (202) 293-7999   e-mail: ability@nod.org   www.nod.org

An organization dedicated to achieving the full participation of people with disabilities in all aspects of community life. Works with a network of local agencies to achieve this goal. Provides technical assistance and maintains an informational database.

National Rehabilitation Association (NRA)
633 South Washington Street
Alexandria, VA 22314
(703) 836-0850   (703) 836-0849 (TTY)
FAX (703) 836-0848   e-mail: info@nationalrehab.org
www.nationalrehab.org

A membership organization for rehabilitation professionals and independent living center affiliates. Includes special divisions for independent living, counseling, job placement, etc. Legislative alerts appear on NRA's web site. Regular membership, $110.00, includes "Journal of Rehabilitation" and newsletter, "Contemporary Rehab."

National Rehabilitation Information Center for Independence (NARIC)
4200 Forbes Boulevard, Suite 202
Lanham, MD 20706
(800) 346-2742   (301) 459-5900   (301) 459-4263
e-mail: naricinfo@heitechservices.com
www.naric.com

A federally funded center that responds to telephone and mail inquiries about disabilities and support services. Maintains "REHABDATA," a database with publications and research references. "RehabWire," a monthly newsletter, is available online only. Some NARIC publications are available on the web site.

National Resource Center for Parents with Disabilities
Through the Looking Glass
2198 Sixth Street, Suite 100
Berkeley, CA 94710
(800) 644-2666   (800) 804-1616 (TTY)   (510) 848-1112
FAX (510) 848-4445   e-mail: TLG@lookingglass.org
www.lookingglass.org

A federally funded center that conducts research on the needs of parents with disabilities. Conducts research on special equipment and techniques of caring for babies. Maintains a national network of parents with disabilities, their families, researchers, and service providers. Convenes a National Task Force on Parents with Disabilities and Their Families, which meets annually. "Keeping Our Families Together," a report of the first Task Force meeting is available in print and alternate formats; $2.00. Publishes quarterly newsletter, "Parenting with a Disability," which provides information about the center's activities, publications in the field, and practical suggestions for parents. Available in print and alternate formats. Free. Also available on the web site.

National Women's Health Information Center (NWHIC)
(800) 994-9662   (888) 220-5446 (TTY)   www.4women.gov

A web site for women with disabilities that includes information on medical conditions, online medical dictionaries, glossaries, and journals.

National Women's Health Network
514 10th Street, NW, Suite 400
Washington, DC 20004
(202) 347-1140   FAX (202) 347-1168
www.womenshealthnetwork.org

A coalition of consumers, health care providers, and researchers who work to provide up-to-date information about women's health issues and to improve women's ability to make informed decisions about their health care. Maintains a clearinghouse to provide information on a wide variety of disorders and conditions that affect women. Membership, $25.00, includes bimonthly newsletter "Network News."

National Women's Health Resource Center
120 Albany Street, Suite 820
New Brunswick, NJ 08901
(877) 986-9472   (732) 828) 8575   FAX (732) 249-4671
e-mail: info@healthywomen.org   www.healthywomen.org

Develops programs and clinical services to meet women's health needs; sponsors conferences; and provides information to encourage women to be active participants in their own health care decisions. Maintains a database on women's health issues and provides responses to telephone inquiries about specific health issues with referrals, resources, and general information. Online database of "women friendly" health care organizations. Bimonthly newsletter, "National Women's Health Report," $30.00. Some publications available online.

Office of Research on Women's Health (ORWH)
National Institutes of Health (NIH)
Building 1
9000 Rockville Pike
Bethesda, MD 20892
(301) 402-1770   FAX (301) 402-1798   e-mail: mc24a@nih.gov
www4.od.nih.gov/orwh

Established in 1990, this organization monitors NIH policy with the goal of promoting research into diseases that are prevalent in women, affect only women, have different effects on women than on men, or have different risk factors or interventions for women. ORWH works to ensure that women are represented in research sponsored by NIH and to develop opportunities for recruitment, retention, and advancement of women in biomedical careers. Some publications are available on the web site.

Older Women's League (OWL)
1750 New York Avenue, NW, Suite 350
Washington, DC 20006
(800) 825-3695   (202) 783-6686   FAX (202) 628-0458 e -
mail: owlinfo@owl-national.org

Advocates on behalf of older women in areas such as health, housing, and financial affairs. Publishes research papers, model bills for state legislative action, books, and videotapes. Membership, $25.00, includes bimonthly newsletter, "The Owl Observer."

Research and Training Center on Independent Living (RTC/IL)
University of Kansas
4089 Dole Life Span Institute
1000 Sunnyside Avenue
Lawrence, KS 66045
(785) 864-4095   (785) 864-0706 (TTY)   FAX (785) 864-5063
e-mail: rtcil@ku.edu   www.rtcil.org

A federally funded center that conducts research and training on the variables that affect independent living. Publications catalogue, free.

Research and Training Center on Rural Rehabilitation
52 Corbin Hall
University of Montana
Missoula, MT 59812
(800) 732-0323 (V/TTY)   (406) 243-5467 (V/TTY)
FAX (406) 243-4730   e-mail muarid@selway.umt.edu   ruralinstitute.umt.edu

A federally funded center that conducts research and training on issues that affect service delivery of rehabilitation in rural areas. Maintains a directory of rural disability services throughout the country. Publishes a newsletter, "The Rural Exchange," free. Available in alternate formats and on the web site.

Sexuality Information and Education Council of the United States (SIECUS)
130 West 42nd Street, Suite 350
New York, NY 10036
(212) 819-9770   FAX (212) 819-9776
e-mail: siecus@siecus.org   www.siecus.org

Provides information and education about sexuality through publications, database, library, symposia, and advocacy. Bimonthly journal, "SIECUS Report," $49.00; full text of past issues available on the web site. Publications catalogue, free.

Society for Disability Studies (SDS)
Department of Disability and Human Development
University of Illinois at Chicago
1640 West Roosevelt Road, #236
Chicago, IL 60608
(312) 355-0550   FAX (312) 413-2918   e-mail: cg16@uic.edu
www.uic.edu/orgs/sds

Membership organization of practitioners, clinicians, and social scientists interested in the study of issues related to disability. Holds an annual meeting. Membership, $95.00; low income, $30.00; includes "Disability Studies Quarterly."

Society for the Scientific Study of Sexuality
PO Box 416
Allentown, PA 18105-0416
(610) 530-2483   FAX (610) 530-2485
e-mail: TheSociety@inetmail.att.net
www.sexscience.org

A multidisciplinary society of professionals who conduct research on sex; includes a special interest group on disability.   Membership, $145.00, includes "Journal of Sex Research;" nonmembers subscription, individuals, $104.00; institutions, $168.00; and quarterly newsletter, "Sexual Science."

Substance Abuse Resources & Disability Issues (SARDI)
Rehabilitation Research and Training Center on Drugs and Disability
School of Medicine, Wright State University
PO Box 927
Dayton, OH 45401-0927
(937) 775-1484 (V/TTY)   FAX (937) 775-1495
www.med.wright.edu/som/sardi

A federally funded research center that investigates the relationship between drug use and disabilities. Free newsletter, "SARDI Online."

United Way of America (UWA)
701 North Fairfax Street
Alexandria, VA 22314
(800) 411-8929 to obtain telephone number of closest United Way office
(703) 836-7100   FAX (703) 683-7840
www.unitedway.org

An umbrella organization of local human service organizations. National office will direct callers to the local United Way, which in turn will provide referral to a specific local service agency.

World Institute on Disability (WID)
510 16th Street, Suite 100
Oakland, CA 94612
(510) 763-4100   (510) 208-9496 (TTY)   FAX (510) 763-4109
e-mail: webpoohbah@wid.org   www.wid.org

A public policy center founded and operated by individuals with disabilities, WID conducts research, public education, and training. It also develops model programs related to disability. It deals with issues such as personal assistance, public transportation, employment, and access to health care. WID's Research and Training Center on Independent Living and Disability Policy is a federally funded center that studies federal independent living initiatives and community integration issues. Publishes a semi-annual newsletter, "Equity," which focuses on economic development and the disability community; "Open Line," a quarterly newsletter which reports on policy developments in access to telecommunications for people with disabilities; and "Impact," a semi-annual newsletter.

Across Borders: Women with Disabilities Working Together
by Diane Driedger, Irene Feika, and Eileen Giron Batres (eds.)
gynergy books
2250 Military Road
Tonawanda, NY 14150
(800) 565-9523   FAX (800) 221-9985
e-mail: utpbook@utpress.utoronto.ca   www.utpublishing.com

This anthology written by women with disabilities discusses their personal lives and political activism in both developed and developing countries. $14.95

After the Diagnosis
by JoAnn LeMaistre
Alpine Guild
PO Box 4846
Dillon, CO 80435
(800) 869-9559   FAX (970) 269-9378
e-mail: information@alpineguild.com
www.alpineguild.com

Written by a woman with multiple sclerosis, this book describes the emotional responses to health changes due to physical disabilities, chronic illness, and aging. $15.95

Bigger Than the Sky: Disabled Women on Parenting 3
by Michele Wates and Rowen Jade (eds.)
Trafalgar Square Publishing
PO Box 257
Howe Hill Road
North Pomfret, VT 05053
(800) 423-4525   (802) 457-1911   FAX (802) 457-1913
e-mail: tsquare@sover.net   www.trafalgarsquarebooks.com

In this anthology, 39 women with disabilities write about their parenting experiences, as birth mothers, adoptive or foster parents, or as mothers not raising children, by choice or circumstances. $17.95

Building Community: A Manual Exploring Issues of Women and Disability
Educational Equity Concepts
100 Fifth Avenue, 8th Floor
New York, NY 10011
(212) 243-1110 (V/TTY)   FAX (212) 627-0407
e-mail: information@edequity.org   www.edequity.org

A collection of readings and activities that explore the relationship between gender and disability bias. Available in standard print, braille, and audiocassette. $25.00.

Dictionary of Rehabilitation
by Myron G. Eisenberg
Springer Publishing Company
536 Broadway
New York, NY 10012
(877) 687-7476   (212) 431-4370   FAX (212) 941-7842
e-mail: springer@springerpub.com www.springerpub.com

This book defines the core terms used in the rehabilitation field. $43.95

Disability and Motherhood
Films for the Humanities & Sciences
PO Box 2053
Princeton, NJ 08543-2053
(800) 257-5126   FAX (609) 275-3767
e-mail: custserv@films.com   www.films.com

This videotape portrays the childbearing and childrearing experiences of three women with disabilities.
25 minutes. $89.95

Double the Trouble, Twice the Fun
Women Make Movies
462 Broadway, Suite 500 WS
New York, NY 10013
(212) 925-0606   FAX (212) 925-2052
e-mail: info@wmm.com   www.wmm.com

In this videotape, interviews are conducted with both lesbians and gays, dispelling the myth that people
with disabilities are asexual. 25 minutes. Purchase, $250.00; rental for three days, $75.00

Enabling Romance: A Guide to Love, Sex, and Relationships for the Disabled
by Ken Kroll and Erica Levy Klein
No Limits Communications
PO Box 220
Horsham, PA 19044
(888) 850-0344   (215) 675-9133
FAX (215) 675-9376   e-mail: kim@leonardmedia.com
www.newmobility.com

Written by a man who has a disability and his wife who does not, this book provides examples of how
people with a variety of disabilities have established fulfilling relationships. $15.95

Encyclopedia of Disability and Rehabilitation
by Arthur E. Dell Orto and Robert P. Marinelli (eds.)
Gale Group
PO Box 9187
Farmington Hills, MI 48333-9187
(800) 877-4253   FAX (800) 414-5043
e-mail: galeord@galegroup.com   www.gale.com

Written by a variety of experts in the field of disability, this reference book includes articles ranging from AIDS to stroke, advocacy to wheelchairs, and aging to work. $140.00

Federal Register
New Orders, Superintendent of Documents
PO Box 371954
Pittsburgh, PA 15250-7954
(866) 512-1800   (202) 512-1530
FAX (202) 512-2250   www.access.gpo.gov/su_docs/aces/aces140.html

A federal publication printed every weekday with notices of all regulations and legal notices issued by federal agencies. Domestic subscriptions, $764.00 annually for second class mailing of paper format; $264.00 annually for microfiche. Also available on the web site at no charge.

If It Weren't for the Honor - I'd Rather Have Walked
by Jan Little
Brookline Books
PO Box 1047
Cambridge, MA 02238-1047
(800) 666-2665   (617) 868-0360
FAX (617) 868-1772   e-mail: brooklinebks@delphi.com
www.brooklinebooks.com

The author recounts her experiences as a person with a disability in the pre-ADA period. $15.95

Imprinting Our Image: An International Anthology by Women with Disabilities
by Diane Driedger and Susan Gray (eds.)
gynergy books
2250 Military Road
Tonawanda, NY 14150
(800) 565-9523   FAX (800) 221-9985
e-mail: utpbook@utpress.utoronto.ca   www.utpublishing.com

This collection of essays written by women with disabilities discusses their changing roles in the family and the community in both developed and underdeveloped countries. $12.95

In Sickness and in Health: Sex, Love, and Chronic Illness
by Lucille Carlton
Delacorte Press, New York, NY

Writing from experience as caregiver for her husband who had Parkinson's disease, the author offers creative solutions for handling the sexual needs of couples coping with a partner's chronic illness. Out of print

Journal of Disability Policy Studies
Pro-Ed
8700 Shoal Creek Boulevard
Austin, TX 78757
(800) 897-3202   FAX (800) 397-7633   www.proedinc.com

A journal, published twice a year, with articles related to legislative policy and regulatory matters as well as articles from a range of academic disciplines. Individuals, $43.00; institutions, $109.00.

Journal of Rehabilitation Research and Development (JRRD)
Scientific and Technical Publications Section
Rehabilitation Research and Development Service
103 South Gay Street, 5th Floor
Baltimore, MD 21202
(410) 962-1800   FAX (410) 962-9670   e-mail: pubs@vard.org
www.vard.org

A bimonthly journal that includes articles on disability, rehabilitation, sensory aids, gerontology, and disabling conditions. Available in standard print and on the web site. Free

Journal of Women and Aging
Haworth Press, Inc.
10 Alice Street
Binghamton, NY 13904
(800) 429-6784   (607) 722-5857   FAX (800) 895-0582
e-mail: getinfo@haworthpressinc.com www.haworthpressinc.com

A multidisciplinary quarterly journal that publishes articles dealing with psychosocial practice, theory, and research. Individuals, $60.00; organizations, $120.00.

Journal of Women's Health
Mary Ann Liebert, Inc., Publishers
2 Madison Avenue
Larchmont, NY 10538
(800) 654-3237   (914) 834-3100   FAX (914) 834-3688
e-mail: info@liebertpub.com   www.liebertpub.com

A bimonthly journal that publishes articles dealing with the conditions and diseases that are prevalent in women. Individuals, $129.00; institutions, $379.00. Online version, individuals, $109.00; institutions, $355.00.

Learning to Act in Partnership: Women with Disabilities Speak to Health Professionals
by Carol Gill and Kristi Kirschner
Rehabilitation Institute of Chicago
345 East Superior Street, Room 106
Chicago, IL 60611
(312) 238-2859   FAX (312) 238-4451
e-mail: bdelhunt@rehabchicago.org   www.rehabchicago.org

In this videotape, women with disabilities discuss their experiences with health care providers. Discussions focus on access, sexuality, mental health, and health care policy. 38 minutes. $150.00

Life on Cripple Creek: Essays on Living with Multiple Sclerosis
by Dean Kramer
Demos Medical Publishing
386 Park Avenue South, Suite 201
New York, NY 10016
(800) 532-8663   (212) 683-0072   FAX (212) 683-0118
e-mail: info@demospub.com   www.demosmedpub.com

Written by a woman who has multiple sclerosis, this book reveals the emotional and practical aspects of living with a chronic disease. $18.95. Orders made on the Demos web site receive a 15% discount.

Making Disability
by Paul Higgins
Charles C. Thomas Publisher
2600 South First Street
Springfield, IL 62794
(800) 258-8980   (217) 789-8980   FAX (217) 789-9130
e-mail: books@ccthomas.com   www.ccthomas.com

Written by a sociologist, this book examines disability as a social phenomenon rather than a defect. It discusses the depiction of disability, experiencing disability, serving individuals with disabilities, and developing disability policy. Hardcover, $57.95; softcover, $39.95.

Making Wise Medical Decisions: How to Get the Information You Need
Resources for Rehabilitation
22 Bonad Road
Winchester, MA 01890
(781) 368-9094   FAX (781) 368-9096
e-mail: info@rfr.org   www.rfr.org

This book includes information about where to go and what to read in order to make informed, rational, medical decisions. It describes how to obtain relevant health information and evaluate medical tests and procedures, health care providers, and health facilities. Includes chapters on special issues facing elders and people with chronic illnesses and disabilities. $42.95 (See last page of this book for order form.)

The Me in the Mirror
by Connie Panzarino
Seal Press, Seattle, WA
(800) 754-0271   e-mail: sealpress@scn.org   www.sealpress.com

Written by a woman who was born with spinal muscular atrophy III, a disease that has resulted in severe mobility impairment, this book provides details about her education, work, familial relationships, and romantic relationships, including her eventual turn to lesbianism. $12.95

Mothers with Disabilities: An Introduction to Issues
Health Resource Center for Women with Disabilities
Rehabilitation Institute of Chicago
345 East Superior Street, Room 106
Chicago, IL 60611
(312) 238-8003   (312) 238-8523 (TTy)   FAX (312) 238-1205
e-mail: jreis@rehabchicago.org

In this videotape, women with mobility impairments discuss their pregnancies, their experiences with the adoption process, and their coping strategies. A psychologist analyzes the overriding issues that the women have presented. 20 minutes. $152.00

Mother To Be: A Guide to Pregnancy and Birth for Women with Disabilities
by Judith Rogers and Molleen Matsumura
Demos Medical Publishing
386 Park Avenue South, Suite 201
New York, NY 10016
(800) 532-8663   (212) 683-0072
FAX (212) 683-0118   e-mail: info@demospub.com   www.demosmedpub.com

This book describes the pregnancy and childbirth experiences of 36 women with a wide variety of disabilities. Suggests practical solutions for the special concerns of women with disabilities during pregnancy and those of their partners, families, and health care providers. Includes a glossary and a bibliography. $29.95 Orders made on the Demos web site receive a 15% discount.

My Body Is Not Who I Am
Aquarius Health Care Videos
266 Main Street, Suite 33B
Medfield, MA 02052
(888) 440-2963   FAX (508) 242-9854
e-mail: orders@aquariusproductions.com
www.aquariusproductions.com

In this videotape, individuals discuss the effects that disability has had on their lives. Includes family relationships, sexuality, and health care. 35 minutes. $150.00

The New Ourselves, Growing Older
by Paula B. Doress-Worters and Diana Laskin Siegal
Simon and Schuster
IBD
PO Box 218
Paramus, NJ 07653
(800) 223-2336   FAX (800) 943-9831   www.simonsays.com

This book provides information and resources for midlife and older women. Topics include aging, sexuality, disabilities, health care, employment, housing, and finances. $20.00

No Pity: People with Disabilities Forging a New Civil Rights Movement
by Joseph P. Shapiro
Random House, Order Department
400 Hahn Road
Westminster, MD 21157
(800) 733-3000   www.randomhouse.com

This book describes the evolution of the disability rights movement and profiles its leaders. $16.00

Past Due: A Story of Disability, Pregnancy, and Birth
by Anne Finger
Seal Press, Seattle, WA

In this autobiographical book, a woman who was disabled by polio analyzes the issues pertinent to disability and pregnancy. Out of print. Available on four-track audiocassette, playable on the National Library Service for the Blind and Physically Handicapped cassette player (see Chapter 1, "ORGANIZATIONS"); RC 44699.

Positive Images
Women Make Movies
462 Broadway, Suite 500 WS
New York, NY 10013
(212) 925-0606   FAX (212) 925-2052
e-mail: info@wmm.com   www.wmm.com

In this videotape, three women (one blind, one deaf, and one with a spinal cord injury) discuss their lives at home, at work, and with family and friends. 58 minutes. Purchase, $295.00; rental for three days, $75.00.

Prenatal Testing and Disability Rights
by Erik Parens and Adrienne Asch (eds.)
Georgetown University Press
3240 Prospect Street, NW
Washington, DC 20007
(202) 687-5889   FAX (202) 687-6340   press.georgetown.edu

This book presents a series of articles written by a multidisciplinary group of researchers who debate the ethics of prenatal diagnosis of genetic disability. Members of the disability rights movement contend that testing for genetic disability devalues the worth of individuals who live with disabilities, while others contend that such testing enables mothers to end their pregnancies and prevent the distress of raising a child with a disability. Hardcover, $65.00; softcover, $27.50

Ragged EDGE
Advocado Press Inc.
Box 145
Louisville, KY 40201
e-mail: editor@ragged-edge-mag.com
www.ragged-edge-mag.com
This bimonthly magazine reports on disability issues from the perspective of disability rights activists. Individuals, $17.50; institutions, $35.00. The "Electronic EDGE" is available at no charge on the web site.

Report on Disability Programs
Business Publishers
8737 Colesville Road, Suite 1100
Silver Spring, MD 20910-3928
(800) 274-6737   (301) 589-5103
FAX (301) 589-8493   e-mail: bpinews@bpinews.com   www.bpinews.com

A biweekly newsletter with information on policies promulgated by federal agencies, laws, and funding sources. $327.00

Reproductive Issues for Persons with Physical Disabilities
by Florence P. Haseltine, Sandra S. Cole, and David B. Gray (eds.)
Brookes Publishing Company, Baltimore, MD
This book provides an overview of sexuality, disability, and reproductive issues across the lifespan for individuals with disabilities, including multiple sclerosis and spinal cord injury. Includes academic articles as well as personal narratives written by individuals with disabilities. Out of print

Resourceful Woman
Health Resource Center for Women with   Disabilities
Rehabilitation Institute of Chicago
345 East Superior Street, Room 106
Chicago, IL 60611
(312) 238-8003   (312) 238-8523 (TTY)
FAX (312) 238-1205   e-mail: jreis@rehabchicago.org

A newsletter dealing with the broad range of issues that affect women with disabilities. Includes a regular column "Resourceful Parenting," which answers readers' questions. Free (contribution requested).

The Self-Help Sourcebook Online
American Self-Help Clearinghouse
100 Hanover Avenue, Suite 202
Cedar Knolls, NJ 07927
(973) 326-6789   FAX (973) 326-9467   www.selfhelpgroups.org

This online database provides information on national and model self-help groups, online mutual help groups and networks, and self-help clearinghouses. Includes ideas on starting self-help groups and opportunities to link with others to develop new groups.

Sexual Concerns When Illness or Disability Strikes
by Carol L. Sandowski
Charles C. Thomas Publisher, Springfield, IL

Written by a social worker who is a certified sex counselor, this book discusses sexuality and issues of self-esteem that arise with illness or disability. Out of print.

Sexual Function in People with Disability and Chronic Illness: A Health Professional's Guide
by Marca Sipski and Craig Alexander
Aspen Publishers, Inc.
PO Box 990
Frederick, MD 21705-9782
(800) 234-1660   www.aspenpub.com

This book discusses many types of disability, their effects on sexuality, reproductive concerns, and treatment methods, as well as providing basic information on general sexual function and dysfunction. Includes spinal cord injury, diabetes, multiple sclerosis, arthritis and other connective tissue diseases, and heart disease. Offers a discussion of the issues faced by the partner of an individual with a disability. $59.00

Sexuality and Disability
Kluwer Academic Publishing
101 Philip Drive
Assinippi Park
Norwell, MA 02061
(866) 269-9527   (781) 871-6600   FAX (781) 871-6528
e-mail: kluwer@wkap.com   www.wkap.com

A quarterly journal with articles on the medical and rehabilitation aspects of sexuality for individuals who have experienced a disability. Individuals, $75.00; institutions, $459.00.

Sexuality and Disability
Sexuality Information and Education Council of the United States (SIECUS)
130 West 42nd Street, Suite 350
New York, NY 10036-7802
(212) 819-9770   FAX (212) 819-9776
e-mail: siecus@siecus.org   www.siecus.org

This annotated bibliography lists general books, books for professionals, curricula, journals and newsletters, teaching aids, databases, and organizations that provide information about sexuality for individuals with disabilities. $3.00 Also available on the web site at no charge.

Staring Back: The Disability Experience from the Inside Out
by Kenny Fries (ed.)
Penguin Putnam, Inc.
(800) 788-6262   www.penguinputnam.com

This anthology includes essays, poems, and works of fiction written by individuals who have a broad range of disabilities. $17.00

Table Manners: A Guide to the Pelvic Examination for Disabled Women and Health Care Providers
by Susan Ferreyra and Katrine Hughes
Planned Parenthood Golden Gate
815 Eddy Street, Suite 300
San Francisco, CA 94109
(415) 441-7858   FAX (415) 776-1449   www.ppgg.org

Written by two women with disabilities, this booklet suggests alternative positions for pelvic examinations; discusses bowel and bladder concerns, spasticity, and hypersensitivity; and describes transfer methods for getting on the examination table. $3.00

Us and Them
Fanlight Productions
4196 Washington Street, Suite 2
Boston, MA 02131
(800) 937-4113   (617) 469-4999   FAX (617) 469-3379
e-mail: fanlight@fanlight.com   www.fanlight.com

This videotape is about relationships between people who have disabilities and those who do not. 32 minutes, black and white. $69.00

Vital Signs: Crip Culture Talks Back
Fanlight Productions
4196 Washington Street, Suite 2
Boston, MA 02131
(800) 937-4113   (617) 469-4999   FAX (617) 469-3379
e-mail: fanlight@fanlight.com   www.fanlight.com

This videotape documentary includes performances, debates, and interviews with disability rights activists who discuss the politics of disability. 48 minutes, open captioned. Purchase, $199.00.

Waist-High in the World
by Nancy Mairs
Houghton Mifflin Company
PO Box 7050
Wilmington, MA 01887
(800) 225-3362   FAX (800) 634-7568   www.hmco.com

Written by a woman who has multiple sclerosis, this book examines her personal experiences as well as general issues for women with disabilities. $15.00

We Are Not Alone: Learning to Live with Chronic Illness
by Sefra Kobrin Pitzele
Workman Publishing, New York, NY
Written by a woman with lupus, this book offers practical advice for coping with chronic diseases and maintaining relationships. It also provides practical suggestions for independent living. Out of print.

What Happened to You?
by Lois Keith (ed.)
W. W. Norton
Paid Orders Department
800 Keystone Industrial Park
Scranton, PA 18512
(800) 223-4830   (717) 346-2029
FAX (800) 458-6515   www.norton.com

This book is an anthology of essays, fiction, and poetry written by women with disabilities. Hardcover, $22.50; softcover, $12.95

What Psychotherapists Should Know about Disability
by Rhoda Olkin
Guilford Publications
72 Spring Street
New York, NY 10012
(800) 365-7006   (212) 431-9800
FAX (212) 966-6708   e-mail: info@guilford.com   www.guilford.com

Written by a clinician who has a disability, this book examines a minority model of disability and describes the disability experience, including how stereotypes and attitudes affect everyday experiences. Includes chapters on laws and social history, families, etiquette with individuals with disabilities, special issues in therapy, and assistive technology. Hardcover, $43.00; softcover, $23.00.

With the Power of Each Breath
Susan E. Browne, Debra Connors, and Nanci Stern
Cleis Press, San Francisco, CA

This collection of articles, written by women with a variety of disabilities, describes their experiences, their emotions, and societal reactions. Out of print

Women and Health
Haworth Press, Inc.
10 Alice Street
Binghamton, NY 13904
(800) 342-9678   (607) 722-5857   FAX (800) 895-0582
e-mail: getinfo@haworthpressinc.com www.haworthpressinc.com

A multidisciplinary quarterly journal that deals with all phases of health care, including disability, rehabilitation, and chronic illness. Individuals, $75.00; institutions, $200.00.

Women and Their Doctors
by John M. Smith
Grove/Atlantic, Berkeley, CA
Written by a gynecologist, this book discusses the abuse of women by the medical system, medical problems experienced by women, when certain procedures are appropriate, and how to select the right gynecologist. Out of print.

Women, Disability and Identity
by Hans Asha
Sage Publications
2455 Teller Road
Thousand Oaks, CA 91320
(800) 818-7243   FAX (805) 375-1700
e-mail: info@sagepub.com   www.sagepub.com

This anthology, with articles on both developing and developed countries, examines the roles women with disabilities have played in society and makes suggestions for improvements. $59.95

Women with Disabilities: Found Voices
by Mary E. Willmuth and Lillian Holcomb (eds.)
Haworth Press, Inc.
10 Alice Street
Binghamton, NY 13904
(800) 342-9678   (607) 722-5857   FAX (800) 895-0582
e-mail: getinfo@haworthpressinc.com www.haworthpressinc.com

This set of essays, written by women with disabilities, offers their perspectives on living with chronic illness. Includes recommendations for finding therapists. Hardcover, $74.95; softcover, $18.95.

Women with Physical Disabilities: Achieving and Maintaining Health and Well-Being
by Danuta M. Krotoski, Margaret A. Nosek, and Margaret A. Turk (eds.)
Brookes Publishing Company, Baltimore, MD

This collection of articles addresses the special issues that women with disabilities face, including self-concept, dating and relationships, sexuality, pregnancy and motherhood, and bowel and bladder control. Out of print.

<u>You Are Not Your Illness</u>
by Linda Noble Topf
Simon and Schuster
IBD
PO Box 218
Paramus, NJ 07653
(888) 866-6631   FAX (800) 943-9831   www.simonsays.com

In this book, the author, who has multiple sclerosis, shares her personal perspectives on living with chronic illness. She describes a step-by-step process for dealing with loss and maintaining feelings of self-worth. $12.00

Chapter 2

COPING WITH DAILY ACTIVITIES

Women in our society carry out a variety of roles and responsibilities; they are mothers, career women, and caregivers for sick or disabled partners or parents. For women with disabilities, these activities may become a challenge. Although the number of products to help people with disabilities live independently has increased dramatically in recent years, especially with the advent of the personal computer, the everyday tasks performed by women with disabilities are often more time consuming than they are for healthy women. And while increasing numbers of women have entered the workforce, it is well known that women are still responsible for the major portion of household activities, even when partners are available to provide assistance. After a discussion of the effects of disabilities on the family, the sections that follow provide information about carrying out basic everyday activities, providing care for others with disabilities, working with a disability, housing and environmental adaptations, and recreation and travel.

HOW DISABILITIES AND CHRONIC CONDITIONS AFFECT THE FAMILY

Diagnosis of a disability or chronic condition in a family member can cause disruption in the healthiest of families. Coping with a crisis situation puts strain on any relationship; coping with the inevitability of a permanent change causes strain between marital partners and places great stress upon children. Stress may be related to providing adequate health care, financial concerns, disruption of familiar patterns of everyday living and work, and sexual relations.

Children in the family are often not told the details of the situation, as parents do not want to frighten them. Without information, however, their imaginations may picture a situation far worse than reality. During the initial crisis, when their mother is in the hospital, the children are often deprived not only of her company but also of their father's, who is tending to the mother's emotional and physical needs (Rustad: 1984).

It is crucial that family members understand the nature of the condition and its effects on daily functioning. Holding realistic expectations for what the affected family member can and cannot do contributes to the individual's ability to cope with the situation. Being overly protective and trying to do everything for the affected family member may result in diminished self-esteem and independence. On the other hand, expecting the individual to carry out activities that are unrealistic or implying that the limitations are "only in the head" creates a great deal of additional stress. People with disabilities and chronic conditions often express the fear of being a burden on family members; when their relatives suggest that they can accomplish tasks that are physically impossible for them, the affected individuals will be reluctant to ask for assistance at any time.

Following the onset of a disability or chronic condition, all family members must be prepared for role changes and accommodations. The woman who has been affected may find that she can no longer carry out the roles in the family that she was accustomed to. For example, if she is no longer able to drive, she will not be able to transport children to activities or go grocery shopping on her own. Her partner or spouse will need to take on additional roles. Children who are old enough should be encouraged to take on some additional household responsibilities. When it is financially feasible, hiring household help can alleviate some of the burdens placed on family members. Some families may qualify for homemaker services provided by government agencies or voluntary organizations.

Often the assistance of a social worker or a psychologist is necessary to help the family restructuring that takes place following the development of a disability or chronic condition. The emotional needs of the spouse or partner must also be considered. Since the spouse or partner has the additional role of providing emotional and physical support for the individual who has developed a disability or chronic condition, he or she will likely need support also. Self-help groups of other caregivers in similar situations may prove helpful. Hulnick and Hulnick (1989) suggest that counselors can help family members "reframe" the context of the situation so that they respond positively, learn and grow from the new situation, and empower themselves to make choices. Local and state governments, private agencies that provide case management services, and voluntary organizations that are dedicated to one disease or disability often have programs to help family members as well as the individuals with disabilities and chronic conditions.

CARING FOR OTHERS WITH DISABILITIES

Women provide most of the "informal" care required by their parents and spouses. Although many caregivers are middle-aged women, as the population lives longer women 65 years or older may simultaneously be providing care for their spouses and for their elderly parents (usually mothers) who may be 85 years or older. These older caregivers themselves may also be experiencing the effects of chronic health problems and disabilities.

Women caring for partners who have disabilities not only face the physical demands such caregiving entails but the emotional issues that spring from changes in the relationship. Cohen, whose husband has multiple sclerosis, describes the "dire straits" in which she and their children lived until her husband moved to a nursing home. Despite participation in multiple sclerosis support groups and well spouse groups, she felt that she experienced a conspiracy of silence about the realities of family caregiving that kept her ignorant of caregiving options. This situation led her to comment:

Well spouses often feel weak, ineffective, and perhaps ashamed and guilt ridden. Our belief systems are threatened. We're forced, or feel we're forced, to go against our beliefs, our habits, our life-styles, and our expectations. (1996, 120)

The extreme stresses she endured caused Cohen to question her role in the marriage, "I don't know to what extent I am still a wife, to what extent I want to be" (1996, 81).

Sons are far less likely than daughters to provide care for their parents. When parents have no daughters, it is usually the daughters-in-law who provide the care, not the sons. When sons do provide assistance, it is often in the domain of financial management. Daughters, accepting their roles as nurturers, may make excuses for their brothers' failure to help by asserting that men's work is their primary function. All the while, these daughters may be juggling their own families and work schedules to provide care for parents (Aronson: 1992).

Adding the role of caregiver to an already overburdened lifestyle may result in great stress. Often the caregiver must take time away from her employment outside the home in order to carry out the necessary caregiving tasks. These tasks include providing transportation, arranging for medical appointments, shopping and other household tasks, and supervising medication. In some instances, helping relatives with disabilities includes helping them with the basic tasks of living, such as bathing, dressing, and eating.

The emotional and physical burden of providing these tasks for an older relative while taking care of her family of procreation often causes conflict for a woman. Children may find that their mother is not available as often as they would like or when she is available, she is too tired to participate in the usual family activities. The sheer quantity of caregiving indicates why caregivers are "women in the middle;" Brody (1990) found that three-quarters of daughters provided care every single day.

Furthermore, the older the caregiver (and therefore her mother), the greater number of hours per week she spent providing care (Brody: 1981).

A study (Richards and Shewchuk: 1996) found that most caregivers of individuals with spinal cord injuries were women, usually wives or mothers. Not only was a majority of this sample clinically depressed, but their positive affect decreased between six months and one year following discharge from the hospital. Not surprisingly, caregivers for individuals who were quadriplegics had higher levels of emotional distress than caregivers of individuals who were paraplegics. While the stress for caregivers of paraplegics declined over time, the stress for caregivers of quadriplegics increased, suggesting that the severity of the condition plays a role in the caregivers' emotional problems. Caregivers spent a substantial part of their day carrying out the tasks associated with caring for the person with spinal cord injury.

Caregiving for a parent may result in feelings of anger, guilt, and depression. Psychological conflicts that existed between mothers and daughters may be rekindled; problems that already existed between spouses may intensify as a result of the additional demands on time and emotions. When caregivers enter into a relationship with the relative's health care provider, additional conflicts may ensue, as the caregiver and the health care provider may hold an opinion contrary to the relative's (Haug: 1994).

As difficult as this situation is for healthy women, women who have disabilities or chronic conditions may feel that they are neglecting their parents if they do not help with the provision of care and services. While they may hold unrealistic expectations for themselves, they may feel guilty for not being able to devote time or energy to their parents. In such situations, locating a case manager for the parent may be the most useful solution. Some case managers are in private practice, while others may be located at publicly funded agencies on aging. Case managers will evaluate the person's needs, recommend appropriate services, and follow up to ensure that the services are being provided.

To relieve the burden on family members, many state departments on aging fund programs that provide assistance to elders living at home who need additional care. Financial assistance is also available. Employment of a home health aide alleviates some of the burdens placed on the family caregiver. Respite care programs, which may include activities outside the home for the care recipient or home health aides to assist with grooming and other daily activities, enable caregivers time to take care of their own needs. In addition, adult day care programs provide transportation and activities for elders with disabilities. Both of these programs may be available from agencies that serve elders, hospitals, or visiting nurse associations. Another option that may prove useful to the woman who finds herself in the role of caregiver is a support group of family members in similar situations. Many of the national voluntary organizations that are dedicated to a single disease or disability sponsor these support groups.

Employers, recognizing the growing needs of their employees in the area of elder care, have begun to provide assistance as well. Flexible time schedules, information and referral services, and on-site adult day care are a few of the programs that are now available at places of employment.

Short term respite programs that enable caregivers to have time to themselves, adult day care programs, utilization of personal attendants or home health aides, and special programs for children and elders have been developed as a way for caregivers to give adequate care and also tend to their own personal needs. Meeting the financial needs of dependent family members often requires the help of an attorney who specializes in family law. The federal Family and Medical Leave Act of 1993 (P.L. 103-3) enables eligible employees to take unpaid leave from work to care for sick relatives without forfeiting their jobs or their benefits. The National Family Caregiver Support Program (NFCSP) was established through the Older Americans Act Amendments of 2000 (P.L. 106-501). It is designed to help family members provide care for elders at home (see Chapter 3, "Laws that Affect Women with Disabilities" for a more detailed description of these act).

References

Aronson, Jane
1992   "Women's Sense of Responsibility for the Care of Older People: 'But Who Else is Going to Do It?'" Gender and Society 6(March):1:8-29

Brody, Elaine M.
1990   Women in the Middle: Their Parent Care Years New York, NY: Springer Publishing Company
1981   "'Women in the Middle' and Family Help to Older People" The Gerontologist 21:5:471-479

Cohen, Marion Deutsche
1996   dirty details: the days and nights of a well spouse Philadelphia, PA: Temple University Press

Haug, Marie R.
1994   "Elderly Patients, Caregivers, and Physicians: Theory and Research on Health Care Triads" Journal of Health and Social Behavior 35(March):1-12

Hulnick, Mary R. and H. Ronald Hulnick
1989   "Life's Challenges: Curse or Opportunity? Counseling Families of Persons with Disabilities" Journal of Counseling and Development 68(November/December):166-170

Richards, J. Scott and Richard Shewchuk
1996   "Caregivers of Persons with Spinal Cord Injury: A Longitudinal Investigation" Research Update Spain Rehabilitation Center, University of Alabama at Birmingham, September

Rustad, Lynne C.
1984   "Family Adjustment to Chronic Illness and Disability in Mid-Life" pp. 222-242 in Myron G. Eisenberg, LaFaye C. Sutkin, and Mary A. Jansen (eds.) Chronic Illness and Disability through the Life Span New York, NY: Springer Publishing Company

ORGANIZATIONS

Caregivers Corner
www.mayoclinic.com

This web site provides information on home adaptation, safety, advance directives, long term care, and other topics for caregivers.

CarePlanner
www2.careplanner.org

Developed by the Centers for Medicare and Medicaid Services and Clinical Tools, Inc., this web site provides a tool that may help individuals with disabilities and chronic conditions, families, and professionals make decisions about health, financial, personal, and caregiver issues. It may be used online, generating an individualized Advice Report.

Children of Aging Parents (CAPS)
1609 Woodbourne Road, Suite 302A
Levittown, PA 19057
(800) 227-7294   (215) 945-6900   FAX (215) 945-6720
www.careguide.net

Helps caregivers find the appropriate care and support for elders as well as for themselves. Sponsors a network of support groups for caregivers. Publishes a variety of training and resource materials for support groups and a national directory of geriatric case managers. Membership, individuals, $20.00; professionals and organizations, $100.00; includes bimonthly newsletter "CAPSule."

Eldercare Locator
National Association of Area Agencies on Aging (NAAAA)
(800) 677-1116   www.eldercare.gov

A nationwide database that provides callers with the phone number for an information and referral service in their local area, which in turn provides the name of a local agency that can help with their specific needs. Free

National Alliance for Caregiving (NAC)
4720 Montgomery Lane, Suite 642
Bethesda, MD 20814
(301) 718-8444   FAX (301) 652-7711   www.caregiving.org

An alliance of several national groups concerned with issues of aging, this organization supports research, outreach programs, and a clearinghouse of resources. The AXA Foundation Family Care Resource Connection database, available on the web site, allows family caregivers to search for information on topics such as medical conditions, hands-on caregiving skills, legal and financial information, coping with caregiving, and community resources. Entries are rated for quality and usefulness.

National Association for Home Care (NAHC)
228 7th Street, SE
Washington, DC 20003
(202) 547-7424   FAX (202) 547-3540   www.nahc.org

Trade association of home care and hospice organizations. Consumer education publications include "How to Choose a Home Care Provider," and "How to Choose a Home Care Agency." Single copies, free. Also available on the web site.

National Family Caregivers Association
10400 Connecticut Avenue, Suite 500
Kensington, MD 20895-3944
(800) 896-3650   (301) 942-6430   FAX (301) 942-2302
e-mail: info@nfcacares.org   www.nfcacares.org

A membership organization for individuals who provide care for others at any stage of their lives or with any disease or disability. Maintains an information clearinghouse. Membership, U.S. family caregivers, free; other individuals, $20.00; professionals, $40.00; nonprofit organizations, $60.00; and group medical practices, home health agencies, etc., $100.00. Membership includes quarterly newsletter, "Take Care!" which provides information and resources for family caregivers.

National Resource Center for Parents with Disabilities
Through the Looking Glass
2198 Sixth Street, Suite 100
Berkeley, CA 94710-2204
(800) 644-2666   (800) 804-1616 (TTY)   (510) 848-1112
FAX (510) 848-4445   e-mail: TLG@lookingglass.org
www.lookingglass.org

Studies the needs of parents with disabilities, including special equipment and techniques of caring for babies. Maintains a national network of parents with disabilities, their families, researchers, and service providers. Convenes a National Task Force on Parents with Disabilities and Their Families, which meets annually. Publishes quarterly newsletter, "Parenting with a Disability," which provides information about the center's activities, publications in the field, and practical suggestions for parents. Available in print and alternate formats. Free. Also available on the web site.

Well Spouse Foundation
30 East 40th Street, Suite PH
New York, NY 10016
(800) 838-0879   (212) 685-8815   FAX (212) 685-8676
e-mail: wellspouse@aol.com   www.wellspouse.org

A network of support groups that provide emotional support to husbands, wives, and partners of people who are chronically ill. Membership, individuals, $25.00; professionals, $50.00; includes bimonthly newsletter, "Mainstay." Publishes pamphlets discussing "Guilt," "Anger," "Isolation," and "Looking Ahead." $1.50 each; $5.00 a set.

<u>Adaptive Baby Care Equipment: Guidelines, Prototypes, and Resources</u> (book)
<u>Adaptive Baby Care Equipment</u> (video)
Through the Looking Glass
2198 Sixth Street, Suite 100
Berkeley, CA 94710
(800) 644-2666   (800) 804-1616 (TTY)   (510) 848-1112
FAX (510) 848-4445   e-mail: TLG@lookingglass.org
www.lookingglass.org

This combination of book and videotape describes products to help parents with disabilities diaper, bathe, dress, feed, and play with their babies. The 12 minute videotape demonstrates successful techniques used by parents with disabilities. $79.00

<u>Beyond Chaos: One Man's Journey Alongside His Chronically Ill Wife</u>
by Gregg Piburn
Arthritis Foundation Distribution Center
PO Box 509
Pembina, ND 58271
(800) 207-8633   FAX (770) 442-9742

This book describes a couple's relationship and how fibromyalgia, a chronic illness, caused changes in the relationship and their lives. It discusses anger, guilt, re-examination of priorities, and increased trust and intimacy in the marriage. $14.95

<u>Caregiver's Handbook: A Complete Guide to Home Health Care</u>
by Visiting Nurse Associations of America
Dorling Kindersley
375 Hudson Street
New York, NY 10014
(877) 342-5357   (212) 213-4800   www.dk.com

This book offers practical advice, emotional support, and information for daily caregiving. Includes illustrated techniques, information on benefits, patient's bill of rights, and a glossary. $14.95

<u>Caregiving: The Spiritual Journey of Love, Loss and Renewal</u>
by Beth Witrogen McLeod
John Wiley and Sons, Consumer Center
10475 Crosspoint Boulevard
Indianapolis, IN 46256
(877) 762-2974   FAX (800) 597-3299
e-mail: customer@wiley.com   www.wiley.com

This book uses caregiver stories, interviews, and literary references to provide strategies for coping with the stress of caring for loved ones. It discusses topics such as emotional stresses, end-of-life concerns, and recovery from loss. $14.95

Caring for Yourself While Caring for Others: Survival and Renewal
by Lawrence M. Brammer
Vantage Press
516 West 34th Street
New York, NY 10001
(800) 882-3273   (212) 736-1767
FAX (212) 736-2273   www.vantagepress.com

This book discusses coping and survival strategies and suggests how to face difficult feelings. Provides community resources and reading lists. $14.95

Coming Home: Basic Information for the Home Caregiver
Terra Nova Films
9848 South Winchester Avenue
Chicago, IL 60643
(800) 779-8491   (773) 881-8491
FAX (773) 881-3368   www.terranova.org

This videotape reviews five basic caregiving concerns: moving and transfer, infection control, nutrition, stress, and talking with the doctor. 51 minutes. Purchase, $129.00; one week rental, $45.00.

dirty details, the days and nights of a well spouse
by Marion Deutsche Cohen
Temple University Press
c/o Chicago Distribution Center
11030 South Langley Avenue
Chicago, IL 60628
(800) 621-2736   FAX (800) 621-8476
e-mail: kh@press.uchicago.edu   www.press.chicago.edu

A frank, personal account, written by a woman whose husband has multiple sclerosis, this book describes her caregiving experiences. Hardcover, $49.95; softcover, $20.95.

Families and Health
National Council on Family Relations (NCFR)
3989 Central Avenue, NE, Suite 550
Minneapolis, MN 55421
(888) 781-9331   (763) 781-9331   FAX (763) 481-9348
e-mail: info@ncfr.org   www.ncfr.org

This videotape discusses how families cope with chronic illness and disability, how they interact with health care professionals, and how the caregiver's management of stress affects the entire family. 90 minutes. $32.95

Family Caregivers
Films for the Humanities & Sciences
PO Box 2053
Princeton, NJ 08543-2053
(800) 257-5126   FAX (609) 275-3767
e-mail: custserv@films.com   www.films.com

This videotape offers suggestions for dealing with the stresses of caregiving and profiles the Well Spouse Foundation (see "ORGANIZATIONS" section above). 30 minutes. $89.95

Family Challenges: Parenting with a Disability
Aquarius Health Care Videos
266 Main Street, Suite 33B
Medfield, MA 02052
(888) 440-2963   FAX (508) 242-9854
e-mail: orders@aquariusproductions.com
www.aquariusproductions.com

In this videotape, the children and spouses of individuals with disabilities describe their relationships and coping strategies. 25 minutes. $195.00

Federal Benefits for Veterans and Dependents

This booklet describes the benefits available under federal laws. $6.00. Also available on the web site at no charge.

Final Negotiations: A Story of Love and Chronic Illness
by Carolyn Ellis
Temple University Press
c/o Chicago Distribution Center
11030 South Langley Avenue
Chicago, IL 60628
(800) 621-2736   FAX (800) 621-8476
e-mail: kh@press.uchicago.edu   www.press.chicago.edu

Written by a woman whose romantic partner became progressively disabled by emphysema, this book describes their relationship as it changes during the course of his disease. It discusses romance and the reversal of roles and coping with the loss of a loved one. Hardcover, $71.50; softcover, $24.95

Helping Yourself Help Others: A Book for Caregivers
by Rosalynn Carter with Susan K. Golant
Random House, Order Department
400 Hahn Road
Westminster, MD 21157
(800) 733-3000   www.randomhouse.com

This book focuses on family caregivers, offering suggestions for everyday problems such as physical and emotional needs, isolation, burnout, and dealing with professional caregivers. $14.00

Hiring Home Caregivers: The Family Guide to In-Home Eldercare
by Helen Susik
Impact Publishers, Inc., San Luis Obispo, CA

This book provides practical information for elders and family members for hiring, supervising, and paying home caregivers. Included are sample forms for recruiting, interviewing, and checking references of potential caregivers as well as employment agreements and suggestions for supervision. Out of print

How to Help Children Through a Parent's Serious Illness
by Kathleen McCue with Ron Bonn
St. Martin's Griffin
c/o VHPS
16365 James Madison Highway
Gordonsville, VA 22942
(888) 330-8477   www.vhpsva.com/bookseller

This book presents practical guidelines to help parents explain their illness to children of different ages, how to understand the children's reactions, and how to seek professional help. Includes a chapter on chronic illness. $13.95

The Other Victim - Caregivers Share Their Coping Strategies
by Alan Drattell
Seven Locks Press
PO Box 25689
Santa Ana, CA 92799
(800) 354-5348   FAX (714) 545-1572

This book is a collection of personal accounts of nine caregivers of individuals with multiple sclerosis. Also includes a resource list of organizations and suggestions for coping. $17.95

Share the Care: How to Organize a Group to Care for Someone Who is Seriously Ill
by Cappy Capossela and Sheila Warnock
Simon and Schuster
IBD
PO Box 218
Paramus, NJ 07653
(888) 866-6631   FAX (800) 943-9831   www.simonsays.com

This book provides guidelines for sharing responsibilities for the care of a person who is seriously ill. $14.00

Surviving Your Spouse's Chronic Illness
by Chris McGonigle
Henry Holt and Company, New York, NY

Building on her own background as a well spouse, the author interviewed more than 40 spouses of women and men with chronic conditions and describes the emotional and psychological aspects of their experiences. Out of print.

<u>With This Body: Caring and Disability in Marriage</u>
by Gillian Parker
Open University Press, Philadelphia, PA

In this book, the author examines the experiences of married couples when one partner becomes chronically ill or disabled. Focuses on the issues of dependence/independence and the effects of pre-existing relationships on caregiver and receiver. Out of print.

WORKING WITH A DISABILITY

Because many women had been full-time homemakers or had low paying, part-time positions prior to their disability, they are unlikely to have private disability insurance or workers' compensation. Many women with disabilities receive one or more types of financial assistance from the government: food stamps, cash assistance, or household assistance.

Many women with disabilities and chronic conditions experience extreme fatigue, which makes them feel unproductive. These women often feel it appears that they are shirking their responsibilities when their physical condition requires that they live at a much slower pace than what they were accustomed to (Hillyer: 1993). Changes in physical abilities may require that women adopt different definitions of productivity without feeling guilty. Women who previously held full-time positions while managing a house and raising children may find it necessary to hire household help, cut back on working hours, and require that family members carry out household chores. Other options that can help eliminate fatigue are flexi-time schedules, job sharing with another person to cut down on hours, and performing work at home to eliminate travel time. Working at home full-time, however, can lead to an increased sense of isolation, a problem that is prevalent among women with disabilities.

One woman who had experienced a severe stroke found that slowing down was not all bad:

> Being forced to slow down is not all negative. The rhythm of my life has changed dramatically. Before, it was governed by the calendar and the clock. Now I follow the natural pace of my body. The tasks of everyday living take me much longer. I have become patient, as have those around me. I have to ration my limited energy and choose carefully who I see and what I do. I have no time to waste on bullshit, but I do have time to smell the flowers. I cherish my solitude, and enjoy the fullness of the company of intimate friends and family. (Sherr Klein: 1992, p. 74)

Work can help contribute to a woman's sense of positive self-esteem as well as her perception of well-being. Nathanson (1980) reported that employment was positively related to self-esteem and the effect was most marked upon women who had few other avenues to enhance their self-esteem. Women with disabilities are likely to have lower levels of education and hence lower self-esteem; therefore, it is likely that this finding is especially applicable to them. Kutner and Gray's (1981) study of women with chronic renal failure found that women who were employed had lower depression scores than women who were homemakers. Furthermore, for many women work also provides a social network; therefore, disruption of employment also disrupts social interactions (Brintnell et al.: 1994).

Women with recently acquired disabilities should think carefully about the type of work they would like to do, being realistic about their physical abilities and their stamina. Vocational assessment and counseling may prove useful to women whose conditions require a position change. Physical location of the place of employment, transportation, and work schedule are all important considerations regarding a particular position.

The Americans with Disabilities Act requires that employers make "reasonable accommodations" for people with disabilities (see Chapter 3, "Laws that Affect Women with Disabilities"). Advances in technology, especially in computer technology that is the core of most office work, have produced a variety of adapted equipment that enables even those with the most limited mobility to continue working. Women with minimal mobility can control their environment through the use of switches, headpointers, joysticks, and sip-and-puff switches; these devices are used in conjunction with special software or adapted hardware. For example, women with high quadriplegia are able to turn electrical devices on and off through the use of a sip-and-puff device. Switches that may be operated by a toe, a foot, or a hand permit entry of data into computers. Headpointers are attached to a headset and consist of pointers with rubber tips that are used to control keys on the keyboard. Joysticks enable women with limited motion to simulate the movement of a mouse.

Speech recognition systems enable women who are severely limited in their mobility to use personal computers in a variety of situations. These systems recognize the user's voice as an alternative way of entering data into computers and may be used to write and to carry out conversations, both on the job and in other settings.

Barrier-free design ensures that women with disabilities can enter and exit the building easily and safely; that bathroom facilities, water fountains, and employee dining rooms are accessible; that aisles and entryways are wide enough to accommodate wheelchairs; that ramps are placed where needed; and that floor coverings are amenable to the use of wheelchairs. Special paint or grit strip paint applied to slippery surfaces or inclines reduces the risk of accidents. Mirrors mounted at hallway intersections and see-through panels in doors may help prevent accidents for employees traveling in wheelchairs. Elevator buttons, public telephones, and light switches should also be accessible to people who use wheelchairs. Staff members who are not disabled should be assigned the responsibility for helping women with disabilities to exit the building in case of an emergency, such as a fire, bomb threat, or toxic leak.

The space underneath the desk should be large enough to accommodate a wheelchair; file cabinets should be lateral so that they are within reach. Special desks and workstations are available to accommodate wheelchairs and adjust to the required height of the user. Where carpets are used, they should be low level pile to allow for easier mobility, and elevators should be large enough to accommodate wheelchairs. Some individuals use standing wheelchairs that offer flexibility in adapting to the workplace as well as improving circulation, reducing pressure sores, and allowing users to make direct eye contact with colleagues without looking up from a seated position.

Transportation has often been a barrier to employment for women with disabilities. Some women with disabilities may be able to operate their own automobiles or vans. Many car manufacturers offer specially adapted vans to carry wheelchairs. Some of these companies also have special purchase or loan programs for people with disabilities. General Motors, Ford, and Chrysler offer financial assistance for the purchase of adaptive equipment such as hand controls, a ramp, or lifts to be installed in vehicles (see "TRAVEL AND TRANSPORTATION ORGANIZATIONS" section in this chapter). Public transportation systems may have regular buses with special equipment to lift wheelchairs, or they may offer transportation in vehicles specially designed for people with disabilities. The entry from the parking lot should provide enough space for wheelchairs to be removed from the vehicle. Level ground or ramps should lead into the building.

Women who require continued medical supervision to manage their conditions should be allowed time to schedule doctors' appointments. Flexibility is often the key, enabling women to work through lunch or later hours one day in order to take time off for medical care another day. Employers who cooperate to accommodate the special needs of women with disabilities and chronic conditions will contribute to a more productive workforce.

References

Brintnell, E. Sharon et al.
1994   "Disruption of Life Roles Following Injury: Impact on Women's Social Networks" Work 4:2:137-146
Hillyer, Barbara
1993   Feminism and Disability Norman, OK: University of Oklahoma Press

Kutner, Nancy G. and Heather L. Gray
1981   "Women and Chronic Renal Failure: Some Neglected Issues" <u>Journal of Sociology and Social Welfare</u> 8:2:320-332
Nathanson, Constance A.
1980   "Social Roles and Health Status among Women: The Significance of Employment" <u>Social Science and Medicine</u> 14A:463-471
Sherr Klein, Bonnie
1992   "We Are Who You Are" <u>Ms.</u> III(November/December):3:70-74
U.S. Department of Labor Women's Bureau
1992   "Women with Work Disabilities" <u>Facts on Working Women</u> March, No. 92.2

ORGANIZATIONS

Apple Computer Disability Resources
www.apple.com/education/k12/disability

The web site describes the built-in accessibility features of Macintosh computers for individuals with physical/motor, hearing, and/or visual disabilities. These features include easy access software, speech recognition, adjustable keyboards, and screen magnification. Provides links to third party solutions. An "Assistive Technology Resource Guide" is available online.

Equal Employment Opportunity Commission (EEOC)
1801 L Street, NW, 10th floor
Washington, DC 20507
(800) 669-3362 to order publications
(800) 669-4000 to speak to an investigator
(800) 800-3302 (TTY)
In the Washington, DC metropolitan area, (202) 275-7377
(202) 275-7518 (TTY)   www.eeoc.gov

Responsible for promulgating and enforcing regulations for the employment section of the ADA. Copies of its regulations are available in standard print and alternate formats.

IBM Special Needs Systems
www.austin.ibm.com/sns

The web site provides information on products and services for individuals with disabilities such as mobility, vision, speech, and hearing loss.

Job Accommodation Network (JAN)
West Virginia University
PO Box 6080
Morgantown, WV 26506-6080
(800) 526-7234 (V/TTY)   (800) 232-9675 (V/TTY)
FAX (304) 293-5407   e-mail: jan@jan.icdi.wvu.edu   www.jan.wvu.edu

Maintains database of products that facilitate accommodation in the workplace. Provides information to employers about practical accommodations which enable them to employ individuals with disabilities.

Microsoft Accessibility Technology for Everyone
www.microsoft.com/enable

The web site describes the built-in accessibility features of Microsoft products, including speech recognition, on screen keyboard programs, keyboard filters, and touch screens. Tutorials are available to enable individuals to customize their equipment.

National Easter Seal Society
230 West Monroe Street, Suite 1800
Chicago, IL 60606-4802
(800) 221-6827   (312) 726-6200   (312) 726-4258 (TTY)
FAX (312) 726-1494   e-mail: info@easter-seals.org
www.easter-seals.org

Helps individuals with disabilities find jobs through its Job Training and Employment Program. Provides day care for children of working parents. Affiliates throughout the country.

9to5, National Association of Working Women
1430 West Peachtree Street, Suite 610
Atlanta, GA 30309
(800) 522-0925
e-mail: hotline9to5@igc.org   www.9to5.org

Works on policy issues that affect working women, such as pregnancy discrimination and sexual harassment. Provides legal advice and offers a hot-line to help women who have job related problems. Membership, $25.00, includes "9to5 Newsline."

Office of Disability Employment Policy
U.S. Department of Labor
Frances Perkins Building
200 Constitution Avenue, NW
Washington, DC 20210
(202) 693-7880   (202) 693-7881 (TTY)   www.dol.gov/odep

Responsible for increasing employment opportunities for adults and youths with disabilities. Maintains the Small Business Self Employment Service to encourage individuals with disabilities to consider becoming entrepreneurs.

Rehabilitation Engineering and Assistive Technology Society of North America/RESNA
1700 North Moore Street, Suite 1540
Arlington, VA 22209
(703) 524-6686   (703) 524-6639 (TTY)   (703) 524-6630
e-mail: natloffice@resna.org   www.resna.org

Multidisciplinary professional membership organization for people involved with improving technology for people with disabilities. Conducts a variety of projects, including research in the area of assistive technology and rehabilitation technology service delivery and technical assistance to statewide programs to develop technology. Membership, regular, $150.00; institutional, $500.00; corporate, $525.00; includes semi-annual journal, "Assistive Technology" and quarterly newsletter, "RESNA News." Special membership rates for consumers and for students, $50.00 without journal; $80.00 with journal.

Vocational Rehabilitation and Employment
Veterans Benefits Administration
U.S. Department of Veterans Affairs (VA)
(800) 827-1000 (connects with regional office)
www.vba.va.gov

Provides education and rehabilitation assistance and independent living services to veterans with service related disabilities through offices located in every state as well as regional centers, medical centers, and insurance centers. Medical services are provided at VA Medical Centers, Outpatient Clinics, Domiciliaries, and Nursing Homes. VONAPP (VA Online Application) enables veterans to apply for benefits on the Internet.

Wider Opportunities for Women (WOW)
1001 Connecticut Avenue, NW, Suite 930
Washington, DC 20036
(202) 464-1596   FAX (202) 464-1660
e-mail: info@WOWonline.org   www.WOWonline.org

Works to achieve economic independence and equity for women and girls. Provides technical assistance online for employers and unions. Free publications list. Membership, $100.00, includes quarterly newsletter, "Women at Work" and discounts on publications.

Women's Bureau
U.S. Department of Labor
200 Constitution Avenue, NW, Room S3002
Washington, DC 20210
(800) 827-5335   (202) 693-67106610
FAX (202) 693-6725   www.dol.gov/wb

Works to improve working conditions for women. Publishes brochures on subjects related to employment, including disability information, medical leave and sexual harassment. Free. Newsletter, "e-News," available in print and on the web site. Free

PUBLICATIONS AND TAPES

Adaptive Technologies for Learning & Work Environments
by Joseph J. Lazzaro
ALA Order Fulfillment
American Library Association
PO Box 932501
Atlanta, GA 31193-2501
(866) 746-7252   FAX (770) 442-9742
e-mail: ala-orders@PBD.com   www.alastore.ala.org

This book explores adaptive technology for those with motor and/or speech impairments, visual impairment, and hearing impairment. It focuses on personal computer hardware, software, computer networks, and online services. It also lists funding sources, training and technical support resources, and vendors. $48.00. Also available on a CD-ROM, $35.00.

Americans with Disabilities Act: Questions and Answers
Equal Employment Opportunity Center (EEOC)
Publications Distribution Center
PO Box 12549
Cincinnati, OH 45212-0549
(800) 669-3362   (800) 800-3302 (TTY)   FAX (513) 489-8692
www.eeoc.gov

This booklet's question and answer format provides explanations of the ADA's effects on employment, state and local governments, and public accommodations. Available in standard print, alternate formats, automated fax system, and on the web site. Free. Also available at www.pueblo.gsa.gov. Click on "Federal Programs."

Careers and the Disabled
Equal Opportunity Publications
445 Broad Hollow Road, Suite 425
Melville, NY 11747
(631) 421-9421   FAX (631) 421-0359   e-mail: info@eop.com
www.eop.com

This magazine provides articles on career guidance and profiles of role-models and lists companies seeking qualified job candidates. A braille insert in each issue describes the articles which appear in print. Offers Online Resume Database which matches readers with advertisers who are recruiting employees. Published three times a year; $12.00.

Computer and Web Resources for People with Disabilities
Alliance for Technology Access
2175 East Francisco Boulevard, Suite L
San Rafael, CA 94901
(415) 455-4575   (415) 455-0491 (TTY)   FAX (415) 455-0654
e-mail: ATAinfo@ataccess.org   www.ataccess.org

This book describes assistive technology and discusses what to consider when making a purchase, the support team members that can provide assistance, and information on sources. Softcover, $20.95; spiral bound, $27.95; CD-ROM (html format), $27.95

Family and Medical Leave Act at the One Year Mark
9to5, National Association of Working Women
231 West Wisconsin Ave, Suite 900
Milwaukee, WI 53203
(800) 522-0925 jobs problem hot-line (414) 274-0925   FAX (414) 272-2870
e-mail: naww9to5@execpc.com   www.9to5.org

This publication reports on the implementation of the law and suggest enforcement strategies. $10.00

Guide to the Family and Medical Leave Act
The National Partnership for Women and Families
National Partnership for Women and Families
1875 Connecticut Avenue, NW, Suite 650
Washington, DC 20009
(202) 986-2600   FAX (202) 986-2539
e-mail: info@nationalpartnership.org   www.nationalpartnership.org

This booklet answers the most frequently asked questions about the law. Available in English and Spanish. Also available on the web site. Free

Key Changes
Fanlight Productions
4196 Washington Street, Suite 2
Boston, MA 02131
(800) 937-4113   (617) 469-4999   FAX (617) 469-3379
e-mail: fanlight@fanlight.com   www.fanlight.com

This videotape portrays Lisa Thorson, a vocalist who experienced a spinal cord injury and continues performing in her chosen profession. 28 minutes. $149.00

Meeting the Needs of Employees with Disabilities
Resources for Rehabilitation
22 Bonad Road
Winchester, MA 01890
(781) 368-9094   FAX (781) 368-9096   e-mail: info@rfr.org
www.rfr.org

This book provides information to help people with disabilities retain or obtain employment. Information on government programs and laws, supported employment, training programs, environmental adaptations, and the transition from school to work are included. Chapters on mobility, vision, and hearing and speech impairments include information on organizations, products, and services that enable employers to accommodate the needs of employees with disabilities. $44.95 (See order form on last page of this book.)

Part of the Team - People with Disabilities in the Workforce
National Easter Seal Society
230 West Monroe Street, Suite 1800
Chicago, IL 60606-4802
(800) 221-6827   (312) 726-6200   (312) 726-4258 (TTY)
FAX (312) 726-1494   e-mail: info@easter-seals.org
www.easter-seals.org

This videotape profiles ten individuals who have overcome physical barriers to employment with cooperation and communication with their employers. $25.00

Ticket to Work and Work Incentives Improvement Act of 1999
Working While Disabled... How We Can Help
Social Security Administration (see "ORGANIZATIONS" section above)
(800) 772-1213   (800) 325-0778 (TTY)   www.socialsecurity.gov

These booklets provide basic information about Social Security employment programs for individuals with disabilities. The Social Security Administration distributes many other titles, including many that are available in standard print, alternate formats, on the web site, and at local Social Security offices. Free

HOUSING AND ENVIRONMENTAL ADAPTATIONS

Housing plays an important role in a woman's ability to remain independent. Most women with disabilities will opt to live in their own home whenever possible. Often this requires financial assistance, household help, environmental modifications, or moving to a more accessible building. The government has provided a number of programs to assist people with disabilities with affordable housing and to protect them from discrimination.

The *Fair Housing Act of 1988* prohibits discrimination in housing due to race, religion, gender, family status, disability, and national origin. It is enforced by the Department of Housing and Urban Development (HUD). It applies to sale and rental of most housing and mortgage lending. New buildings constructed after March 13, 1991 that have an elevator and four or more units must be accessible to individuals with disabilities. Tenants with disabilities have the legal right to make modifications to rental housing at their own expense in order to meet their needs. However, the residence must be restored to its original condition "within reason" when the tenant moves. In addition, HUD has established programs to house individuals with disabilities who are homeless. When individuals with disabilities file a complaint, HUD will provide interpreters, materials on cassette or in braille, and assistance in reading and filling out forms.

Public housing is a major resource for women with disabilities and older women with low income. *Section 8* Certificates and Vouchers provide federal subsidies to income-eligible households to help defray housing costs in the private rental market. Section 8 subsidies may also be used in group residences. Local public housing authorities administer the program. *Section 803* of the National Affordable Housing Act of 1990, HOPE for Elderly Independence, combines tenant-based rental housing certificates and rental vouchers with supportive services to enable frail elders who have not been receiving any form of housing assistance to continue living in the community.

Section 202 of the *Housing and Community Development Act of 1987,* Direct Loan Program for Housing for the Elderly or Handicapped, provides loans to nonprofit organizations to sponsor development of housing for elders and persons with disabilities, including units eligible for Section 8 rent subsidies. Under amendments to the *Housing and Community Development Act of 1987* (P.L. 100-242), the Department of Housing and Urban Development provides direct loans for the development of projects for elders and individuals with disabilities. These developments may consist of apartments or group homes for up to 15 residents.

In 2000, HUD released the final rule that allows individuals and families to use Section 8 vouchers for home ownership. Public housing authorities who participate in the Homeownership Program can allow individuals and families to convert current Section 8 vouchers from rental to mortgage supplements and allow individuals and families who are eligible in the future to choose between mortgage and rental subsidies.

The *Rural Housing Service* of the U.S. Department of Agriculture offers a variety of home ownership programs for individuals who are elderly, disabled, or low-income and who live in rural areas, including direct loan and loan guarantee programs, home repair loan and grant programs, and rental assistance (see "ORGANIZATIONS" section below). Fannie Mae, a private company, offers HomeChoice, Community Living, and Retrofitting mortgages that make home ownership and home modifications possible for individuals with disabilities or who have family members with disabilities living with them (see "ORGANIZATIONS" section below).

Home Equity Conversion Mortgages, sometimes called reverse mortgages, allow elders to convert the equity in their homes into cash that will enable them to meet housing expenses. These mortgages are insured by HUD in the event that the lender defaults. The reverse mortgage does not have to be repaid until the mortgagee moves or dies. Homeowners must be age 62 or older, occupy their own home as a principal residence, and own the home free and clear or nearly so. Reverse mortgage payment options include "tenure," monthly payments to homeowners as long as they use their homes as principal residences; "term," which provides monthly payments for a specified period; and "line-of-credit," which allows homeowners to draw on their equity up to a maximum amount.

Women who feel that they have experienced discrimination in housing may file complaints with HUD or a state or local fair housing agency, or they may file a civil suit.

Other housing options for women with disabilities include assisted living facilities, such as board and care homes, adult care homes, and residential care facilities. Many cities have residential hotels for older women with services, such as housekeeping, security, and social activities. Continuing care retirement communities provide housing choices ranging from independent apartment living with services, such as congregate meals and activities, to 24-hour nursing care. Shared housing programs include shared group residences and programs which match elders who need some assistance to remain at home with younger people who need inexpensive housing. Accessory housing, independent housing units built on to single family homes or erected on the property of a single family home, is another option for elders who wish to live independently but need supportive services.

Women with disabilities who wish to remain in their own homes may find that environmental adaptations enable them to do so. For example, the installation of ramps, elevators, and special lifts to climb the stairs may be sufficient for those with mobility impairments. Lowered kitchen counters and appliances facilitate cooking for women who use wheelchairs. Other adaptive design features include accessible routes, light switches, electrical outlets, and thermostats; bathrooms with walls sturdy enough to install grab bars; and kitchens and bathrooms with sufficient space to maneuver wheelchairs.

Many architects now specialize in designing buildings and dwelling units that meet the needs of people with disabilities. The state office on disability, the architectural access board, or the local or state professional society of architects should be able to provide a list of qualified architects.

Assistive devices for dressing, such as elastic shoelaces, velcro closures, and buttoning aids, are especially useful for women with mobility impairments. Foam hair rollers, water pipe foam insulation, or layers of tape are used to build up the handles of items as varied as toothbrushes, pens, pencils, eating utensils, paint brushes, and crochet hooks.

Remote controls turn on and off lights and televisions and open and close garage doors. Telephones with voice dialers permit the storage of frequently called telephone numbers and automatic dialing. Speaker phones allow individuals with poor motor control or tremors to carry on a telephone conversation comfortably.

Although some of the publications described below mention a specific disability or age, they include suggestions that are applicable for individuals of all ages and with a variety of conditions. Suppliers of personal and home health care aids, recreational products, and mobility aids for more than one type of condition or disability are listed. Many hospital pharmacies as well as large department and discount stores now sell home health products such as wheelchairs, bathroom safety devices, canes, and walkers. Some of this equipment may also be available on a rental or loan basis from community health agencies.

ORGANIZATIONS

ABLEDATA
8630 Fenton Street, Suite 930
Silver Spring, MD 20910
(800) 227-0216   www.abledata.com

This federally funded center responds to telephone, mail, and e-mail inquiries about disabilities, assistive products, and support services. Most publications may be downloaded from the web site. Free

Architectural and Transportation Barriers Compliance Board (ATBCB)
1331 F Street, NW, Suite 1000
Washington, DC 20004
(800) 872-2253   (800) 993-2822 (TTY)   (202) 272-0080
(202) 272-0082 (TTY)   FAX (202) 272-0081
e-mail: info@access-board.gov www.access-board.gov

A federal agency charged with developing standards for accessibility in federal facilities, public accommodations, and transportation facilities as required by the Americans with Disabilities Act and other federal laws. Provides technical assistance, sponsors research, and distributes publications. Publishes a quarterly newsletter, "Access America." Publications available in standard print, alternate formats, and on the web site. Free

Center for Universal Design
North Carolina State University
Box 8613
Raleigh, NC 27695-8613
(800) 647-6777   (919) 515-3082 (V/TTY)
FAX (919) 515-7330   e-mail: cud@ncsu.edu   www.design.ncsu.edu/cud

A federally funded research and training center that works toward improving housing and product design for people with disabilities. Provides technical assistance, training, and publications. Some publications are available on the web site.

Fair Housing Accessibility FIRST
(888) 341-7781 (V/TTY)   e-mail: contact@fairhousingfirst.org
www.fairhousingfirst.org

This program, funded by the Department of Housing and Urban Development (HUD), provides guidance, training, and educational materials about the Fair Housing Act. A training curriculum has been developed, and technical assistance is available.

Fannie Mae
(800) 732-6643   www.fanniemae.com

This private company offers mortgage products designed to help individuals with disabilities attain home ownership. Publishes "A Home of Your Own Guide," for housing educators and counselors who work with individuals with disabilities; available through the Fannie Mae Distribution Center, (800) 471-5554. Free. Also available on the web site.

GE Answer Center
(800) 626-2000   (800) 833-4322 (TTY)

This consumer information center provides assistance to individuals with disabilities as well as to the general public. Appliance controls marked with braille or raised dots are available for individuals who are blind or visually impaired, free. Two brochures, "Appliance Help for Those with Special Needs," and "Basic Kitchen Planning for the Physically Handicapped," are free. The center is open 24 hours a day, seven days a week.

National Association of Home Builders (NAHB)
National Research Center, Economics and Policy Analysis Division
400 Prince George's Boulevard
Upper Marlboro, MD 20772
(301) 249-4000   FAX (301) 249-0305   www.nahbrc.org

The research section of the home building industry trade organization produces publications and provides training on housing and special needs.

National Council of State Housing Agencies (NCSHA)
444 North Capitol Street, NW, Suite 438
Washington, DC 20001
(202) 624-7710   FAX (202) 624-5899   www.ncsha.org

Membership organization of state housing agencies. Web site offers a "State Housing Finance Agency Directory" that lists assistance available for home modifications and home ownership programs.

National Home of Your Own Alliance
Center for Housing and New Community Economics
Institute on Disability
University of New Hampshire
7 Leavitt Lane, Suite 101
Durham, NH 03824
(800) 220-8770   alliance.unh.edu

The web site provides extensive information about housing for individuals with disabilities, including the Section 8 Homeownership Rule; "A Home of Your Own Guide" for prospective home owners; and information about state housing coalitions, funding sources, and other resources.

Office of Fair Housing and Equal Opportunity
U.S. Department of Housing and Urban Development (HUD)
451 7th Street, SW, Room 5204
Washington DC 20140
(800) 669-9777   (800) 927-9275 (TTY)
(202) 927-9275 (TTY)   www.hud.gov/fheo.html

This agency enforces the Fair Housing Act and will inform callers how to file a complaint with one of the ten regional HUD offices. Information about the Fair Housing Act and a complaint form are available on the web site.

Rural Housing Service National Office
U.S. Department of Agriculture
Room 5037, South Building
14th Street and Independence Avenue, SW
Washington, DC 20250
(202) 720-4323   www.rurdev.usda.gov/rhs

Provides home ownership, renovation, and repair programs for individuals with disabilities who live in rural areas.

Accessible Home Design: Architectural Solutions for the Wheelchair User
PVA Distribution Center
PO Box 753
Waldorf, MD 20604-0753
(888) 860-7244   (301) 932-7834
FAX (301) 843-0159   www.pva.org

Focusing on areas such as kitchens, bathrooms, and multiple levels, this book provides practical and economical designs to make homes accessible. $22.95

A Consumer's Guide to Home Adaptation
Adaptive Environments Center
374 Congress Street, Suite 301
Boston, MA 02210
(617) 695-1225 (V/TTY)   FAX (617) 482-8099
e-mail: adaptive@adaptiveenvironments.org
www.adaptenv.org

This workbook enables people with disabilities to plan the modifications necessary to adapt their homes. Describes how to widen doorways, lower countertops, etc. $12.00

Designs for Independent Living
The Less Challenging Home
Appliance Information Service
Whirlpool Corporation
Benton Harbor, MI 49022
(800) 253-1301   (800) 334-6889 (TTY)   www.whirlpool.com

The first brochure provides information on adaptations for the home environment and major appliances. Free. The second brochure provides suggestions for incorporating accessible design when building or remodeling kitchens and bathrooms. Describes building materials and appliances and includes charts indicating appliance features that are helpful to users with disabilities. Free

Directory of Accessible Building Products
National Association of Home Builders (NAHB)
National Research Center, Economics and Policy Analysis Division
400 Prince George's Boulevard
Upper Marlboro, MD 20772
(301) 249-4000   FAX (301) 430-60180   www.nahbrc.org

This directory describes and illustrates products available for use by individuals with disabilities. $5.00

Easy Things to Make -- To Make Things Easy: Simple Do-It-Yourself Home Modifications for Older People and Others with Physical Disabilities
by Doreen Greenstein
Brookline Books
PO Box 1047
Cambridge, MA 02238-1047
(800) 666-2665   (617) 868-0360
FAX (617) 868-1772   e-mail: brooklinebks@delphi.com
www.brooklinebooks.com

This book describes low-cost home modifications and suggests adaptations for everyday activities. Large print. $15.95

Home Safety Checklist for Older Consumers
U.S. Consumer Product Safety Commission
Washington, DC 20207-0001
(800) 638-2772   (301) 504-0580   FAX (301) 504-0281
e-mail: info@cpsc.gov   www.cpsc.gov

Provides information on simple, inexpensive repairs and safety recommendations. Available in English and Spanish. Free. Also available on the web site.

How to Build Ramps for Home Accessibility
Metropolitan Center for Independent Living
1600 University Avenue West, Suite 16
St. Paul, MN 55104
(651) 603-2029   www.wheelchairramp.org

The manual and videotape provide step-by-step instruction in building modular ramps and steps. Manual, $15.00. May also be downloaded from web site. Videotape, $20.00.

Kitchen Design for the Wheelchair User
PVA Distribution Center
PO Box 753
Waldorf, MD 20604-0753
(888) 860-7244   (301) 932-7834
FAX (301) 843-0159   www.pva.org

This booklet shows how kitchens may be designed for easy access by wheelchair users. Three sample designs are provided. Free. Also available on the web site.

Mealtime Manual for People with Disabilities and Aging
by Judith L. Klinger
Slack Incorporated
6900 Grove Road
Thorofare, NJ 08086
(856) 848-1000   FAX (856) 853-5991   www.slackinc.com

This book provides information on meal planning and preparation for individuals with mobility and visual impairments. Includes hands-on skills and suggests many assistive devices. $25.95

Retrofitting Homes for a Lifetime
National Association of Home Builders (NAHB)
National Research Center, Economics and Policy Analysis Division
400 Prince George's Boulevard
Upper Marlboro, MD 20772
(301) 249-4000   FAX (301) 430-6180   www.nahbrc.org

This publication enables remodelers and homeowners to assess needed modifications; provides an accessibility checklist; suggests financing alternatives; and makes recommendations for working with builders. $15.00

Shared Housing for the Elderly
by Dale Jaffe (ed.)
Greenwood and Heinemann Publishing Group
88 Post Road West
Westport, CT 06881
(800) 225-5800   (203) 226-3571   FAX (603) 431-2214
www.greenwood.com

A collection of articles about the advantages and problems of shared housing programs. $57.95

VENDORS OF ASSISTIVE DEVICES

The following vendors sell assistive devices that help people remain independent. Those that specialize in a specific type of product have a notation under the listing. Otherwise, their product line is broad, usually including personal, health care, and aids and devices for the home. Unless otherwise noted, the catalogues are free.

Access with Ease
PO Box 1150
Chino Valley, AZ 86323
(800) 531-9479   (928) 636-9469
e-mail: kmjc@northlink.com   www.shop.store.yahoo.com/capability

adaptAbility
75 Mill Street
Colchester, CT 06415
(800) 243-9232   FAX (800) 566-6678
e-mail: cservice@ssww.com   www.ssww.com

Aids that make dressing, eating, and bathing easier. Exercise and fitness activities and hot and cold therapy.

Dynamic Living, Inc.
426 Hayden Station Road
Windsor, CT 06095
(888) 940-0605   FAX (860) 683-2694
e-mail: info@dynamic-living.com   www.dynamic-living.com

Enrichments
Sammons Preston Roylan
PO Box 5071
Bollingbrook, IL 60440
(800) 323-5547   FAX (800) 547-4333
e-mail: sp@sammonspreston.com   www.sammonspreston.com

Independent Living Aids, Inc. (ILA)
200 Robbins Lane
Jericho, NY 11753
(800) 537-2118   FAX (516) 752-3135
e-mail: can-do@independentliving.com
www.independentliving.com

Living Better with Arthritis
Aids for Arthritis, Inc.
35 Wakefield Drive
Medford, NJ 08055
(800) 654-0707   FAX (609) 654-8631   www.aidsforarthritis.com

A mail order catalogue of products with dressing, bathing, and grooming aids and kitchen, housekeeping, and recreation equipment.

LS & S Group
PO Box 673
Northbrook, IL 60065
(800) 468-4789   (847) 498-9777
e-mail: info@lssonline.net   www.lssgroup.com

Medela Inc.
1101 Corporate Drive
McHenry, IL 60050
(800) 435-8316   FAX (800) 995-7867
e-mail: customer.service@medela.com
www.medela.com

Sells breastfeeding products, including electric breastpumps and the PedalPump, a breastpump powered by a foot pedal.

Medic Alert Foundation International
2323 Colorado Avenue
Turlock, CA 95382
(888) 633-4298   In CA, (209) 668-3333
FAX (209) 669-2495   www.medicalert.org

Medical identification bracelet for people with serious medical conditions.

Oxo International
75 Ninth Avenue, Fifth Floor
New York, NY 10011
(800) 545-4411   FAX (877) 523-7186   e-mail: info@oxo.com
www.oxo.com

Sells a wide variety of Oxo household and gardening tools with built-up handles, including vegetable peelers, can openers, trowels, and scissors.

Radio Shack/Tandy Corporation
500 One Tandy Center
100 Throckmorton Street
Fort Worth, TX 76102
(817) 390-3700   www.radioshack.com

Radio Shack products for individuals with disabilities, such as talking watches and clocks and assistive listening aids, are included in the company's regular catalogues.

Rolli-Moden Designs
12225 World Trade Drive, Suite T
San Diego, CA 92128
(800) 707-2395   (858) 676-1825   FAX (858) 676-0820
e-mail: rm@roli-moden.com   www.rolli-moden.com

Sells dress and casual clothing and accessories designed for wheelchair users. Free catalogue.

Sears Home HealthCare Catalog
7700 Brush Hill Road
Hinsdale, IL 60521
(800) 326-1750   (800) 733-7249 (TTY)

Sells health care and rehabilitation products.

TRAVEL AND RECREATION

Both travel and recreation provide relief from tension, relaxation, and social interactions. Individuals who participate in recreational activities have an increased sense of self-worth and well-being. For individuals who are seriously ill, recreation diverts attention from the illness and provides opportunities for socialization. Some individuals with disabilities need assistance in order to continue with their favorite recreational pastimes. Others may develop an interest in new activities more appropriate to their current condition.

In the aftermath of World War II, rehabilitation programs were developed to treat those returning home with physical and mental disabilities. Competitive sports were included in the program of the first spinal cord injury center opened in England in 1944 (DePauw and Gavron: 1995). During the 1950s, wheelchair sports expanded throughout Europe to the United States, and individuals with other disabilities became involved in national and international sports organizations. For individuals who have engaged in sports throughout their lives, the advent of disability seems to signal an end to valued activities. Those who receive care in rehabilitation facilities are more apt to discover the adaptations available in equipment and techniques that make sports opportunities accessible. Sports enthusiasts may choose activities such as skiing, basketball, running, golf, scuba diving, baseball, horseback riding, archery, and sailing, to name just a few examples.

The *Americans with Disabilities Act* (ADA) of 1990 mandates accessibility to recreation facilities and athletic programs, from aerobic training classes and local parks to football stadiums and other venues. Advances in technology have led to the development of racing wheelchairs, special hand and foot prostheses, and adapted ski equipment such as sit-skis. All-terrain vehicles (ATVs), adapted with lifts, hand controls, or safety harnesses, enable individuals with mobility impairments to participate in many outdoor recreation activities. Organizations that specialize in adaptive recreation programs are listed below (see "ADAPTIVE SPORTS AND RECREATION ORGANIZATIONS"). The ADA also requires that fixed route buses and rail transportation be accessible and usable by individuals with disabilities. However, deadlines for implementation of the ADA's regulations vary from six to seven years for private intercity transit to as long as 20 years for Amtrak and commuter rail stations.

The Federal Aviation Administration requires each airline to submit a company-wide policy for travelers with disabilities. Passengers may call ahead to request early boarding, special seating, or meals which meet dietary restrictions. Airport facilities are designed to offer accessible restrooms, elevators, electric carts or wheelchairs, and first aid stations. The *Air Carrier Access Act of 1986* (ACAA) includes regulations that cover the needs of travelers with disabilities, such as access to commuter planes, accessible lavatories, wheelchair storage, and sensitivity training for all airline personnel. Contact the airlines to obtain a written statement of the special services they provide. Individuals who believe that their rights have been denied may file a complaint within 45 days of the incident with the Aviation Protection Division, U.S. Department of Transportation, C-75 Room 4107, Washington, DC 20590, (202) 366-2220; (202) 765-7687 (TTY); e-mail: airconsumer@ost.dot.gov. Air Travel Consumer Report is a web site that provides information on the rights of individuals with disabilities with regard to new security regulations put into place in late 2001 (see "ORGANIZATIONS" section).

Amtrak offers a 15% discount on most one-way, round trip, and All Aboard America rail fares for individuals with disabilities. Passengers must present proof of disability, such as a certificate of legal blindness or a letter from a physician specifying the nature of the disability. Greyhound allows passengers with disabilities requiring assistance with personal hygiene, eating, medications, or while the bus is in motion to request a free ticket for a companion (certain restrictions apply). There is no charge for guide dogs for individuals who are visually impaired, blind, or deaf.

Travel agencies that plan special trips for people with disabilities are available throughout North America. Many major hotel chains, airlines, and car rental companies provide special assistance to people with disabilities and often have special toll-free numbers for users of teletypewriters (TTYs). Some companies offer specially trained travel companions to people with disabilities who need an escort. In the United States, many state tourism offices provide information about accessible attractions for prospective visitors with disabilities. Auto clubs both here and abroad are also good sources for such information.

Individuals with disabilities and elders are eligible for special entrance passes to federal recreation facilities. The *Golden Access Passport* is a free lifetime pass available to any U.S. citizen or permanent resident, regardless of age, who is blind or permanently disabled. It admits the permit holder and passengers in a single, private, noncommercial vehicle to any parks, monuments, historic sites, recreation areas, and wildlife refuges which usually charge entrance fees. If the permit holder does not enter by car, the Passport admits the permit holder, spouse, and children. The permit holder is also entitled to a 50% discount on charges such as camping, boat launching, and parking fees. Fees charged by private concessionaires are not discounted. Golden Access Passports are available only in person, with proof of disability, such as a certificate of legal blindness. Since the Passport is available at most federal recreation areas, it is not necessary to obtain one ahead of time. A *Golden Age Passport* offers the same benefits to persons age 62 or older, with proof of age.

The Disabled Sportsmen's Access of 1998 (P.L. 105-261) will lead to the accessibility to outdoor recreation programs on military installations for individuals with disabilities. The outdoor recreation programs include sports such as fishing, trapping, hunting, wildlife observation, boating, and camping.

Rehabilitation hospitals and centers offer driver evaluation services such as clinical testing and observation to determine an individual's need for adaptive equipment or training. Many Department of Veterans Affairs Medical Centers (VAMC) offer driver evaluation services, driver training, and information services to veterans with disabilities through the Rehabilitation Medicine Service at their facilities. The Internal Revenue Service allows individuals to include in medical expenses the cost of special hand controls and other special equipment installed in a car to be used by a person with a disability. Individuals may also consider as a medical expense the difference between the cost of a car designed to hold a wheelchair and the cost of the car without modification. Contact the Internal Revenue Service (see "ORGANIZATIONS" section below) to obtain Publication 502 "Medical and Dental Expenses." Major automobile manufacturers offer reimbursement for adaptive equipment installed on new vehicles. Programs for special adaptive equipment offered by automobile manufacturers are listed in the "ORGANIZATIONS" section below.

Reference

DePauw, Karen P. and Susan J. Gavron
1995   Disability and Sport Champaign, IL: Human Kinetics

TRAVEL AND TRANSPORTATION ORGANIZATIONS

Access-Able Travel Service
PO Box 1796
Wheat Ridge, CO 80034
(303) 232-2979   FAX (303) 239-8486   www.access-able.com

Provides information on accommodations, access guides, entertainment, tours, and transportation. Free monthly newsletter available by e-mail.

Access Outdoors
www.accessoutdoors.org

This web site provides information about organizations that offer accessible outdoor recreation experiences, adaptive recreation products, and organizations that provide assistance in creating accessible programs. A service of Wilderness Inquiry.

ADED - Association for Driver Rehabilitation Specialists
711 South Vienna Street
Ruston, LA 71270
(800) 290-2344   (318) 257-5055
FAX (318) 255-4175   www.driver-ed.org

Certifies members to conduct driver evaluation and training for individuals with disabilities.

Air Travel Consumer Report
(800) 778-4838   (800) 455-9880 (TTY)
www.airconsumer.ost.dot.gov/report.htm

This web site includes information about the rights of passengers with disabilities. The rights of individuals with disabilities regarding new security regulations put in place in late 2001 are described in a fact sheet on the web site. The toll-free number provides assistance to travelers with disability-related air travel service problems. Assistance is available seven days a week from 7:00 a.m. to 11:00 p.m., Eastern time.

Amtrak
(877) 268-7252   (800) 523-6590 (TTY)

Provides 15% discount on most fares, including accessible sleeping accommodations, for individuals with disabilities. Also applies to companion fare. On-board services and special meals available upon request with advance notice. Request "Access Amtrak: A Guide to Amtrak Services for Travelers with Disabilities." Available in standard print and alternate formats. Free

Architectural and Transportation Barriers Compliance Board (ATBCB)
1331 F Street, NW, Suite 1000
Washington, DC 20004
(800) 872-2253   (800) 993-2822 (TTY)   (202) 272-0080
(202) 272-0082 (TTY)   FAX (202) 272-0081   www.access-board.gov

Maintains a database on accessible transportation, including a computerized, annotated bibliography. Publishes brochures on subjects such as "Air Carrier Policies on Transport of Battery Powered Wheelchairs."

Auto Channel
(877) 275-4226   www.ican.com

Provides a step-by-step evaluation to enable consumers with disabilities to choose the vehicle that meets their needs.

Automobility
DaimlerChrysler Corporation
PO Box 5080
Troy, MI 48007-5080
(800) 255-9877   (800) 922-3826 (TTY)
FAX (810) 597-3501   www.automobility.daimlerchrysler.com

Provides $750 to $1000 reimbursement (on eligible models) on the purchase of alerting devices for people who are deaf or hearing impaired and assistive equipment for vehicles purchased to transport individuals who use wheelchairs.

Ford Mobility Motoring Program
(800) 952-2248   (800) 833-0312 (TTY)
FAX (800) 292-7842
www.ford.com/en/ourServices/specialBuyingPrograms/mobilityMotoringProgram/default.htm

This program funds assistive equipment conversion up to $1000. Provides toll-free information line, free videotape that describes the program, list of assessment centers that determine equipment needs, and referrals to sources for additional assistance.

General Motors Mobility Assistance Center
100 Renaissance Center, PO Box 100
Detroit, MI 48265
(800) 323-9935   (800) 833-9935 (TTY)
www.gm.com/automotive/vehicle_shopping/gm_mobility

This program reimburses customers up to $1000 for vehicle modifications or adaptive driving devices for new or demo vehicles. Includes alerting devices for drivers who are deaf or hearing impaired, such as emergency vehicle siren detectors and enhanced turn signal reminders.

Greyhound Lines, Inc.
PO Box 660362
Dallas, TX 75266-0362
(800) 231-2222 (General Information)
(800) 752-4841 (ADA Assist Line)
(800) 345-3109 (TTY)   www.Greyhound.com

Provides assistance to travelers with disabilities upon request. Call ADA Assist line at least 48 hours in advance of travel. Information also available on web site; click on "Travel Planning for Passengers with Disabilities."

Internal Revenue Service (IRS)
(800) 829-1040   (800) 829-4059 (TTY)
www.irs.ustreas.gov

The IRS provides technical assistance about tax credits and deductions related to accommodations for disabilities. To request Publication 502, "Medical and Dental Expenses," call (800) 829-3676; (800) 829-4059 (TTY). These publications are available on the web site.

Mobility International USA (MIUSA)
PO Box 10767
Eugene, OR 97440
(541) 343-1284 (V/TTY)   FAX (541) 343-6812
e-mail: info@miusa.org   www.miusa.org

Promotes the participation of individuals with disabilities in international and educational exchange programs, such as workcamps, conferences, and internships. Membership, $35.00, includes semi-annual newsletter, "Over the Rainbow."

MossRehab ResourceNet
www.mossresourcenet.org

This web site offers information on accessible travel for individuals with disabilities. Click on "Accessible Travel."

National Mobility Equipment Dealers Association
11211 North Nebraska Avenue, Suite A-5
Tampa, FL 33612
(800) 833-0427   (813) 977-6603   FAX (813) 977-6402
www.nmeda.org

The members of this organization are car dealers, manufacturers, driver evaluators, and insurance companies. Provides local referrals to members who are adaptive equipment dealers and rates members' competencies in equipment installation and conversion.

National Park Service
U.S. Department of the Interior, Office of Public Affairs
1849 C Street, NW, Room 3045
Washington, DC 20240   (202) 208-6843   www.nps.gov

Operates the Golden Access Passport program for people who have disabilities. Free brochure.

Project Action Accessible Traveler's Database
www.projectaction.org/paweb/index.htm

This database offers information on accessible transportation services, including accessible car and van rental companies, rural and urban transit operators, major hotel chains, and national toll-free numbers.

Society for Accessible Travel and Hospitality (SATH)
347 Fifth Avenue, Suite 610
New York, NY 10016
(212) 447-7284   FAX (212) 725-8253   www.sath.org

Advocates for accessibility for individuals with disabilities and serves as a clearinghouse for information on barrier-free travel. Membership, individuals, $45.00; seniors and students, $30.00.

Transportation Security Administration (TSA)
U.S. Department of Transportation
400 Seventh Street, SW
Washington, DC 20590
www.tsa.gov

Created by Congress under the Transportation Security Act, passed after the attack on the World Trade Center on September 11, 2001, this agency is responsible for establishing regulations to enhance passenger security related to all types of transportation. The web site has information specific to travelers who have disabilities.

Wheelers Accessible Van Rental
(800) 456-1371   www.wheelerz.com

Rents mini-vans accessible to wheelchair users throughout the country.

Wilderness Inquiry
808 14th Avenue SE
Minneapolis, MN 55414
(800) 728-0719 (V/TTY)   In Minneapolis and St. Paul, (612) 676-9400
(612) 676-9475 (TTY)   FAX (612) 676-9401
www.wildernessinquiry.org

Sponsors trips into wilderness areas for individuals with disabilities or chronic conditions. Request schedule of current trips.

ADAPTIVE SPORTS AND RECREATION ORGANIZATIONS

Access to Recreation
8 Sandra Court
Newbury Park, CA 91320
(800) 634-4351   (805) 498-7535
FAX (805) 498-8186   www.accesstr.com

Sells assistive devices that help people with disabilities enjoy sports and recreational activities, such as swimming aids, fishing equipment, fitness equipment and home gyms, golf clubs, wheelchair ramps, bowling aids, and adapted games.

Achilles Track Club
42 West 38th Street, 4th Floor
New York, NY 10018
(212) 354-0300   FAX (212) 354-3978
www.achillestrackclub.org

Promotes running as a recreational activity and competitive sport for individuals with disabilities. Chapters in many states and foreign countries. Membership is free. Publishes newsletter, "The Achilles Heel."

American Canoe Association
7432 Alban Station Boulevard, Suite B-232
Springfield, VA 22150
(703) 451-0141   FAX (703) 451-2245
e-mail: aca@acanet.org   www.acanet.org

Certifies instructors in adaptive paddling course for canoeing, kayaking, and coastal kayaking. Will refer individuals with disabilities to certified instructors in local area. Provides information on equipment adaptations.

Breckenridge Outdoor Education Center
PO Box 697
Breckenridge, CO 80424
(970) 453-6422   FAX (970) 453-4676
e-mail: boec@boec.org   www.boec.org

Offers year-round adaptive outdoor learning experiences for children and adults with disabilities and provides training for therapists and educators.

Challenged Athletes Foundation (CAF)
2148 Jimmy Durante Boulevard, #B
Del Mar, CA 92014
(858) 793-9293
e-mail: execdir@challengedathletes.org
www.challengedathletes.org

The foundation provides grants to individual athletes with disabilities for training, equipment, or travel to competitions.

Disabled Sports, U.S.A.
451 Hungerford Drive, Suite 100
Rockville, MD 20850
(301) 217-0960   FAX (301) 217-0968   e-mail: dsusa@dsusa.org
www.dsusa.org

Nationwide network of chapters sponsors recreational activities such as skiing, camping, hiking, biking, horseback riding, and mountain climbing. Offers adaptive fitness instructor training to therapists, exercise instructors, and program directors. Membership, $25.00, includes subscription to "Challenge Magazine."

Disabled Sports U.S.A. Volleyball
921 North Village Lake Road
DeLand, FL 32724
e-mail: chris@dsusav.org   www.dsusav.org

Promotes the participation in volleyball by athletes who are amputees or have limb disabilities.

Fishing Has No Boundaries
PO Box 175
Hayward, WI 54843
(800) 243-3462   (715) 634-3185
e-mail: fhnbinc@cheq.net   www.fhnbinc.org

Provides opportunities for individuals with disabilities to fish and teaches them about adaptive devices for fishing. Events sponsored by community organizations.

Handicapped Scuba Association (HSA)
1104 El Prado
San Clemente, CA 92672
(949) 498-4540   e-mail: hsa@hsascuba.com   www.hsascuba.com

This organization trains and certifies scuba diving instructors to work with individuals with disabilities; teaches able-bodied divers to accompany divers with disabilities; and certifies divers with disabilities in "open water" diving. All contributors become members.

Job Accommodation Network (JAN)
West Virginia University
PO Box 6080
Morgantown, WV 26506-6080
(800) 526-7234 (V/TTY)   (800) 232-9675 (V/TTY)
FAX (304) 293-5407   e-mail:jan@jan.icdi.wvu.edu
www.jan.wvu.edu/links/adalinks.htm

The web site listed above lists laws, Supreme Court decisions, guidebooks, and other materials related to the Americans with Disabilities Act, which covers access to recreation and travel.

National Ability Center
PO Box 682799
Park City, UT 84068-2779
(435) 649-3991 (V/TTY)   FAX (435) 658-3992
e-mail: nac@nac1985.org   www.nationalabilitycenter.org

Offers year-round sports and recreation experiences for children and adults with disabilities.

National Easter Seal Society
230 West Monroe Street, Suite 1800
Chicago, IL 60606
(800) 221-6827   (312) 726-6200   (312) 726-4258 (TTY)
FAX (312) 726-1494   e-mail: info@easter-seals.org
www.easter-seals.org

Offers 140 camping and recreation facilities for children and adults with disabilities across the U.S. Day, residential, and respite programs are available.

National Sports Center for the Disabled
PO Box 1290
Winter Park, CO 80482
(970) 726-1540   FAX (970) 726-4112   e-mail: info@nscd.org
www.nscd.org

Offers year round recreation programs for children and adults with disabilities and offers training programs for recreation professionals.

National Wheelchair Basketball Association
(501) 834-8513   www.nwba.org

This organization of more than 175 teams across the U.S. and Canada provides opportunities for organized competition in men's, women's, and youth divisions.

North American Riding for the Handicapped Association (NARHA)
PO Box 33150
Denver, CO 80233
(800) 369-7433   (303) 452-1212   FAX (303) 252-4610
e-mail: narha@narha.org   www.narha.org

This professional association promotes therapeutic horseback riding for individuals with disabilities and accredits riding programs. Membership, $40.00, includes membership directory and subscription to two newsletters, "NARHA Strides," published quarterly, and "NARHA News," published eight times a year.

<u>Sailors with Special Needs</u>
United States Sailing Association
15 Maritime Drive, PO Box 1260
Portsmouth, RI 02871
(401) 683-0800   www.ussailing.org/swsn

Promotes competitive and recreational sailing for individuals with disabilities.

<u>United States Golf Association</u> (USGA)
PO Box 708
Far Hills, NJ 07931-0708
(908) 234-2300   www.usga.org

The association's web site lists golf programs for individuals with disabilities. Also provides "A Modification of The Rules of Golf for Golfers with Disabilities," including those who have mobility impairments.

<u>Universal Wheelchair Football Association</u>
c/o John B. Kraimer
9555 Plainfield Road
Blue Ash, OH 45236
(513) 792-8625   (513) 745-8300 (TTY)
FAX (513) 792-8624   e-mail: john.kraimer@uc.edu

Promotes football for individuals with disabilities. Provides rules upon request.

<u>Wheelchair Sports, USA</u>
3595 East Fountain Boulevard, Suite L-1
Colorado Springs, CO 80910
(719) 574-1150   FAX (719) 574-9840   e-mail: wsusa@aol.com
www.wsusa.org

This organization provides opportunities for individuals who use wheelchairs to compete in team and individual sports at local, regional, and international levels. The sports include archery, track and field, basketball, fencing, quad rugby, racquetball, shooting, sled hockey, swimming, table tennis, waterskiing, and weightlifting. Membership fees vary by region and number of sports selected.

PUBLICATIONS AND TAPES

Accessible Gardening for People with Physical Disabilities: A Guide to Methods, Tools, and Plants
by Janeen R. Adil
Woodbine House
6510 Bells Mill Road
Bethesda, MD 20817
(800) 843-7323   FAX (301) 897-5838
e-mail: info@woodbinehouse.com   www.woodbinehouse.com

Written for people with a variety of mobility impairments, this book provides information on making existing gardens more accessible and creating new gardens. Sources for obtaining supplies are included. $16.95

Access Travel: Airports
Federal Citizens Information Center
PO Box 100
Pueblo, CO 81002
(888) 878-3256   FAX (719) 948-9724
e-mail: cic.info@pueblo.gsa.gov   www.pueblo.gsa.gov

This brochure lists facilities and services for people with disabilities in airport terminals worldwide. Free. Also available on the web site.

Barrier-Free Travel: A Nuts & Bolts Guide for Wheelers and Slow Walkers
by Cindy Harrington
C & C Creative Concepts
PO Box 278
Ripon, CA 95366
FAX (209) 599-9482   e-mail: horizons@emerginghorizons.com
www.emerginghorizons.com

This book provides information on accessible recreation and vacation destinations with many tips to insure a successful trip. Includes resource list. $18.69

Challenge
Fanlight Productions
4196 Washington Street, Suite 2
Boston, MA 02131
(800) 937-4113   (617) 469-4999
FAX (617) 469-3379   e-mail: fanlight@fanlight.com   www.fanlight.com

This videotape features individuals with disabilities participating in sports such as wheelchair tennis, golf, skiing, and rock climbing. 28 minutes. Purchase, $195.00; rental for one day, $50.00; rental for one week, $100.00.

Conditioning with Physical Disabilities
by Kevin Lockette and Ann Keyes Ebersole
Human Kinetics
1607 North Market Street
PO Box 5076
Champaign, IL 61825-5076
(800) 747-4457   FAX (217) 351-1549
e-mail: orders@hkusa.com   www.humankinetics.com

This illustrated guide describes easy and safe exercises for individuals with physical disabilities. Step-by-step instructions are provided. $23.95

Disability and Sport
by Karen P. DePauw and Susan J. Gavron
Human Kinetics
PO Box 5076
Champaign, IL 61825-5076
(800) 747-4457   FAX (217) 351-1549
e-mail: orders@hkusa.com   www.humankinetics.com

This book reviews the development of the sports movement for individuals with disabilities. Describes sports modifications, lists disability sports organizations, discusses coaching athletes with disabilities, and provides information about publications. Includes biographies of athletes with disabilities. $40.00

The Disabled Driver's Mobility Guide
c/o Kay Hamada, Traffic Safety and Engineering
American Automobile Association (AAA)
1000 AAA Drive
Heathrow, FL 32746
(407) 444-7961   FAX (407) 444-7956

This book provides information about adaptive equipment, driver training, and travel information services. $8.95

Emerging Horizons
C & C Creative Concepts
PO Box 278
Ripon, CA 95366
FAX (209) 599-9482   e-mail: horizons@emerginghorizons.com
www.emerginghorizons.com

This quarterly magazine focuses on accessible travel for individuals with mobility impairments. $14.95. Available in print and online.

Guide to Wheelchair Sports and Recreation
PVA Distribution Center
PO Box 753
Waldorf, MD 20604-0753
(888) 860-7244   (301) 932-7834   FAX (301) 843-0159
www.pva.org

This book describes the wide range of wheelchair sports and lists manufacturers of equipment and Paralyzed Veterans of America (PVA) chapters that offer such sports. Available in English and Spanish. Free

New Horizons for the Air Traveler with a Disability
Federal Citizens Information Center
PO Box 100
Pueblo, CO 81002
(888) 878-3256   FAX (719) 948-9724
e-mail: cic.info@pueblo.gsa.gov   www.pueblo.gsa.gov

This booklet provides information about the Air Carrier Access rules and other regulations that affect air travelers. Free. Also available on the web site.

Sports 'N Spokes
2111 East Highland Avenue, Suite 180
Phoenix, AZ 85016
(888) 888-2201   (602) 224-0500   FAX (602) 224-0507
e-mail: pvapub@aol.com   www.sportsnspokes.com

A magazine that features articles about sports activities for people who use wheelchairs. Published eight times a year. $21.00

Wheelchair Basketball Book and Videotapes
PVA Distribution Center
PO Box 753
Waldorf, MD 20604-0753
(888) 860-7244   (301) 932-7834   FAX (301) 843-0159
www.pva.org

This instruction manual and videotape series covers individual skills and team play. Available in English and Spanish. Complete set, $75.00; separately: book, $21.95; videotape I, individual skills, $29.95; videotape II, team play, $29.95.

<u>A World of Options: A Guide to International Exchange, Community Service, and Travel for Persons with Disabilities</u>
by C. Bucks (ed.)
Mobility International USA (MIUSA)
PO Box 10767
Eugene, OR 97440
(541) 343-1284 (V/TTY)   FAX (541) 343-6812
e-mail: info@miusa.org   www.miusa.org

This book lists educational exchange programs, international workcamps, and accessible travel opportunities.   Personal experiences are used to describe these programs.   Individuals, $35.00; organizations, $45.00.

Chapter 3
LAWS THAT AFFECT WOMEN WITH DISABILITIES

(For laws related to housing, see Chapter 2, "Coping with Daily Activities")

Laws that affect women with disabilities cover a wide range of issues, including health care, financial benefits, rehabilitation, civil rights, transportation, access to public buildings, and employment. For those who are not specialists in the law, it is sometimes difficult to keep abreast of the laws and their amendments. At the same time, women with disabilities may be able to continue living independently if they are aware of their rights and know how to locate services and equipment provided by government programs or financial assistance to reimburse private providers.

In 1990, the *Americans with Disabilities Act* (ADA) was passed. Considered the most important piece of civil rights legislation in recent years, the ADA (P.L. 101-336) increases the steps employers must take to accommodate employees with disabilities and requires that new buses and rail vehicles, facilities, and public accommodations be accessible. The ADA defines disability as "a physical or mental impairment that substantially limits one or more of the major life activities..." [such as speaking, hearing, seeing, or walking]; "a record of such impairment;" or "being regarded as having such an impairment." Thus, individuals who have been cured of cancer or mental illness may still be regarded by others as having a disability and may experience discrimination. Others may have a physical condition that does not limit activity, such as disfiguring scars from injuries incurred in an automobile accident, but are regarded as disabled. Individuals in these situations are covered by the law.

The major provisions of the ADA are as follows:
- Prohibits discrimination against individuals with disabilities who are otherwise qualified for employment and requires that employers make "reasonable accommodations." "Reasonable accommodations" include making existing facilities accessible and job restructuring (e.g., reassignment to a vacant position, modification of equipment, training, provision of interpreters and readers). Employers are protected from "undue hardship" in complying with this provision; the financial situation of the employer and the size and type of business are considered when determining whether an accommodation would constitute "undue hardship." The provisions of this section apply to employers with 15 or more employees. (For a more detailed discussion of the employment aspects of the ADA, see Meeting the Needs of Employees with Disabilities, described in "PUBLICATIONS AND TAPES" section below)
- Prohibits discrimination by public entities (i.e., local and state governments) and requires that individuals with disabilities be entitled to the same rights and benefits of public programs as other individuals.
- Requires that bus and railroad transportation systems address the needs of individuals with disabilities by purchasing adapted equipment, modifying facilities, and providing special transportation services that are comparable to regular transportation services. Effective dates vary with the type of transportation system.
- Requires that public accommodations, businesses, and services be accessible to individuals with disabilities. Public accommodations are broadly defined to include places such as hotels and motels, theatres, museums, schools, shopping centers and stores, banks, restaurants, and professional service providers' offices. After

January 26, 1993, most new construction for public accommodations must be accessible to individuals with disabilities.

• Mandates that telephone companies provide relay services 24 hours a day, seven days a week, for individuals with hearing or speech impairments. Relay services enable individuals who have text telephones (TT's; formerly called telecommunication devices for the deaf or TDD's) or another computer device that is capable of communicating across telephone lines to communicate with individuals who do not have such devices.

Copies of the ADA and all federal laws are available from Senators and Representatives. Agencies charged with formulating regulations and standards include the Architectural and Transportation Barriers Compliance Board, the Department of Transportation, the Equal Employment Opportunity Commission, the Federal Communications Commission, and the Attorney General. Regulations for enforcing individual sections of the ADA are available from the federal agencies charged with promulgating them and in the "Federal Register" (see "PUBLICATIONS" section below). In addition, many private agencies that work with individuals with disabilities have copies of the ADA available for distribution to the public.

In 1999, the Supreme Court ruled in Olmstead, Commissioner, Georgia Department of Human Resources, et al. v. L.C. et al. that the ADA requires community placement instead of institutionalization whenever possible. The case was brought by two women who were both mentally retarded and mentally ill. Both had lived in state mental institutions for many years. Now their mental health professionals were recommending that they be placed in community-based treatment, but the state refused, saying it was more cost effective to keep the women hospitalized. The Supreme Court rejected the state's argument, citing Congress's intent that isolation and segregation were discrimination per se, and returned the case to the lower level court to determine appropriate relief. As a result of the Olmstead ruling, governments must place individuals in the community settings rather than in institutions whenever possible. This includes elders, who are often placed in nursing homes even though supplemental in-home services could allow them to remain in their own homes.

In 2002, the Supreme Court unanimously ruled that the ADA does not protect individuals with impairments that prevent them from carrying out manual tasks related to their jobs. In the case of Toyota Motor Manufacturing of Kentucky v. Williams, the Court said that workers must show that an impairment has substantial effect beyond the workplace in order to be covered by the ADA.

Other major laws that affect women with disabilities include the *Rehabilitation Act of 1973* (P.L. 93-112) and its amendments, which are the centerpieces of federal law related to rehabilitation. States must submit a vocational rehabilitation plan to the Rehabilitation Services Administration indicating how the designated state agency will provide vocational training, counseling, and diagnostic and evaluation services required by the law. Subsequent reauthorizations of and amendments to the Rehabilitation Act expanded the services provided under this law. For example, the "Client Assistance Program" authorizes states to inform clients and other persons with disabilities about all available benefits under the Act and to assist them in obtaining all remedies due under the law (P.L. 98-221). "Comprehensive Services for Independent Living" (P.L. 95-602) expands rehabilitation services to individuals with severe disabilities, regardless of their vocational potential, making services available to many people who are no longer in the work force. The Act broadly defines services as any "service that will enhance the ability of a handicapped individual to live independently or function within his family and community..." These services may include counseling, job placement, housing, funds to make the home accessible, funds for prosthetic devices, attendant care, and recreational activities.

Section 503 of the Rehabilitation Act requires any contractor that receives more than $10,000.00 in contracts from the federal government to take affirmative action to employ individuals with disabilities. The Office of Federal Contract Compliance Programs within the Department of Labor is responsible for enforcing this provision (see "ORGANIZATIONS" section below). *Section 504* prohibits any program that receives federal financial assistance from discriminating against individuals with disabilities who are otherwise eligible to benefit from their programs. Virtually all educational institutions are affected by this law, including private postsecondary institutions which receive federal financial assistance under a wide variety of programs. Programs must be physically accessible to individuals with disabilities, and construction begun after implementation of the regulations (June 3, 1977) must be designed so that it is in compliance with standard specifications for accessibility. Federal agencies must develop an affirmative action plan for hiring, placing, and promoting individuals with disabilities and for making their facilities accessible. The Civil Rights Division of the Department of Justice is responsible for enforcing this section.

The *Rehabilitation Act Amendments of 1992* (P.L. 102-569) establish state rehabilitation advisory councils composed of representatives of independent living councils, parents of children with disabilities, vocational rehabilitation professionals, and business; the role of these councils is to advise state vocational rehabilitation agencies and to prepare an annual report for the governor. The Amendments required that each state agency establish performance and evaluation standards by September 30, 1994.

Supplemental Security Income (SSI) is a federal minimum income maintenance program for elders and individuals who are blind or disabled and who meet a test of financial need. Monthly *Social Security Disability Insurance* (SSDI) benefits are available to individuals who are disabled and their dependents, including widowed spouses who are disabled and are 50 years or older (with certain qualifications). To be eligible, individuals must have paid Social Security taxes for a specified number of years (dependent upon the applicant's age); must not be working; and must be declared medically disabled by the state disability determination service or through an appeals process. The disability must be expected to last at least 12 months or to result in death. Individuals who are blind and age 55 to 65 may receive monthly benefits if they are unable to carry out the work (or similar work) that they did before age 55 or becoming blind, whichever is later. Individuals who apply for disability insurance from the Social Security Administration must undergo an evaluation carried out by a state disability evaluation team, composed of physicians, psychologists, and other health care professionals. Social Security disability benefits are not retroactive, so it is important to apply for them immediately after becoming disabled. Social Security disability benefits payments do not begin until six full months after the date that the Social Security office has determined that disability began. At age 65, disability benefits are called retirement benefits even though the dollar amount of benefits remains the same.

The Social Security Administration will provide an estimate of the disability and retirement benefits which any individual has accrued. Since these benefits are based on an average of lifetime earnings under Social Security, it is important to verify that the Social Security Administration has accurate employment records. Women should call the Social Security Administration at (800) 772-1213 to obtain a copy of a "Request for Earnings and Benefit Estimate Statement." Once it is completed and returned, the Social Security Administration will send an estimate of expected benefits. These benefits may be reduced by other government benefits, such as workers' compensation and government pensions.

Women who have received Social Security Disability Insurance for two consecutive years are eligible for *Medicare*, a federal health insurance program which has two parts, hospital insurance and medical insurance. Hospital care and some follow-up care is covered by Medicare Part A. Part B, medical insurance, is paid for by monthly premiums which vary with the type of insurance purchased. Women with low incomes may qualify for a program in which their state pays Medicare premiums and may cover deductibles and coinsurance payments. However, Medicare does not cover eyeglasses (except for recipients who have undergone cataract surgery), low vision aids, or hearing aids. *Medicaid* is a health insurance plan for individuals who are considered financially needy (i.e., recipients of financial benefits from governmental assistance programs, such as Aid to Families with Dependent Children or Supplemental Security Income). Medicaid is a joint federal/state program. While federal law requires that each state cover hospital services, skilled nursing facility services, physician and home health care services, and diagnostic and screening services, states have great discretion in other areas. Payments for prosthetics and rehabilitation equipment vary greatly from state to state.

The *Ticket to Work and Work Incentives Improvement Act of 1999* (P.L. 106-170) created new options and incentives for states to offer a Medicaid buy-in for workers with disabilities and extends Medicare coverage for an additional four and one-half years for people on disability who return to work.

The *Consolidated Omnibus Budget Reconciliation Act of 1985* (P.L. 99-272), more commonly known as COBRA, provides group health insurance continuation to individuals whose work or family status changes due to unemployment, divorce, or a spouse's death or retirement. COBRA requires that employers of 20 or more workers, including local and state governments, provide employees and their families with the option of continuing their group health insurance coverage for 18 months (longer under certain circumstances). This protection was later extended to federal employees and their families. Under COBRA, the individual must pay the entire monthly premium (both the employee and employer portions) and may be charged an administrative fee.

The *Health Insurance Portability and Accountability Act of 1996* (P.L. 104-191), also known as the Kennedy-Kassebaum law, protects individuals from being denied health insurance due to a pre-existing medical condition when they move from one job to another or if they become unemployed. "Portability" means that once individuals have been covered by health insurance, they are credited with having medical coverage when they enter a new plan. Group health plans, health insurance plans such as HMOs, Medicare, Medicaid, military health plans, Indian Health Service medical care, and public, state, or federal health benefits are considered creditable coverage (Fuch et al.: 1997). Coverage of a pre-existing medical condition may not be limited for more than 12 months for individuals who enroll in the health plan as soon as they are eligible (18 months for those who delay enrollment). Although the Act creates federal standards, the states have considerable flexibility in their requirements for insurers. The Departments of Treasury, Health and Human Services, and Labor are responsible for enforcing the provisions of the Act.

The *Family and Medical Leave Act* of 1993 (P.L.103-3) requires that employers with 50 or more employees at a worksite or within 75 miles of a worksite must permit eligible employees 12 workweeks of unpaid leave during a 12 month period in order to care for a spouse, son or daughter, or parent who has a serious health condition. During this period of leave, the employer must continue to provide group health benefits for the employee under the same conditions as the employee would have received while working. Upon return from leave, the employee must be restored to the same position s/he had prior to the leave or to a position with equivalent pay, benefits, and conditions of employment. Special regulations apply to employees of school systems and private schools and employees of the federal civil service.

The medical and social service benefits available from organizations receiving federal assistance are guaranteed by federal laws and protected by the Office of Civil Rights of the Department of Health and Human Services (HHS). When a woman feels that her rights have been violated, a complaint should be filed with the regional office of HHS (see "ORGANIZATIONS" section below).

The *Technology-Related Assistance for Individuals with Disabilities Act Amendments of 1994* (P.L. 103-218) strengthens the original Act, passed in 1988. The Act mandates state-wide programs for technology-related assistance to determine needs and resources; to provide technical assistance and information; and to develop demonstration and innovation projects, training programs, and public awareness programs. The amendments set priorities for consumer responsiveness, advocacy, systems change, and outreach to underrepresented populations such as the poor, individuals in rural areas, and minorities.

The *Help America Vote Act of 2002* (P.L. 107-252) requires that each polling place have at least one voting machine that is accessible to individuals with disabilities.

The *Telecommunications Act of 1996* (P.L. 104-104) has several sections that apply to individuals with disabilities. Section 254 redefines "universal service" to include schools, health facilities, and libraries and requires that the Federal Communications Commission (FCC) work with state governments to determine what services must be made universally available and what is considered "affordable." Section 255 of the Act requires that manufacturers of telecommunications equipment and providers of telecommunications services ensure that equipment and services are accessible to and usable by individuals with disabilities. If these provisions are not "readily achievable," manufacturers and service providers must ensure that their equipment and services are compatible with the special equipment used by individuals with disabilities to make them accessible. Section 713 requires that video services be accessible to individuals with hearing impairments via closed captioning and to individuals with visual impairments via descriptive video services. Section 706 requires that the FCC encourage the development of advanced telecommunications technology that provides equal access for individuals with disabilities, especially school children. The FCC is authorized to establish regulations and time tables for implementing these sections. The Architectural and Transportation Barriers Compliance Board (ATBCB) was required to issue guidelines within 18 months of the Act's passage on January 31, 1996.

The *Older Americans Act* (P.L. 89-73) requires that each state office designated to serve elders submit a plan to the Commissioner of the Administration on Aging. This plan must discuss the development of joint programs with the state agency primarily responsible for serving people with disabilities in order to meet the needs of elders with disabilities. The Act also requires that legal services be provided to elders and that each state employ someone to develop legal services to ensure that elders receive these services. Such services could include representing clients in obtaining Social Security benefits and providing legal counseling. The *Older Americans Act Amendments of 2000* (P.L. 106-501) included funding for the National Family Caregiver Support Program. It is designed to assist caregivers through information and assistance, counseling, support groups and training, respite services, and supplemental services. More than $141 million in grants were made to states for fiscal year 2002.

The federal government allows special tax credits for people who are totally disabled and additional standard deductions for those who are legally blind. Legal blindness is defined as acuity of 20/200 or less in the better eye with the best possible correction or a field of 20 degrees or less diameter in the better eye. Tax deductions for business expenses include disability related expenditures, and deductions for medical expenses include special equipment, such as wheelchairs. Contact the Internal Revenue Service (see "ORGANIZATIONS" section below) to obtain publications that explain these benefits, including Publication 501, "Exemptions, Standard Deduction, and Filing Information," and Publication 524, "Credit for the Elderly or the Disabled.".

All states and many local governments have adopted their own laws regarding accessibility. Information about these laws may be obtained from the state or local office serving people with disabilities. In many areas, special legal services for people with disabilities are available, often with fees on a sliding scale. Check with the local bar association or with a law school. Some lawyers specialize in the legal needs of people with disabilities.

The Internet supplies the text of many federal laws and information about federal programs. Individuals who have a connection to the Internet via their university, workplace, or a commercial online service (such as America Online, Delphi, Compuserve, Prodigy, etc.) may search the information available on the Internet by typing "telnet fedworld.gov" and selecting from the menu.

References

Fuch, Beth C. et al.
1997   <u>The Health Insurance Portability and Accountability Act of 1996: Guidance</u> Washington DC:
        Library of Congress, Congressional Research Service

ORGANIZATIONS

Architectural and Transportation Barriers Compliance Board (ATBCB)
1331 F Street, NW, Suite 1000
Washington, DC 20004-1111
(800) 872-2253   (800) 993-2822 (TTY)   (202) 272-5434
(202) 272-0082 (TTY)   FAX (202) 272-0081
e-mail: info@access-board.gov   www.access-board.gov

A federal agency charged with developing standards for accessibility in federal facilities, public accommodations, and transportation facilities as required by the Americans with Disabilities Act and other federal laws. Provides technical assistance, sponsors research, and distributes publications. Publishes a quarterly newsletter, "Access America." Free. Publications available in standard print, alternate formats, and on the web site.

Clearinghouse on Disability Information
Office of Special Education and Rehabilitative Services (OSERS)
Department of Education
Room 3132, Switzer Building
Washington, DC 20202-2524
(800) 872-5327   (800) 437-0833 (TTY)   (202) 205-8241
FAX (202)) 401-0689   www.ed.gov/offices/OSERS

Responds to inquiries about federal legislation and programs for people with disabilities and makes referrals.

Client Assistance Program (CAP)
U.S. Department of Education
Rehabilitation Services Administration
330 C Street, SW, Switzer Building, Room 3223
Washington, DC 20202
(202) 205-9315

Established by the Rehabilitation Act of 1973, as amended, CAP provides information and advocacy for individuals with disabilities served under the Act and Title I of the Americans with Disabilities Act. Assistance is also provided to facilitate employment.

Commission on Mental and Physical Disability Law
American Bar Association
740 15th Street, NW, 9th Floor
Washington, DC 20005-1022
(202) 662-1570   (202) 662-1012 (TTY)
FAX (202) 662-1032   e-mail: cmpdl@abanet.org   www.abanet.org

Operates a Disability Legal Research Service, which provides searches of databases of laws, legal cases, and recent developments in the field of disability. Provides technical consultations on rights, enforcement, and other issues related to the Americans with Disabilities Act.

<u>Disability Rights Education and Defense Fund</u> (DREDF)
2212 6th Street
Berkeley, CA 94710
(510) 644-2555   (510) 644-2626 (TTY)
FAX (510) 841-8645   e-mail: dredf@dredf.org   www.dredf.org

Provides technical assistance, information, and referrals on laws and rights; provides legal representation to people with disabilities in both individual and class action cases; trains law students, parents, and legislators. ADA Hotline [(800)-466-4232 (V/TTY)] provides information on the Americans with Disabilities Act. Quarterly newsletter, "Disability Rights News," available in standard print, alternate formats, and on the web site. Free

<u>Disability Rights Section</u>
U.S. Department of Justice, Civil Rights Division
950 Pennsylvania Avenue, NW
Washington, DC 20530
(800) 514-0301   (800) 514-0383 (TTY)
FAX (202) 307-1198   www.usdoj.gov/crt/ada/adahom1.htm

Responsible for enforcing Titles II and III of the Americans with Disabilities Act. Copies of its regulations are available in standard print, alternate formats, and on the web site. Callers may request publications, obtain technical assistance, and speak to an ADA specialist.

<u>Equal Employment Opportunity Commission</u> (EEOC)
1801 L Street, NW, 10th Floor
Washington, DC 20507
(800) 669-3362 to order publications
(800) 669-4000 to speak to an investigator
(800) 800-3302 (TTY)
In the Washington, DC metropolitan area, (202) 275-7377
(202) 275-7518 (TTY)   www.eeoc.gov

Responsible for promulgating regulations for the employment section of the ADA. Copies of its regulations are available in standard print and alternate formats. Individuals who feel their employment rights under the ADA have been violated should file a complaint with the EEOC.

<u>Federal Communications Commission</u> (FCC)
445 12th Street, SW
Washington, DC 20554
(888) 225-5322   (888) 835-5322 (TTY)   (202) 418-0190
(202) 418-2555 (TTY)   www.fcc.gov

Responsible for developing regulations for telecommunication issues related to federal laws, including the ADA and the Telecommunications Act of 1996.

<u>Internal Revenue Service</u> (IRS)
(800) 829-1040   (800) 829-4059 (TTY)
www.irs.ustreas.gov

The IRS provides technical assistance about tax credits and deductions related to accommodations for disabilities. To receive Publication 554, "Older Americans Tax Guide," Publication 501, "Exemptions, Standard Deduction, and Filing Information;" Publication 907, "Tax Highlights for Persons with Disabilities;" and Publication 524, "Credit for the Elderly or the Disabled," call (800) 829-3676; (800) 829-4059 (TTY). These publications are available on the web site.

Job Accommodation Network (JAN)
West Virginia University
PO Box 6080
Morgantown, WV 26506-6080
(800) 526-7234 (V/TTY)   (800) 232-9675 (V/TTY)
FAX (304) 293-5407   e-mail:jan@jan.icdi.wvu.edu
www.jan.wvu.edu/links/adalinks.htm

The web site listed above lists laws, Supreme Court decisions, guidebooks, and other materials related to the Americans with Disabilities Act.

Justice for All
www.jfanow.org

This web site provides alerts regarding Congressional actions on issues related to disabilities. Web site provides instructions for signing up for alerts.

National Council on Disability (NCD)
1331 F Street, 10th Floor
Washington, DC 20004
(202) 272-2004   (202) 272-2074 (TTY)   FAX (202) 272-2022
e-mail: mquigley@ncd.gov   www.ncd.gov

An independent federal agency mandated to study and make recommendations about public policy for people with disabilities. Holds regular meetings and hearings in various locations around the country. Publishes monthly newsletter, "NCD Bulletin," available in standard print, alternate formats, and on the web site. Free

Nolo Law for All
Nolo Press
950 Parker Street
Berkeley, CA 94710
(800) 992-6656   (510) 549-1976   FAX (800) 645-0895
www.nolo.com

This web site provides information on legal topics, updates legislation and court decisions, and features articles from "Nolo News." Free publications catalogue.

Office for Civil Rights
U.S. Department of Health and Human Services
200 Independence Avenue, SW
Washington, DC 20201
(877) 696-6775   (202) 619-0700   (202) 863-0101 (TTY)
FAX (202) 619-3818   www.hhs.gov

Responsible for enforcing laws and regulations that protect the rights of individuals seeking medical and social services in institutions that receive federal financial assistance. Individuals who feel their rights have been violated may file a complaint with one of the ten regional offices located throughout the country. Calling (800) 368-1019 connects you with the regional office closest to you.

Office of Civil Rights
Federal Transit Administration
400 7th Street, SW, Room 9102
Washington, DC 20590
(888) 446-4511   (202) 366-3472
FAX (202) 366-3475   e-mail: ada.assistance@fta.dot.gov
www.fta.dot.gov

Responsible for investigating complaints covered by regulations set forth in the Americans with Disabilities Act regarding the transportation of individuals with disabilities. Call the ADA Assistance Line, (888) 446-4511, to request a complaint form or to obtain a copy of the Americans with Disabilities Act regulations that apply to the Department of Transportation.

Office of Civil Rights
U.S. Department of Education
300 C Street, SW
Washington, DC 20202
(800) 421-3481   (877) 521-2172 (TTY)   (202) 205-5413
FAX (202) 205-9862   www.ed.gov/offices/OCR

Responsible for enforcing laws and regulations designed to protect the rights of individuals in educational institutions that receive federal financial assistance. Individuals who feel their rights have been violated may file a complaint with one of the ten regional offices located throughout the country.

Office of Fair Housing and Equal Opportunity
U.S. Department of Housing and Urban Development (HUD)
451 7th Street, SW, Room 5204
Washington DC 20140
(800) 669-9777   (800) 927-9275 (TTY)   (202) 927-9275 (TTY)
www.hud.gov/fheo.html

This agency enforces the Fair Housing Act and will inform callers how to file a complaint with one of the ten regional HUD offices. Information about the Fair Housing Act and a complaint form are available on the web site.

Office of Federal Contract Compliance Programs (OFCCP)
U.S. Department of Labor, Employment Standards Administration
200 Constitution Avenue, NW, Room C-3325
Washington, DC 20210
(888) 378-3227   (202) 219-9475   FAX (202) 219-6195
www.dol.gov/dol/esa/ofccp/index.htm

Reviews contractors' affirmative action plans; provides technical assistance to contractors; investigates complaints; and resolves issues between contractors and employees. Ten regional offices throughout the country serve as liaisons with the national office and with district offices under their jurisdiction.

Office of General Counsel
U.S. Department of Transportation
400 7th Street, SW
Washington, DC 20590
(202) 366-9306   (202) 755-7687 (TTY)   FAX (202) 366-9313
www.dot.gov

Responsible for providing information and interpretation of the regulations for transportation of individuals with disabilities required by the Rehabilitation Act and the Americans with Disabilities Act. Regulations available in standard print or on audiocassette. Free

Rehabilitation Services Administration (RSA)
U.S. Department of Education
400 Maryland Avenue, SW, Room 3329-MES
Washington, DC 20202-2251
(202) 205-5482   FAX (202) 205-9874
www.ed.gov/offices/OSERS/RSA

The principal federal agency mandated to carry out the provisions of the Rehabilitation Act of 1973 and its amendments.

Social Security Administration (SSA)
6401 Security Boulevard
Baltimore, MD 21235
(800) 772-1213   (800) 325-0778 (TTY)
www.socialsecurity.gov

Special rules enable people with disabilities who receive Supplemental Security Income (SSI) and Social Security Disability Insurance (SSDI) to continue receiving these benefits and Medicare or Medicaid while they are working. Call the number listed above and ask for the work incentives expert to learn about the rules for these programs. A special web site for women (www.socialsecurity.gov/women) has information that is especially pertinent to women.

Thomas
Library of Congress
thomas.loc.gov

This online service provides a database of recent laws and pending legislation, as well as information about the committees of Congress and the text of the "Congressional Record." Searches for legislation and laws may be done by topic or public law number.

<u>U.S. Department of Housing and Urban Development</u> (HUD)
451 7th Street, SW, Room 5240
Washington, DC 20410
(202) 708-1112   (202) 708-1455 (TTY)
www.hud.gov (HUD Section 504 One-Stop Web Site)
HUD Discrimination Hotline: (800) 669-9777; (800) 927-9275 (TTY)

Operates programs to make housing accessible, including loans for developers of independent living and group homes and loan and mortgage insurance for rehabilitation of single or multifamily units. Individuals who feel their rights have been violated may file a complaint with one of the ten regional offices located throughout the country.

The ADA: Questions and Answers
Equal Employment Opportunity Center (EEOC)
Publications Distribution Center
PO Box 12549
Cincinnati, OH 45212-0549
(800) 669-3362   (800) 800-3302 (TTY)
FAX (513) 489-8692   www.eeoc.gov

This booklet's question and answer format provides explanations of the ADA's effects on employment, state and local governments, and public accommodations. Available in standard print, alternate formats, and on the web site. Free. Also available at www.pueblo.gsa.gov.

The Appeals Process
Disability Benefits
How We Decide if You Are Still Disabled
Social Security Disability Programs Can Help
Social Security: What You Need to Know When You Get Disability Benefits
Your Right to Question the Decision to Stop Your Disability Payments
Social Security Administration (see "ORGANIZATIONS" section above)
(800) 772-1213   (800) 325-0778 (TTY)   www.socialsecurity.gov

These booklets provide basic information about Social Security programs for individuals with disabilities. The Social Security Administration distributes many other titles, including many that are available in standard print, alternate formats, on the web site, and at local Social Security offices. Free

Directory of Legal Aid and Defender Offices
National Legal Aid and Defender Association
1625 K Street, NW, 8th Floor
Washington, DC 20006
(202) 452-0620   FAX (202) 872-1031   www.nlads.org

A directory of legal aid offices throughout the U.S. Includes chapters on disability protection/advocacy, health law, and senior citizens. Updated biennially. $90.00

Disability Resource Library
DND Press
600 Turnstone Trace
New Smyrna Beach, FL 32168
(386) 423-2077   FAX (386) 426-8956
e-mail: infor@dndpress.com   www.dndpress.com

This CD-ROM includes the full text of the Americans with Disabilities Act as well as other federal laws related to disabilities; ADA settlement agreements; technical assistance letters from the Department of Justice; and a glossary. $69.95

The Disability Rights Movement: From Charity to Confrontation
by Doris Zames Fleischer and Frieda Zames
Temple University Press
c/o Chicago Distribution Center
11030 South Langley Avenue
Chicago, IL 60628
(800) 621-2736   (215) 204-8787
FAX (800) 621-8476   e-mail: tempress@astro.mail.temple.edu
www.temple.edu/tempress

This book presents the history of the disability rights movement in the United States. It discusses deinstitutionalization and independent living, legislation, education, and technology. Includes the Americans with Disabilities Act and Section 504 of the Civil Rights Act. $24.95

Fact Sheet: The Family and Medical Leave Act, the Americans with Disabilities Act, and Title VII of the Civil Rights Act of 1964
Equal Employment Opportunity Commission (EEOC)
Publications Distribution Center
PO Box 12549
Cincinnati, OH 45212-0549
(800) 669-3362   (800) 800-3302 (TTY)   FAX (513) 489-8692
www.eeoc.gov

This fact sheet provides information about key federal legislation. Free. Also available on the web site.

Federal Benefits for Veterans and Dependents
Federal Citizens Information Center
PO Box 100
Pueblo, CO 81002
(888) 878-3256   FAX (719) 948-9724
e-mail: cic.info@pueblo.gsa.gov www.pueblo.gsa.gov

This booklet describes the benefits available under federal laws. $6.00. Also available on the web site. Click on "Federal Programs."

Federal Register
New Orders, Superintendent of Documents
PO Box 371954
Pittsburgh, PA 15250-7954
(866) 512-1800   (202) 512-1530   FAX (202) 512-2250
e-mail: gpoaccess@gpo.gov   www.access.gpo.gov/su_docs/aces/aces140.html

A federal publication printed every weekday with notices of all regulations and legal notices issued by federal agencies. Domestic subscriptions, $764.00 annually for second class mailing of paper format; $264.00 annually for microfiche. Access to the Federal Register is available through the Internet at the address listed above at no charge.

A Guide to Disability Rights Laws
Federal Citizens Information Center
PO Box 100
Pueblo, CO 81002
(888) 878-3256   FAX (719) 948-9724
e-mail: cic.info@pueblo.gsa.gov   www.pueblo.gsa.gov

This brochure summarizes federal laws that are applicable to individuals with disabilities and lists the agencies that enforce them. Free. Also available on the web site.

Guide to the Family and Medical Leave Act: Questions and Answers
National Partnership for Women and Families
1875 Connecticut Avenue, NW, Suite 650
Washington, DC 20009
(202) 986-2600   FAX (202) 986-2539
e-mail: info@nationalpartnership.org
www.nationalpartnership.org

This booklet answers the most frequently asked questions about the law. Available in English and Spanish. Free. Also available on the web site.

Health Benefits Under COBRA
Federal Citizens Information Center
PO Box 100
Pueblo, CO 81002
(888) 878-3256   FAX (719) 948-9724
e-mail: cic.info@pueblo.gsa.gov   www.pueblo.gsa.gov

This booklet describes the coverage provided by the Consolidated Omnibus Budget Reconciliation Act (COBRA). $.50 Also available on the web site.

Health Insurance Resource Manual: Options for People with a Chronic Disease or Disability
by Dorothy E. Northrop and Stephen Cooper
Demos Medical Publishing
386 Park Avenue South, Suite 201
New York, NY 10016
(800) 532-8663   (212) 683-0072   FAX (212) 683-0118
e-mail: info@demospub.com   www.demosmedpub.com

This book provides an overview of health insurance plans; government programs such as Social Security, Medicare, Medicaid, and the federal laws that affect health insurance; and resources for conducting research on health insurance options. $24.95. Orders made on the Demos web site receive a 15% discount.

Insurance Solutions--Plan Well, Live Better: A Workbook for People with Chronic Illnesses or Disabilities
by Laura D. Cooper
Demos Medical Publishing
386 Park Avenue South, Suite 201
New York, NY 10016
(800) 532-8663   (212) 683-0072   FAX (212) 683-0118
e-mail: info@demospub.com   www.demosmedpub.com

This book enables readers to find and evaluate insurance options. Includes checklists, worksheets, and exercises. $24.95. Orders made on the Demos web site receive a 15% discount.

Medicare & You
Centers for Medicare and Medicaid Services (CMS)
formerly Health Care Financing Administration (HCFA)
7500 Security Boulevard
Baltimore, MD 21244
(877) 267-2323   (866) 226-1819 (TTY)   (410) 786-3000
www.medicare.gov

This booklet provides basic information about Medicare including eligibility, enrollment, coverage, and options. Available in English and Spanish in standard print and alternate formats. Free. Also available on the web site.

Meeting the Needs of Employees with Disabilities
Resources for Rehabilitation
22 Bonad Road
Winchester, MA 01890
(781) 368-9094   FAX (781) 368-9096   e-mail: info@rfr.org
www.rfr.org

This book provides information to help people with disabilities retain or obtain employment. Information on government programs and laws, supported employment, training programs, environmental adaptations, and the transition from school to work are included. Chapters on mobility, vision, and hearing and speech impairments include information on organizations, products, and services that enable employers to accommodate the needs of employees with disabilities. $44.95 (See order form on last page of this book.)

Mental and Physical Disability Law Reporter
Commission on Mental and Physical Disability Law
American Bar Association
740 15th Street, NW, 9th Floor
Washington, DC 20005
(202) 662-1570   (202) 662-1012 (TTY)
FAX (202) 662-1032   e-mail: hammillj@staff.abanet.org
www.abanet.org

A bimonthly journal with court decisions, legislative and regulatory news, and articles on treatment, accessibility, employment, education, federal programs, etc. Individual subscription, $314.00; organizational subscription, $374.00. Reprints of articles from back issues available.

The National Partnership for Women and Families Guide to the Family and Medical Leave Act
National Partnership for Women and Families
1875 Connecticut Avenue, NW, Suite 710
Washington, DC 20009
(202) 986-2600   FAX (202) 986-2539
e-mail: info@nationalpartnership.org www.nationalpartnership.org

This booklet answers the most frequently asked questions about the law. Available in English and Spanish. Also available on the web site. Free

Removing Barriers to Health Care: A Guide for Health Professionals
Center for Universal Design
North Carolina State University
Box 8613
Raleigh, NC 27695-8613
(800) 647-6777   (919) 515-3082 (V/TTY)   FAX (919) 515-7330
e-mail: cud@ncsu.edu   www.design.ncsu.edu/cud

This booklet provides guidelines for access to health care facilities. Reviews the design standards of the Americans with Disabilities Act and suggests methods for courteous interactions with individuals with disabilities. Free. Also available on the web site.

Report on Disability Programs
Business Publishers
8737 Colesville Road, Suite 1100
Silver Spring, MD 20910-3928
(800) 274-6737   (301) 589-5103   FAX (301) 589-8493
e-mail: bpinews@bpinews.com   www.bpinews.com

A biweekly newsletter with information on policies promulgated by federal agencies, laws, and funding sources. $297.00

Social Security, Medicare & Pensions: Get the Most Out of Your Retirement and Medical Benefits
by Joseph Matthews and Dorothy Matthews Berman
Nolo Press
950 Parker Street
Berkeley, CA 94710
(800) 728-3555   (510) 549-1976
FAX (800) 645-0895   e-mail: order@nolo.com   www.nolo.com

This book provides information on Social Security, Medicare and Medicaid, Supplemental Security Income, veterans' benefits, and civil service benefits. It also discusses a variety of Internet sites related to these topics. $29.99

<u>Social Security: What Every Woman Should Know</u>
Federal Citizens Information Center
PO Box 100
Pueblo, CO 81002
(888) 878-3256   FAX (719) 948-9724
e-mail: cic.info@pueblo.gsa.gov   www.pueblo.gsa.gov
www.socialsecurity.gov/womne

This booklet discusses how benefits are affected by disability, widowhood, divorce, retirement, or other special situations. Free. Also available on both web sites.

<u>A Summary of Department of Veterans Affairs Benefits</u>
(800) 827-1000   www.va.gov

This booklet is available from any VA regional office. Free

Chapter 4

ARTHRITIS

Although rheumatoid arthritis and osteoarthritis are two common rheumatic diseases found in women, the conditions develop at different stages of life and have different symptoms. Some women may have both conditions. Since osteoarthritis usually affects women later in life, it is described below in the section titled "Arthritis in Older Women."

Rheumatoid arthritis is a chronic, systemic, inflammatory disease that can affect the entire body but is most commonly found in the hands, wrists, and feet. It is estimated that over two million Americans have the disease (National Institute of Arthritis and Musculoskeletal and Skin Diseases: 1998). It occurs three times more frequently in women than in men. Many American women experience limitations in activities of daily living due to arthritis and rheumatism.

The disease affects the synovium, which is the membrane that lines the joints and provides them with nourishment and lubrication. Rheumatoid arthritis causes the synovium to become inflamed (synovitis), swollen, and painful. Eventually the bone cartilage is affected, causing pain and further damaging joints. Fatigue, depression, weight loss, and anemia are common. Rheumatoid arthritis may also cause inflammation in other body organs, affecting the blood vessels and the outer lining of the heart and lungs. Although rheumatoid arthritis can occur in children (juvenile rheumatoid arthritis), onset peaks between the ages of 20 and 50 (Arthritis Foundation: 1994a). Eighty percent of the women who develop rheumatoid arthritis are between the ages of 35 and 50 (Lipsky: 1994). Some researchers have linked an inherited tendency to develop rheumatoid arthritis with genetic markers controlling immune system function, while others suspect that infections trigger the development of rheumatoid arthritis (Arthritis Foundation: 1994a).

Rheumatoid arthritis subsides and flares unpredictably, causes severe pain, and may lead to substantial or complete disability. In contrast to many other forms of arthritis, rheumatoid arthritis develops symmetrically, affecting the same joint on both sides of the body (knees, wrists, knuckles, etc.). The stages of functional incapacity include normal activity with no restrictions; adequate function with some pain and moderate restrictions; limited ability to work or to provide self care; confinement to bed; or requiring the use of a wheelchair (Bennett: 1988).

Diagnosing rheumatoid arthritis is difficult. Many individuals describe their condition as "flu-like," citing muscle aches and fatigue. Since symptoms vary among individuals, other rheumatic diseases may be considered initially. Blood tests and x-rays are commonly used, as well as criteria established by the American College of Rheumatology. These criteria include joint swelling and pain for more than six weeks, marked joint and muscle stiffness in the morning, evidence of bone damage, nodules characteristic of rheumatoid arthritis under the skin, and the presence of a rheumatoid antibody in the blood. This antibody, called a rheumatoid factor, is found in 80 to 90% of individuals diagnosed with rheumatoid arthritis (Shlotzhauer and McGuire: 1993). About a fifth of the individuals with rheumatoid arthritis develop pea sized nodules under the skin, which are actually inflamed blood vessels. These nodules appear sporadically during the course of the disease. Although they rarely cause problems, they are indicative of an acute form of the disease.

Some individuals with rheumatoid arthritis develop a related rheumatic condition known as Sjogren's syndrome, which affects the tear, salivary, and other moisture producing glands. Corneal erosions, conjunctivitis, and inflammation of the front of the eye are complications of the lack of tears. Sjogren's syndrome is ten times more frequent in women than in men (American College of Rheumatology: no date). Treatment options include artificial tears and ointments or pellets placed between the eyelid and eyeball that dissolve slowly, releasing moisture to the eye. Dry mouth (xerostomia), which may cause swallowing problems and tooth decay, may be treated with prescription medication. Its symptoms can be relieved by the use of artificial saliva and sugarless gum or candy.

In the United States, autoimmune diseases such as rheumatoid arthritis, multiple sclerosis, and lupus affect a disproportionate number of women, nearly 79% of the 8.5 million individuals affected (Whitacre et al.: 1999). Researchers believe that differences in women's immune responses; the effects of sex hormones such as estrogen, progesterone, and testosterone; and genetic influences may account for this gender gap. In 1999, the National Multiple Sclerosis Society established the Task Force on Gender, MS, and Autoimmunity; members included basic and clinical scientists, to review current data and make research recommendations (see Chapter 10, "Multiple Sclerosis").

Multipurpose Arthritis and Musculoskeletal Diseases Centers, created by the National Arthritis Act of 1975, were established across the United States. Fourteen centers investigated the roles of physiological treatment and psychosocial interventions in the care of individuals with rheumatic diseases (Freeman et al.: 1996). By fiscal year 2001 these centers will be replaced by Multidisciplinary Clinical Research Centers in Arthritis, Musculoskeletal and/or Skin Diseases.

TREATMENT

Early diagnosis and treatment are key to the prevention of inflammation and deformities of the joints and the pain that are associated with rheumatoid arthritis. Treatment includes medications, rest, and exercise to restore and protect joint and muscle function. Women who fear disability due to arthritis sometimes delay seeking treatment, placing themselves at greater risk for potential damage. Pain is the major manifestation of arthritis; therefore, pain management should be a prime concern for both women and their health care providers.

There are several categories of drugs used to treat rheumatoid arthritis. *Nonsteroidal anti-inflammatory drugs* (NSAIDs) such as aspirin have been the most common medications used to treat arthritis, because they reduce joint inflammation and pain. Side effects of treatment with NSAIDs include stomach irritation, constipation, nausea, fluid retention, dizziness, and blood clotting problems. According to the Arthritis Foundation (1996), being female confers a greater risk of developing an ulcer while taking NSAIDs, although many other factors may contribute to ulcers as well. NSAIDs such as ibuprofen and naproxen are similar to aspirin but may have fewer side effects, although they have been implicated in gastrointestinal bleeding and renal problems (Fenner: 1992).

Cox-2 inhibitors are a new subcategory of NSAIDS that reduce arthritis pain and inflammation without the gastrointestinal side effects of traditional NSAIDS. Celecoxib (Celebrex) was approved by the Food and Drug Administration (FDA) in 1998 for use by individuals with rheumatoid arthritis and osteoarthritis. After reports of bleeding complications in patients who also take warfarin, an anticoagulant used in the treatment of heart disease and stroke, it was recommended that these individuals be monitored to determine whether adjustment in the warfarin dose is needed. In 2002, after a long term safety study, the FDA mandated that the geriatric section of celecoxib labeling warn of the risk of serious gastrointestinal and renal effects in elders (Food and Drug Administration: 2002).

Aspirin is a salicylate, another subcategory of NSAIDS, that may also cause gastrointestinal problems and bleeding tendencies and affect kidney function. Chemically modified salicylates, or nonacetylated salicylates, are usually safer and do not increase bleeding tendencies. Drugs in this category include choline salicylate (Arthropan), choline magnesium trisalicylate (Trilisate), and salsalate (Disalcid).

Disease-modifying antirheumatic drugs (DMARDS) relieve painful swollen joints, and slow joint damage. Methotrexate (Rheumatrex), leflunomide (Arava), and azathioprine (Imuran) are among the DMARDs. The American College of Rheumatology recommends that DMARD therapy be initiated in patients whose symptoms have not abated despite three months of treatment with NSAIDs. It may take several months of treatment with DMARDS to notice improvement. The Arthritis Foundation (1994b) reports that methotrexate has been shown to maintain control of the disease over periods of more than five years in a larger proportion of people with rheumatoid arthritis than those treated with other medications. Individuals who take methotrexate are monitored carefully for liver function and white blood cell counts. Contraindications for methotrexate therapy include kidney, lung, and heart disease. Abstention from drinking alcohol during methotrexate treatment is advised.

Biologics are a new category of drugs used in the treatment of rheumatoid arthritis. They reduce joint inflammation by blocking the action of tumor necrosis factor (TNF), a protein that causes inflammation. Anakinra (Kineret) was approved by the FDA in 2001 for the treatment of rheumatoid arthritis. The patient or a health care provider injects the drug daily, sometimes resulting in a mild swelling of the injection site. Another biologic, etanercept (Enbrel), is also injected subcutaneously. The drug is not recommended for pregnant women. In May 1999, the FDA and the manufacturer issued warnings about prescribing etanercept to patients with active infections, those who had recurring infections, and those with conditions that predisposed them to infection, such as diabetes.

Analgesics may be prescribed to reduce pain when there is little inflammation. Acetaminophen is the most commonly used analgesic. It is available in generic and brand-name (Anacin, Execedrin, Tylenol) forms. Narcotic analgesics (Darvon, Ultram) may be used for severe and chronic pain. Individuals who have swallowing problems should ask their physicians or pharmacists if liquid forms of these medications are available. A hollow handled medicine spoon is useful when taking these liquids. Topical analgesics are creams or salves, such as BenGay, Zostrix, Capzasin-P, or Icy Hot, which are rubbed on to affected areas to stimulate or irritate nerve endings, distracting attention from musculoskeletal pain.

The role of exercise in increasing endurance for women with arthritis has receiving increased attention. Jurisson (1991) reports that a decrease in symptoms is an unexpected benefit of exercises, such as walking, aquatics, and riding a stationary bicycle. Individuals with arthritis benefit from a daily routine combining strengthening, range of motion, and endurance exercises followed by rest and relaxation.

A program of physical therapy may include heat and cold treatments, massage, and relaxation training. Heat treatments may include hot baths or showers, hot packs, heat lamps, electric pads or mitts, paraffin wax applications, or blown hot air. Cold compresses or ice bags may also be effective. Transcutaneous electrical nerve stimulation (TENS) may be used to relieve pain. The physical therapist may recommend the use of canes, walkers, or crutches to reduce the body's weight on joints. Physical therapists may also provide instruction in using the joints more safely; for example, pushing with the whole arm or side of the body rather than with the hand only. Splints or orthotics, which are devices used for support and to improve function in movable parts of the body, may be prescribed to stabilize weak joints and prevent them from becoming permanently stiff or bent. The physical therapist may also recommend rest to relieve inflammation and pain, although too much rest may lead to stiffness and poor joint movement. It is necessary to achieve a balance between rest during flares and activity during remissions.

If medication and physical therapy are insufficient for pain management and there is evidence of joint damage, orthopedic surgery may be required, such as knee, hip, shoulder, and wrist arthroplasty (total replacement) or arthrodesis (joint fusion). Prosthetic joints may wear out, and the risk of infection requires careful medical monitoring over time. Since multiple joint damage is common in individuals with rheumatoid arthritis, it is crucial to evaluate functional capacities before surgery. For example, will a woman undergoing a knee replacement be able to use crutches during the recuperative period? If wrist, elbow, or shoulder joints are painful, how will she ambulate with crutches? Women treated with corticosteroids are more susceptible to infection and thinning of the skin. Aspirin treatment may interfere with blood clotting factors and should be discontinued at least a week before surgery to avoid bleeding during surgery and postoperatively. Individuals should consider giving their own blood prior to surgery so that it is available if needed during or after the operation. It may be wise to start performing exercises prior to surgery to help with recovery. A physical therapist should be consulted before engaging in such an exercise program. Individuals contemplating surgery must also be evaluated for their ability and motivation to participate in a long postoperative rehabilitation program.

ARTHRITIS IN OLDER WOMEN

Osteoarthritis, the most common type of arthritis in older women, is a chronic, nonsystemic, noninflammatory form of arthritis which results in the breakdown of the cartilage that covers the ends of the bones and other joint tissue. Osteoarthritis occurs in more than 20 million Americans (National Institute of Arthritis and Musculoskeletal and Skin Diseases: 2002). Age is a major risk factor in the development of osteoarthritis, and it is more common in women over the age of 54 than men (Arthritis Foundation: 1994b). An x-ray survey of women revealed that while 30% of women ages 45 to 64 showed evidence of osteoarthritis, 68% of women over age 65 had developed the condition (Brandt: 1994).

Osteoarthritis does not affect the entire body but most commonly occurs in the joints of the fingers, hips, and knees, and the discs of the spine. It is a degenerative disease, formerly thought to be related to the overuse and abuse of joints through the "wear and tear" of aging. Actually, activity seems to protect joints. Lorig and Fries (1990) report that studies of individuals engaged in activities that put stress on joints, such as long distance runners and those who operate pneumatic drills, are at no greater risk for osteoarthritis. Obesity is a far greater risk factor for osteoarthritis of the knee. The Arthritis Foundation (1994b) reports that controlling or losing weight may reduce this risk, citing a study in which women who lost as little as 11 pounds over a ten year span halved their risk for osteoarthritis of the knee.

The most common signs of osteoarthritis are painful bony growths in the joints of the fingers. Osteoarthritis may also occur in a single joint due to injury or infection. Sports injuries, for example, may increase the risk of developing osteoarthritis. Osteoarthritis develops gradually, resulting in mild to severe disability. A woman's medical history and findings from a physical examination are often sufficient to suspect that she has osteoarthritis. X-rays, which detect the growth of bony spurs or the narrowing of space between joints due to wearing away of cartilage, are used to confirm a diagnosis of osteoarthritis.

The most common medications used to treat osteoarthritis by reducing pain are analgesics and nonsteroidal anti-inflammatory drugs (NSAIDs). Researchers who have compared these two options found that there was no difference in the relief of symptoms, although NSAIDS are more expensive and have greater risk of side effects (Brandt: 1993). It is recommended that these drugs be taken with meals in order to reduce stomach irritation. Rofecoxib (Vioxx) was approved in 1999 for use by individuals with osteoarthritis for the relief of pain. The Food and Drug Administration has approved two drugs for treating osteoarthritis of the knee, hyaluronan (Hyalgan) and hylan G-F20 (Synvisc), which are injected into the knee joint to reduce the pain that occurs when joint fluid breaks down due to this disease. Relief lasts between six and 12 months. Glucosamine sulfate and chondroitin sulfate, popular alternative therapies used by many individuals with arthritis, are approved as drugs in Europe and South America, but are available as dietary supplements only in the United States. Advocates claim that glucosamine stimulates growth and maintains the strength of cartilage. The National Institutes of Health is currently conducting clinical trials of both supplements.

Range of motion exercises strengthen joints and reduce the loss of physical functioning. Walking and swimming help women maintain flexible joints and also provide aerobic exercise that is good for the entire body and the sense of well-being. Swimming is particularly good for women whose knees and hips are affected. Exercise in the water reduces the stress on these major joints while increasing cardiovascular health and endurance.

Severe osteoarthritis in the hip may require total hip replacement surgery, to restore function and relieve pain. Since total hip replacements last an average of 15 years (Lorig and Fries: 1990), it is important to think about facing the pain, risk, and costs of repeating the procedure. It is wise to participate in a rehabilitation program following this surgery. Physical and occupational therapy services may be provided at a rehabilitation center, outpatient clinic, or in the home.

More than 650,000 Americans undergo knee arthroscopy each year in the hope of alleviating the pain of osteoarthritis (Owings and Kozak: 1998). In this procedure, the orthopedic surgeon flushes the knee joint with fluid to remove loose debris, repairs tears, or smooths rough cartilage. A recent randomized, placebo-controlled trial designed to measure the efficacy of this procedure reported that patients who underwent the procedure had no less pain or better function that those who had placebo surgery (Moseley et al.: 2002).

Knee replacement surgery has become more common and successful in recent years. The complication rate of knee replacement surgery is reduced when surgeons are experienced in the procedure and operate at facilities where at least 40 procedures are performed each year (Kass-Bartelmes: 2002). Maintaining a healthy weight and exercising daily will contribute to post-surgical success. Older women should investigate the benefits of joint replacement surgery very carefully, seeking more than one opinion, and taking their time in making a decision.

SEXUAL FUNCTIONING

The woman coping with rheumatoid arthritis may experience problems with sexual functioning, becoming self-conscious about body image due to weight gain associated with use of steroid drugs. In addition, she may experience deformed joints; fatigue; and lack of energy. A loss of self-esteem commonly occurs. Some women may avoid sexual relations, fearing pain or rejection. Depression, resulting from chronic arthritic pain, may also cause decreased interest in sexual activity (Ehrlich: 1973). A partner who fears causing pain may hesitate to initiate sexual relations, reinforcing the woman's feeling of rejection. If neither partner is willing to discuss these feelings, relationships suffer. Communication between partners is key to living with a chronic disease as well as to maintaining sexual function.

Vaginal dryness, a complication often experienced by women with rheumatoid arthritis (Fries: 1995), may cause painful intercourse. A commercial, water soluble lubricant may alleviate this problem. Hormone replacement therapy reduces estrogen deficiency, a cause of vaginal dryness. Estrogen-based topical creams for vaginal dryness are also available. However, once the woman has experienced pain during intercourse, she may avoid future sexual encounters because of her fears. Medications prescribed to reduce pain may also reduce libido. Anti-inflammatory medication should be scheduled so that it will provide maximum relief during sexual relations. Fatigue and a diminished range of motion may also affect sexual function. A warm bath or shower may help to relax joints and muscles. A water bed or flotation mattress may make movement less painful and reduce stress on joints. Experimenting with new positions for intercourse that put less stress on the affected joints may be helpful. Placing a pillow under the hips or wearing knee pads may relieve stress on these joints. Regular exercise may help reduce weakness, contribute to weight control, and increase feelings of well-being.

FAMILY PLANNING, PREGNANCY, AND CHILDREARING

Women who do not wish to become pregnant should choose contraceptive methods with care. Birth control pills are reliable and may be preferable for women whose manual dexterity makes barrier methods difficult to use.

Since rheumatoid arthritis affects women of childbearing age, couples must weigh the decision to have children carefully. They must evaluate the risk to both mother and fetus, the effects of treatment, and the effects on the family. Medications may affect fertility in the woman experiencing a flare. It is a good idea to seek obstetric care from a physician with experience in the management of high risk pregnancies who will work with the rheumatologist to provide the best possible care.

Although it is safe to continue taking most arthritis medications during pregnancy, it is important to discuss their use with both rheumatologist and obstetrician. Weinblatt (1993) suggests that women wishing to conceive should discontinue treatment with methotrexate for at least one menstrual cycle prior to attempting conception. The Arthritis Foundation (1999) recommends that methotrexate be discontinued 90 days prior to a planned pregnancy and throughout the course of pregnancy in order to prevent birth defects. Nor should methotrexate be taken when breastfeeding. Immunosuppressive drugs should be continued during pregnancy only if the mother's health is at serious risk (Kean and Buchanan: 1990). Salicylates, such as aspirin, should be discontinued several weeks before the due date to avoid blood clotting problems and anemia in the mother. Salicylates should not be taken after delivery if the mother is breastfeeding, because they are excreted in breast milk. It is recommended that NSAIDs be prescribed at the lowest possible dose during the first four months of gestation. They, too, are excreted in breast milk and should be discontinued while the mother is nursing her baby. Corticosteroids, injected into affected joints rather than taken orally, may be used to control inflammation with little effect on the fetus. Cases of nerve deafness in the infant caused by antimalarials have also been reported (Klipple and Cecere: 1989). It is recommended that a woman who takes leflunomide use birth control to prevent pregnancy. She should stop taking the drug if she wishes to become pregnant, and she will need to take a drug to eliminate the leflunomide from her system (Arthritis Foundation: 1999).

Generally, women with rheumatoid arthritis deliver their babies with no complications. However, women with hip deformities who cannot spread their legs wide enough for a vaginal delivery will require a cesarean delivery (Rogers and Matsumura: 1991). Cervical spine x-rays, taken before conception, will show potential problems if intubation is necessary for the administration of anesthesia. Regional anesthesia, such as an epidural, may be preferred for delivery if there is any evidence of cervical subluxation (slippage of the joints).

Klipple and Cecere (1989) report that 70% of women with rheumatoid arthritis experience some remission of their symptoms while pregnant and that subsequent pregnancies also follow this course. Remission of rheumatoid arthritis symptoms will most likely end after the baby's birth, returning the mother to her pre-pregnancy status. More than 90% of the women in one of their studies experienced a relapse within six to eight months after delivery.

The pregnant woman with rheumatoid arthritis should develop a schedule that allows for rest periods during the day, eight to ten hours of sleep per night, and the opportunity to sit down for rest frequently during the course of the day. She should continue the exercise routine she followed prior to pregnancy and may find that swimming provides an ideal workout, protecting weight-bearing joints from the stress of weight gain associated with pregnancy. A woman may need assistance during the period of adjustment to motherhood, especially if a probable flare of symptoms occurs. Siblings may resent the new baby not only for the attention being paid to their new sister or brother, but also because their mother's symptoms have flared and she is exhausted and in pain.

Couples should consider the potential for stress on the partner due to the extra duties necessitated by the mothers's fatigue during pregnancy. Increased fatigue, stiffness, and pain after delivery; and a possible combination of postpartum depression with disappointment at the return of rheumatic disease activity are potential problems for the mother. Financial matters may be an issue if the couple is dependent on the wife's earnings and she is unable to return to work. The physical duties of baby care, such as lifting, bathing, and carrying the infant, must be planned in advance in the event the disease flares after delivery.

Women with rheumatoid arthritis may find that maternity and baby clothes need adaptations for easier use. Maternity clothes can be adapted with velcro closures. Bending over to tie shoes can be avoided when elastic shoelaces are substituted for conventional laces. Maternity or nursing brassieres with front hooks or velcro fasteners eliminate the problem of fastening hooks in the rear. A baby sling relieves the strain of carrying the infant. A nursing pillow used to support the baby and a breast pump operated by foot are useful when breastfeeding. When the child is sick, an ear thermometer which is larger and therefore easier to hold may be substituted for a conventional thermometer; large medicine droppers or a bottle may be used to give medications.

Women with arthritis face additional challenges in childrearing. Not only must they cope with the responsibilities of home and family, but often they must cope with pain and lack of energy too. It is difficult for children to understand when a parent cannot attend a sports event or prepare refreshments for a school activity due to an arthritis flare. Young children sometimes think that a mother's illness is in some way their fault. Children also fear that they, too, will develop the condition. If mothers find it difficult to discuss a chronic condition with their children, it may be helpful for the family to work with a social worker, physical therapist, or other health professional. Many support groups invite families to attend their meetings in order to provide them with emotional support and practical information. The group setting may help family members understand functional losses as well as fatigue and pain of arthritis. Providing respite care for women with arthritis and their families in the form of babysitting and cleaning services may prove to be extremely valuable.

PSYCHOLOGICAL ASPECTS OF ARTHRITIS

Women with arthritis must learn how to adjust to the flares and remissions associated with their particular condition; to cope with pain; and to determine the best medical treatment for their specific needs. Arthritis is often a "hidden" disease, since symptoms such as fatigue and morning stiffness are unpredictable. When the symptoms are active, the woman may be in obvious pain; when rested or when treatment reduces pain, it is hard for others to understand her limitations. It is important for the physician to explain these aspects of arthritis.

When arthritis makes work and activities of daily living difficult, it may affect interpersonal relationships both on the job and at home. If the woman is tired, in pain, or unable to move about easily, she may experience emotional problems, such as depression, loss of self-esteem, and worry, which in turn make everyday life even more difficult. These problems combined with mood changes due to medication may also lead to sexual dysfunction (Gerber: 1988). The Arthritis Foundation recommends learning stress reduction or relaxation techniques and participating in recreational activities and social groups.

Arthritis also affects the dual roles of women as workers outside the home and homemakers. Allaire (1992) reports that little role disability is encountered by women with mild arthritis, but that women with more severe disease are likely to have both employment and household disability. Allaire (1992) recommends that rehabilitation interventions address both employment and homemaker goals. Her subjects with severe disease activity tried to maintain their roles as homemakers through a combination of adaptive aids, help from partners and children, and changing their standards for household tasks, such as cleaning and meal preparation. A study of gender differences in osteoarthritis suggests that caregiving responsibilities may delay a woman's decision to undergo knee or hip replacement surgery (Freeman et al.: 1996).

PROFESSIONAL SERVICE PROVIDERS

Services for women with arthritis are provided by a variety of health care professionals. In addition, voluntary organizations provide information, education, and support groups.

Internists or *family physicians*, who provide primary care, may diagnose and approve treatment for rheumatoid arthritis. Often they refer individuals to a rheumatologist for confirmation of the diagnosis and with whom they will coordinate treatment. *Rheumatologists* are physicians who specialize in the treatment of rheumatic diseases, which are inflammations and degenerations of joints and connective tissues. Rheumatologists may serve as case coordinators for women who receive treatment from a multidisciplinary team. *Orthopedic surgeons* or *plastic surgeons* may perform surgery to repair or replace joints damaged by arthritis. *Physiatrists* are physicians who specialize in rehabilitation medicine, often arranging for treatment from physical and occupational therapists.

Obstetricians are physicians who provide primary care during pregnancy, labor and delivery, and postpartum. Some may be specialists in treating women with high risk pregnancies due to chronic disease; they should work with rheumatologists to provide multidisciplinary care during pregnancy.

Physical therapists develop an exercise program to control some arthritic symptoms; keep joints flexible; build up and preserve muscle strength; and help protect joints from further stress. *Occupational therapists* teach new techniques to perform everyday activities, such as washing and dressing, homemaking, and recreation. They may make suggestions regarding safety and sources of assistive devices, such as reaching tools, built-up kitchen utensils, and writing aids.

Social workers provide information about financial and medical benefits, housing, and community resources. They conduct individual, family, or group counseling and may refer individuals to self-help or peer counseling groups.

Rehabilitation counselors help individuals with arthritis develop a plan that will enable them to continue functioning and working. Some individuals will need assistance in returning to their previous position or retraining to obtain a different type of position. Rehabilitation counselors help make the contacts and placements necessary to attain these goals.

WHERE TO FIND SERVICES

The health care professionals who provide services to women with rheumatoid arthritis and osteoarthritis work in hospitals, rehabilitation centers, home health agencies, private and public agencies, independent living centers, and as private practitioners. Individual and group counseling may be available through a local hospital, community health center, senior center, or from mental health professionals in private practice. Patient education programs are offered by hospitals, universities, and chapters of the Arthritis Foundation in order to help individuals live as independently as possible. These courses often result in reduction in pain, dependency, and depression (National Resource Center on Health Promotion and Aging: 1989). Common topics in these courses are education about arthritis, exercise, emotional support, and discussions of how individuals can advocate for themselves within the health care system and participate in choosing treatment options. The Arthritis Foundation offers a six week self-help course, which has been found to increase participants' perception of their own control over the disease, which in turn improves their health status (Haggerty: 1995). Exercise programs in heated pools are also sponsored by local chapters of the Arthritis Foundation. Some women attend pain clinics which teach behavior modification techniques to control the effect of pain.

Women who are severely disabled by arthritis often require home health services. These services are provided by nurses or home health aides; special homemaker services; Meals on Wheels programs; chore services such as housecleaning; and adult day activity programs. The services are often free to individuals with low incomes, or the fees may be on a sliding scale.

Women with rheumatoid arthritis or osteoarthritis require hospitalization when joint replacement surgery is necessary. After surgery, they may move to a rehabilitation unit within the hospital where the surgery was performed or to a rehabilitation hospital. Most rehabilitation centers also offer out-patient services.

ASSISTIVE DEVICES AND ENVIRONMENTAL ADAPTATIONS

Many individuals with arthritis use assistive devices to make everyday living easier. These devices may be specially designed, or they may be common items found in medical supply or hardware stores. They may be purchased in local stores or through mail order catalogues. Schweidler (1984) identifies four basic functions of assistive devices for people with arthritis: to compensate for lost function; to alleviate joint stress; to decrease energy demands; and to increase safety.

The physical therapist or occupational therapist may recommend using an assistive device only at times when functioning is difficult. Women with arthritis must keep their joints flexible yet protect them from stress. It is also important to learn to use the assistive device correctly to avoid stress on other joints.

Devices such as can and jar openers compensate for a weak grasp. Long-handled tongs, utensils with built-up handles, and other adapted equipment will make it easier to continue homemaking activities. Special lamps are controlled with a pat of the hand. A pen with a thick barrel is easier to use than a slim design, because it reduces stress on finger joints. Dressing aids, such as button hooks, elastic shoe laces, a long-handled shoe horn, sock-aid, or zipper pulls, and clothing with velcro fasteners, elastic waistbands, or snaps enable a woman to conserve energy when dressing. Reachers may be used to pick up items that have fallen to the floor or to reach items in overhead cabinets. It is easier to open and close doors when doorknobs are replaced with levers, push locks, or push-pull latches. Swing clear hinges on doors provide the clearance to accommodate wheelchairs and walkers, which some women with arthritis use in order to ambulate. Adjustable height sinks and toilets are valuable additions in the bathroom as are grab bars, long-handled bath brushes, and bath benches for safety in the tub or shower. A cane may make walking safer by promoting balance. Battery powered chairs help individuals who cannot walk long distances or stand for long periods of time continue activities, such as visiting museums and attending sports events. Assistive devices for recreational activities include cardholders, bookstands, and adapted gardening tools that reduce bending and ease grasping.

An automobile with power steering, brakes, windows and seat controls reduces stress on joints. General Motors, Ford, and DaimlerChrysler offer financial assistance for the purchase of adaptive equipment such as hand controls, a ramp, or lifts to be installed in vehicles (see Chapter 2, "TRAVEL AND TRANSPORTATION ORGANIZATIONS"). Special van services or special parking placards for individuals with arthritis may help solve some transportation problems. Architectural adaptations such as ramps, railings, chairlifts, and elevators may make independent mobility easier.

Although most assistive devices are nonprescription items, some may be covered by third-party payment with prior approval.

References

Allaire, Saralynn H.
1992   "Employment and Household Work Disability in Women with Rheumatoid Arthritis" Journal of Applied Rehabilitation Counseling 23:1:44-51

American College of Rheumatology
No date   Fact Sheet: Sjogren's Syndrome Atlanta, GA: American College of Rheumatology

Arthritis Foundation
1999   Rheumatoid Arthritis Atlanta, GA: The Arthritis Foundation
1996   Aspirin and Other NSAIDS Atlanta, GA: The Arthritis Foundation
1994a   Rheumatoid Arthritis Atlanta, GA: The Arthritis Foundation
1994b   Osteoarthritis Atlanta, GA: The Arthritis Foundation

Bennett, J. Claude
1988   "Clinical Features" pp. 87-92 in H. Ralph Schumacher, Jr. (ed.) Primer on the Rheumatic Diseases Atlanta, GA: Arthritis Foundation

Brandt, Kenneth D.
1994   "Osteoarthritis" pp. 1692-1698 in Kurt J. Isselbacher et al. (eds.) Harrison's Principles of Internal Medicine New York, NY: McGraw Hill
1993   "NSAIDs in the Treatment of Osteoarthritis: Friends or Foes?" Bulletin on the Rheumatic Diseases 42:6:1-4

Ehrlich, George E.
1973   Total Management of the Arthritic Patient Philadelphia, PA: J.B. Lippincott Company

Fenner, Helmut
1992   "Nonsteroidal Anti-inflammatory Drugs: Benefit/Risk Evaluation in Rheumatic Diseases" Journal of Rheumatology 19:(Supplement 32):98-99

Food and Drug Administration
2002   "Labeling Changes for Arthritis Drug Celebrex" FDA Talk Paper June 7

Freeman, Julia B. et al.
1996   "Advances Brought by Health Services Research to Patients with Arthritis: Summary of the Workshop on Health Services Research in Arthritis: From Research to Practice" Arthritis Care and Research 9 (April):2:142-150

Fries, James F.
1995   Arthritis: A Take Care of Yourself Health Guide Reading, MA: Addison-Wesley-Longman Publishing Company

Gerber, Lynn H.
1988   "Rehabilitative Therapies for Patients with Rheumatic Disease" pp. 301-307 in H. Ralph Schumacher, Jr. (ed.) Primer on the Rheumatic Diseases Atlanta, GA: Arthritis Foundation

Haggerty, Maureen
1995   "Taking Control" Advance/Rehabilitation 4(January)6:35-38

Jurisson, Mary L.
1991   "Rehabilitation in Rheumatic Diseases What's New" Western Journal of Medicine 154:5:545-548

Kass-Bartelmes, Barbara L.
2002   "Managing Osteoarthritis: Helping the Elderly Maintain Function and Mobility" Research in Action Rockville, MD: Agency for Healthcare Research and Quality

Kean, W.F. and W.W. Buchanan
1990   "Pregnancy and Rheumatoid Arthritis" Baillieres Clinical Rheumatology 4(1):125-40

Klipple, Gary L. and Fred A. Cecere
1989   "Rheumatoid Arthritis and Pregnancy" Rheumatic Disease Clinics of North America 15:2:213-239

Lipsky, Peter E.
1994   "Rheumatoid Arthritis" pp. 1648-1655 in Isselbacher, Kurt J. et al. (eds.) Harrison's Principles of Internal Medicine New York, NY: McGraw Hill

Lorig, Kate and James F. Fries
1990   The Arthritis Helpbook Reading, MA: Addison-Wesley Publishing Company

McNeil, John M.
1993   Americans with Disabilities: 1991-92 U.S. Bureau of the Census, Current Population Reports, P70-33 Washington, DC: U.S. Government Printing Office

Moseley, J. Bruce et al.
2002   "A Controlled Trial of Arthroscopic Surgery for Osteoarthritis of the Knee" New England Journal of Medicine 347:2(July 11):81-88

National Institute of Arthritis and Musculoskeletal and Skin Diseases
2002   Handout on Health: Osteoarthritis Bethesda, MD
1998   Handout on Health: Rheumatoid Arthritis Bethesda, MD

National Resource Center on Health Promotion and Aging
1989   "Arthritis: Positive Approaches Offer New Hope" Perspectives in Health Promotion and Aging 4:(November-December)6

Rogers, Judith and Molleen Matsumura
1991   Mother To Be: A Guide to Pregnancy and Birth for Women with Disabilities New York, NY: Demos Publications

Schweidler, Helen
1984   "Assistive Devices, Aids to Daily Living" pp. 263-276 in Gail Kershner Riggs and Eric P. Gall (eds.) Rheumatic Diseases, Rehabilitation and Management Boston, MA: Butterworth

Shlotzhauer, Tammi L. and James L. McGuire
1993   Living with Rheumatoid Arthritis Baltimore, MD: Johns Hopkins University Press

Weinblatt, Michael E.
1993   "Methotrexate in Rheumatoid Arthritis" Bulletin on the Rheumatic Diseases 42:4:4-7 Atlanta, GA: The Arthritis Foundation

Whitacre, Caroline C. et al.
1999   "A Gender Gap in Autoimmunity" Science 283:5406(26Feb99):1277-1278

ORGANIZATIONS

American Academy of Orthopaedic Surgeons
6300 North River Road
Rosemont, IL 60018-4262
(800) 346-2267   (847) 823-7186
FAX (847) 823-8125   orthosinfo.aaos.org   www.aaos.org

A professional organization for orthopaedic surgeons and allied health professionals. Web site offers a "Find a Surgeon" link. The "Surgery Center" link provides information on types, benefits, and risks of surgery as well as preparing for surgery, hospitalization, and recovery. Surgery animations demonstrate procedures such as arthroscopy and hip, knee, and shoulder replacements. Fact sheets that relate to surgery and arthritis are available on the web site. A quarterly e-mail newsletter, "Your Orthopaedic Connection," is available upon request.

American Autoimmune Related Diseases Association (AARDA)
22100 Gratiot Avenue
East Detroit, MI 48021
(800) 598-4668   (586) 776-3900   e-mail: aarda@aol.com
www.aarda.org

Provides information on autoimmune diseases including rheumatoid arthritis, type 1 diabetes, and multiple sclerosis, Sjogren's syndrome. Web site offers brief explanations of conditions. Offers telephone support and referrals.

American Chronic Pain Association (ACPA)
PO Box 850
Rocklin, CA 95677
(800) 533-3231   FAX (916) 632-3208   e-mail: acpa@pacbell.neet
www.theacpa.org

Organizes groups throughout the U.S. to provide support and activities for people who experience chronic pain. Membership, $30.00 first year, $15.00 thereafter; includes quarterly newsletter, "ACPA Chronicle."

American College of Rheumatology
1800 Century Place, Suite 250
Atlanta, GA 30345
(404) 633-3777   FAX (404) 633-1870
e-mail: acr@rheumatology.org   www.rheumatology.org

A professional membership organization for rheumatologists who treat or study all forms of arthritis. The web site provides a geographical listing of rheumatologists. Offers fact sheets on rheumatic diseases such as osteoarthritis, rheumatoid arthritis, and gout. Free. Also available on the web site.

American Pain Foundation
201 North Charles Street, Suite 710
Baltimore, MD 2120
(888) 615-7246   FAX (410) 385-1832   www.painfoundation.org

This organization provides educational materials and advocates on behalf of people who are experiencing pain. Promotes research and advocates to remove barriers to treatment for pain. Distributes patient educational materials, free, and has information about the causes of pain and treatment as well as links to related sites on its web site.

Arthritis Center
www.mayoclinic.com

This "Condition Center," found on the Mayo Clinic web site, provides information on many forms of arthritis as well as Healthy Lifestyle Planners for weight management, exercise, and stress management.

Arthritis Foundation
PO Box 7669
Atlanta, GA 30357-0669
(800) 283-7800   (404) 872-7100
FAX (404) 872-0457   www.arthritis.org

Supports research; offers referrals to physicians; provides public and professional education. Chapters throughout the U.S.; toll-free number connects to local chapter. Some chapters offer arthritis classes, clubs, and exercise programs. Membership, $20.00, includes the Arthritis Foundation's "Drug Guide," chapter newsletter and magazine, "Arthritis Today." Also available by subscription, $12.95. Members receive discounts on purchases of publications. Many brochures are available on the web site. Several brochures are available in Spanish.

MEDLINEplus: Osteoarthritis
www.nlm.nih.gov/medlineplus/osteoarthritis.html
MEDLINEplus: Rheumatoid Arthritis
www.nlm.nih.gov/medlineplus/rheumatoidarthritis.html

These web sites provide links to sites for information about arthritis, treatment, alternative therapy, clinical trials, disease management, specific conditions/aspects, everyday living, organizations, and research. They include an interactive tutorial. Some information available in Spanish. Provide links to MEDLINE research articles and related MEDLINEplus pages.

National Aging Institute Information Center (NAIC)
330 Independence Avenue, SW, Room 4656
Washington, DC 20201
(202) 619-7501   FAX (202) 401-7620   www.aoa.gov/naic

Provides information and statistics related to research conducted by the National Institute on Aging. Free publications list. Many publications available on the web site.

National Chronic Pain Outreach Association (NCPOA)
PO Box 274
Millboro, VA 24460-9606
(540) 862-9437   FAX (540) 862-9485   www.chronicpain.org

A national clearinghouse for information about chronic pain. Refers individuals to support groups on chronic pain throughout the U.S. Produces publications and audiocassettes on a variety of topics related to chronic pain. Membership, individuals, $25.00; professionals, $50.00; includes quarterly newsletter, "Lifeline."

National Institute of Arthritis and Musculoskeletal and Skin Diseases Information Clearinghouse
1 AMS Circle
Bethesda, MD 20892
(877) 226-4267   (301) 495-4484
(301) 565-2966 (TTY)   FAX (301) 718-6366
e-mail: niamsinfo@mail.nih.gov   www.niams.nih.gov

Distributes bibliographies, fact sheets, catalogues, and directories to the public and professionals. Free. Many of the publications are available on the web site in English and Spanish. NIAMS supports clinical research, individual research, and specialized research centers, which conduct basic and clinical research; provide professional, public, and patient education; and sponsor community-related activities.

Sjogren's Syndrome Foundation
8120 Woodmont Avenue, Suite 530
Bethesda, MD 20814
(800) 475-6473   FAX (301) 718-0322
e-mail: ssf@idt.net   www.sjogrens.com

Provides information to individuals and professionals through support groups and conferences. Membership, $25.00, includes newsletter, "The Moisture Seekers," published 9 times per year, and discounts on publications.

Spine-health.cm
1840 Oak Avenue, Suite 112
Evanston, IL 60201
www.spine-health.com

This web site provides information on coping with chronic back pain, treatment, pain management, and rehabilitation. Also offers a physician directory on the web site.

All about Osteoarthritis
by Nancy E. Lane and Daniel J. Wallace
Oxford University Press
2001 Evans Road
Cary, NC 27513
(800) 451-7556   FAX (919) 677-1303
e-mail: custserv@oup-usa.org   www.oup-usa.org

This book describes the disease, treatments, alternative therapies, when surgery may be necessary, and how patients can help themselves. It also contains detailed illustrations showing how joints degenerate. $25.00

Arthritis
Films for the Humanities & Sciences
PO Box 2053
Princeton, NJ 08543-2053
(800) 257-5126   FAX (609) 275-3767
e-mail: custserv@films.com   www.films.com

This videotape discusses osteoarthritis, rheumatoid arthritis, and juvenile arthritis through profiles of individuals who use conventional and alternative therapies. Health care professionals provide information about a variety of treatments. 50 minutes. $89.95

The Arthritis Action Program
by Michael E. Weinblatt
Simon and Schuster
IBD
PO Box 218
Paramus, NJ 07653
(888) 866-6631   FAX (800) 943-9831   www.simonsays.com

This book describes common forms of arthritis, including osteoarthritis. Discusses treatment strategies, complementary therapies, exercises, pain management, and the role of physical and occupational therapists. $14.00

Arthritis and Exercise Information Package
National Institute of Arthritis and Musculoskeletal and Skin Diseases Information Clearinghouse
(877) 226-4267   www.niams.nih.gov

This packet provides articles on the role of exercise in the treatment of arthritis. 33 range-of-motion, strengthening, and endurance exercises are illustrated. Includes glossary. Free

Arthritis Answers
Arthritis Foundation (see "ORGANIZATIONS" above)
(800) 283-7800   www.arthritis.org

This booklet provides basic information about arthritis. Includes signs, symptoms, diagnosis, types, treatment, and research. Available in English and Spanish. Free

Arthritis: A Take Care of Yourself Health Guide
by James F. Fries
Perseus Books Group
Customer Service Department
5500 Central Avenue
Boulder, CO 80301
(800) 386-5656   FAX (720) 406-7336
e-mail: westview.orders@perseusbooks.com
www.perseusbooksgroup.com

This book describes major forms of arthritis and methods of managing the condition through exercise and new pain medications. Includes charts that help individuals make pain relief decisions. $16.00

The Arthritis Foundation's Guide to Alternative Therapies
by Judith Horstman
Arthritis Foundation Distribution Center
PO Box 509
Pembina, ND 58271
(800) 207-8633   FAX (770) 442-9742

This book describes nearly 90 alternative therapies for arthritis. Discusses the risks and benefits of therapies such as homeopathy, acupuncture, dietary supplements, and chiropractic, providing clinical evidence, research, and medical opinion. $24.95

The Arthritis Helpbook
by Kate Lorig and James J. Fries
Perseus Books Group
Customer Service Department
5500 Central Avenue
Boulder, CO 80301
(800) 386-5656   FAX (720) 406-7336
e-mail: westview.orders@perseusbooks.com
www.perseusbooksgroup.com

This book focuses on techniques that help reduce pain and increase dexterity. Includes information on prescription and over-the-counter medications, exercises, and nutrition. $19.95

Arthritis of the Hip and Knee: The Active Person's Guide to Taking Charge
by Ronald J. Allen, Victoria Anne Brander, and S. David Stulberg
Peachtree Publishers
1700 Chattahoochee Avenue
Atlanta, GA 30324
(800) 241-0113   FAX (800) 875-8909
e-mail: orders@peachtree-online.com   www.peachtree-online.com

This handbook, written by a patient who has had two hip replacements, an orthopedic surgeon, and a physiatrist, discusses the causes, treatment options, and progression of osteoarthritis. Includes information on hip replacement, post-operative physical therapy, the role of exercise, and advice on everyday activities. $14.95

Aspirin and Other NSAIDs
Arthritis Foundation (see "ORGANIZATIONS" above)
(800) 283-7800   www.arthritis.org

Using a question and answer format, this booklet discusses NSAIDs and possible side effects. Free

Connect and Control
Arthritis Foundation (see "ORGANIZATIONS" above)
(800) 283-7800   www.arthritis.org

This online, interactive, self-management guide provides a personalized exercise program based on an individual's answers to a series of questionnaires. Weekly e-mails provide activities and information on additional topics such as nutrition, pain management, treatment options, emotional support, and managing stress and depression. Free

Coping with Osteoarthritis
by Robert H. Phillips
Penguin Putnam, Inc., Inside Sales
(800) 788-6262   FAX (607) 775-5586   www.penguinputnam.com

Written by a psychologist, this book provides information for individuals and their families on coping with the condition and improving quality of life. $14.95

Coping with Rheumatoid Arthritis
by Robert H. Phillips
Penguin Putnam, Inc., Inside Sales
(800) 788-6262   FAX (607) 775-5586   www.penguinputnam.com

Written by a psychologist, this book discusses strategies for improving the quality of life; advice for dealing with the emotional aspects of this chronic condition; suggestions for activities and lifestyle changes; and information for family members. $9.95

Feeling Good with Arthritis
Info Vision
102 North Hazel Street
Glenwood, IA 51534
(800) 237-1808   FAX (888) 735-2622

This videotape discusses the importance of exercise, medical treatment, diet, and attitude. Individuals with rheumatoid arthritis and osteoarthritis describe their experiences. 60 minutes. $25.00

Guide to Intimacy with Arthritis
Arthritis Foundation (see "ORGANIZATIONS" above)
(800) 283-7800   www.arthritis.org

Reprinted from "Arthritis Today," this article offers answers to concerns related to sexuality and arthritis. Free. Also available on the web site.

Guide to Pain Management: Natural and Medical Therapies
Arthritis Foundation Distribution Center
PO Box 509
Pembina, ND 58271
(800) 207-8633   FAX (770) 442-9742

This book provides information about using high-tech methods, medications, and alternative therapies to relieve pain. Includes a pain rating scale. $24.95

Knee Replacement Information Package
National Institute of Arthritis and Musculoskeletal and Skin Diseases Information Clearinghouse
(see "ORGANIZATIONS" above)
(877) 226-4267   www.niams.nih.gov

This packet provides articles which discuss knee replacement surgery, pre- and post-operative care, and activities after surgery. Includes glossary. Free

Living Well: Taking Care of Yourself in the Middle and Later Years
by James J. Fries
Perseus Books Group
Customer Service Department
5500 Central Avenue
Boulder, CO 80301
(800) 386-5656   FAX (720) 406-7336
e-mail: westview.orders@perseusbooks.com
www.perseusbooksgroup.com

This book presents a program for keeping in physical and mental shape while living with osteoarthritis. $18.00

Living with Rheumatoid Arthritis
by Tammi L. Shlotzhauer and James L. McGuire
Johns Hopkins University Press
2715 North Charles Street
Baltimore, MD 21218
(800) 537-5487   (410) 516-6900   FAX (410) 516-6968
e-mail: all inside@jhupbooks.com   www.press.jhup.edu

Written by two rheumatologists, this book covers the physical aspects of rheumatoid arthritis and medical and surgical treatment, describes coping techniques, suggests exercises, and provides information about everyday activities. $16.95

130

<u>Managing Your Activities</u>
<u>Managing Your Fatigue</u>
<u>Managing Your Health Care</u>
<u>Managing Your Pain</u>
<u>Managing Your Stress</u>
Arthritis Foundation (see "ORGANIZATIONS" above)
(800) 283-7800   www.arthritis.org

This series of brochures describes self-management techniques for coping with arthritis. "Managing Your Activities" suggests methods that will enable individuals to reduce stress on joints affected by arthritis and provides tips for self-help techniques and assistive devices. "Managing Your Fatigue" discusses fatigue, a common symptom in individuals with rheumatic disease. "Managing Your Health Care" describes the roles various health care professionals play in treating individuals with rheumatic diseases. Provides guidelines for making the most of office visits and a list of questions to ask physicians. "Managing Your Pain" discusses pain management strategies such as medication, exercise, assistive devices, heat and cold treatments, massage, and relaxation techniques. "Managing Your Stress" describes how stress can lead to physical and emotional reactions and discusses stress management techniques such as deep breathing, progressive relaxation, guided imagery, and visualization. Free. Also available on the web site.

<u>Mayo Clinic on Arthritis</u>
Mayo Clinic Health Information Division
PO Box 609
Calverton, NY 11933
(800) 291-1128   www.health-store.com

This book provides information for individuals with osteoarthritis or rheumatoid arthritis. Includes treatments; alternative therapies; exercises; tips for joint protection, pain control, and weight management; coping techniques; and suggestions for everyday activities, recreation and travel, and employment. $16.95

Mother To Be: A Guide to Pregnancy and Birth for Women with Disabilities
by Judith Rogers and Molleen Matsumura
Demos Medical Publishing
386 Park Avenue South, Suite 201
New York, NY 10016
(800) 532-8663   (212) 683-0072
FAX (212) 683-0118   e-mail: info@demospub.com   www.demosmedpub.com

This book describes the pregnancy and childbirth experiences of 36 women with a wide variety of disabilities including rheumatoid arthritis. Suggests practical solutions for the special concerns of individuals with disabilities during pregnancy and those of their partners, families, and health care providers. Includes a glossary and a bibliography. $29.95   Orders made on the Demos web site receive a 15% discount.

The New Sjogren's Syndrome Handbook
by Steven Carsons and Elaine K. Harris (eds.)
Sjogren's Syndrome Foundation
8120 Woodmont Avenue, Suite 530
Bethesda, MD 20814
(800) 475-6473   FAX (301) 718-0322
e-mail: ssf@idt.net   www.sjogrens.com

This book provides practical suggestions for living more comfortably with this chronic condition. $25.00.

Osteoarthritis
Arthritis Foundation (see "ORGANIZATIONS" above)
(800) 283-7800   www.arthritis.org
This booklet describes the causes, diagnosis, and treatment of osteoarthritis. Includes "joint saver" tips to reduce pain. Available in English and Spanish. $1.00

Osteoarthritis and Rheumatoid Arthritis
Films for the Humanities & Sciences
PO Box 2053
Princeton, NJ 08543-2053
(800) 257-5126   FAX (609) 275-3767
e-mail: custserv@films.com   www.films.com

This videotape describes the differences between these two conditions as well as medical and surgical treatments. 19 minutes. $99.95

Osteoporosis and Arthritis: Two Common but Different Conditions
NIH Osteoporosis and Related Bone Diseases National Resource Center (ORBD)
1232 22nd Street, NW
Washington, DC 20037
(800) 293-2356   (202) 223-0344   (202) 466-4315 (TTY)
FAX (202) 223-2237   e-mail: orbdnrc@nof.org   www.osteo.org

132

This brochure provides an overview of the risk factors, physical effects, treatment options, and pain management strategies associated with osteoporosis, osteoarthritis, and rheumatoid arthritis. Free. Also available on the web site.

People with Arthritis Can Exercise (PACE)
Pool Exercise Program (PEP)
Arthritis Foundation Distribution Center
PO Box 509
Pembina, ND 58271
(800) 207-8633   FAX (770) 442-9742
www.arthritis.org

Videotape exercise programs developed by the Arthritis Foundation. "PACE Level 1" is a gentle exercise program for individuals with significant joint disease; 30 minutes. "PACE Level 2" is a moderate exercise program designed to increase endurance for individuals with mild arthritis; 40 minutes. "PEP" presents pool exercises to perform in chest level water; 50 minutes. $19.50 each

Questions and Answers about Arthritis Pain
National Institute of Arthritis and Musculoskeletal and Skin Diseases Information Clearinghouse
(see "ORGANIZATIONS" section above)
(877) 226-4267   www.niams.nih.gov

This booklet discusses short-term and long term management of chronic arthritis pain, alternative therapies, and coping strategies. Free. Also available on the web site.

Questions and Answers about Hip Replacement
National Institute of Arthritis and Musculoskeletal and Skin Diseases Information Clearinghouse
(see "ORGANIZATIONS" section above)
(877) 226-4267   www.niams.nih.gov

This booklet discusses the surgical procedure, possible complications, recovery, and rehabilitation. Free. Also available on the web site.

Rheumatoid Arthritis
Arthritis Foundation (see "ORGANIZATIONS" above)
(800) 283-7800   www.arthritis.org

This booklet describes rheumatoid arthritis and explains how it differs from other forms of arthritis. Discusses diagnostic tests and treatment with medications, rest, exercise, and surgery. Free. Also available on the web site.

Rheumatoid Arthritis Information Packet
National Institute of Arthritis and Musculoskeletal and Skin Diseases Information Clearinghouse
(see "ORGANIZATIONS" section above)
(877) 226-4267   www.niams.nih.gov

This information packet describes the development and progress of rheumatoid arthritis; its symptoms, diagnosis and treatment; and current research. Free

Sexual Function in People with Disability and Chronic Illness: A Health Professional's Guide
by Marca Sipski and Craig Alexander
Aspen Publishers, Inc.
PO Box 990
Frederick, MD 21705-9782
(800) 234-1660   www.aspenpub.com

This book discusses the effects of disability on sexuality, reproductive concerns, treatment methods, and information on general sexual function and dysfunction. Includes spinal cord injury, diabetes, multiple sclerosis, arthritis and other connective tissue diseases, and heart disease. $59.00

Sjogren's Syndrome
Arthritis Foundation (see "ORGANIZATIONS" above)
(800) 283-7800   www.arthritis.org

This booklet explains the causes, symptoms, diagnosis, and treatment for this related condition. Free. Also available on the web site.

The Sjogren's Syndrome Survival Guide
by Teri P. Rumpf and Katherine Morland Hammitt
New Harbinger Publications
5674 Shattuck Avenue
Oakland, CA 94609
(800) 748-6273   (510) 652-0215
FAX (510) 652-5472   e-mail: customerservice@newharbinger.com
www.newharbinger.com

Written by two women who have Sjogren's syndrome, this book contains information on the condition, treatments, research, and resources. $15.95

Understanding Osteoarthritis
Fanlight Productions
4196 Washington Street, Suite 2
Boston, MA 02131
(800) 937-4113   (617) 469-4999   FAX (617) 469-3379
e-mail: fanlight@fanlight.com   www.fanlight.com

This videotape describes the condition, its treatment, pain relief, and lifestyle changes. Interviews with people living with arthritis are included. 19 minutes. $199.00

Xerostomia (Dry Mouth) Video
Sjogren's Syndrome Foundation
8120 Woodmont Avenue, Suite 530
Bethesda, MD 20814
(800) 475-6473   FAX (301) 718-0322
e-mail: ssf@idt.net   www.sjogrens.com

This videotape discusses the causes of dry mouth and current treatment options. 30 minutes. $35.00.

RESOURCES FOR ASSISTIVE DEVICES

Listed below are publications that provide information about assistive devices and catalogues that specialize in devices for people with arthritis. Generic catalogues that sell some aids for people with arthritis are listed in Chapter 2, " COPING WITH DAILY ACTIVITIES."

Living Better with Arthritis
Aids for Arthritis, Inc.
35 Wakefield Drive
Medford, NJ 08055
(800) 654-0707   FAX (609) 654-8631   www.aidsforarthritis.com

A mail order catalogue of products with dressing, bathing, and grooming aids and kitchen, housekeeping, and recreation equipment. Free. Also available on the web site.

Sears Home Healthcare Catalog
7700 Brush Hill Road
Hinsdale, IL 60521
(800) 326-1750   (800) 733-7249 (TTY)

Sells health care and rehabilitation products.

Chapter 5

CORONARY HEART DISEASE

Contrary to popular belief, coronary heart disease is the leading cause of death in American women as well as men. In 1996, 49.2% of women's deaths were due to coronary heart disease (American Heart Association: 1998a). Although men have heart attacks at a younger age, women's risk of heart disease or stroke increases as they age. When women enter menopause, the protective effects of estrogen decline, increasing the risk for coronary heart disease. Historically, clinical trials have studied only men, leading to questions about their validity for women. Differences in age at diagnosis, symptoms, risk factors, diagnostic test accuracies, and mortality rates between women and men must be carefully considered (Redberg: 1998).

Coronary heart disease (CHD), also called ischemic heart disease or coronary artery disease, is the result of arteriosclerosis or "hardening of the arteries," a generic term that describes narrowing of the arteries. The walls of the arteries thicken and lose elasticity, due to the formation of plaque. Atherosclerosis, a type of arteriosclerosis, affects larger arteries and is an underlying cause of most heart disease.

High blood cholesterol, obesity, and lack of physical activity are the risk factors for heart disease that are particular problems for women. Diabetes and smoking are additional risk factors that increase women's chances of developing coronary heart disease. A large study (Canto et al.: 2002) comparing the treatment of men and women who had suffered heart attacks found that women were less likely to receive such treatment as aspirins, beta-blockers, angioplasty, and hear t bypass surgery than men. The risk of death from coronary heart disease is significantly greater for women with diabetes than it is for men with diabetes (Lee et al.: 2000).

Too much cholesterol in the blood leads to a build-up of fatty deposits in the arteries, increasing the risk of heart attack. Cholesterol levels in the blood may be lowered by limiting saturated fat in the diet and substituting polyunsaturated fats from vegetable sources. Some individuals require medication to lower blood cholesterol levels satisfactorily, although some of these medications affect liver function and should be taken with caution.

In women, estrogen appears to affect cholesterol levels. Low density lipoproteins (LDL) carry fat and cholesterol through blood vessels, causing the build-up of fatty deposits while high density lipoproteins (HDL) remove cholesterol from the blood. LDL is often referred to as the "bad" cholesterol, and HDL, the "good" cholesterol. Estrogen is thought to increase HDL and decrease LDL levels.

Hormone replacement therapy (HRT), used to treat the symptoms of menopause, has long been thought to improve women's cardiovascular systems. HRT uses either estrogen alone or with progestin to reduce hot flashes or flushes, sweats, and sleeplessness. However, a large clinical study of the effects of this therapy in preventing heart disease, breast and colorectal cancer, and osteoporosis was halted due to evidence that the risks outweighed benefits. The Women's Health Initiative study showed a 26% increase in breast cancer, a 41% increase in stroke, and a 29% increase in heart attacks, as well as a doubling of blood clots in legs and lungs, in the women who used hormone therapy (Women's Health Initiative: 2002). Another study (Herrington et al.: 2000) found that neither estrogen alone or in combination with progesterone affected the progression of coronary artery disease among women who already had the disease.

Individuals who are overweight increase their risk for high blood pressure and diabetes. Losing weight helps to decrease cholesterol levels in the blood, lower blood pressure, and improve blood glucose tolerance. A low fat diet accompanied by aerobic exercise will help individuals lose weight and reduce their risk of heart disease.

The National High Blood Pressure Education Program recently updated its guidelines for the prevention and reduction of high blood pressure. It recommends reduction of daily sodium consumption to less than 2400 milligrams; moderate physical exercise, limiting alcohol intake to no more than 24 ounces of beer, 10 ounces of wine, or two ounces of whiskey per day; maintaining normal weight; daily consumption of more than 3500 milligrams of dietary potassium; and eating meals that are reduced in fat and rich in vegetables, fruits, and low-fat dairy products (Whelton et al.: 2002).

The cardiovascular benefits of exercise have been demonstrated in studies of men with heart disease. Although women who exercise benefit through weight reduction and associated improvement in blood pressure and blood cholesterol levels, women traditionally participate less in recreational sports and tend to become physically inactive as they age (Limacher: 1998).

Individuals with diabetes have an increased risk of coronary heart disease and an increased rate of heart attack. About four-fifths of individuals with diabetes die of premature cardiovascular disease, usually myocardial infarction (National Institutes of Health: 1989). Diabetes is a greater risk factor for coronary heart disease in women than in men. Not only does the risk for coronary disease double in women with diabetes in comparison with those without diabetes, these women are more likely to die after heart attack (Sowers: 1998). Diabetes undermines the effects of estrogen, leading to high blood pressure, high cholesterol, and atherosclerosis. The use of insulin has been implicated in the higher rate of fatal coronary heart disease in women with diabetes. To reduce the risk of heart disease, individuals with diabetes should maintain good control of their blood glucose (see Chapter 6, "Diabetes"), stop smoking, reduce high blood pressure and high cholesterol, and if necessary, lose weight.

TYPES OF CORONARY HEART DISEASE

Angina pectoris is caused by a lack of oxygen-rich blood to the heart; its symptoms are chest, arm, back, neck, or jaw pain. Eighty-five percent of angina is caused by coronary heart disease; the remaining 15% may be attributed to heart valve disease, spasms in artery walls, or abnormalities in the heart chamber (Texas Heart Institute: 1996). Women may not exhibit the classic signs of angina; they are more likely to have "atypical" chest pain, complaining of pain in the abdomen, breathing problems, nausea, or unexplained fatigue. This atypical pain may be attributed to noncardiac conditions such as arthritis or osteoporosis. Stable angina may occur with exertion, but the pain subsides quickly with rest. Unstable angina is characterized by frequent episodes and severe discomfort. Unstable angina is diagnosed through physical examination, electrocardiogram (ECG), exercise stress tests, and thallium stress tests. Exercise stress tests measure heart function but do not indicate where or how badly arteries are blocked; they are helpful in determining treatment options. In an exercise stress test, electrodes are placed on the chest, and the individual walks on a motor-driven treadmill, as the speed and incline are increased at regular intervals. The ECG is monitored carefully, and blood pressure is checked regularly. Exercise requires the heart to work harder; if there are blockages in the arteries, the ECG will show changes to its normal wave patterns. Exercise stress tests tend to be less accurate in women (American Heart Association: 1998b).

The thallium scan is used to determine the location of the blockage. Thallium, a radioactive isotope, is injected into a vein while the individual is walking on the treadmill; it travels through the bloodstream to the heart. With the individual lying flat, an imaging scan is performed to show the movement of the thallium throughout the heart muscle; areas that do not receive blood appear as "holes." However, in women, breast tissue may affect the clarity of the scan. It has recently been suggested that exercise-thallium testing of individuals who are symptom-free after coronary artery bypass grafts may predict subsequent myocardial infarction or death. Routine screening of these individuals has been discouraged in the past (Lauer et al.: 1998). Noninvasive tests, such as the thallium scan, are more expensive than the exercise stress test; women may be referred less frequently for these tests.

Unstable angina may be treated with medication, angioplasty (a procedure that is used to reduce arterial blockage), or coronary bypass surgery. Medications include aspirin, nitroglycerin, and beta-blockers. Aspirin prevents the formation of blood clots; side effects are usually avoided by taking buffered or coated aspirin. Nitroglycerin dilates blood vessels, increases blood flow, and lowers blood pressure, reducing the work of the heart. It may be taken orally, in ointments, or through a patch placed on the arm. When taken as a tablet, nitroglycerin is placed under the tongue and allowed to dissolve so that it enters the bloodstream rapidly. Relief is usually felt within a minute or two. Side effects include dizziness and tingling. Beta-blockers slow the heart rate and reduce the amount of oxygen it needs. Side effects include fatigue and dizziness, impotence, depression, diarrhea, or skin rashes; these conditions are relieved by reducing the dose or discontinuing the medication. Beta-blockers should be discontinued slowly over time to avoid complications. Calcium channel blockers help increase the blood supply to the heart and reduce its need for oxygen. They are effective in treating stable angina and have few side effects.

Cardiac catheterization is a test used to assess blood flow and the extent of blockage; a catheter is inserted into an artery in the arm or groin, threaded up through the artery to the heart, and a dye is injected. The procedure is monitored by x-ray which allows the physician to visualize the blockage. The resulting pictures are called arteriograms; about 1,359,000 were performed in 1999 (American Heart Association: 2001). When Schulman and his colleagues (1999) assessed the effects of sex and race on physicians' referrals for cardiac catheterization, they found that women and blacks were less likely to be referred for this procedure.

A *myocardial infarction* occurs when the blood cannot reach the heart muscle due to a partial or total blockage of the coronary arteries. The damage is irreversible. Common symptoms are intense chest pain, a cold sweat, dizziness, and shortness of breath. Individuals experiencing these symptoms should seek medical attention immediately. Two tests are used to determine the diagnosis of myocardial infarction, the electrocardiogram (ECG) and blood tests, which reveal the presence of cardiac enzymes released when heart muscle cells are injured. Electrodes, connected to the electrocardiograph, are placed on the individual's chest, arms, and legs. The electrocardiogram measures the electrical activity within the heart and records it as a tracing on a strip of moving paper; abnormalities are detected by comparing the tracing with recordings of normal heart activity.

Myocardial infarction is usually first treated in the hospital emergency room. Morphine may be administered to relieve chest pain. If an electrocardiogram detects abnormal heartbeat rhythms, known as arrhythmias, they are treated with medications such as lidocaine, or defibrillation (shock therapy) is used to interrupt the abnormal rhythm and return the heartbeat to normal. A pacemaker, a mechanical device that provides regular electrical stimulation to the heart, may be attached temporarily or permanently implanted. Once the physician has confirmed that a myocardial infarction has occurred, the drugs streptokinase or tissue plasminogen activator (tPA) are used to dissolve the blood clot that precipitated the heart attack. Streptokinase or tPA must be given, through a catheter or direct injection, soon after the attack in order to dissolve the clot. Some individuals develop blood clots in the heart after myocardial infarction; these clots may enter the bloodstream and cause damage to other organs. To counter clot formation, anticoagulants or blood thinners such as warfarin (Coumadin) are prescribed. Individuals taking anticoagulants are prone to excessive bleeding and must be carefully monitored. Aspirin should be avoided when taking anticoagulants, because it is also an anticoagulant, but acetaminophen may be taken. Individuals spend several days in an intensive care unit (ICU) for careful monitoring by ECG. Medications are administered through an intravenous line in a vein in the arm, and oxygen is usually administered. Following the stay in the ICU, the individual will be transferred to a less intensively monitored unit for additional care and initial cardiac rehabilitation services.

In late 2002, the National Heart, Lung and Blood Institute announced the results of a major clinical trial, called ALLHAT (Antihypertensive and Lipid-Lowering Treatment to Prevent Heart Attack Trial). It compared calcium channel blockers (CCBs), ACE inhibitors, and alpha blockers with conventional diuretics. Researchers found that the rates of nonfatal myocardial infarction and fatal heart attack were identical in participants treated with CCBs, ACE inhibitors, and diuretics. (The alpha blocker study was stopped early due to findings that individuals taking alpha blockers experienced more heart problems than those taking diuretics.) Since diuretics lower blood pressure, reduce the risk of heart attack, are well-tolerated by most individuals, and are less costly, the researchers recommended that diuretics should be the initial treatment for lowering blood pressure (ALLHAT: 2002). The research methodology of this study has been criticized by physicians who specialize in hypertension and contradicted by a large Australian study that found that ACE inhibitors were superior to diuretics (Brookes: 2003). However, an analysis of 42 clinical studies published from 1995 to 2002 found much the same results as the ALLHAT study; low dose diuretics were the most effective initial treatment for lowering blood pressure (Pasty et al.: 2003).

There are two interventions that may improve blood flow to the heart in individuals with angina or myocardial infarction. *Percutaneous transluminal coronary angioplasty* (PTCA) is a non-surgical procedure used to open blocked arteries. A catheter is inserted into an artery in the arm or groin and carefully threaded through the aorta to the site of the blocked artery. This procedure is performed with the guidance of a fluoroscope, an x-ray camera. A tiny balloon, attached to the tip of another catheter, is passed through the first catheter. It is inflated to compress the plaque on the artery, opening the blocked area, then deflated, and removed. When it is successful, the benefits of angioplasty include pain reduction, a return to normal activity level, and a decrease in the need for medication. About 419,000 PTCA procedures were performed in the United States in 1995 (American Heart Association: 1998a). Angioplasty is not without risk; the procedure may damage the artery or increase angina. According to the Agency for Health Care Policy and Research (1994), about 40% of arteries become blocked again within six months. An individual may then require emergency bypass surgery, have a heart attack, or die.

Coronary artery bypass grafts (CABG) may be recommended for the individual who has severe blockages in the left coronary artery or in several blood vessels. Cardiac catheterization and angioplasty procedures are used to determine the degree and location of coronary artery blockage and its effect on heart function. A vein removed from the individual's leg or a mammary artery removed from the chest, is transplanted between the aorta and the coronary artery above the blockage. Grafts using mammary arteries remain open longer than those using veins (Selwyn and Braunwald: 1994). Coronary artery bypass graft surgery is "open-heart" surgery; a heart-lung machine is used to maintain blood flow and respiration while surgery takes place. Currently, however, about 30% of these procedures are done "off-pump," by stabilizing the heart and operating on it while it is pumping and circulating blood. Preliminary findings indicate that this off-pump coronary artery bypass (OPCAB) surgery reduces neurological damage associated with the use of the heart-lung machine, fluid retention, and the need for blood transfusions (Johns Hopkins Medicine: 2003). By improving blood flow to the heart, coronary artery bypass grafts have been found to relieve anginal pain fully in about 70% of individuals and partially in another 20% (Texas Heart Institute: 1996), but they do not halt atherosclerosis. Other arteries may become clogged, angina may return, or the individual may have a heart attack.

Coronary artery bypass graft surgery has been shown to have a lower death rate for people with either Type 1 or 2 blood flow and respiration while surgery takes place. By improving blood flow to the heart, coronary artery bypass grafts have been found to relieve anginal pain fully in about 70% of individuals and partially in another 20% (Texas Heart Institute: 1996), but they do not halt atherosclerosis. Other arteries may become clogged, angina may return, or the individual may have a heart attack.

Lange and Hillis (1998) claim that many patients undergo angiography and bypass surgery despite the fact that these procedures do not reduce the incidence of subsequent myocardial infarction or death. Four large, randomized studies that compared aggressive treatment (angiography followed by surgery) with conservative management (medical therapy or noninvasive testing) showed that although aggressive management is chosen by most physicians, the results do not justify their choices. Factors influencing physicians' choices include insistence on aggressive management by the patient and family; skepticism regarding the trials' results; habit; and the availability of facilities, trained personnel, and reimbursement (Lange and Hillis: 1998). A study by Steingart and associates (1991) found that although women experienced greater functional disability than men from coronary artery disease, women were less likely than men to have undergone cardiac catheterization or cardiac bypass surgery.

Coronary artery bypass graft surgery has been shown to have a lower death rate for people with either Type 1 or 2 diabetes who were on drug therapy than PTCA (National Heart, Lung, and Blood Institute: 1995). The mortality rates for individual who were not diabetic or who had diabetes but were not taking medication were about the same. A study comparing outcomes of patients who had bypass surgery with those who had PTCA found that patients who had bypass surgery had better function, better quality of life, and more relief from angina. The differences were attributed to restenosis or narrowing of the affected artery in PTCA patients (Borkon et al.: 2002).

Coronary stenting is an alternative when arteries become blocked (restenosis) after an initial balloon angiography. A stent is a tiny tube that is implanted in the blood vessel in order to keep it open and clear. More than two-thirds of individuals undergoing procedures to open blocked arteries have had stents implanted since the procedure was approved in 1994 (Topol: 1998). When researchers compared individuals with restenosis who had had either a second balloon angioplasty or coronary stenting, they found that the rate of restenosis was less in those who had had the stenting procedure (Erbel et al.: 1998).

The recent multicenter Stent or Surgery (SoS) Trial (SoS Investigators: 2002) conducted in Europe and Canada reported that the use of stents reduced the need for repeat surgical procedures compared to balloon angioplasty, but that the rate of restenosis remains higher than in individuals treated with coronary artery bypass surgery (CABG).

Two individuals with the same clinical symptoms may opt for different treatments. For example, individuals with chronic, stable angina may react differently to the same severity of pain. Those affected should be aware that surgery to perform coronary artery bypass graft may not result in increased survival time, but it may result in relief of symptoms. Nease and colleagues (1995) studied 220 individuals with angina and found that individuals with the same level of pain opted for different outcomes. While some opted for symptom relief through surgery with the knowledge that their survival time would be shorter, others chose to live longer and endure their pain.

The recovery period before a return to work is usually four to six weeks, longer if a job requires strenuous physical exertion. During recovery, individuals are encouraged to alternate light physical exercise, such as walking, with periods of rest. Leg swelling that occurs when a vein is removed may be relieved by wearing an elastic stocking, elevating the leg, avoiding prolonged sitting, and walking. Individuals will be advised to make lifestyle changes such as giving up smoking; reducing cholesterol, saturated fats, and sodium in their diet; reducing stress; losing weight; and engaging in aerobic exercise.

A study comparing survival rates of individuals 65 years or older found that women have lower survival rates than men after experiencing a myocardial infarction (Vaccarino et al.: 2000). Therefore, keeping abreast of the latest medical advice and discussing it with a trusted physician is especially important for women at risk for this disease.

In *congestive heart failure*, the heart cannot pump enough blood to maintain normal circulation. Blood backs up into the lungs, causing congestion in the lungs and body tissues, and excess water and salt are retained in the kidneys. Congestive heart failure may be caused by chronic hypertension, damage to the heart muscle (myocardial infarction), defective or damaged heart valves, or congenital heart disease. Common symptoms of congestive heart failure are edema (swelling in the ankles, legs or feet), shortness of breath, and fatigue. Chest x-rays, which detect the presence of fluid in the lungs, and echocardiograms, which provide information on heart function, are used to diagnose the condition. The physician uses the echocardiogram to determine whether the symptoms are due to valve, muscle, or artery damage or a congenital heart defect. Cardiac catheterization and coronary angiography may also be used to confirm a diagnosis.

The goals for treating congestive heart failure are to increase the pumping function of the heart, decrease the work load on the heart, and control retention of salt and water. Digitalis strengthens heart muscle function; individuals taking digitalis must be monitored carefully for cardiac rhythm disorders. Side effects may include ringing in the ears, blurred vision, and nausea. Both angiotensin-converting enzyme (ACE) inhibitors and calcium channel blockers dilate blood vessels, lowering blood pressure and reducing the heart's workload. Diuretics are used to eliminate salt and water from the body. Potassium levels are monitored in individuals taking diuretics, since low levels may cause fatigue, weakness, or cardiac rhythm disorders. Individuals may be advised to supplement their diet with foods rich in potassium, such as bananas, broccoli, and potatoes. Rest, moderate restriction of physical activity, and mild sedation to reduce anxiety are helpful in decreasing cardiac work load (Braunwald: 1994).

SEXUAL FUNCTIONING

Most individuals with cardiac disease may resume sexual activity within a month or two after heart attack or heart surgery. Many reports indicate that the energy expended in sexual intercourse is equivalent to climbing two flights of stairs. The individual's ability to withstand this amount of activity can be measured by a treadmill test or the use of a Holter recorder (a portable ECG monitor). Despite these readiness tests, nearly a quarter of individuals do not become sexually active after myocardial infarction and about a third of those who have coronary artery bypass grafts engage in less sexual activity than prior to their surgery (Papadopoulos: 1991).

In many individuals, psychological responses to heart surgery or heart attack affect sexual activity. Although studies have shown that the actual incidence of death during sexual activity is low, women with coronary heart disease (as well as men) fear resumption of intercourse (Stitik and Benevento: 1997). Studies of the sexual function of individuals who have undergone procedures such as CABG or PTCA have focused on men; statistics are generally unavailable for female cardiac patients. Anxiety, fear, and depression may affect libido; a woman or her partner may fear precipitating another heart attack or anginal chest pain. A woman whose self-esteem is affected by invalidism and a partner who is also the caregiver may find it difficult to return to the role of lovers.

Some couples find that using different positions for coitus, such as the healthy partner on top or a side-by-side position, requires less energy and causes less muscle fatigue. Since digestion places strain on the heart, it is recommended that couples wait several hours after a heavy meal before engaging in sexual activity. To avoid fatigue, couples might plan to have sex in the morning, when energy levels are higher. Cardiac exercise programs help women increase physical strength and provide a sense of well-being that boosts their self-image and confidence in performing sexually.

Sexual counseling should be a part of cardiac rehabilitation programs. Physicians and other health care professionals should be willing and prepared to initiate conversations with individuals during follow-up office visits. Since coronary heart disease affects women later in life, professionals should be careful to avoid ageism when counseling these patients, thinking that they are no longer sexually active. Referrals may also be made to sex therapists.

PSYCHOLOGICAL ASPECTS OF CORONARY HEART DISEASE

Since many women are unaware of heart attack symptoms, they may delay seeking medical care for symptoms such as chest pain, attributing it to stress, heartburn, or other noncardiac causes. Atypical symptoms such as abdominal pain, breathing difficulty, unexplained fatigue, or nausea may accompany chest pain, leading to misinterpretation of their condition. Denial may also lead to a woman's delay in seeking care.

Once the immediate threat to life caused by a heart attack has been overcome, the woman with heart disease often experiences anxiety due to fears for her future health, and family relationships. She may become depressed due to a combination of physical weakness, dependence on others, and fatigue. Women with coronary heart disease are more likely to be widowed, living alone, and have difficulty in allowing others to become caretakers. Medications used to treat the acute symptoms of heart attack may affect her memory, and she may refuse necessary medication for fear of becoming addicted to the drugs. These fears may become worse upon discharge from the hospital. A woman who has spent time in a coronary care or surgical intensive care unit may miss the security of close monitoring and observation and feel defenseless at home. Minor chest pain or indigestion may be misinterpreted as precursors of another heart attack. In many cases, these pains may be attributed to the muscle aches that accompany a cardiac exercise regimen.

Women who are accustomed to physical activity chafe at the enforced six to eight week rest period that is prescribed to allow the heart to heal and form scar tissue. Gradually, they are allowed to resume moderate exercise; fatigue and lack of energy decrease with time.

Although anxiety, fear, and feelings of uselessness are common in the weeks following a heart attack, they should abate in time; however, if the individual becomes apathetic, has trouble concentrating, takes no interest in her appearance or formerly pleasurable activities, tires easily, has difficulty sleeping, or expresses feelings of inadequacy, she may be seriously depressed. Changes in medication may be required, or the individual may be referred for counseling. A recent study found that sertraline, a new antidepressant, is safely used in individuals with angina or myocardial infarction (Glassman et al.: 2002). Ziegelstein and colleagues (2000) also report that individuals with depression take medications less often than prescribed compared with those who are not depressed.

Family members may fear that their actions will precipitate another attack, or they may feel guilty about causing the attack in the first place. Family members may be overprotective, interfering with recommended timelines for resumption of activity. Both the woman and her family may have concerns about medical bills and lifestyle changes to diet, daily routine, and physical activities.

It is important that health care professionals provide opportunities for women and their families to discuss their fears and ask questions. Cardiac rehabilitation programs offer individual and group counseling for participants and their families. Individuals who are referred to support programs often find that they receive encouragement and practical advice from other participants in exercise programs. Mended Hearts is a support program for individuals with heart disease (see "ORGANIZATIONS" section below). Nutrition classes offer counseling and instruction in "heart-healthy" meal preparation, providing information and motivation to follow dietary recommendations.

The effects of stress in everyday activities may be ameliorated by engaging in routine exercise and learning relaxation techniques. In addition to cardiac rehabilitation services, community organizations such as YMCA's, local recreation programs, and adult education centers offer aerobics training and stress reduction classes. Stress management or relaxation audiotapes use visual imagery and meditation to help individuals cope with stress.

PROFESSIONAL SERVICE PROVIDERS

Primary care physicians, who are often internists, oversee the individual's general health. Internists are physicians who specialize in the diagnosis and treatment of the body's internal organs, such as the heart, lungs, and kidneys. Internists make referrals to specialists such as cardiologists for further tests and treatment. *Cardiologists* are physicians who specialize in diagnosing and treating heart disease. They perform diagnostic tests such as exercise stress tests and angiograms and procedures such as coronary angioplasty. *Cardiovascular surgeons* are physicians who perform operations such as coronary artery bypass surgery, heart valve replacements, and heart transplants.

The *cardiac rehabilitation team* is a multidisciplinary group of health care professionals made up of physicians, nurses, physical and occupational therapists, dietitians, and psychologists or social workers.

WHERE TO FIND SERVICES

Cardiac rehabilitation programs have several goals: exercise training, risk factor modification, and psychological well-being. Candidates for cardiac rehabilitation services are those who have had heart attacks or heart surgery and those with congestive heart failure. A physician's referral is required for cardiac rehabilitation services. Of the 13.5 million Americans affected by coronary heart disease, only 11 to 20% have enrolled in cardiac rehabilitation programs (Wenger et al.: 1995). Nearly 4.7 million individuals with congestive heart failure may also benefit from cardiac rehabilitation. Benefits from cardiac rehabilitation are increased exercise tolerance, symptom modification, blood lipid level reduction, lowered blood pressure, weight loss, and smoking cessation.

Although cardiac rehabilitation usually starts prior to hospital discharge, the bulk of the program takes place in outpatient settings in the hospital or medical center, community center, or, in some cases, in the workplace. After an initial medical evaluation, an individualized plan is designed. Exercise training is the key ingredient of cardiac rehabilitation programs. Individuals who participate in three 20 to 40 minute sessions of aerobic exercise per week are reported to receive the most benefit (Wenger et al.: 1995). Elders, who often receive fewer services due to age bias, also gain functional improvement when enrolled in exercise programs (Hellman and Williams: 1994).

Although various studies report that women are less likely than men to be referred to cardiac rehabilitation programs, once they are referred, their participation differs from men's. Psychosocial factors, such as depression and social inhibition, and physical function issues, such as low exercise tolerance and pain, differ. Halm and colleagues (1999) reported that women who were referred to cardiac rehabilitation programs but did not participate cited lack of transportation and insurance coverage and the presence of exercise equipment in the home as reasons for nonparticipation. When Moore and colleagues (1998) examined women's patterns of exercise after cardiac rehabilitation, they found that they were exercising far less than recommended. These researchers suggest that cardiac rehabilitation programs for women be devised that would remove these obstacles and promote successful participation.

While some individuals will discontinue smoking on their own after a heart attack, most require a program that combines education, behavior modification, and counseling. Nutrition education and training, behavior modification, and physical exercise may help most individuals lower their blood lipid levels, but some will require medication. Weight reduction is best accomplished with nutrition education and exercise training; exercise alone is not sufficient. In order to reduce blood pressure, individuals must employ a combined strategy of sodium restriction, weight reduction, and exercise training along with medication. The combination of diet, weight loss, and exercise may lead to reduced need for medication.

Wenger and her colleagues (1995) reported that although exercise training alone provides improvement in the individual's sense of well-being, the added components of education, counseling, and psychosocial interventions result in even greater benefits, such as social adjustment and stress reduction. Women with depression who participate in cardiac rehabilitation programs demonstrate improvement in quality of life as well as exercise tolerance and weight reduction (Lavie et al.: 1999).

In choosing a cardiac rehabilitation program, individuals should consider its location, schedule, service options, and cost. Distance and availability of private or public transportation and parking may affect the individual's ability to participate in a program that meets three or more times per week. Some people prefer group services rather than individual exercise plans; group interaction and social supports provide motivation for adherence to an exercise schedule. Medical insurance may cover the cost of cardiac rehabilitation. Less expensive programs may be found in a community setting such as a YMCA or other community organization. The American Association of Cardiovascular and Pulmonary Rehabilitation offers a national directory of cardiac rehabilitation programs (see "ORGANIZATIONS" section below).

Diseases of the circulatory system, which included heart disease, hypertension, and cerebrovascular disease, were the most prevalent conditions of women age 65 and over who used home health care services in 1996 (Munson: 1999). Skilled nursing services, physical therapy, occupational therapy, and homemaker services may be provided by public and private clinics; local hospitals; home health agencies such as visiting nurse associations; state, federal, and private agencies which serve elders; Veterans Affairs Medical Centers; and therapists in private practice. Meals on Wheels provides nutritious meals to those who are unable to prepare meals themselves or who are alone for long periods of time.

HOW TO RECOGNIZE A HEART ATTACK AND GET HELP

Many women are unfamiliar with the warning signs of a heart attack. Here are both classic and less-common symptoms:

• Pain in the center of the chest that continues for more than a few minutes, goes away and returns. The woman may describe a feeling of chest fullness, squeezing, or uncomfortable pressure.

• Pain that radiates to the neck, shoulders, or arms.

• Lightheadedness, sweating, fainting, shortness of breath accompanying chest pain or discomfort.

• Less common signals include abdominal or stomach pain; unexplained weakness, fatigue, or anxiety; pallor, cold sweat, or palpitations; both shortness and difficulty breathing; and nausea or dizziness.

When a heart attack is suspected, follow these recommendations:

• If you know that the individual has heart disease, assume she is having a heart attack if chest pain does not respond to antacids or if angina does not respond to a nitroglycerin (take up to three tablets over a five minute interval; if not effective, call 911).

• If heart attack is suspected, call 911 (or drive to the hospital if quicker). While waiting for emergency help, have her stop any activity and sit or lie down with her head slightly elevated. Check to see if she is wearing a medication alert bracelet.

• The American Heart Association (1996) recommends that the individual chew two aspirins thoroughly and swallow, with a glass of water. Aspirin, a blood thinner, may dissolve small blood clots before the individual arrives at the hospital.

References

Agency for Health Care Policy and Research
1994   Managing Unstable Angina Rockville, MD: Agency for Health Care Policy and Research
ALLHAT (Antihypertensive and Lipid-Lowering Treatment to Prevent Heart Attack Trial
2002   "Major Outcomes in High-Risk Hypertensive Patients Randomized to Angiotensin-Converting Enzyme Inhibitor or Calcium Channel Blocker vs. Diuretic" JAMA 288:23(December 18):2981-2997

American Heart Association
2001   2002 Heart and Stroke Statistical Update Dallas, TX: American Heart Association
1998a   1999 Heart and Stroke Statistical Update Dallas, TX: American Heart Association
1998b   Clinician's Guide to Fighting Cardiovascular Diseases in Women Dallas, TX: American Heart Association
1996   The American Heart Association Guide to Heart Attack: Treatment, Recovery, and Prevention Dallas, TX: American Heart Association

Borkon, A. Michael et al.
2002   A Comparison of the Recovery of Health Status after Percutaneous Coronary Intervention and Coronary Artery Bypass" Annals of Thoracic Surgery 74:5(November):1526-1530

Braunwald, Eugene
1994   "Heart Failure" pp. 998-1009 in Kurt J. Isselbacher et al. (eds.) Harrison's Principles of Internal Medicine New York, NY: McGraw Hill, Inc.

Brookes, Linda
2003   "ALLHAT -- Criticisms and Contradictions" Medscape Cardiology February 21

Canto, John et al.
2002   "The Association of Sex and Payer Status on Management and Subsequent Survival in Acute Myocardial Infarction" Archives of Internal Medicine 162:5(March 11):587-593

Erbel, Raimund et al.
1998   "Coronary-Artery Stenting Compared with Balloon Angioplasty for Restenosis After Initial Balloon Angioplasty" New England Journal of Medicine 339:23(December):1678

Glassman, Alexander H. et al.
2002   "Sertraline Treatment of Major Depression in Patients with Acute MI or Unstable Angina" JAMA 288:6(August 14):701-709

Halm, M. et al.
1999   "Women and Cardiac Rehabilitation: Referral and Compliance Patterns" Journal of Cardiovascular Nursing 13:3(April):83-92

Hellman, E.A. and M.A. Williams
1994   "Outpatient Cardiac Rehabilitation in Elderly Patients" Heart-Lung 23:6:506-512

Herrington, David M. et al.
2000   "Effects of Estrogen Replacement on the Progression of Coronary-Artery Atherosclerosis" New England Journal of Medicine 343:8(August 24):522-529

Johns Hopkins Medicine
2003   "Bypass Without Missing a Beat" Health After 50 14:11(January):1

Lange, Richard A. and L. David Hillis
1998   "Use and Overuse of Angiography and Revascularization for Acute Coronary Syndromes" New England Journal of Medicine 338:25(June 18):1838-1839

Lauer, M.S. et al.
1998   "Prediction of Death and Myocardial Infarction By Screening with Exercise-thallium Testing After Coronary-Artery-Bypass Grafting" Lancet 351(9103):615-22

Lee, Warren L. et al.
2000   "Impact of Diabetes on Coronary Artery Disease in Women and Men" Diabetes Care 23:7(July):962-968Lavie, C.J. et al.
1999   "Effects of Cardiac Rehabilitation and Exercise Training Programs in Women with Depression" American Journal of Cardiology 83:10(May 15):1480-1483, A7

Limacher, M.C.
1998   "Exercise and Cardiac Rehabilitation in Women" Cardiology Review 6:4(July):240-248

Moore, S.M. et al.
1998   "Women's Patterns of Exercise Following Cardiac Rehabilitation" Nursing Research 47:6(November-December):318-324

Munson, M.L.
1999   "Characteristics of Elderly Home Health Care Users: Data from the 1996 National Home and Hospice Care Survey" Advance Data from Vital and Health Statistics, No. 309 Hyattsville, MD: National Center for Health Statistics

National Heart, Lung, and Blood Institute
1995   "Bypass Over Angioplasty for Patients with Diabetes" HeartMemo Bethesda, MD: National Heart, Lung, and Blood Institute

National Institutes of Health
1989   Heart Attacks Washington, DC: National Institutes of Health Clinical Center

Nease, Robert F. Jr. et al.
1995   "Variation in Patient Utilities for Outcome of the Management of Chronic Stable Angina: Implications for Clinical Practice Guidelines" Journal of the American Medical Association 273(15):1185-1190

Papadopoulos, Chris
1991   "Sex and the Cardiac Patient" Medical Aspects of Human Sexuality August:18-21

Pasty, Bruce M. et al.
2003   "Health Outcomes Associated with Various Antihypertensive Therapies Used as First-Line Agents" JAMA 239:19(May 21):2534-2544

Redberg, Rita F.
1998   "Coronary Artery Disease in Women: Understanding the Diagnostic and Management Pitfalls" Medscape Women's Health Journal 3:5

Schulman, Kevin A. et al.
1999   "The Effect of Race and Sex on Physicians' Recommendations for Cardiac Catheterization" New England Journal of Medicine 340:8(February 25):618-626

Selwyn, Andrew P. and Eugene Braunwald
1994   "Ischemic Heart Disease" pp. 1077-1085 in Kurt J. Isselbacher et al. (eds.) Harrison's Principles of Internal Medicine New York, NY: McGraw Hill, Inc.

SoS Investigators

2002   "Coronary Artery Bypass Surgery vs. Percutaneous Coronary Intervention with Stent Implantation in Patients with Multivessel Coronary Disease" <u>Lancet</u> 360:9338 (September 28):965-970Sowers, James R.

1998   "Diabetes Mellitus and Cardiovascular Disease in Women" <u>Archives of Internal Medicine</u> 158(Mar 23):617-621

Steingart, R.M. et al.

1991   "Sex Differences in the Management of Coronary Artery Disease" <u>New England Journal of Medicine</u> 325:4(July 25):226-230

Stitik, Todd P. and Barbara T. Benevento

1997   "Cardiac and Pulmonary Disease" pp. 303-335 in Marca L. Sipski and Craig J. Alexander (eds.) <u>Sexual Function in People with Disability and Chronic Illness: A Health Professional's Guide</u> Frederick, MD: Aspen Publishers, Inc.

Texas Heart Institute

1996   <u>Heart Owner's Handbook</u> New York, NY: John Wiley & Sons, Inc.

Topol, Eric J.

1998   "Coronary-Artery Stents--Gauging, Gorging, and Gouging" <u>New England Journal of Medicine</u> 339:23(December):1704

Vaccarino, V. et al.

2000   "Long-term Outcome of Myocardial Infarction in Women and Men: A Population Perspective" <u>American Journal of Epidemiology</u> 152:10(November 15): 965-973

Wenger, N.K. et al.

1995   <u>Cardiac Rehabilitation as Secondary Prevention</u> Clinical Practice Guideline. Quick Reference Guide for Clinicians, No. 17 Rockville, MD: Agency for Health Care Policy and Research Pub. No. 96-0673

Whelton, Paul K. et al.

2002   "Clinical and Public Health Advisory from the National High Blood Pressure Education Program" <u>JAMA</u> 288:15(October 16):1882-1888

Women's Health Initiative

2002   "Risks and Benefits of Estrogen Plus Progestin in Healthy Postmenopausal Women" <u>JAMA</u> 288:3(July 17):321-333

ORGANIZATIONS

American Association of Cardiovascular and Pulmonary Rehabilitation
401 North Michigan Avenue
Chicago, IL 60611
(312) 321-5146   FAX (312) 245-1085
e-mail: aacvpr@asba.com   www.aacvpr.org

This organization's web site offers a directory of cardiac rehabilitation programs.

American Heart Association
7272 Greenville Avenue
Dallas, TX 75231-4596
(800) 242-8721   (214) 373-6300   FAX (214) 706-1341
www.women.americanheart.org   www.americanheart.org

Promotes research and education and publishes professional and public education brochures. Local affiliates. Membership fees vary. Web site offers a women's forum, where women write about their experiences with heart disease. Click on "Healthy lifestyles," then "Women's online forum." "Choose to Move" is a 12 week, self-paced exercise program for women. To register, click on "Healthy Lifestyles" at left of home page, then click on "Choose to Move," or send an e-mail to ctm@heart.org. Registrants receive a handbook in the mail. Free

Heart and Blood Vessels Center
www.mayoclinic.com

This web site provides information on many aspects of heart disease and stroke and offers healthy lifestyle planners for weight, exercise, stop smoking, and stress management.

Heart Center Online
www.heartcenteronline.com

This web site offers patient guides to heart conditions such as congestive heart failure, angina, coronary artery disease, and heart attack. Includes interactive tools to calculate ideal weight, nutrition, and calories burned; illustrations and animations; and discussion boards.

Heart Failure Online
www.heartfailure.org

This web site provides information on preventing and treating heart failure. Includes answers to common questions, a glossary, and "My Pill Box," a link that enables individuals to create a daily/weekly/monthly cardiac medication schedule.

Heart Failure Society of America
Court International, Suite 240S
2550 University Avenue West
St. Paul, MN 55114
(651) 642-1633   FAX (651) 642-1502   e-mail: info@hfsa.org
www.hfsa.org
The web site provides answers to common questions about heart failure, including risks, symptoms, diagnosis, stages, and treatment.

HeartInfo.org
www.heartinfo.org

This web site offers patient guides to conditions such as hypertension, heart attack symptoms and warning signs, bypass surgery, angioplasty, congestive heart failure, and cardiac catheterization. Includes a nutrition guide, recipes, drug information, and a fitness guide.

Heartmates
PO Box 16202
Minneapolis, MN 55416
(612) 558-3331   FAX (952) 929-6395
e-mail: heartmates@heartmates.com   www.heartmates.com

Developed by a social worker whose husband has heart disease, the web site includes resources for the emotional needs of spouses and family members of individuals who have had a heart attack.

MEDLINEPlus: Arrhythmia
www.nlm.nih.gov/medlineplus/arrhythmia.html

This web site provides links to sites for general information about arrhythmia, prevention and screening, diagnosis/symptoms, disease management, specific conditions/aspects, treatment, research, clinical trials, and organizations. Includes interactive tutorials on arrhythmia, atrial fibrillation, and pacemakers. Provides links to MEDLINE research articles and related MEDLINEplus pages.

MEDLINEPlus: Coronary Heart Disease
www.nlm.nih.gov/medlineplus/coronarydisease.html

This web site provides links to sites for general information about coronary heart disease, prevention and screening, diagnosis/symptoms, specific conditions/aspects, treatment, research, clinical trials, statistics, nutrition, and organizations. Includes interactive tutorials on echocardiograms and echocardiography stress tests. Provides links to MEDLINE research articles and related sites.

Mended Hearts
7272 Greenville Avenue
Dallas, TX 75231
(214) 706-1442   FAX (214) 706-5231   www.mendedhearts.org

This affiliate of the American Heart Association has chapters in many states. It offers support to individuals with heart disease through monthly meetings, raises funds for medical equipment and scholarships, and trains volunteers to visit individuals who have undergone heart surgery. Membership, individuals, $17.00; family, $24.00; includes quarterly newsletter, "Heartbeat."

National Diabetes Education Program (NDEP)
National Institute of Diabetes and Digestive and Kidney Diseases (NIDDKD)
31 Center Drive, MSC 2560
Washington, DC 20892
(800) 438-5383   (301) 496-3583   www.ndep.nih.gov

A joint project of the National Institutes of Health and the Centers for Disease Control and Prevention, this program aims to prevent the increase in diabetes in this country through partnerships with other organizations that will provide public information about the disease. Free. In conjunction with the American Diabetes Association, the NDEP is conducting a campaign called "Be Smart about Your Heart: Control the ABCs of Diabetes" to increase public awareness of the link between diabetes and heart disease. The web site has information about diabetes, and the program has produced public information materials, including cookbooks.

National Hypertension Association
324 East 30th Street
New York, NY 10016
(212) 889-3557   FAX (212) 447-7032   www.nathypertension.org

Conducts research, promotes public and professional education, and provides hypertension work-site detection programs. General information packet, free.

NHLBI Health Information Net
National Heart, Lung, and Blood Institute
PO Box 30105
Bethesda, MD 20824-0105
(800) 575-9355   (301) 592-8573   (240) 629-3255 (TTY)
FAX (240) 629-3246   e-mail: nhlbinfo@nhlbi.nih.gov   www.nhlbi.nih.gov

The NHLBI conducts research and national education programs and issues clinical guidelines on topics such as high blood pressure and high cholesterol. It is currently sponsoring a campaign to raise the awareness of heart disease in women called "The Heart Truth." The NHLBI Health Information Net distributes publications about cardiovascular disease. Free publications list. Many publications and a publication list are available on web site. Free

Pacemaker Club
12 Mars Lane
Fredericton, New Brunswick
Canada E3C 1M9
e-mail: info@pacemakerclub.com   www.pacemakerclub.com

The web site offers information and support to individuals with pacemakers.

<u>Women's Health Initiative</u> (WHI)
National Heart, Lung and Blood Institute
National Institutes of Health
6705 Rockledge Drive, Suite 300
Rockledge One, MSC 7966
Bethesda, MD 20892-7966
(301) 402-2900   FAX (301) 480-5158   e-mail: nmo9@nih.gov
www.nhlbi.nih.gov/whi/index.html   www.whi.org

This major women's health research project enrolled 162,000 women, ages 50 to 79, in order to study the major causes of death, disability, and the quality of life in post-menopausal women. Heart disease is one of the conditions included in the study. The portion of the study that examined the effects of estrogen replacement therapy (ERT) was stopped in July, 2002, because it was determined that the health risks outweighed the benefits. The web sites include information about the findings of the study to date as well as references to articles that came out of the study.

<u>YourSurgery.com</u>
yoursurgery.com

This multimedia site uses simple diagrams and animation to show how various chest procedures are done. Click on "Chest," then on procedure, including "Cardiac Catheterization," "Coronary Artery Bypass Graft," and "Diagnostic and Interventional Angiography."

About Your Bypass Surgery: Our Guide to Understanding Coronary Artery Bypass Graft Surgery
American Heart Association (see "ORGANIZATIONS" section above)
(800) 242-8721   www.americanheart.org

This brochure discusses treatment of coronary artery disease using bypass graft surgery. Describes pre-surgical preparation and post-surgical care and makes suggestions for recuperating at home. Free

Advances in Cardiac Surgery
Aquarius Health Care Videos
266 Main Street, Suite 33B
Medfield, MA 02052
(888) 440-2963   FAX (508) 242-9854
e-mail: orders@aquariusproductions.com
www.aquariusproductions.com

In this videotape, cardiac surgeons describe new, minimally invasive techniques and which patients qualify for them. 28 minutes. $195.00

After Your Heart Attack: Our Guide to Help You Recover
American Heart Association (see "ORGANIZATIONS" section above)
(800) 242-8721   www.americanheart.org

This booklet discusses the physical effects of heart attack as well as depression, returning to work, family members' emotions, and how to reduce risk factors. Free

Cardiac Comeback 1, 2, 3
Info Vision
102 North Hazel Street
Glenwood, IA 51534
(800) 237-1808   FAX (888) 735-2622

This series of three videotapes provides beginning, intermediate, and advanced exercise programs for individuals with heart disease. Set of three, $59.00

Cleveland Clinic Heart Advisor
PO Box 420235
Palm Coast, FL 32142-0235
(800) 829-2506

This monthly newsletter discusses coronary care, including information on surgical techniques, medications, risk factors, and research. $34.00

Controlling High Blood Pressure: A Guide for Older Women
Alliance for Aging Research
2021 K Street, NW, Suite 305
Washington, DC 20006
(800) 639-2421   (202) 293-2856   FAX (202) 785-8574
e-mail: info@agingresearch.org   www.agingresearch.org

This booklet discusses how high blood pressure affects health and the lifestyle changes and medications that may help control it. Free. Also available on the web site.

Coping with Heart Illness
by Wayne M. Sotile
Human Kinetics
1607 North Market Street
PO Box 5076
Champaign, IL 61825-5076
(800) 747-4457   (217) 351-5076
FAX (217) 351-2674   e-mail: orders@humankinetics.com
www.humankinetics.com

This series of three videotapes features physicians and patients discussing psychosocial aspects of cardiac rehabilitation such as depression, sexuality, lifestyle changes, and family issues. $49.95

Coronary Artery Disease in Women: What All Physicians Need to Know
by Pamela Charney (ed.)
American College of Physicians
190 North Independence Mall West
Philadelphia, PA 19106
(800) 523-1546, ext. 2600   (215) 351-2600   www.acponline.org

This book discusses the prevention, diagnosis, and management of coronary artery disease in women. Summarizes the results of research into the differences between women and men with coronary artery disease. $43.00

Diabetes, Heart Disease and Stroke
American Heart Association (see "ORGANIZATIONS" section above)
(800) 242-8721   www.americanheart.org

This booklet discusses diabetes as a risk factor for heart disease and stroke and the role of weight management, physical activity, and nutrition in managing diabetes. Free

Harvard Heart Letter
PO Box 420379
Palm Coast, FL 32142-0379
(800) 829-9171   e-mail: harvardhhl@palmcoastd.com
www.health.harvard.edu

This monthly newsletter reports on treatment, nutrition, and research. $28.00

Health Heart Handbook for Women
NHLBI Health Information Net
(see "ORGANIZATIONS" section above)
(800) 293-2356   www.nhlbi.nih.gov

This book discusses the risk factors for heart disease, describes the warning signs of a heart attack, and includes recipes for heart healthy meal preparations. Includes information on recent research. $4.00 May be downloaded from the web site at no charge.

The Heart Depression Connection
by Windsor Ting and Gregory Fricchione
McGraw-Hill Order Services
PO Box 182604
Columbus, OH 43272-3031
(877) 833-5524   FAX (614) 759-3749
e-mail: pbg.ecommerce_custserv@mcgraw-hill.com
books.mcgraw-hill.com

Written by a cardiologist and a psychiatrist, this book explores the interrelationship of depression and cardiovascular disease. $24.95

Heart Illness and Intimacy: How Caring Relationships Aid Recovery
by Wayne M. Sotile
Real Talk, Inc.
1396 Old Mill Circle
Winston-Salem, NC 27103
(336) 794-0230   www.sotile.com

This book describes the psychological effects of heart disease on the individual, spouse, and family. Includes discussions of personality, attitude, sexuality, and stress reduction. $15.00

Heartmates
The Heartmates Journal
PO Box 16202
Minneapolis, MN 55416
(612) 558-3331   FAX (952) 929-6395
e-mail: heartmates@heartmates.com   www.heartmates.com

"Heartmates" is a guide for spouses and families of individuals with heart disease, $18.95. "The Heartmates Journal" is an interactive guide to recovery, $14.95.

Heart Owner's Handbook
by The Texas Heart Institute
John Wiley & Sons, Inc.
10475 Crosspoint Boulevard
Indianapolis, IN 46256
(877) 762-2974   FAX (800) 597-3299
e-mail: customer@wiley.com   www.wiley.com

This book provides information on the cardiovascular system, symptoms and treatment of heart disease, and cardiac rehabilitation. Also describes the risk factors for heart disease and how to control them. Includes recipes for "heart-smart" cooking. $16.95

Heart Truth Fact Sheets
NHLBI Health Information Net
(see "ORGANIZATIONS" section above)
(800) 575-9355   www.nhlbi.nih.gov

Excerpted from the "Health Heart Handbook for Women," this series of fact sheets includes "The Heart Truth for Women: An Action Plan," "The Heart Truth for Women: If You Have Heart Disease," and "When Delicious Meets Nutritious: Recipes for Heart Health." Single copies, free. web

The Hypertension Sourcebook
by Mary McGowan and Jo McGowan Chopra
McGraw-Hill Order Services
PO Box 182604
Columbus, OH 43272-3031
(877) 833-5524   FAX (614) 759-3749
e-mail: pbg.ecommerce_custserv@mcgraw-hill.com
books.mcgraw-hill.com

This book provides information about the causes of hypertension and lifestyle changes that can reduce it. Also includes an evaluation of medications and home monitors. $17.95

Living with Congestive Heart Failure
American Heart Association (see "ORGANIZATIONS" section above)
(800) 242-8721   www.americanheart.org

This brochure discusses the causes and symptoms of congestive heart failure. Describes treatment with medications, lifestyle changes, and surgery. Free

Living with Your Pacemaker
American Heart Association (see "ORGANIZATIONS" section above)
(800) 242-8721   www.americanheart.org

This booklet describes how pacemakers work, problems that may occur, and tips for proper operation. Free

Mayo Clinic Heart Book
by Bernard J. Gersh (ed.)
Harper Collins
PO Box 588
Dunmore, PA 18512
(800) 242-7737   www.harpercollins.com

This book describes a variety of heart conditions and discusses the risks of coronary artery disease, common tests, and treatments. Includes a medication guide. $30.00

The New American Heart Association Cookbook
Random House, Order Department
400 Hahn Road, PO Box 100
Westminster, MD 21157
(800) 733-3000   www.randomhouse.com

This cookbook provides low fat, low cholesterol recipes. Hardcover, $30.00; softcover, $6.99.

The New Living Heart
by Michael E. DeBakey and Antonio M. Gotto, Jr.
Adams Media Corporation
260 Center Street
Holbrook, MA 02343
(800) 872-5627   (508) 767-8100
www.adamsmedia.com

This book discusses heart conditions such as coronary heart disease, atherosclerosis, congestive heart failure, and stroke. Includes information on surgical and medical treatment and rehabilitation. $18.95

Portrait of the Heartmate
Heartmates, Inc.
PO Box 16202
Minneapolis, MN 55416
(612) 929-3331   FAX (612) 929-6395
e-mail: heartmates@outtech.com   www.heartmates.com

This videotape discusses the psychosocial recovery needs of families when a family member has an acute or chronic cardiac condition. Five 20 minute programs. $59.95

Psychosocial Interventions for Cardiopulmonary Patients: A Guide for Health Professionals
by Wayne M. Sotile
Human Kinetics
1607 North Market Street
PO Box 5076
Champaign, IL 61825-5076
(800) 747-4457   (217) 351-5076   FAX (217) 351-2674
e-mail: orders@hkusa.com   www.humankinetics.com

This book provides practical strategies for teaching patients how to manage the emotional stress of heart and lung disease. $39.00

Recovering From Heart Problems Through Cardiac Rehabilitation
Agency for Healthcare Research a;nd Quality (AHRQ)
Publications Clearinghouse
PO Box 8547
Silver Spring, MD 20907
(800) 358-9295   e-mail: info@ahrq.gov   www.ahrq.gov

This booklet discusses the goals of cardiac rehabilitation and how to choose a cardiac rehabilitation program. Includes sample recordkeeping guide. Available in English and Spanish. Free. Also available on the web site.

The Sensuous Heart: Sex After a Heart Attack or Heart Surgery
by Suzanne Cambre
Pritchett and Hull Associates
3440 Oakcliff Road, NE, Suite 110
Atlanta, GA 30340
(800) 241-4925   (770) 451-0602   www.p-h.com

This booklet answers questions about the resumption of sexual activity after heart attack or heart surgery. Includes information about comfortable positions and the effects of medications. $3.85

Sex and Heart Disease
American Heart Association (see "ORGANIZATIONS" section above)
(800) 242-8721   www.americanheart.org

This brochure provides guidelines for resuming sexual activity after heart attack or heart surgery. Discusses the effects of age, medications, and psychological factors on sexual interest and activity. Free

Success with Heart Failure: Help and Hope for Those with Congestive Heart Failure
by Marc Silver
Perseus Books Group Customer Service
5500 Central Avenue
Boulder, CO 80301
(800) 386-5656   FAX (720) 406-7336
e-mail: westview.orders@perseusbooks.com
www.perseusbooks.com

This book describes current treatments for heart failure, including heart transplantation. It discusses the psychological effects of a prognosis of heart failure and reviews the importance of diet and exercise. $20.00

Surviving Transplantation: A Personal Guide for Organ Transplant Patients, Their Families, Friends and Caregivers
by John Craven and Susan Farrow
www.psychiatry.med.uwo.ca/survive/frmain.htm

This web publication discusses waiting and recovery from an organ transplant and understanding and dealing with stress associated with the procedure as well as strategies for working with health professionals. Free

Women and Heart Disease
by Desmond G. Julian and Nanette Kass Wenger (eds.)
Elsevier Health science Division
11830 Westline Industrial Drive
St. Louis, MO 63146
(800) 545-2522   FAX (800) 568-5136
e-mail: custserv.ehs@elsevier.com   www.us.elsevierhealth.com

This book presents a collection of articles that include information on the general aspects of heart disease as well as issues specifically related to women. These topics include heart conditions related to pregnancy, contraception, and the impact of sex hormones on cardiovascular physiology. $145.00

Chapter 6

DIABETES

Diabetes mellitus is a term that applies to a variety of disorders related to the production or utilization of insulin, a substance that is necessary to metabolize the glucose (sugar) that the body needs for energy. As a result of diabetes, the body is unable to maintain normal glucose levels. *Hypoglycemia* is a condition where the level of glucose is too low. It occurs when the individual does not eat soon enough or eats too little, uses too much insulin, or engages in overactivity. Hypoglycemia may lead to an insulin reaction; symptoms may include feeling shaky or sweaty, headache, hunger, irritability, and dizziness. Insulin shock sometimes occurs if an insulin reaction is not treated quickly; in these cases individuals may lose consciousness. *Hyperglycemia* is a condition where the level of glucose in the blood is too high. Symptoms include extreme thirst, a dry mouth, excessive urination, blurred vision, and lethargy. Sometimes when an individual who has had an insulin reaction takes food high in sugar to replace glucose in the body, too much glucose is released, resulting in high blood glucose levels (hyperglycemia). The combination of too much sugar without enough insulin to use it properly may gradually lead to diabetic coma if warning signs are not monitored; diabetic coma usually occurs only in individuals with insulin-dependent diabetes.

As the prevalence of diabetes has increased, it has become a major health problem in the United States and an important contributor to the cost of health care. From 1990 to 2000, the number of individuals with diagnosed diabetes increased 49% (Centers for Disease Control and Prevention: 2002a). Seventeen million Americans or 6.2% of the population have diabetes; of these 5.9 million have the disease but have not been diagnosed. Over nine million American women (8.9%) have diabetes (Centers for Disease Control and Prevention: 2002b).

Women who have diabetes are at risk during pregnancy, as are their fetuses, and must take special precautions. In addition, some women develop diabetes during pregnancy (gestational diabetes mellitus) and are at risk for the disease following pregnancy as well (see "Types of Diabetes," "Sexual Functioning," and "Family Planning, Pregnancy, and Childrearing" sections below).

Diabetes was the third most frequent primary diagnosis for individuals who visited outpatient departments in non-federal hospitals in 1994 (Lipkind: 1996). More than half (57.5%) of the 13.2 million patient visits to physicians in 1989 that had a primary diagnosis of diabetes were made by women (Schappert: 1992). Diabetes and its complications are responsible for many hospital stays and have a large economic impact on society. Direct medical expenses for diabetes care totaled 44.1 billion dollars in 1997. Factoring in the cost of lost work productivity and premature mortality increased the cost of the disease by an additional 54 billion dollars. On a per capita basis, individuals with diabetes spent on average $10,071 in 1997 for medical care compared to $2,669 for individuals without diabetes (American Diabetes Association: 1998).

Currently, there is no cure for diabetes; however, there are means to control the disease and to decrease the risk of the numerous associated complications. Early diagnosis and intervention are crucial steps in maintaining proper control of diabetes.

Transplantations of the pancreas (the gland responsible for secreting insulin), although no longer considered experimental, are performed only in a select group of patients. Currently, transplantations are performed on patients who have end-stage renal disease, have a history of serious metabolic complications, have had or plan to have a kidney transplant as well, or have serious clinical difficulty with insulin injections. In addition, they must not present an excessive risk for this type of surgery (American Diabetes Association: 2000a). Both pancreas transplantation alone or in conjunction with kidney transplantation have high rates of success (Larsen: 2002). When successful, pancreas transplantation results in the elimination of insulin injections. Rejection of transplanted tissue and the need for large amounts of immunosuppressive drugs are important factors that have prevented this type of transplantation from becoming standard procedure. Because people with diabetes are especially prone to infection, transplantation involves more risks for this population than for other individuals. Research to improve the management of diabetes through innovative administration of insulin and drugs that improve the body's use of insulin is ongoing. Transplantation of islet cells in the pancreas that are responsible for insulin production is also under investigation.

TYPES OF DIABETES

The two major types of diabetes mellitus are referred to as type 1 and type 2. In *type 1*, the pancreas does not produce insulin. Individuals with type 1 diabetes must take regular injections of insulin. For this reason, type 1 is also referred to as Insulin-Dependent Diabetes Mellitus (IDDM). This variant of the disease was formerly called juvenile-onset diabetes, because it is usually diagnosed at a young age. Symptoms of type 1 diabetes include extreme thirst, weight loss despite increased appetite, weakness and fatigue, and blurred vision.

In the United States there are an estimated 300,000 to 500,000 individuals with insulin-dependent diabetes mellitus (IDDM) (National Institute of Diabetes and Digestive and Kidney Diseases: 1990). In addition to daily insulin injections, individuals with IDDM must carefully watch their diet and coordinate meals with insulin doses to maintain a balanced glucose level. Insulin may be injected by syringe or by "jet injectors" that do not use actual needles. Some individuals, especially those who are on erratic schedules that prevent them from eating on a regular schedule, use insulin pumps that automatically provide insulin throughout the day. The use of insulin pumps often results in improved control of blood glucose levels over other methods. Prior to eating, pump users determine the amount of insulin they need and program the pump to release that amount.

In *type 2* diabetes, the body produces some insulin but does not produce enough or does not utilize it properly. Because type 2 diabetes usually does not require insulin injections, it is also referred to as noninsulin-dependent diabetes mellitus (NIDDM). This type of the disease is often called adult-onset or maturity-onset diabetes, because it is most frequently diagnosed after age forty. It is estimated that over 90% of the cases of diabetes in the United States are type 2 (National Center for Health Statistics: 1987).

Although the causes of type 2 diabetes are not known, obesity (80 to 90% of all individuals with type 2 diabetes are obese) and a family history of diabetes are predisposing factors. Symptoms of noninsulin-dependent diabetes include fatigue, frequent urination, excessive thirst, and vaginal infections in women. Individuals who have these symptoms should make an appointment for a physical examination. However, diabetes is sometimes present when no symptoms are evident (Williams: 1983). Tests for glucose in urine or a blood glucose test conducted during a routine physical examination are often the first indications of diabetes.

In many cases, type 2 diabetes can be controlled through both diet and exercise. For obese individuals who have diabetes, a change in diet and reduction of caloric intake may make a dramatic difference in blood glucose levels. Research suggests that individuals with type 2 diabetes may lower their blood glucose and insulin levels throughout the day by increasing the frequency and decreasing the size of their meals. This strategy slows the rate of carbohydrate absorption. A possible disadvantage is that obese individuals who use this dietary plan may have a tendency to gain weight (Jenkins: 1995).

A subtype of diabetes caused by a defect in the mitochondrial DNA has recently been discovered. Called maternally inherited diabetes and deafness (MIDD) because the mitochondrial DNA is inherited only from the mother, this type of diabetes is associated with deafness and may be either type 1 or type

2 diabetes (Kobayashi et al.: 1997). In most cases, individuals with this type of diabetes are not obese. If they have type 2 diabetes, they usually do not need insulin in the early stages of the disease, although they may need it as the disease progresses. Protein in the urine, a sign of kidney disease, is sometimes diagnosed in individuals with MIDD; this clinical symptom is caused by the mutation, not the diabetes (Jansen et al.: 1997). A study of individuals with MIDD found that subjects treated with a dietary supplement, coenzyme Q10, had better outcomes in terms of beta cell production (the cells produced by the pancreas that are responsible for insulin production) and hearing than members of a control group (Suzuki et al.: 1998).

Diet and exercise for people with either type of diabetes should be planned with a physician's advice to ensure that all medical conditions are taken into account. The goals of dietary restrictions are to reduce total body weight and to minimize the intake of glucose. The American Diabetes Association has produced many publications about diet for people with diabetes, including "Exchange Lists" (developed jointly with the American Dietetic Association), which list foods with similar caloric and nutrient contents (see "PUBLICATIONS AND TAPES" section below).

Exercise helps the body to utilize the glucose and thus is an important part of the plan to control diabetes. In some individuals with type 2 diabetes, the muscle cells that are receptors for glucose do not work efficiently; exercise enables muscle cells to use the glucose efficiently without requiring more insulin (Cantu: 1982). Exercise also reduces fat, which is known to reduce the body's sensitivity to insulin. After consulting with a physician, even individuals who have been sedentary can begin a gradual exercise program by starting to take brief daily walks. A regular exercise regimen has been shown to be useful in reducing the required levels of daily insulin injections.

When diet and exercise are insufficient to control type 2 diabetes, oral medications are prescribed. Sulfonylureas are a type of medication that causes the pancreas to produce increased amounts of insulin. Side effects of this type of medication include hypoglycemia and hyperinsulinemia, a condition in which too much insulin is in the bloodstream. Hyperinsulinemia is a risk factor for vascular disease and heart attack. In addition, sulfonylureas often fail to work after a number of years, as the pancreas can no longer produce sufficient insulin. When this occurs, individuals must begin injecting insulin. Several drugs that use different mechanisms to control diabetes are currently being tested.

One drug that has been available throughout much of the world since the late 1950s, metformin (Glucophage), has recently been approved for use in the United States. Although it is not clear exactly how metformin works, it is effective in lowering blood glucose levels and has no serious side effects, unless the individual has kidney disease at the outset. Another drug recently approved by the Food and Drug Administration is acarbose, a carbohydrase inhibitor. Carbohydrases are the enzymes that break down carbohydrates and turn them into glucose. The side effects of acarbose are bloating, gas, and diarrhea, which may subside after six months of taking the drug (American Diabetes Association: 1995).

Although testing urine for sugar was previously used to monitor glucose levels, this method is not as accurate as testing the blood directly. People with both types of diabetes use home blood glucose monitoring equipment to measure glucose levels; this involves putting a drop of blood from a fingertip on a specially treated strip designed to react to the glucose. The color of the strip indicates the level of glucose that is present. A digital display or speech output indicates the blood glucose level, and some monitors record the date and time of the reading. Illness, even a simple cold, can affect how the body uses insulin; glucose monitoring is even more important at these times. Log booklets enable individuals to keep a record of their blood glucose levels and to analyze their diets and schedules to determine what causes them to have varying levels of blood glucose. Home blood glucose monitors are inexpensive and are quite compact, making them suitable for travel and to take to work or school.

Diabetes adds a financial burden that is often not covered by medical insurance. Although the initial cost of a blood glucose monitor is relatively low, the cost of the strips that are used to test the blood, supplies to inject insulin, and special foods increase a woman's expenditures substantially. The financial burden of managing diabetes often prevents women with low to moderate income from taking proper care of themselves. Some women are forced to sacrifice normal expenditures in order to meet these expenses.

Both types of diabetes have the same potential long term health effects. It is essential that everyone with diabetes be aware of the proper management of their disease and all of the potential complications. Complications of diabetes include greater risks of heart disease (see Chapter 5 "Coronary Heart Disease"), stroke, infections, and nephropathy (kidney disease); circulatory problems that can be especially problematic for legs and feet (resulting in amputation in extreme cases); neuropathy or nerve disease which causes tingling, numbness, double vision, pain, or dizziness; and vision problems. Good control of blood glucose levels can help to prevent these long term complications.

Among the leading vision problems caused by diabetes is diabetic retinopathy. Visual impairment occurs when the small blood vessels in the retina are damaged and fail to nourish the retina adequately. One consequence of this process is bleeding inside the eye. If detected early, diabetic retinopathy can sometimes be treated successfully by laser therapy. In other cases, complex surgical procedures are performed in the attempt to restore useful vision. To manage their diabetes, many people with visual impairments use a wide range of adapted equipment, such as glucometers, scales, and thermometers with speech output; syringe magnifiers; special insulin gauges; and special syringes that automatically measure insulin doses.

The Diabetes Control and Complications Trial (DCCT) (1993) reported the results of a study which monitored 1,441 individuals with type 1 diabetes who were assigned to receive either conventional therapy (one or two injections of insulin daily) or intensive therapy (three or more injections of insulin daily). Results indicate that the intensive therapy group had significantly lower incidence of retinopathy, nephropathy, and neuropathy. The chief adverse effect of intensive therapy was increased episodes of severe hypoglycemia. In a follow-up study, the DCCT investigators (2000a) reported that the effects of intensive therapy continued to decrease the rates of retinopathy and nephropathy four years later.

A British study carried out over a period of 20 years (UK Prospective Diabetes Study Group: 1998a) found that intensive control had similar benefits for individuals with type 2 diabetes. Individuals whose diabetes was controlled by sulfonylureas or insulin also had increased episodes of hypoglycemia. Obese individuals treated with metformin had lower risks for diabetes complications and fewer episodes of hypoglycemia than individuals treated with sulfonylureas or insulin (UK Prospective Diabetes Study Group: 1998b).

Women with diabetes may notice a dramatic increase in blood glucose two to five days before menstruation begins. During the week before menstruation begins, the levels of estrogen and progesterone are at their highest levels; since these two hormones exert an anti-insulin effect, it takes more than the usual amount of insulin to control blood glucose. Once menstruation begins and the levels of these hormones drop, blood glucose levels also drop. Women must experiment with insulin dosages to determine the adjustments that are necessary during the various phases of the menstrual cycle (Jovanovic et al.: 1987).

Women with diabetes are especially susceptible to vaginal infections. When blood glucose is high, yeast infections are more likely. Vaginal infections are a common symptom of undiagnosed diabetes. Uncontrolled diabetes may also result in missed menstrual periods.

Menopause results in a decreased need for insulin due to decreased levels of estrogen and progesterone and may result in low blood glucose levels. Because women with type 1 diabetes have usually had the disease for 20 years or more when they reach menopause, they are likely to have developed neuropathy and not to be sensitive to the symptoms of hypoglycemia (Jovanovic et al.: 1987).

Gestational diabetes mellitus (GDM) occurs in approximately three percent of all pregnancies in the United States, usually in the third trimester of pregnancy (Engelau et al.: 1995). Factors related to the development of gestational diabetes include age at pregnancy, obesity, number of pregnancies, and family history of diabetes (King: 1998). A study of women who had developed gestational diabetes during pregnancy found that more than a third (35.6%) developed gestational diabetes in their next pregnancy (MacNeill et al.: 2001).

The American Diabetes Association (2000b) recommends that all women be assessed for the risk factors for gestational diabetes at their first prenatal visit. Recent efforts to screen all pregnant women for gestational diabetes between the 24th and 28th week of pregnancy have resulted in a dramatic decrease in the perinatal* mortality rate among pregnant women with this form of diabetes. Screening for gestational diabetes consists of an oral glucose tolerance test (OGTT), in which the mother ingests glucose and has her blood glucose tested one hour afterward. If the result is abnormal (140mg/dl or higher), she must return for a fasting oral glucose tolerance test and have her blood glucose tested after an overnight fast of at least eight hours and at one, two, and three hours after ingesting the glucose. Insulin does not cross the placenta, but glucose does, causing the baby's pancreas to produce extra insulin (American Diabetes Association: 1996a). Macrosomia, a condition in which the baby's weight is abnormally high and a possible complication of gestational diabetes, may cause injury to the baby if the delivery is difficult; it may also result in obesity in childhood.

Treatment for gestational diabetes usually consists of dietary therapy and self-monitoring of blood glucose. If the woman is still hyperglycemic, she may be treated with insulin (Centers for Disease Control: 1991). In some instances when the woman has difficulty controlling blood glucose, she may be hospitalized.

Half or more of all women who develop gestational diabetes will develop diabetes at some point later in life. Unmodifiable risk factors for developing type 2 diabetes after gestational diabetes include ethnicity, age, pre-pregnancy weight, number of pregnancies, family history of diabetes, and degree of hyperglycemia both during and immediately following pregnancy. Modifiable factors include obesity, weight gain, and subsequent pregnancies (Dornhorst and Rossi: 1998). Women with gestational diabetes should be screened for diabetes at six to eight weeks after delivery and have annual screenings thereafter. Women with gestational diabetes should be educated about the symptoms of diabetes and should consult a physician if the symptoms appear.

SEXUAL FUNCTIONING

It has been suggested that the sexual functioning of women with diabetes may be affected in several ways, including reduced sexual libido and ability to achieve orgasm. The relatively few studies that have been carried out on this subject have resulted in contradictory findings. Some studies have found that women with diabetes do have reduced libido and are less likely to achieve orgasm (Erol et al.: 2002), while other studies find no significant differences between women with diabetes and those who do not have diabetes (Schreiner-Engel: 1983; Wilson Young and Barthalow Koch: 1989). Methodological differences among the studies and the use of self-reports limit the validity of these studies.

Depression upon the diagnosis of the disease may interfere with sexual desire. The woman's partner may also be depressed and, without adequate information about the disease, may avoid sexual relations. Diabetes that is out of control may result in vaginal infections and lack of vaginal lubrication, causing painful intercourse. Neuropathy, which usually occurs only after a woman has had diabetes for many years, may affect the genitals and cause lack of sensation or painful intercourse.

*shortly before and after birth, usually defined as the 29th week of gestation until 4 weeks after birth

Women with diabetes are able to become pregnant, although historically the rate of complications has been much higher for women with diabetes than for those who do not have diabetes. Rates of congenital malformations of babies born to mothers with overt or established diabetes (diabetes that was not caused by the pregnancy) are significantly higher than healthy mothers (Sheffield et al.: 2002). Malformations include those of the central nervous system, skeleton, heart, and kidneys (Centers for Disease Control: 1991). Rates of cesarean delivery, spontaneous abortion, and preterm labor are high, as are risks to the mother's health. Acceptable blood glucose levels for pregnant women are lower than normal, because hyperglycemia is associated with increased morbidity and mortality for both the mother and the fetus. Achieving this tight control often results in episodes of hypoglycemia. Women with diabetes may use most of the methods of birth control that other women use. Birth control pills should be low dosage, and women who have high blood pressure should not use them (Jovanovic et al.: 1987).

Gestational diabetes accounts for most of the cases of diabetes in pregnancy (88%), noninsulin-dependent diabetes accounts for 8% of the cases, and insulin-dependent diabetes for 4%. Mothers with gestational diabetes and those with noninsulin-dependent diabetes were older than mothers whose pregnancies were not complicated by diabetes. Both age and obesity were associated with the development of gestational diabetes (Engelau et al.: 1995).

Women who have advanced diabetic retinopathy are at risk for exacerbating the disease if they become pregnant. A study (Chew et al.: 1995) found that women whose diabetes was poorly controlled and who had retinopathy at conception were more likely to have progression of their retinopathy during pregnancy than women who had no retinopathy or only microaneurysms. The researchers recommended that women with diabetes and retinopathy who are contemplating pregnancy bring their diabetes into tight control prior to conception.

Women with diabetes who have kidney disease or nephropathy who become pregnant may experience an acceleration of the progression of the disease (Purdy et al.: 1996) and are at risk for preeclampsia (Centers for Disease Control: 1991), a condition which occurs in the third trimester of pregnancy or during labor. For these reasons, it is often recommended that women with diabetes who have kidney disease not become pregnant (Jovanovic et al.: 1987). Preeclampsia involves elevation of blood pressure, protein in the urine, abdominal pain, edema (abnormal accumulation of fluids), visual disturbances, and headache. Preeclampsia often requires preterm delivery of the baby. Eclampsia, a condition that occurs in about five percent of the cases of preeclampsia, causes convulsions and coma and may be life threatening (Margolis and Greenwood: 1993). Women with nephropathy who do decide to become pregnant must monitor not only their blood glucose but also their blood pressure, keeping it at 130/85 or lower, according to John Kitzmiller, a physician who specializes in the care of pregnant women with diabetes. Blood pressure may be kept in control through the use of medications, although pregnant women with diabetes may not use all of the blood pressure medications available to the general population, as some of these medications may affect the fetus and glycemic control. Recommended medications are methyldopa, prazosin, or clonidine (American Diabetes Association: 1996b).

Women who plan to become pregnant are advised to seek preconception counseling and care in order to be certain that their blood glucose is maintained at levels that will minimize risks to themselves and their babies. Preconception and perinatal care have proven to be successful in reducing infant morbidity and mortality as well as reducing the number of cesarean section deliveries (Catalano: 1988). Glycemic control affects the formation of organs during the first weeks of pregnancy. Therefore, having blood glucose in control before becoming pregnant and maintaining excellent control is crucial to the health of the baby. Jovanovic (1987) recommends that pregnant women with diabetes test their blood glucose five to ten times daily.

Rosenn and colleagues (1991) compared a group of women who attended a preconception program with those who attended a program early in their pregnancy. Those who attended the program before conceiving achieved better glycemic control and experienced lower rates of spontaneous abortion. These clinicians suggested that the results may have differed for the two groups because it often takes several weeks to attain optimal glycemic control and fetal organs had already begun developing during this period in the pregnant group. Despite the recognized importance of preconceptual planning, many women who have diabetes do not receive this counseling from their physicians. A study found that less than half of women who sought care after becoming pregnant had ever received any advice about pregnancy from their physicians (Janz et al.: 1995).

Women with type 1 diabetes must adjust their insulin dosage throughout their pregnancy. During the first trimester of pregnancy, diabetes is often unstable; stability in the next trimester is followed by an increased need for insulin at about 24 weeks. The increased need for insulin is due to the production of pregnancy related hormones, such as estrogen and progesterone, which act as insulin antagonists (Steel et al.: 1994). The Diabetes Control and Complications Trial (2000b) found that women with type 1 diabetes who received either intensive or conventional therapy were at great risk for retinopathy during their pregnancy and one year postpartum. Although the increased risk was not long term, the finding suggests that women should have regular ophthalmic examinations during this period.

A study (Towner et al.: 1995) of pregnant women with type 2 diabetes who had not received preconception counseling found that the rate of congenital anomalies among this group of women was similar to the rate for women with type 1 diabetes. Control of blood glucose and the mother's age at onset of diabetes were the only variables that had a significant influence upon congenital anomalies. Type of treatment (dietary regimen, insulin injections, or oral agents) did not result in significantly different rates of anomalies.

Macrosomia, a condition in which babies' birth weight is abnormally high, occurs in approximately a quarter of all babies born to women with diabetes. Macrosomia is associated with protracted labor, skeletal and nerve injuries, perinatal asphyxia, and high rates of hypoglycemia in the infants (Cordero and Landon: 1993). The cause of macrosomia in women with diabetes is not fully understood. Studies have revealed little relationship between the mother's glycemic control and macrosomia, although it is known that the fetus's own pancreas produces excess amounts of insulin in the third trimester and causes the growth of the fetus (Schwartz et al.: 1994). Macrosomia may necessitate cesarean delivery. Often these babies become obese in childhood and develop glucose intolerance at an early age.

A long term study (Weiss et al.: 2000) followed the offspring of mothers with type 1 diabetes and the offspring of mothers who did not have diabetes. Children were examined between the ages of 5 and 15. The study concluded that children of mothers with type 1 diabetes were significantly more likely to develop diabetes later in life than the children of mothers who did not have diabetes.

DIABETES IN OLDER WOMEN

Diabetes is an age-related disease, having a greater prevalence in older age groups. Over 17% of women age 60 or over have diabetes, either diagnosed or undiagnosed (Hennessy and Beckles: 2001). Since a large proportion of individuals who have diabetes are not aware that they have the disease, it is important that older individuals be tested for the presence of the disease. The American College of Obstetricians and Gynecologists has recently recommend that older women over 45 years old undergo a fasting blood glucose test every three years.

Diabetes is a greater risk factor for coronary heart disease in women than in men. Post-menopausal women with diabetes have twice the risk of developing coronary heart disease as women who do not have diabetes (Sowers: 1998). Diabetes causes a greater disability among women 60 years or older than it does for men with diabetes over 60. Nearly one-third of women (32%) in this group had difficulty walking a quarter of a mile, climbing stairs, or doing housework. The proportion of women with diabetes who had these disabilities was significantly greater than men and women without diabetes in the same age group (Gregg et al.: 2000).

The costs of the supplies used to monitor and control diabetes have been barriers for some individuals, especially those on limited or fixed incomes. Medicare now pays for the cost of supplies for all beneficiaries who have diabetes, whether or not they take insulin. Supplies include blood glucose monitors, lancets, test strips, insulin, etc.

PSYCHOLOGICAL ASPECTS OF DIABETES

Although shock, fear, and depression are normal reactions to diabetes at first, these emotions may subside once the woman understands how to control the disease. Because diabetes affects so many parts of the body, it also affects many aspects of daily life. In addition to prescribed changes in diet and exercise, women with diabetes must always be aware of the symptoms that indicate hyperglycemia or hypoglycemia. Women who must take daily injections of insulin may have to overcome a fear of needles; talking with others who have experienced this fear and overcome it may prove extremely valuable.

Changes in daily routines are never accepted readily. For women with diabetes, changes in lifestyle and the need to monitor glucose may cause great stress. Social events and travel must be carefully planned to ensure that meals will comply with special diets.

A study by Anderson et al. (2001) reviewed a large number of studies to determine if individuals with diabetes experienced depression at higher rates than individuals without the disease. Indeed, individuals with diabetes were twice as likely to experience clinical depression (requiring treatment) as those without the disease; women and those whose diabetes was not in control were most likely to experience depression. A national study (Edege and Zheng: 2003) confirmed the finding that people with diabetes were twice as likely to have major depression as those without the disease. Perceptions of worsening health was associated with depression, and females with diabetes were twice as likely as males to have major depression.

Diabetes has a great effect on family relationships as well. The need to make a change in lifestyle may be upsetting not only to the woman herself, but also to her partner and to her children. Planning diets carefully means extra time devoted to shopping and cooking; exercising also takes time away from other family activities. Involving family members in these activities can channel positive energy into helping the woman with diabetes instead of isolating her from her family. All family members should also learn about blood glucose monitoring and insulin injection as well as recognizing the symptoms of insulin reaction and the necessary measures to counter it.

A common fear of mothers is that they will have an insulin reaction when home alone with their babies or young children. Teaching young children how to recognize signs of an insulin reaction and how to call for emergency help may prove to be lifesaving. Numerous incidents have been reported where small children dialed "911" and saved their mothers' lives.

The diagnosis of diabetes may result in the fear that most food is off limits and that it will be impossible to enjoy eating. Recent policy recommendations from the American Diabetes Association (1994) indicate that the use of simple sugars such as sucrose (table sugar) is not off limits and that they do not cause greater or more rapid rises in blood glucose than other carbohydrates. Scientific evidence suggests that sucrose has a similar effect on blood glucose as bread, rice, and potatoes. It is important to keep in mind the total amount of carbohydrates consumed and that simple sugars must be used in place of other carbohydrates in the diet. With the new food labeling laws mandated by the federal government, this calculation becomes much easier, as the amount of carbohydrates per serving must be indicated on the food label. In order to control the amount of carbohydrates, many foods, including desserts and candies, are sweetened with artificial sweeteners or fruit juices.

A number of food manufacturers cater to the dietary needs of individuals with diabetes, and their products are often available in the dietetic food section of large supermarkets. Health food or natural food stores also carry many products that are amenable to the diet of people with diabetes. Perseverance in tracking down the right foods will allow for an interesting and varied diet; however, the shock and depression that follow the diagnosis of diabetes may limit the individual's emotional endurance. Support from a family member or close friend can help women with diabetes to carry out this endeavor.

Public libraries are a good source for the myriad cookbooks that have been written especially for people with diabetes. Discovering the variety of interesting recipes, including those for dessert and candies, should prove to be a psychological boost for women who fear being restricted to bland meals.

Diligent efforts to control glucose by following the recommended dosages of insulin or diets do not always result in the desired response. Women whose glucose is out of control should learn not to feel guilty; they may need to have their insulin or medication dosage and diet modified by a health care professional.

A common response to adult-onset or type 2 diabetes is that "It's just a touch of diabetes." This response can be extremely dangerous when the woman fails to properly monitor and control the disease. Women with diabetes and their family members must discuss the disease and its potential effects so that they understand the importance of the prescribed dietary regimen, exercise, and blood glucose monitoring.

Older women with diabetes may experience other disabling conditions or diseases; the additional diagnosis of diabetes may cause them to have grave concerns about their health and their ability to live independently. Widows and older women who live alone may be especially vulnerable to this response. Their physicians may tell them not to worry about the diabetes, because it takes many years to develop serious complications. This attitude may contribute to the woman's denial of her disease and result in exacerbation of the symptoms of hyperglycemia discussed above.

PROFESSIONAL SERVICE PROVIDERS

Because diabetes is a systemic disease, it has a wide range of effects. As a result, many types of health care professionals are involved in caring for women with diabetes.

Family physicians and *internists* are the physicians in charge of coordinating the various aspects of care for individuals with diabetes. *Diabetologists* (endocrinologists) are physicians who specialize in the treatment of individuals with diabetes. *Obstetricians/gynecologists* care for women who are pregnant and treat conditions affecting women's reproductive organs; diabetes makes women susceptible to vaginal infections and puts them at high risk during pregnancy. Obstetricians should work with internists or diabetologists, neonatologists, and diabetes educators to ensure the health of both the mother and the fetus. Some women get their prenatal care from specialists in high risk pregnancies. *Nephrologists* are physicians who treat people with kidney disease, which is a common complication of diabetes. *Ophthalmologists* are physicians who specialize in diseases of the eye. If diabetic retinopathy is detected, individuals are often referred to subspecialists called retina and vitreous specialists.

Certified diabetes educators (CDE) are health care professionals certified by the American Association of Diabetes Educators to teach individuals with diabetes how to effectively manage their disease. Certified diabetes educators may be physicians or nurses. Many are dietitians or nutritionists who help people with diabetes plan a diet to control their blood glucose levels.

Psychologists, social workers, and other counselors help people with diabetes and their family members adjust to the regimen prescribed to control the diabetes.

WHERE TO FIND SERVICES

In some areas, special treatment centers for diabetes and dialysis centers for people with kidney disease are available. Diabetes treatment centers often have special divisions for the monitoring and care of pregnant women with diabetes. The special physicians listed above practice in hospitals or have private practices. Affiliates of the American Diabetes Association (ADA) exist in every state. These affiliates may provide publications, educational programs, and referrals to local resources. The national office (described in the "ORGANIZATIONS" section below) can provide the address and phone number of local affiliates. The ADA also has information about local support groups. Understanding that others with diabetes continue to live fulfilling lives can be an extremely important benefit of attending support groups. People with diabetes who have vision problems may obtain services from public or private rehabilitation agencies serving individuals who are visually impaired or blind.

ASSISTIVE DEVICES

Individuals with insulin-dependent diabetes use a variety of devices to administer their insulin, such as syringes; insulin pens which combine the insulin dose and injector; needle-free jet injectors; and insulin pumps, which automatically deliver insulin slowly throughout the day and night through a plastic tube attached to a needle. Equipment to measure blood glucose is necessary for both type 1 and type 2 forms of diabetes. Some health insurance policies will pay some of the costs for glucose monitors and test strips. It is wise to check with the insurance carrier before purchasing such equipment.

Supplies and equipment to help individuals with diabetes to monitor and manage their disease are usually available at pharmacies or medical supply stores. Mail order catalogues also sell these supplies.

HOW TO RECOGNIZE AN INSULIN REACTION AND GIVE FIRST AID

Individuals experiencing an insulin reaction may feel shaky or dizzy, sweat profusely, complain of a headache, or act irritable. Family members of the woman with diabetes, including her children, should learn the signs of insulin reaction. Suggestions for giving first aid to individuals who have had an insulin reaction are:

> • Give the individual some food, such as orange juice, milk, or even sugar itself, to replace the low blood sugar level. Many individuals with diabetes carry sugar packets, glucose tablets, or candy with them for use in emergencies.
> • If the individual is unconscious, rub honey or another sugary substance into the mouth, between the teeth and cheek.

Frequent insulin reactions should be reported to the physician. It is recommended that individuals with diabetes wear a medical identification bracelet so that emergency care personnel will know that they have diabetes.

References

American Diabetes Association

2000a   "Pancreas Transplantation for Patients with Diabetes Mellitus" <u>Diabetes Care</u> 23(January):Supplement 1:S85

2000b   "Gestational Diabetes Mellitus" <u>Diabetes Care</u> 23(January):Supplement 1:S77-79

1998   "Economic Consequences of Diabetes Mellitus in the U.S. in 1997" <u>Diabetes Care</u> 21:2(February):296-309

1996a   "Why Worry about Gestational Diabetes?" <u>Diabetes Forecast</u> 49(March):3:46-47

1996b   "Pregnancy and Beyond" <u>Diabetes Forecast</u> 49(September):9:31-32

1995   "Surge Protector" <u>Diabetes Forecast</u> 48(May)5:23-24

1994   "Nutrition Recommendations and Principles for People with Diabetes Mellitus" <u>Diabetes Care</u> 17(May)5:519-522

Anderson, Ryan J. et al.

2001   "The Prevalence of Comorbid Depression in Adults with Diabetes: A Meta-analysis" <u>Diabetes Care</u> 24:6(June):1069-1078

Cantu, Robert C.

1982   <u>Diabetes and Exercise</u> New York, NY: E.P. Dutton

Catalano, Patrick M.

1988   "Diabetic Pregnancy: Is It Time to Enjoy the Fruits of Our Labor?" <u>Diabetes Care</u> 11(November):292-293

Centers for Disease Control and Prevention

2002a   <u>Diabetes: Disabling, Deadly, on the Rise</u> Atlanta, GA: Centers for Disease Control and Prevention

2002b   <u>National Diabetes Fact Sheet: General Information and National Estimates on Diabetes in the United States 2000</u> Atlanta, GA: Centers for Disease Control and Prevention

1991   <u>The Prevention and Treatment of Complications of Diabetes</u> Atlanta, GA: Public Health Service

Chew, Emily et al.

1995   "Metabolic Control and Progression of Retinopathy" <u>Diabetes Care</u> 18(May):5:631-637

Cordero, Leandro and Mark B. Landon

1993   "Infant of the Diabetic Mother" <u>Clinics in Perinatology</u> 20(September)3:635-648

Diabetes Control and Complications Trial

2000a   "Retinopathy and Nephropathy in Patients with Type 1 Diabetes Four Years after a Trial of Intensive Therapy" <u>New England Journal of Medicine</u> 342:6(February 10):381-389

2000b   "Effect of Pregnancy on Microvascular Complications in the Diabetes Control and Complications Trial" <u>Diabetes Care</u> 23:8(August):1084-1091

1993   "The Effect of Intensive Treatment of Diabetes on the Development and Progression of Long-Term Complications in Insulin-Dependent Diabetes Mellitus" <u>New England Journal of Medicine</u> 329(September 30):14:977-986

Dornhorst, Anne and Michela Rossi
1998   "Risk and Prevention of Type 2 Diabetes in Women with Gestational Diabetes" <u>Diabetes Care</u> 21:Supplement 2(August): B43-B49

Edege, L. E. and D. Zheng
2003   "Independent Factors Associated with Major Depressive Disorder in a National Sample of Individuals with Diabetes" <u>Diabetes Care</u> 26:1(January):104-111

Engelau, Michael et al.
1995   "The Epidemiology of Diabetes and Pregnancy in the U.S., 1988" <u>Diabetes Care</u> 18(July):7:1029-1033

Erol, B. et al.
2002   "Sexual Dysfunction in Type II Diabetic Females: A Comparative Study" <u>Journal of Sex and Marital Therapy</u> 28(Supplement):55-63

Gregg, Edward W. et al.
2000   "Diabetes and Physical Disability among Older Adults" <u>Diabetes Care</u> 23:9(September):1272-1277

Hennessy, C.H. and G.L.A. Beckles
2001   "The Older Years" pp. 147-167 in G.L.A. Beckles and P.E. Thompson-Reid (eds.) <u>Diabetes and Women Across the Life Stages</u> Centers for Disease Control and Prevention

Jansen, J.J. et al.
1997   "Mutation in Mitochondrial tRNA (Leu(UUR)) Gene Associated with Progressive Kidney Disease" <u>Journal of the American Society of Nephrology</u> 8:7(July):1118-1124

Janz, Nancy K. et al.
1995   "Diabetes and Pregnancy" <u>Diabetes Care</u> 18(February)2:157-165

Jenkins, David J. A.
1995   "Nutritional Principles and Diabetes" <u>Diabetes Care</u> 18(November)11:1491-1498

Jovanovic, Lois, June Biermann, and Barbara Toohey
1987   <u>The Diabetic Woman</u> Los Angeles, CA: Jeremy P. Tarcher

King, Hilary
1998   "Epidemiology of Glucose Intolerance and Gestational Diabetes in Women of Childbearing Age" <u>Diabetes Care</u> 21:Supplement 2(August): B9-B13

Kobayashi, Tetsuro et al.
1997   "In Situ Characterization of Islets in Diabetes with a Mitochondrial DNA Mutation at Nucleotide Position 3243" <u>Diabetes</u> 46:1-(October):1567-15710

Larsen, J.
2002   "Pancreas and Kidney Transplantation" <u>Current Diabetes Report</u> 2:4(August):359-364

Lipkind, Karen L.
1996   "National Hospital Ambulatory Medical Care Survey: 1994 Outpatient Department Summary" <u>Advance Data from Vital and Health Statistics</u>, No. 276, Hyattsville, MD: National Center for Health Statistics, June 11

MacNeill, Stephanie et al.
2001   "Rates and Risk Factors for Recurrence of Gestational Diabetes" <u>Diabetes Care</u> 24:4(April):659-662

Margolis, Alan J. and Sadja Greenwood
1993   "Gynecology and Obstetrics" pp. 560-613 in Lawrence M. Tierney, Jr. et al. (eds.) <u>Current Medical Diagnosis and Treatment</u> Englewood Cliffs, NJ: Appleton and Lange

National Center for Health Statistics
1987 "Health Practices and Perceptions of U.S. Adults with Noninsulin-Dependent Diabetes. Data from the 1985 National Health Interview Survey of Health Promotion and Disease Prevention" Advance Data from Vital and Health Statistics, No. 141, DHHS Pub. No. (PHS) 87-1250. Public Health Service, Hyattsville, MD September 23, 1987

National Institute of Diabetes and Digestive and Kidney Diseases
1990 Insulin-Dependent Diabetes Bethesda, MD: National Diabetes Information Clearinghouse

Purdy, Lisa P. et al.
1996 "Effect of Pregnancy on Renal Function in Patients with Moderate-to-Severe Diabetic Renal Insufficiency" Diabetes Care 19(October):10:1067-1074

Rosenn, Barak et al.
1991 "Pre-Conception Management of Insulin-Dependent Diabetes: Improvement of Pregnancy Outcome" Obstetrics and Gynecology 77(June):6:846-849

Schappert, Susan M.
1992 "Office Visits for Diabetes Mellitus: United States, 1989" Advance Data from Vital and Health Statistics No. 211, DHHS Pub. No. (PHS) 92-1250. Hyattsville, MD: Public Health Service March 24, 1992

Schreiner-Engel, Patricia
1983 "Diabetes Mellitus and Female Sexuality" Sexuality and Disability 6(Summer):2:83-92

Schwartz, Robert et al.
1994 "Hyperinsulinemia and Macrosomia in the Fetus of the Diabetic Mother" Diabetes Care 17(July):7:640-649

Sheffield, J.S. et al.
2002 "Maternal Diabetes Mellitus and Infant Malformations" Obstetrics and Gynecology 100:5 Part 1(November):925-930

Sowers, James R.
1998 "Diabetes Mellitus and Cardiovascular Disease in Women" Archives of Internal Medicine 158:617-621

Steel, Judith M. et al.
1994 "Insulin Requirements During Pregnancy in Women with Type I Diabetes" Obstetrics and Gynecology 83(February):2:253-258

Suzuki, S. et al.
1998 "The Effects of Coenzyme Q10 Treatment on Maternally Inherited Diabetes and Deafness and Mitochondrial DNA 3243 (A to G) Mutation" Diabetologia 41:5(May):584-588

Towner, Dena et al.
1995 "Congenital Malformations in Pregnancies Complicated by NIDDM" Diabetes Care 18(November):1:1446-1451

UK Prospective Diabetes Study Group
1998a "Intensive Blood-Glucose Control with Sulphonylureas or Insulin Compared with Conventional Treatment and Risk of Complications in Patients with Type 2 Diabetes" The Lancet 352(September 12):837-853

1998b "Effect of Intensive Blood-Glucose Control with Metformin on Complications in Overweight Patients with Type 2 Diabetes" The Lancet 352(September 12):854-865

Weiss, Peter et al.
2000 "Long-Term Follow-Up of Infants of Mothers with Type 1 Diabetes" Diabetes Care 23:7(July):9o5-911

Williams, T. Franklin
1983   "Diabetes Mellitus in Older People" pp. 411-415 in William Reichel (ed.) <u>Clinical Aspects of Aging</u> Baltimore, MD: Williams and Wilkins
Wilson Young, Elaine and Patricia Barthalow Koch
1989   "Research Comparing the Dyadic Adjustment and Sexual Functioning Concerns of Diabetic and Nondiabetic Women" <u>Health Care for Women International</u> 10:377-394

ORGANIZATIONS

<u>American Association of Diabetes Educators</u> (AADE)
100 West Monroe Street, Suite 400
Chicago, IL 60603-1901
(800) 338-3633   (312) 644-2233   FAX (312) 424-2427
www.aadenet.org

Membership organization for health care professionals who work with people with diabetes. Holds annual meeting. Membership, $85.00, includes a bimonthly journal, "The Diabetes Educator," Journal only, $45.00.

<u>American Association of Kidney Patients</u>
100 South Ashley Drive, Suite 280
Tampa, FL 33602
(800) 749-2257   FAX (813) 223-0001
e-mail:AAKPnat@aol.com   www.aakp.org

Advocates on behalf of patients with kidney disease; sponsors local patient and family support groups; holds conferences and seminars. Membership, patients/families, $25.00; professionals, $35.00; includes quarterly newsletter, "aakpRENALIFE."

<u>American Autoimmune Related Diseases Association</u> (AARDA)
22100 Gratiot Avenue
East Detroit, MI 48021
(800) 598-4668   (586) 776-3900   e-mail: aarda@aol.com
www.aarda.org

Provides information on autoimmune diseases including type 1 diabetes, multiple sclerosis, Sjogren's syndrome, and rheumatoid arthritis. Web site offers brief explanations of conditions. Offers telephone support and referrals.

<u>American Diabetes Association</u> (ADA)
1701 North Beauregard Street
Alexandria, VA 22311
(800) 342-2383   In the Washington area, DC, (703) 549-1500
FAX (703) 836-7439   e-mail: askADA@diabetes.org
www.diabetes.org

National membership organization with local affiliates. Publications for both professionals and consumers, including cookbooks and guides for the management of diabetes (see "PUBLICATIONS AND TAPES" section below). Membership, $24.00, includes discounts on publications, a subscription to "Diabetes Forecast" (Also available on disc from the National Library Service.) Many local affiliates offer their own publications, sponsor support groups, and conduct professional training programs. The web site includes featured articles from "Diabetes Forecast" and the medical journal "Diabetes Care." In conjunction with the American College of Cardiology, the ADA is sponsoring a campaign called "Make the Link," to increase public awareness about the link between diabetes and heart disease. More information is available at www.diabetes.org/make the link.

American Dietetic Association (ADA)
216 West Jackson Boulevard
Chicago, IL 60606
(800) 877-1600   (312) 899-0040   FAX (312) 899-1758
e-mail: hotline@eatright.org   www.eatright.org

Consumers may receive a referral to a registered dietitian or receive information about nutrition on the telephone or on the web site. Available in English and Spanish.

American Kidney Fund
6110 Executive Boulevard, Suite 1010
Rockville, MD 20852
(800) 638-8299   e-mail: helpline@akfinc.org
www.kidneyfund.org

Provides public and professional education and financial aid to individuals who have chronic kidney problems.

Amputee Coalition of America (ACA)
National Limb Loss Information Center
900 East Hill Avenue, Suite 285
Knoxville, TN 37915
(888) 267-5669   (423) 524-8772   FAX (423) 525-7917
e-mail: info@amputee-coalition.org
www.amputee-coalition.org

Provides education and support services to individuals with amputations through a network of peer support groups, educational programs for health professionals, and a database of resources. Membership, individuals, $25.00; professionals, $50.00; amputee support groups, $75.00; includes magazine, "In-Motion." Guides for organizing peer support groups and peer visitation programs also available.

CDC Division of Diabetes Translation
PO Box 8728
Silver Spring, MD 20910
(877) 232-3422   FAX (301) 562-1050
e-mail: diabetes@cdc.gov   www.cdc.gov/diabetes

The Centers for Disease Control Division of Diabetes Translation conducts research related to the prevalence of diabetes; assesses clinical practices in order to develop optimal treatment; and works with state health departments to develop diabetes control programs.

Diabetes Action Network, National Federation of the Blind
1412 I-70 Drive SW, Suite C
Columbia, MO 65203
(573) 875-8911   FAX (573) 875-8902   e-mail: ebryant@trib.net
www.nfb.org/diabetes.htm

A national support and information network. Publishes a quarterly magazine, "Voice of the Diabetic," which includes personal experiences, medical information, recipes, and resources. Available in standard print, four-track audiocassette, and on the web site. Free. Also available, "Diabetes Resources: Equipment, Services and Information," a list of adaptive equipment; available in alternate formats, $5.00; order from: National Federation of the Blind, 1800 Johnson Street, Baltimore, MD 21230. Also available on the web site.

Diabetes Education Network
www.htinet.com/den/index.html

This web site provides links to service organizations; information about treatment, research, and clinical trials; and support organizations.

Diabetes Exercise and Sports Association (DESA)
formerly International Diabetic Athletes Association
PO Box 1935
Litchfield Park, AZ 85340
(800) 898-4322   (623) 535-4593   FAX (623) 535-4741
e-mail: desa@diabetes-exercise.org   www.diabetes-exercise.org

An organization that provides education for individuals with diabetes who participate in sports and fitness activities, family members, and service providers through conferences, workshops, and publications. Membership, individuals, $30.00; corporate, $150.00; includes quarterly newsletter, "The Challenge."

Diabetes-Sight.org
www.diabetes-sight.org

Sponsored by Prevent Blindness America, this web site provides information for individuals and professionals about prevention of vision loss due to diabetes. Includes interactive tools such as a quiz, vision loss simulation, and tour of the eye's anatomy as well as research summaries and preferred practice guidelines.

Diabetic Retinopathy Foundation
350 North LaSalle Drive, Suite 800
Chicago, IL 60610
www.retinopathy.org

Supports research and public awareness in an effort to prevent diabetic retinopathy. Web site offers information about diabetic retinopathy and links to other web sites.

Juvenile Diabetes Research Foundation International (JDRF)
120 Wall Street, 19th Floor
New York, NY 10005
(800) 533-2873   (212) 785-9500
FAX (212) 785-9595   e-mail: info@jdrfcure.org   www.jdrf.org

Supports research and provides information to individuals with diabetes and their families. Chapters in many states and affiliates in other countries. Membership, $25.00, includes quarterly magazine, "Countdown" and discounts on books.

MEDLINEplus: Diabetes
www.nlm.nih.gov/medlineplus/diabetes.html

This web site provides links to sites for general information about diabetes, symptoms and diagnosis, treatment, alternative therapy, clinical trials, disease management, organizations, and research. Includes an interactive tutorial. Some information available in Spanish. Provides links to MEDLINE research articles and related MEDLINEplus pages.

National Diabetes Education Program (NDEP)
National Institute of Diabetes and Digestive and Kidney Diseases (NIDDKD)
31 Center Drive, MSC 2560
Washington, DC 20892
(800) 438-5383   (301) 496-3583   www.ndep.nih.gov

A joint project of the National Institutes of Health and the Centers for Disease Control and Prevention, this program aims to prevent the increase in diabetes in this country through partnerships with other organizations that will provide public information about the disease. In conjunction with the American Diabetes Association, the NDEP is conducting a campaign called "Be Smart about Your Heart: Control the ABCs of Diabetes" to increase public awareness of the link between diabetes and heart disease. The web site has information about diabetes, and the program has produced public information materials, including cookbooks. Free

National Diabetes Information Clearinghouse (NDIC)
1 Information Way
Bethesda, MD 20892
(800) 860-8747   (301) 654-3327   FAX (301) 907-8906
e-mail: ndic@info.niddk.nih.gov   www.niddk.nih.gov/health/diabetes/ndic.htm

Responds to information requests from the public and professionals. Maintains a database of publications and brochures. Publishes newsletter, "Diabetes Dateline," free. web
Free list of publications. Many publications are available on the web site. Free

National Institute of Diabetes and Digestive and Kidney Diseases (NIDDKD)
National Institutes of Health
31 Center Drive, MSC 2560
Building 31, Room 9A-04
Bethesda, MD 20892
(301) 496-3583   www.niddk.nih.gov

Funds basic and clinical research in the causes, prevention, and treatment of diabetes. Free list of publications. The web site contains fact sheets and patient education materials. Publications available in English and Spanish. Free

National Kidney and Urologic Diseases Information Clearinghouse (NKUDIC)
3 Information Way
Bethesda, MD 20892
(800) 891-5390   (301) 654-4415   FAX (301) 907-8906
e-mail: nkudic@info.niddk.nih.gov   www.niddk.nih.gov

Responds to requests from the public and professionals about diseases of the kidneys and urologic system. Publishes quarterly newsletter, "KU Notes," free. Free list of publications.

National Kidney Foundation (NKF)
30 East 33rd Street
New York, NY 10016
(800) 622-9010   FAX (212) 689-9261
e-mail: info@kidneyfund.org   www.kidney.org

A professional membership organization that provides professional and public education; produces literature on kidney disease; and promotes kidney transplantation and organ donation.

Neuropathy Association
60 East 42nd Street, Suite 942
New York, NY 10165
(800) 247-6968   (212) 692-0662
e-mail: info@neuropathy.org   www.neuropathy.org

This organization serves individuals who experience neuropathy and their family members through the support of research into the causes and treatments of neuropathy, education, and dissemination of information. Membership, $25.00, includes newsletter and informational materials.

American Diabetes Association Complete Guide to Diabetes
American Diabetes Association
Order Fulfillment
PO Box 930850
Atlanta, GA 31193-0850
(800) 232-6733   FAX (404) 442-9742

This book provides information about type 1 and type 2 diabetes, including how to maintain good blood glucose levels, selecting health care providers, planning an exercise program, and enjoying sex. $29.95

The American Dietetic Guide to Eating Right When You Have Diabetes
American Dietetic Association
PO Box 97215
Chicago, IL 60678-7215
(800) 877-1600, ext. 5000   (312) 899-0040, ext. 5000
FAX (312) 899-4899   www.eatright.org

This book provides information on healthy eating for individuals with diabetes, including detailed sample menu plans for a range of calories; tips on reducing fat and sugar in foods; a fast-food restaurant guide; and an ethnic food guide. $14.95

Coping with Limb Loss
by Ellen Winchell
Avery Publishing Group, Garden City Park, NY

Written by a woman who had a limb amputated, this book provides information about surgery, prosthetics, and rehabilitation as well as practical coping strategies. Out of print

Diabetes and Pregnancy: What to Expect
American Diabetes Association (ADA)
Order Fulfillment
PO Box 930850
Atlanta, GA 31193-0850
(800) 232-6733   FAX (404) 442-9742   www.diabetes.org

This book provides information about insulin therapy, blood glucose monitoring, exercise, and nutrition during pregnancy. $9.95

Diabetes and the Kidneys
American Kidney Fund
6110 Executive Boulevard, Suite 1010
Rockville, MD 20852
(800) 638-8299   (301) 881-3052   FAX (301) 881-0898
e-mail: helpline@akfinc.org   www.kidneyfund.org

A booklet that describes how diabetes affects the kidneys' function and measures that may be taken to slow down the course of kidney disease. Available in standard print and large print. Free

Diabetes and Vision Loss: Special Considerations
by Marla Bernbaum
in "Meeting the Needs of People with Vision Loss: A Multidisciplinary Perspective"
Resources for Rehabilitation
22 Bonad Road
Winchester, MA 01890
(781) 368-9094   FAX (781) 368-9096   e-mail: info@rfr.org
www.rfr.org

Provides information on the psychosocial implications and special rehabilitation needs of individuals with vision loss due to diabetes. Also available on audiocassette. $24.95 (See order form on last page of this book.)

The Diabetes Carbohydrate and Fat Gram Guide
by Lea Ann Holzmeister
American Dietetic Association (ADA)
PO Box 97215
Chicago, IL 60678-7215
(800) 877-1600, ext. 5000   (312) 899-0040, ext. 5000
FAX (312) 899-4899   www.eatright.org

This book lists the carbohydrate and fat content of foods, including packaged foods and foods purchased at fast food restaurants. $14.95

The Diabetes Home Video Guide: Skills for Self Care
Joslin Diabetes Center
Publications Department
One Joslin Place
Boston, MA 02215
(800) 344-4501   FAX (617) 732-2562   www.joslin.org

This videotape covers exercise, blood glucose monitoring, nutrition, medications, lifestyle changes, and emotions. Uses people who have diabetes, not actors. 2 hours. Available in English and Spanish. $20.00

Diabetes Self-Management
PO Box 52890
Boulder, CO 80321
(800) 234-0923   www.diabetes-self-mgmt.com

A bimonthly magazine that helps people with diabetes manage their disease. Tips on diet, foot care, medical news, etc. $24.00 Web site provides information on diabetes and health, sports and fitness, and recipes.

Diabetes Type 2 & What to Do
by Virginia Valentine, June Biermann and Barbara Toohey
McGraw-Hill Order Services
PO Box 182604
Columbus, OH 43272-3031
(877) 833-5524   FAX (614) 759-3749
e-mail: pbg.ecommerce_custserv@mcgraw-hill.com
books.mcgraw-hill.com

Written in question and answer format, this book addresses the effects of type 2 diabetes including information on diet and nutrition, exercise, emotional aspects, and paying for medical care. Many case examples are presented throughout the book. Includes reading list and Internet resources. Virginia Valentine and June Biermann have diabetes. $16.95

Diabetic Retinopathy: Information for Patients
National Eye Institute (NEI)
Building 31, Room 6A32
Bethesda, MD 20892
(301) 496-5248   www.nei.nih.gov

This booklet discusses the symptoms of diabetic retinopathy; treatment; vitrectomy; and research. Large print. Free

The Diabetic Woman
by Lois Jovanovic-Peterson, June Biermann, and Barbara Toohey
Penguin Putnam, Newark, NJ

This book focuses on the special issues facing women with diabetes. In addition to generic information about the disease, the book answers questions about menstruation, pregnancy, and sexual relations. Lois Jovanovic-Peterson is a physician who has type 1 diabetes; June Biermann has type 2 diabetes. Out of print

The Diabetic's Book
by June Biermann and Barbara Toohey
Penguin Putnam, Inc., Inside Sales
(800) 788-6262   FAX (607) 775-5586   www.penguinputnam.com

This book answers basic questions about diabetes, including diet, exercise, management of the disease, emotional responses, and other aspects of daily life. June Biermann has type 2 diabetes. $13.95

Exchange Lists for Meal Planning
American Diabetes Association (ADA)
Order Fulfillment
PO Box 930850
Atlanta, GA 31193-0850
(800) 232-6733   FAX (404) 442-9742   www.diabetes.org

This guide lists foods based on carbohydrate, protein, and fat content. $2.50 Discounts available on bulk orders.

The First Year: Type 2 Diabetes
by Gretchen Becker
Distributed by Publishers Group West
1700 Fourth Street
Berkeley, CA 94710
(800) 788-3123   FAX (510) 528-3444   www.pgw.com

Written by a woman who has type 2 diabetes, this practical guide includes basic information that people ask about when they are first diagnosed with diabetes. Includes information that helps to cope with the physical, social, and psychological aspects of diabetes. $14.95

Gestational Diabetes
National Health Video
11312 Santa Monica Boulevard
Los Angeles, CA 90025
(800) 543-6803   (310) 268-2809   FAX (310) 477-8198
e-mail: healthvid@aol.com   www.nhv.com

This videotape discusses gestational diabetes and the role of diet in preventing and treating the condition. Available in English and Spanish. 17 minutes. $89.00

Gestational Diabetes: Caring for Yourself and Your Baby
International Diabetes Center
Attn: IDC Publishing
3800 Park Nicollet Boulevard
Minneapolis, MN 55416
(888) 637-2675   (612) 993-3874   FAX (612) 993-1302
e-mail: idcpub@hsmnet.com   www.idcdiabetes.com

This booklet provides guidelines for nutrition, weight gain, and insulin use for women who develop diabetes during pregnancy. $3.00

Gestational Diabetes: What to Expect
American Diabetes Association (ADA)
Order Fulfillment
PO Box 930850
Atlanta, GA 31193-0850
(800) 232-6733   FAX (404) 442-9742   www.diabetes.org

This book provides information about blood glucose monitoring, exercise, and nutrition during pregnancy. $9.95

Good Health with Diabetes through Exercise
Joslin Diabetes Center
Publications Department
One Joslin Place
Boston, MA 02215
(800) 344-4501   FAX (617) 732-2562   www.joslin.org

This booklet, written for those who use insulin and those who do not, tells how to get started on an exercise plan, what pitfalls to avoid, and how to integrate exercise with food and medications. $4.50

I Hate to Exercise
American Diabetes Association (ADA)
Order Fulfillment
PO Box 930850
Atlanta, GA 31193-0850
(800) 232-6733   FAX (404) 442-9742

This book promotes the value of 30 minutes of exercise a day to strengthen muscles, and heart and how to control diabetes. $14.95

The Johns Hopkins Guide to Diabetes for Today and Tomorrow
by Christopher D. Saudek, Richard R. Rubin, and Cynthia Shump
Johns Hopkins University Press
2715 North Charles Street
Baltimore, MD 21218
(800) 537-5487   (410) 516-6900   FAX (410) 516-6968
e-mail: all inside@jhupbooks.com   www.press.jhup.edu

Written by a physician, a psychologist, and a nurse who specialize in treating individuals with diabetes, this book provides basic information on diabetes and its treatment, emotional and social aspects of the disease, complications, and sexuality and reproduction. $16.95; large print, $22.95.

Living with Diabetes $1.75 per copy
Living with Diabetic Retinopathy $1.75 per copy
Resources for Rehabilitation
22 Bonad Road
Winchester, MA 01890
(781) 368-9094   FAX (781) 368-9096   e-mail: info@rfr.org
www.rfr.org

Designed for distribution by professionals to people with diabetes, these large print (18 point bold type) publications describe the condition, service providers, organizations, devices, and publications. Minimum purchase 25 copies. (See order form on last page of this book.)

Living with Diabetes: A Winning Formula
Info Vision
102 North Hazel Street
Glenwood, IA 51534
(800) 237-1808   FAX (888) 735-2622

This videotape provides information about diet, weight loss, insulin, and self-monitoring of blood glucose. 35 minutes. $25.00

Living with Low Vision: A Resource Guide for People with Sight Loss
Resources for Rehabilitation
22 Bonad Road
Winchester, MA 01890
(781) 368-9094   FAX (781) 368-9096   e-mail: info@rfr.org
www.rfr.org

A large print (18 point bold type) comprehensive directory that helps people with sight loss locate the services that they need to remain independent. Chapters describe products that enable people to keep reading, working, and carrying out their daily activities. $46.95 (See order form on last page of this book.)

Managing Diabetes on a Budget
by Leslie Y. Dawson
American Diabetes Association (ADA)
Order Fulfillment
PO Box 930850
Atlanta, GA 31193-0850
(800) 232-6733   FAX (770) 442-9742   www.diabetes.org

This book provides advice on finding the best buys on supplies and medications, cooking tips, and general diabetes management. $7.95

Managing Your Gestational Diabetes
by Lois Jovanovic-Peterson with Morton B. Stone
John Wiley & Sons, Inc.
10475 Crosspoint Boulevard
Indianapolis, IN 46256
(877) 762-2974   FAX (800) 597-3299
e-mail: customer@wiley.com   www.wiley.com

This book provides information about controlling diabetes associated with pregnancy and reducing health risks to both the mother and the child. Lois Jovanovic-Peterson is a physician who has diabetes and is a mother herself. $12.95

<u>Mayo Clinic on Managing Diabetes</u>
by Maria Collazo-Clavell (ed.)
Mayo Clinic Health Information Division
PO Box 609
Calverton, NY 11933
(800) 291-1128   www.health-store.com

This book provides a basic introduction for newly diagnosed patients and family members. Includes information on pregnancy and "20 Tasty Recipes for People with Diabetes." $14.95

<u>Medical Management of Pregnancy Complicated by Diabetes</u>
by Lois Jovanovic
McGraw-Hill Order Services
PO Box 182604
Columbus, OH 43272-3031
(877) 833-5524   FAX (614) 759-3749
e-mail: pbg.ecommerce_custserv@mcgraw-hill.com
books.mcgraw-hill.com

This book provides information on how women with diabetes should plan for their pregnancy and how to control their diabetes during pregnancy. $39.95

<u>Sexual Function in People with Disability and Chronic Illness: A Health Professional's Guide</u>
by Marca Sipski and Craig Alexander
Aspen Publishers, Inc.
PO Box 990
Frederick, MD 21705-9782
(800) 234-1660   www.aspenpub.com

This book discusses many types of disability, their effects on sexuality, reproductive concerns, and treatment methods, as well as providing basic information on general sexual function and dysfunction. Includes spinal cord injury, diabetes, multiple sclerosis, arthritis and other connective tissue diseases, and heart disease. Offers a discussion of the issues faced by the partner of an individual with a disability. $59.00

<u>Surviving Transplantation: A Personal Guide for Organ Transplant Patients, Their Families, Friends and Caregivers</u>
by John Craven and Susan Farrow
www.psychiatry.med.uwo.ca/survive/frmain.htm

This web publication discusses waiting and recovery from an organ transplant and understanding and dealing with stress associated with the procedure as well as strategies for working with health professionals. Free

The Type 2 Diabetic Woman
by M. Sara Rosenthal
McGraw-Hill Order Services
PO Box 182604
Columbus, OH 43272-3031
(877) 833-5524   FAX (614) 759-3749
e-mail: pbg.ecommerce_custserv@mcgraw-hill.com
books.mcgraw-hill.com

This book describes the physical and emotional needs of women with type 2 diabetes, including issues such as sex and pregnancy. $17.95

The Uncomplicated Guide to Diabetes Complications
by Marvin E. Levin and Michael A. Pfeifer
American Diabetes Association (ADA)
Order Fulfillment
PO Box 930850
Atlanta, GA 31193-0850
(800) 232-6733   FAX (404) 442-9742   www.diabetes.org

This book covers the major complications that diabetes may cause, including nephropathy, heart disease, stroke, and neuropathy. Special issues such as obesity, pregnancy, and hypoglycemia are also discussed. $16.95

Weight Loss: A Winning Battle
Joslin Diabetes Center
Publications Department
One Joslin Place
Boston, MA 02215
(800) 344-4501   FAX (617) 732-2562   www.joslin.org

This booklet provides information that helps people control their weight and offers strategies for losing weight. $3.50

Weight Management for Type II Diabetes: An Action Plan
by Jackie Labat and Annette Maggi
John Wiley and Sons, Consumer Center
10475 Crosspoint Boulevard
Indianapolis, IN 46256
(877) 762-2974   FAX (800) 597-3299
e-mail: customer@wiley.com   www.wiley.com

This book provides recommendations for lifestyle changes for weight control and good diabetes management. $15.95

What to Eat When You Get Diabetes
by Carolyn Leontos
John Wiley and Sons, Consumer Center
10475 Crosspoint Boulevard
Indianapolis, IN 46256
(877) 762-2974   FAX (800) 597-3299
e-mail: customer@wiley.com   www.wiley.com

Written by a dietitian, this book provides guidance to people with type 2 diabetes.   Includes
information about weight loss, calories, portion size, and carbohydrates. $15.95

Women and Diabetes
by Laurinda M. Poirer and Katherine M. Coburn
American Diabetes Association (ADA)
Order Fulfillment
PO Box 930850
Atlanta, GA 31193-0850
(800) 232-6733   FAX (404) 442-9742   www.diabetes.org

This book addresses how diabetes affects women's careers and their role at home.   It discusses
pregnancy, child rearing, sexuality, menopause, and emotions. $14.95

Women and Diabetes
National Health Video
11312 Santa Monica Boulevard
Los Angeles, CA 90025
(800) 543-6803   (310) 268-2809   FAX (310) 477-8198
e-mail: healthvid@aol.com   www.nhv.com

This videotape discusses the relationship between diabetes and puberty, menstruation, pregnancy, and
menopause as well as its psychological effects and effects on sexual functioning. 18 minutes. $89.00

Women and Diabetes Across the Life Stages
CDC Division of Diabetes Translation
PO Box 8728
Silver Spring, MD 20910
(877) 232-3422   FAX (301) 562-1050
e-mail: diabetes@cdc.gov   www.cdc.gov/nccdphp/ddt/ddthome.htm

This book presents a series of papers related to women in the reproductive years, middle years, and
older years. It presents data on incidence and prevalence of the disease as well as risk factors, social
behavior, and concomitant diseases. Free. Also available on the web site.

Chapter 7

EPILEPSY

Epilepsy is a condition in which the brain's cells undergo abnormal electrical activity, causing disturbances in the nervous system. An epileptic seizure occurs when there is an excessive discharge of electrical impulses from these nerve cells. To be classified as epilepsy, these seizures must be recurring events. Individuals who have isolated incidents of seizures do not have epilepsy. Epilepsy is not a single disease or condition, nor is it contagious. It often develops in people whose families have no history of epilepsy, although children of individuals with epilepsy are thought to have a greater chance of developing this condition (Epilepsy Foundation of America: 1993).

It is estimated that about two million Americans have epilepsy (National Information Center for Children and Youth with Disabilities: 2002). Although most studies indicate that epilepsy is somewhat more prevalent in men than women (Kurtz: 1991), the condition can be very serious for women of childbearing age and for their fetuses. Yerby (1991) states that 40% of all Americans with epilepsy are potential mothers. The onset of epilepsy often coincides with puberty and the beginning of menstruation in girls and is related to the hormones produced by the reproductive system (Kurtz: 1991). Epilepsy is the most common neurological disorder of pregnancy, occurring in one out of 200 pregnancies (Morrison and Rieder: 1993).

In order to diagnose their specific type of epileptic seizures and syndromes, women are often asked to come to the physician's office with a family member or other individual who has witnessed their seizures. Patients, family members, or friends should provide the physician with a detailed description of the seizure activity, including onset, frequency, any changes in the seizures, duration, and medication usage. Severe head trauma, stroke, and infections in the central nervous system are the greatest risks for epilepsy. When an individual over age 20 has a seizure for the first time, a brain tumor should be suspected (Epilepsy Foundation of America: 1992).

The electroencephalograph (EEG) is used to determine where in the brain the seizure activity is taking place. Sometimes the EEG does not pick up the brain's electrical changes, or the woman may not experience any seizure activity while being monitored. In some instances, a woman may be hospitalized so that a 24 hour EEG recording may be made. Blood tests and tests of spinal fluid are conducted to determine if an infection has caused the seizure. Computerized tomography scans (CTs) or magnetic resonance imaging (MRIs) may be performed to detect the presence of tumors, scar tissue, or blood clots that could be the cause of seizures.

Some individuals with epilepsy who are candidates for surgery are participating in research to locate areas of abnormal brain metabolism. Positron emission tomography (PET) allows researchers to observe the brain's metabolic activity by measuring the brain's use of glucose, oxygen, and carbon dioxide. Positron emission tomography may also reveal the effects of antiepileptic drugs (National Institute of Neurological Disorders and Stroke: 1984).

TYPES OF SEIZURES

Generalized seizures affect both hemispheres of the brain and may lead to loss of consciousness, convulsions, and loss of memory. Two types of generalized seizures are the tonic-clonic and absence seizures.

A *tonic-clonic seizure* (previously called a grand mal seizure) is a generalized seizure with loss of consciousness. The individual may cry out, fall, and lie rigid. The woman's body may jerk, and she may lose bladder and bowel control. She may bite her tongue, and saliva may appear around the mouth. When the woman regains consciousness, she may feel sore or stiff. She may or may not have any warning of the impending episode. She will not remember the seizure, and she may experience a headache and drowsiness, sometimes taking several days to return to her normal functioning (Dichter: 1994).

An *absence seizure* (previously called a petit mal seizure) is characterized by sudden onset and a blank stare. These seizures last a short time but may occur many times a day, beginning and ending abruptly. The individual is unaware of her surroundings and may not respond when spoken to, although sometimes speaking to her will stop the absence seizure.

If only one hemisphere of the brain is affected, the seizure is called a *partial* (or *focal*) *seizure*. Symptoms of a partial seizure include an involuntary turning of the head, loss of speech, sweating, pallor, dilation of the pupils, and light flashes. Tingling or numbness in the face or fingers or hearing buzzing noises may also occur. Individuals do not lose consciousness during a partial seizure.

Complex partial seizures, which sometimes affect the temporal lobes (at the side of the brain near the ears), can also occur in several other areas of the brain. Women having a complex partial seizure appear to be in a trance accompanied by involuntary motor activities, called automatisms. They lose consciousness and have no control over these movements, which may include lip and tongue smacking, mimicry, hand movements, or repetitive utterances.

The individual is conscious during a *simple partial seizure*, but she cannot control body movements. An arm or leg may jerk or tremble. Seizure activity occurs in the part of the brain which controls vision, hearing, sensation, or memory. She may feel disoriented or fearful, or she may experience odd sensations on one side of the body.

An *aura* is an unusual feeling experienced by many people with epilepsy prior to a seizure. The individual may feel sick or apprehensive, have aural or visual hallucinations, or notice a peculiar odor or taste. The individual retains memory of the sensation even if she loses consciousness. The aura often serves as a warning that a seizure is about to take place, allowing her to move away from potential hazards before the onset of a major seizure.

TREATMENT OF EPILEPSY

Most individuals with epilepsy use antiepileptic drugs to control seizures. The choice of antiepileptic drug is determined by the type of seizure, other clinical aspects of the seizure, the drug's side effects, cost, and method of administration. Smith (1990) recommends that drug therapy begin with a single antiepileptic drug, although the individual experiencing more than one type of seizure may need more than one drug to gain control of the seizures. Drugs such as carbamazepine (Tegretol), phenobarbital (Luminal and others) and phenytoin (Dilantin) are used to treat tonic-clonic seizures; valproic acid (Depakene, Depakote) is effective in treating a variety of seizures (Brodie and Dichter: 1996). On December 1, 1999, the Food and Drug Administration approved a new drug called levetiracetam (Keppra) for use in combination with other antiepileptic drugs to control partial seizures. Although dizziness and sleepiness are possible side effects, clinical trials did not disclose any harmful interaction with other medications or liver damage. Blood tests are used to monitor the efficacy of the chosen drug.

It is important for women with epilepsy to maintain a fixed schedule for taking medication. Missing a dose, ceasing to take medication, or taking the wrong dosage may lead to seizure activity. Women taking antiepileptic medication should tell physicians treating them for other conditions about their epilepsy medicine and inquire about interactions with both over-the-counter products and prescription drugs such as antibiotics, birth control pills, pain medications, decongestants, and cimetidine (Tagament HB), used to treat stomach problems. Two-thirds of the individuals who are treated successfully with antiepileptic drugs may be weaned off these medications (Brodie and Dichter: 1996).

Side effects of antiepileptic drugs may include nausea, fatigue, slurring of words, staggering, or allergic reactions (a rash or hives). Some women experience emotional changes, while others may note memory, learning, or behavior problems. Effects on appearance are not uncommon, including alopecia (hair loss) and weight gain (McGuire: 1991). Women should ask the physician about each drug's side effects and what to do if a reaction occurs.

Experimental drugs are available through special testing programs at medical epilepsy centers. The Epilepsy Foundation will direct individuals to a local center (see "ORGANIZATIONS" section below).

Surgery may be considered when the seizures always originate in one part of the brain; if medication has been unsuccessful; or when surgery will not affect vision, speech, movement, or memory. In resective surgery, the portion of the brain that causes the seizures is removed. In a lobectomy, all or part of the temporal, frontal, parietal, or occipital lobes is removed in order to reduce partial seizures. Sixty-five to 85% of individuals who have temporal lobectomies are free of seizures (Epilepsy Foundation: 1998a). Individuals who experience drop attacks, seizures that cause them to drop to the floor, may undergo surgery to interrupt the nerve pathways by cutting into the hemispheres of the brain in a procedure called a corpus callostomy (Gumnit: 1997). Individuals considering surgery must understand that although surgical procedures may reduce the number and frequency of drop attacks, most individuals will still require medication to bring remaining seizure activity under control (Gumnit: 1997).

Tyler (1990) believes that surgery is not considered as often as it should be because the danger of such surgery is overestimated and the benefits underestimated. In addition, family physicians sometimes lack knowledge of specialized epilepsy surgery centers. The National Institute of Neurological Disorders and Stroke (1988) reports that more than 100,000 individuals with partial seizures who do not respond to medical therapy are candidates for surgery. Women should ask physicians about the risks and benefits of surgery in their own situation. If a physician cannot supply the information, women should ask for a referral to another specialist or contact the National Institute of Neurological Disorders and Stroke for information on surgical procedures. The National Institutes of Health Consensus Development Conference on Surgery for Epilepsy (1990) discussed selection of patients for surgery, diagnostic methods, choices of surgical procedures, and outcome measures. Although controlled trials had not been conducted and investigations differed in their patient criteria and procedures, the panel agreed that surgery is an alternative option when seizures cannot be controlled by medication. A study found that nearly six years after individuals with epilepsy had undergone surgery, two-thirds had had no more than one seizure or experienced only auras compared with 11% of patients who had not had surgery (Vickrey et al.: 1995). The subjects who had surgery were also taking less medication than they had prior to surgery.

In a recent study, Wiebe and colleagues (2001) conducted a randomized, controlled trial of temporal-lobe surgery and concluded that surgery was superior to medical treatment. Nearly 60% of the patients who had had surgery were free of seizures impairing awareness compared with only eight percent of those treated with AEDs.

Brain surgery should never be undertaken without serious investigation into the pro's and con's. Talking with other women who have chosen surgery and those who have not may help the woman make the best possible decision for her health.

In 1997, the Food and Drug Administration (FDA) approved the use of the NeuroCybernetic Prosthesis System, an implantable electronic nerve stimulator for use in seizure control. Called vagus nerve stimulation (VNS), the device is programmed to deliver short bursts of electrical energy to the brain via the vagus nerve. A magnet is used to activate the generator if seizure seems to be imminent. Hoarseness and changes in voice quality are common side effects. The Epilepsy Foundation (2001) reports that about a third of the individuals who use VNS have a major improvement in seizure control, about a third have some improvement, and the remainder experience no improvement. VNS is used in addition to medication.

EPILEPSY IN OLDER WOMEN

The hormonal fluctuations associated with menopause may cause changes in seizure patterns. Some women with epilepsy require adjustments to their medication regimen. Seizures in older women may be the result of systemic illness; the use of medications such as analgesics and antihistamines; or the withdrawal of sedative drugs. The incidence of epilepsy increases in later life, with nearly 20% of newly diagnosed cases of epilepsy occurring in post-menopausal women (Usiskin: 1991). It is crucial to identify any primary medical conditions that may precipitate seizures. Examples of systemic illnesses which may cause seizure activity include strokes (which may cause acute seizures followed by recurring seizure activity) and either primary or metastatic brain tumors. Once seizures symptomatic of systemic illness have been distinguished from epilepsy, they should be treated by managing the precipitating event without the use of antiepileptic drugs (Troupin and Johannessen: 1990).

Antiepileptic drugs affect the supply of calcium to an older woman's bones, contributing to the development of osteoporosis. Consequently they are more vulnerable to fractures if a seizure results in a fall. Tonic-clonic seizures pose additional problems for elders who also have heart or pulmonary disease. Stress on the heart, pain, or breathing problems are potential aftereffects of such seizures (Devinsky: 1994).

Older women with chronic epilepsy may be affected by pharmacologic changes, such as changes in metabolism related to the aging process, and may require adjustment in their usual seizure therapy. Side effects of medication, such as balance problems, confusion, and drowsiness, may put them at risk for falls. Because older women often take drugs for a variety of conditions, those with epilepsy must be concerned about the interaction of these drugs and antiepileptic drugs. For example, cimetidine (Tagamet HB), used to treat stomach problems common in elders, is now available for over-the-counter purchase. However, cimetidine raises the levels of many antiepileptic drugs (Gumnit: 1997). Some antibiotics taken with antiepileptic drugs are also toxic. Women should be certain to ask their physicians about the possible interaction among the various drugs they are taking.

SEXUAL FUNCTIONING

In the past, individuals with epilepsy were forbidden by law to marry, due to false beliefs about the role of heredity and mental function. Now that there is a better understanding of epilepsy, these laws no longer exist. Marriage and childbearing rates in women with epilepsy do not differ from those for women without epilepsy (Epilepsy Foundation of America: 1987).

In some individuals, epilepsy reduces libido and therefore sexual activity. Antiepileptic medications, such as barbiturates, may suppress libido; a change of medication may be helpful. Women with epilepsy may fear close relationships, because they do not feel comfortable disclosing their condition. Some women may fear that sexual activity will cause seizures and that the seizures will be detrimental to their sexual relations. A commercial, water soluble lubricant may alleviate problems such as vaginal dryness or spasms reported by many women. Usiskin (1991) reports that some women confuse the physical characteristics of a seizure with orgasm. Although talking about epilepsy may be difficult at first, it is important to inform anyone who spends time with the woman, including sexual partners, about the condition and what to do if a seizure occurs.

190

FAMILY PLANNING, PREGNANCY, AND CHILDREARING

Hormonal fluctuations may affect seizure patterns throughout a woman's life. Puberty may signal an end to some types of seizures or mark the beginning of other seizure disorders. *Catamenial epilepsy* is the term used to describe exacerbations which occur just before or at the onset of menstruation. Women with epilepsy whose seizures originate in the temporal lobes may have more reproductive disorders than women who do not have epilepsy (Epilepsy Foundation: 1998b).

Women who choose oral contraceptives for birth control should tell their physicians if they take antiepileptic drugs. Certain antiepileptic drugs, such as phenobarbital, impair the effectiveness of birth control pills. The physician should recommend an oral contraceptive that will be most effective for birth control while still taking measures to prevent seizure activity. Women who use certain antiepileptic drugs are advised to use barrier methods of contraception, such as spermicidal cream, diaphragm, or condom, in addition to hormonal contraception. Since 1991 another method of contraception available in this country is Norplant, the implantation of a synthetic progesterone that prevents ovulation for as long as five years. Although side effects are minimal, women who take certain antiepileptic drugs such as Dilantin or Tegretol are advised against using Norplant (Murphy: 1993). Women have filed suit against the manufacturer of Norplant for pain and scarring associated with its removal. Fertility rates are reduced in women with epilepsy, especially in those who have complex partial seizures (Kurtz: 1991).

At least 90% of women with epilepsy who are treated with antiepileptic drugs deliver infants with no birth defects (Epilepsy Foundation: 1998c). However, pregnancy in women with epilepsy is considered high risk and requires special management by neurologists and obstetricians. Women with epilepsy who plan to become pregnant should discuss their medications with their physician prior to conception. If they wait until after conception, the fetus may already have fully formed organs and the opportunity to alter drug therapy may have passed (Crawford: 1993). Since all antiepileptic drugs have been implicated in an increase in birth defects, and some cause developmental delays of the central nervous system (Morrison and Rieder: 1993), prepregnancy counseling should include a discussion of the risk factors for both mother and child.

The probability of prematurity, neonatal and perinatal death, stillbirth, and hemorrhage in the fetus is higher for women with epilepsy than for women who do not have epilepsy (Crawford: 1993). The risk of birth defects is two to three times higher for the children of women with epilepsy who are taking medication to control seizures than for women who do not have epilepsy. Birth defects are one to two times more frequent in the children of women with epilepsy who are not taking seizure medication than in the children of women who do not have epilepsy (Epilepsy Foundation: 1998c). The most common birth defects are cleft lip, cleft palate, and congenital heart conditions. Women who take antiepileptic drugs such as valproate or carbamazepine, commonly prescribed drugs for epilepsy management despite recent controversy over their safety during pregnancy (Morrison and Rieder: 1993), have a higher risk of delivering a child with spina bifida (Treiman: 1993). Gumnit (1997) advises women who are taking antiepileptic drugs to take folic acid supplements prior to becoming pregnant and throughout the pregnancy to reduce the risk of spina bifida in their offspring. Ultrasound tests may detect the presence of this congenital malformation.

Seizures are likely to increase in frequency during pregnancy in a large proportion of mothers. There is some debate over the ability to predict increased frequency of seizures. Montouris and colleagues (1979) indicate that frequency of seizures during the two years prior to pregnancy is a good predictor of seizures during pregnancy. However, Yerby (1991) states that it is difficult to predict which women will be likely to have increased seizures, as they are not related to type of epilepsy, its duration, or seizures during previous pregnancies. It is known that there is greater risk to the fetus for mothers who have seizures during pregnancy than those who do not. Some mothers deliberately reduce the dosage of their antiepileptic drugs during pregnancy because of their fears of the drugs' effect on the fetus, and therefore may be subject to having seizures. It is known that the metabolic changes that occur during pregnancy cause the antiepileptic drugs to be less effective, even when their dosage remains constant. If the mother has a seizure while pregnant and her breathing is affected, a lack of oxygen to the fetus may be a concern; if she falls, she may also cause harm to herself and to the fetus. Mothers who experience tonic-clonic seizures are especially at risk for falling. These generalized seizures may result in the suppression of fetal heart beat, and, less commonly, miscarriage. Partial seizures do not present the same risk unless they become generalized to the whole brain (Yerby: 1991).

If a woman has been seizure free for years, she and her physician may decide to decrease antiepileptic drugs gradually over a period of time before she conceives. If this strategy is not possible due to seizure activity, the use of a single antiepileptic drug in the lowest effective dose to maintain seizure control is recommended (International League Against Epilepsy: 1993).

Some women develop their first seizures during pregnancy, a condition called gestational epilepsy. Three-quarters of these women will have seizures after pregnancy; many of these women have vascular abnormalities or tumors which are activated by the changes that occur during pregnancy (Montouris et al.: 1979).

Women should be carefully monitored during pregnancy and may expect to require some adjustment in antiepileptic medication. Infants born to mothers with epilepsy who take certain antiepileptic drugs may develop hemorrhagic disease due to an insufficient levels of vitamin K. This disorder may be prevented by the administration of vitamin K to the mother prior to delivery and to the newborn after delivery. Blood clotting studies should be performed to ensure that clotting times have become normal. Babies born to mothers who have taken barbiturates such as phenobarbital to control seizure activity during pregnancy may exhibit excessive sleepiness or drug withdrawal after delivery.

Crawford (1993) reports that children whose mothers have epilepsy are more likely to develop the condition than those whose fathers have epilepsy. The risks are greater if both parents or other family members have epilepsy. A genetics specialist can offer information on risks, based on the family's epilepsy history. The fact remains, however, that most women with epilepsy give birth to children who do not develop the condition.

If the mother is not free of seizures, it is important that she have sufficient assistance with child care to avoid seizure related accidents to both herself and the child. A mother may choose bottle feeding over breastfeeding so that this duty can be shared with a partner or child care assistant. The lack of sleep encountered by new mothers may trigger a seizure. Women who experience an aura or another warning sign prior to a seizure should consider using a personal emergency response system to summon help before they lose consciousness. A woman who adapted her child care patterns describes them as follows:

> As a mother with frequent seizures, I was very concerned for the baby, but I managed to keep things simple. When he cried, I'd hold him while sitting on the floor. That's how I fed and changed him, too. I'd wait to bathe him until my husband was home. Then we'd both give him a bath, which was fun. (Epilepsy Foundation of America: 1996)

In addition to these suggestions, women should also consider wearing a medical identification bracelet indicating that they have epilepsy so that emergency assistance may be provided appropriately.

Seeing their mother experience a seizure can be very frightening to children. As soon as they are old enough to understand, parents should explain the mother's condition to their children. Children should learn how to summon help if their mother has a seizure and what they can do to help her. Most telephones may be pre-programmed for emergency calls to fire, police, and rescue squads. Usiskin (1991) describes how she taught her own children to cope with her seizures by assigning them each a role, such as placing a cloth under her face to prevent abrasion. Learning that their mother is not in pain during the seizures can be very comforting information for the children.

PSYCHOLOGICAL ASPECTS OF EPILEPSY

Various studies have concluded that depression is more common among people with epilepsy than among the general population. Although these studies have been conducted by psychiatrists, neurologists, and general practitioners, they are all remarkably consistent in reaching this conclusion (Robertson: 1991).

The diagnosis of epilepsy is difficult to accept:

> Some individuals are more disabled by the fact that they have epilepsy than by the seizures themselves and unduly restrict their activities or withdraw from social interactions (Dichter: 1994, 2233).

Depression in women with epilepsy may be due to the stresses of living with epilepsy; employment problems; or the inability to drive. They may complain of fatigue or feeling sad; may sleep poorly; or may be unable to concentrate. These symptoms may be related to having epilepsy, or they may signal a problem with medication. Masland (1985) found that disability in individuals with epilepsy was related to the disruption caused by the seizures; the effects of associated neurological impairments, including those caused by drugs; reactions of society; and the individual's self-concept.

Snyder's study (1990) of individuals age 18 or over who had had epilepsy for at least one year found that the need to take medications regularly and not knowing when a seizure would occur caused the greatest amount of stress. Ostracism, which has often been cited as a cause of stress, was not a high stressor for these subjects. Individuals who ranked their health as good were more likely to take measures to control their health than were subjects who ranked their health as poor; such measures included relaxation techniques and biofeedback, although the efficacy of these measures is not known.

Upton (1993) reports that perceived support from both family and friends was a factor in the emotional adjustment of individuals with epilepsy. He also found that gender was unrelated to social support or emotional adjustment. Upton and Thompson (1992) found that those subjects who used "wish fulfilling fantasies" as a coping mechanism, that is they wished for a miracle that would cure them, had low levels of self-esteem and acceptance of the condition and high levels of anxiety and depression. Those who coped through "cognitive restructuring," finding positive aspects to the condition such as developing inner strength, were most likely to accept the condition and have lower levels of anxiety, depression, and social avoidance. Participating in a self-help group or discussing negative feelings with a physician, psychologist, or social worker may be helpful. Some people also use stress reduction and relaxation techniques.

Unemployment and underemployment are among the most serious social problems of individuals with epilepsy. It is important that employers understand the effects of epilepsy and antiepileptic drugs. Although unpredictable seizures are hazardous in certain environments, they are less significant than the ignorance and fear of employers and employees. It is equally important that unfounded myths and stereotypes be confronted so that women with epilepsy have the opportunity they deserve in the workplace. However, it is often difficult for them to choose when to disclose their condition. Poor self-image may have a negative effect on the skills necessary to seek employment and interpersonal relationships. The combination of self-stigma, perceived and actual societal stigma, and the lack of social skills and confidence leads to a tendency to blame epilepsy for every failure in life.

The lack of a driver's license can be a significant barrier to employment, activities of everyday living, and social life for women with epilepsy. In most states, individuals must be free of seizures for six months to one year in order to be eligible for a driver's license. A letter from a physician which states that seizures are under control may be required.

It is often difficult for women with epilepsy to purchase health, life, or automobile insurance. Even when insurance is available, the premiums may be very high or exclusions may be made for claims relating to epilepsy.

PROFESSIONAL SERVICE PROVIDERS

Women who experience a seizure will first see a *primary care physician*. Hospitalization may be required to observe the individual for progressive symptoms or additional seizures. An outpatient visit may be sufficient if the seizure occurred more than a week before medical consultation and was an isolated event. The primary care physician may initiate treatment at this time.

If initial treatment does not achieve seizure control in about three months, a woman should be referred to a *neurologist* for a thorough evaluation. A neurologist is a physician who diagnoses and treats conditions involving the brain and nervous system, including epilepsy. A *neurosurgeon* performs any necessary brain surgery.

If seizures are not under control within nine months of treatment, referral to a comprehensive treatment center is recommended. The National Association of Epilepsy Centers has established guidelines for these specialized epilepsy treatment centers (Gumnit: 1990). Women who wish to become pregnant should be treated jointly by their neurologist and their *obstetrician*. Together these physicians and the woman can develop a plan to manage seizures and to protect the health of the woman and her fetus.

Social workers provide information about financial and medical benefits, housing, and community resources. They conduct individual, family, or group counseling and may refer individuals to self-help or peer counseling groups.

Rehabilitation counselors coordinate services such as vocational rehabilitation, education, and training for women with epilepsy. The rehabilitation counselor can serve as an advocate with prospective employers who may be uninformed or fearful about hiring an individual with epilepsy. Women with epilepsy who are unemployed or underemployed should apply to their state vocational rehabilitation agency for assistance with career planning, training, and placement.

A study (Morrell and colleagues: 2000) of a wide range of health care providers who are likely to treat women with epilepsy found that most were unfamiliar with the relationship between epilepsy and menstruation, female hormones, infertility, and sexual dysfunction. Liporace and D'Abreu (2003) suggest that optimal care for women with epilepsy requires the collaboration of neurologists, obstetricians/gynecologist, internists, and other practitioners.

WHERE TO FIND SERVICES

Physicians who treat people with epilepsy are often located in private practices. Women who live in metropolitan areas will find neurological clinics and comprehensive epilepsy centers available at major hospitals or universities. Comprehensive epilepsy centers and programs around the country provide medical care; conduct multidisciplinary research; train physicians, nurses, and other caregivers; and help to organize community services. They are usually affiliated with university medical centers and serve a designated geographic area. The Epilepsy Foundation will refer individuals to local affiliates.

ENVIRONMENTAL ADAPTATIONS

Women whose seizures are under control have no restrictions on their recreational activities. However, it is important to take extra precautions with activities such as swimming, waterskiing, scuba, and sky diving, since the occurrence of a seizure is very dangerous while engaged in these activities. It is a good idea for women to wear an identification bracelet or necklace or carry a wallet card which indicates that they have epilepsy. When traveling, it is wise to carry a letter from a physician describing the seizure disorder and medications currently used. A medication routine may need to be adjusted when travel affects sleep schedules. A pill organizer or medication calendar helps individuals remember to take medications according to the dosage schedule that will be most effective in controlling seizures.

Personal safety should be considered in everyday activities. Lowering the temperature of the water and sitting down to shower may prevent injury if a seizure occurs while bathing. Wall-to-wall carpeting and padding on sharp corners reduce the risk of injury in falls. In the kitchen, using appliances such as food processors and blenders lowers the risk of injuries due to sharp knives. Using a microwave oven reduces burns and substituting plastic cups and dishes prevents cuts when a seizure occurs. Safety gates at the top of staircases; automatic shut-off switches on appliances such as irons, power tools, and lawnmowers; and barriers in front of fireplaces, hot radiators, and heaters, will also prevent injuries.

HOW TO RECOGNIZE A SEIZURE AND GIVE FIRST AID

Epileptic seizures have been mistakenly identified as heart attacks, drunkenness, and drug overdoses. It is important for all health professionals, rehabilitation professionals, and the general public to recognize epileptic seizures and to know simple first aid for epilepsy.

- Remove hard or sharp items that are in the vicinity.
- Loosen the collar to make breathing easier.
- Place a flat, soft cushion, folded jacket, or sweater under the individual's head.
- Gently turn her head to the side to help keep the airway clear. Do not try to place any object between the teeth of anyone experiencing a seizure.
- Do not try to stop her jerking movements.
- Check to see if she is wearing an identification bracelet or necklace or carrying an identification card which states that she has epilepsy.
- Remain with her until the seizure ends and offer assistance, if needed.
- If she seems confused, offer to call a family member, friend, or taxi to help her get home.
- If the seizure continues for more than five minutes, if another seizure begins shortly after the first, or if she does not regain consciousness after the jerking movements have ceased, call an ambulance. If she has other medical conditions such as heart disease or diabetes or she is pregnant, it is also wise to call an ambulance.
- If the individual is having an absence seizure, she may have a dazed appearance, stare into space, or exhibit automatic behavior such as shaking an arm or leg.

Speak quietly and calmly and move her away from any dangerous areas, such as a flight of stairs or a stove. Remain with her until she regains consciousness.

References

Brodie, Martin J. and Marc A. Dichter
1996   "Antiepileptic Drugs" The New England Journal of Medicine 335(January):3:168-175
Crawford, Pamela
1993   "Epilepsy and Pregnancy" Seizure 2:87-90
Devinsky, Orrin
1994   A Guide to Understanding and Living with Epilepsy Philadelphia, PA: F.A. Davis Company
Dichter, Mark A.
1994   "The Epilepsies and Convulsive Disorders" pp. 2223-2244 in Kurt J. Isselbacher et al. (eds.) Harrison's Principles of Internal Medicine New York, NY: McGraw Hill
Epilepsy Foundation
2001   VNS Therapy for Epilepsy Landover, MD: Epilepsy Foundation
1998a   Surgery for Epilepsy Landover, MD: Epilepsy Foundation
1998b   Hormones and Epilepsy Landover, MD: Epilepsy Foundation
1998c   Epilepsy & Pregnancy Landover, MD: Epilepsy Foundation
1996   Safety and Seizures Landover, MD: Epilepsy Foundation of America
1993   Questions and Answers About Epilepsy Landover, MD: Epilepsy Foundation of America
1992   Seizure Recognition and Observation Landover, MD: Epilepsy Foundation of America
1987   Epilepsy: Part of Your Life Landover, MD: Epilepsy Foundation of America
Gumnit, Robert J.
1997   Living Well with Epilepsy New York, NY: Demos Vermande
1990   "Interplay of Economics, Politics, and Quality in the Care of Patients with Epilepsy: The Formation of the National Association of Epilepsy Centers" Appendix I in Dennis B. Smith (ed.) Epilepsy: Current Approaches to Diagnosis and Treatment New York, NY: Raven Press
International League Against Epilepsy, Commission on Genetics, Pregnancy and the Child
1993   "Guidelines for the Care of Women of Childbearing Age with Epilepsy" Epilepsia 34(4):588-589
Kurtz, Zarrina
1991   "Sex Differences in Epilepsy: Epidemiological Aspects" in Michael R. Trimble (ed.) Women and Epilepsy Chichester, England: John Wiley & Sons
Liporace, J. and A. D'Abreu
2003   "Epilepsy and Women's Health: Family Planning, Bone Health, Menopause, and Menstrual-Related Seizures" Mayo Clinic Proceedings 78:4(April):497-506
Masland, R.L.
1985   "Psychosocial Aspects of Epilepsy" pp. 357-377 in Roger J. Porter (ed.) The Epilepsies Stoneham, MA: Butterworth-Heineman
McGuire, A.M.
1991   "Quality of Life in Women with Epilepsy" pp. 13-30 in Michael R. Trimble (ed.) Women and Epilepsy Chichester, England: John Wiley & Sons
Montouris, Georgia D., Gerald M. Fenichel, and L. William McLain
1979   "The Pregnant Epileptic: A Review and Recommendations" Archives of Neurology 36-(October):601-603

Morrell, Martha J. et al.
2000   "Health Issues for Women with Epilepsy: A Descriptive Survey to Assess Knowledge and Awareness among Healthcare Providers" Journal of Women's Health & Gender-Based Medicine 9:9:959-965

Morrison, C. and M. J. Rieder
1993   "Practices of Epilepsy during Pregnancy: A Survey of Canadian Neurologists" Reproductive Toxicology 7:1:55-59

Murphy, Eileen
1993   "Norplant: A New Birth Control Option for Women with Disabilities" Resourceful Woman 2(Fall)3:1,5

National Information Center for Children and Youth with Disabilities
2002   Epilepsy Fact Sheet 2002 Washington, DC

National Institute of Neurological Disorders and Stroke
1988   The Surgical Management of Epilepsy Bethesda, MD: National Institute of Neurological Disorders and Stroke

1984   Positron Emission Tomography: Emerging Research Opportunities in the Neurosciences Bethesda, MD: National Institute of Neurological Disorders and Stroke

Robertson, Mary M.
1991   "Depression in Epilepsy" pp. 223-242 in Michael R. Trimble (ed.) Women and Epilepsy Chichester, England: John Wiley & Sons

Smith, Dennis B.
1990   "Antiepileptic Drug Selection in Adults" pp. 111-138 in Dennis B. Smith (ed.) Epilepsy: Current Approaches to Diagnosis and Treatment New York, NY: Raven Press

Snyder, Mariah
1990   "Stressors, Coping Mechanisms, and Perceived Health in Persons with Epilepsy" International Disability Studies 12:3:100-103

Treiman, D.M.
1993   "Current Treatment Strategies in Selected Situations in Epilepsy" Epilepsia 34 Suppl 5:S17-23

Troupin, Alan S. and Svein I. Johannessen
1990   "Epilepsy in the Elderly" pp. 141-153 in Dennis B. Smith (ed.) Epilepsy: Current Approaches to Diagnosis and Treatment New York, NY: Raven Press

Tyler, Allen R.
1990   "The Role of Surgery in Therapy for Epilepsy" pp. 173-182 in Dennis B. Smith (ed.) Epilepsy: Current Approaches to Diagnosis and Treatment New York, NY: Raven Press

Upton, Dominic
1993   "Social Support and Emotional Adjustment in People with Chronic Epilepsy" Journal of Epilepsy 6:2:105-111

Upton, Dominic and Pamela J. Thompson
1992   "Effectiveness of Coping Strategies Employed by People with Chronic Epilepsy" Journal of Epilepsy 5:2:119-127

Usiskin, Susan C.
1991   "The Woman with Epilepsy" pp. 3-12 in Michael R. Trimble (ed.) Women and Epilepsy Chichester, England: John Wiley & Sons

Vickrey, Barbara G. et al.
1995   "Outcomes in 248 Patients Who Had Diagnostic Evaluations for Epilepsy Surgery" The Lancet 346(December 2):1445-1449

Wiebe, Samuel et al.
2001   "A Randomized, Controlled Trial of Surgery for Temporal-Lobe Epilepsy" <u>New England Journal of Medicine</u> 345:5(August 2):311-318

Yerby, Mark S.
1991   "Pregnancy and Teratogenesis" pp. 167-192 in Michael R. Trimble (ed.) <u>Women and Epilepsy</u> Chichester, England: John Wiley & Sons

ORGANIZATIONS

AED (Antiepileptic Drug) Pregnancy Registry
Massachusetts General Hospital
(888) 233-2334   www.aedpregnancyregistry.org

This project is recruiting women who are taking antiepileptic drugs for a study of the fetal risks of the drugs during pregnancy. Requires three toll-free interviews.

American Epilepsy Society
342 North Main Street
West Hartford, CT 06117
(860) 586-7505   FAX (860) 586-7550   e-mail: info@aes.org
www.aes.org

A professional society of neurologists interested in seizure disorders and epilepsy. Promotes research on these conditions. Articles from their publication "Epilepsy Currents" are available on the web site.

Brain Injury Association
105 North Alfred Street
Alexandria, VA 22314
Family Helpline (800) 444-6443   (703) 236-6000   FAX (703) 236-6001
e-mail: publicrelations@biausa.org   www.biausa.org

Provides information and support for individuals with head injury, their families, and professionals. (Seizures are often precipitated by a head injury.) Local affiliates. Membership, $35.00, includes newsletter, "TBI Challenge!" published six times a year, and discounts on publications, conferences, and seminars. Also publishes the "National Directory of Brain Injury Rehabilitation Services;" $16.00. Many publications available on the web site, free.

Brain Resources and Information Network (BRAIN)
National Institute of Neurological Disorders and Stroke (NINDS)
PO Box 5801
Bethesda, MD 20824
(800) 352-9424   FAX (301) 402-2186
e-mail: braininfo@ninds.nh.gov   www.ninds.nih.gov

Supports clinical and basic research, maintains national specimen banks for the study of brain and other tissue, and publishes professional and public education materials. The web site has information about the disease and clinical studies. Many publications available on the web site and in print, free. Click on "Disorders," and then "Request Mailed Brochures." Some publications available in Spanish.

Citizens United for Research in Epilepsy (CURE)
730 North Franklin Street, Suite 404
Chicago, IL 60610
(312) 255-1800   FAX (312) 255-1809
e-mail: info@CUREepilepsy.org   www.CUREepilepsy.org

This grass roots organization supports increased funding from the government for research and raises funds for private funding of research. Information about applications for grants available on web site.

Epilepsy.com
e-mail: bwissler@comcast.net   www.epilepsy.com

Established by physicians, this web site includes information about the disease, stories by people who have the disease, and a special section for women that includes information about folic acid, preparing for pregnancy, and epilepsy medications and breast feeding.

Epilepsy Foundation (EF)
4351 Garden City Drive, Suite 406
Landover, MD 20785-2267
(800) 332-1000   (301) 459-3700   FAX (301) 577-2684
e-mail: postmaster@efa.org   www.epilelsyfoundation.org

Provides information and education, advocacy, research support, and services to individuals with epilepsy, their family members, and professionals. Some publications and audio-visual materials are available in Spanish. Membership, $25.00, includes discount on publications and videotapes, and quarterly newsletter, "EpilepsyUSA." Some brochures available on the web site or in print, free. Local affiliates. Sponsors e-community chat rooms, including a special one for women. Also sponsors the "Epilepsy Foundation Gene Discovery Project," which enrolls families with histories of epilepsy in research studies. Individuals may register online at the web site. The "National Epilepsy Library" is a professional library for physicians and other health professionals. Maintains the Epilepsy and Seizure Disorders Information database of articles and publications on medical and psychosocial aspects of epilepsy.

Epilepsy-L
home.ease.lsoft.com/Archives/Epilepsy-L.html

This e-mail support group enables participants to "chat" with others who have seizure disorders and their family members.

MEDLINEplus: Epilepsy
www.nlm.nih.gov/medlineplus/epilepsy.html

This web site provides links to sites for general information about epilepsy, symptoms and diagnosis, treatment, alternative therapy, clinical trials, disease management, nutrition, children with epilepsy, organizations, and research. Provides links to MEDLINE research articles and related MEDLINEplus pages.

National Association of Epilepsy Centers (NAEC)
5775 Wayzata Boulevard, Suite 225
Minneapolis, MN 55416
(703) 525-4526   FAX (703) 525-1560
e-mail: contact@naecepilepsy.org   naecepilepsy.org

An organization of epilepsy centers that helps to develop standards for medical and surgical treatment of epilepsy and for the facilities and programs that serve individuals with epilepsy. The NAEC also advises government and industry officials about the needs of people with epilepsy and offers technical assistance to the centers serving these individuals.

<u>National Easter Seal Society</u>
230 West Monroe Street, Suite 1800
Chicago, IL 60606
(800) 221-6827   (312) 726-6200   (312) 726-4258 (TTY)
FAX (312) 726-1494   e-mail: info@easter-seals.org   www.easter-seals.org

Provides information and services to individuals with epilepsy, their families, and professionals. Local affiliates.

<u>National Stroke Association</u>
9707 East Easter Lane
Englewood, Colorado 80112-5112
(800) 787-6537   (303) 649-9299   FAX (303) 649-1328
e-mail: info@stroke.org   www.stroke.org

Assists individuals with stroke and educates their families, physicians, and the general public about stroke and the risk of seizures. Suggested minimum membership, $25.00, includes quarterly newsletter, "Stroke Smart," and discount on publications. Those unable to pay may receive the newsletter at no cost.

The Brainstorms Companion: Epilepsy in Our View
by Steven C. Schachter
Lippincott Williams & Wilkins
PO Box 1600
Hagerstown, MD 21741
(800) 441-4526   FAX (301) 223-2400
e-mail: lrorders@lww.com   www.lww.com

In this book, information about epilepsy is presented through the experiences of family members, friends, and associates of people with the condition. Information about types of seizures and living safely with epilepsy is also discussed. $35.00

The Brainstorms Women and Epilepsy in Our Lives
by Kaarkuzhali Babu Krishnamurthy et al.
Lippincott Williams & Wilkins
PO Box 1600
Hagerstown, MD 21741
(800) 441-4526   FAX (301) 223-2400
e-mail: lrorders@lww.com   www.lww.com

In this book, women tell their stories of coping with epilepsy in every stage of life including the reproductive years. $35.00

The Center of Her Storm
Fanlight Productions
4196 Washington Street, Suite 2
Boston, MA 02131
(800) 937-4113   (617) 469-4999   FAX (617) 469-3379
e-mail: fanlight@fanlight.com www.fanlight.com

This videotape focuses on a 24 year old woman who has complex partial seizures due to epilepsy. It follows her through her daily activities and life following surgery for the disease. 55 minutes. $199.00

Directory of Prescription Drug Patient Assistance Programs
Pharmaceutical Manufacturers Association
1100 15th Street, NW
Washington, DC 20005
(800) 762-4636   www.phrma.org

A list of members that offer certain drugs at low or no cost to uninsured or underinsured patients. Most programs require that a physician make the request. Free. Also available on the web site.

Driving: Information for People with Seizure Disorders
Epilepsy Foundation (see "ORGANIZATIONS" section above)
(800) 213-5821   www.epilepsyfoundation.org

This videotape describes how people whose seizures are under control may obtain a driver's license and offers practical advice to those who cannot drive due to uncontrolled seizures.   13 minutes. Available in English and Spanish. $19.95.

Epilepsy and the Family
Epilepsy Foundation (see "ORGANIZATIONS" section above)
(800) 213-5821   www.epilepsyfoundation.org

In this videotape, family members discuss medical and family challenges.   12 minutes. $16.95

Epilepsy and the Family
by Richard Lechtenberg
Harvard University Press
79 Garden Street
Cambridge, MA 02138
(800) 405-1619   (401) 531-2800   FAX (800) 406-9145
e-mail: hup@harvard.edu   www.hup.harvard.edu

In addition to basic information on epilepsy, this book discusses children growing up with a parent or sibling who has epilepsy and $15.95.

Epilepsy A to Z: A Glossary of Epilepsy Terminology
by Peter W. Kaplan, Pierre Loiseau, Robert S. Fisher, and Pierre Jallon
Demos Medical Publishing
386 Park Avenue South, Suite 201
New York, NY 10016
(800) 532-8663   (212) 683-0072
FAX (212) 683-0118   e-mail: info@demospub.com   www.demosmedpub.com

This book provides definitions and discussions of terms used in epilepsy including diagnostic procedures and medical and surgical treatments.   References to other source materials are also provided. $34.95 Orders made on the Demos web site receive a 15% discount.

Epilepsy: 199 Answers
by Andrew N. Wilner
Demos Medical Publishing
386 Park Avenue South, Suite 201
New York, NY 10016
(800) 532-8663   (212) 683-0072
FAX (212) 683-0118   e-mail: info@demospub.com   www.demosmedpub.com

This guide answers patients' questions about the condition, tests, medications, and research and provides information on driving, work, first aid, and safety.   Includes a medical history form and seizure calendar. $19.95 Orders made on the Demos web site receive a 15% discount.

Epilepsy: The Untold Stories
by Paul J. Joseph and Mark R. Brown
Fanlight Productions
4196 Washington Street, Suite 2
Boston, MA 02131
(800) 937-4113 (617) 469-4999 FAX (617) 469-3379
e-mail: fanlight@fanlight.com www.fanlight.com

This videotape, featuring six individuals who have temporal lobe epilepsy, describes how complex partial seizures affect their lives. Also discusses clinical aspects, diagnosis, and treatment of epilepsy. 27 minutes. $149.00

First Aid for Seizures
Epilepsy Foundation (see "ORGANIZATIONS" section above)
(800) 213-5821 www.epilepsyfoundation.org

Printed in both English and Spanish, this poster gives simple first aid instruction for people experiencing a seizure. $2.05

A Guide to Understanding and Living with Epilepsy
by Orrin Devinsky
F.A. Davis Company
404-420 North 2nd Street
Philadelphia, PA 19123
(800) 323-3555 FAX (215) 440-3016
e-mail: orders@fadavis.com www.fadavis.com

This book discusses medical aspects of epilepsy and its diagnosis and treatment. Also describes epilepsy in children and in adults and legal and financial issues. $26.95

The Legal Rights of Persons with Epilepsy
Epilepsy Foundation (see "ORGANIZATIONS" section above)
(800) 213-5821 www.epilepsyfoundation.org

This book summarizes legal issues that affect individuals with epilepsy, such as employment, federal benefits, vocational rehabilitation, access to health care, and driving. $14.95

Living Well with Epilepsy
by Robert J. Gumnit
Demos Medical Publishing
386 Park Avenue South, Suite 201
New York, NY 10016
(800) 532-8663 (212) 683-0072
FAX (212) 683-0118 e-mail: info@demospub.com www.demosmedpub.com

Written for health professionals and individuals with epilepsy, this book discusses diagnosis and management of seizure disorders. $19.95   Orders made on the Demos web site receive a 15% discount.

Medicines for Epilepsy
Epilepsy Foundation (see "ORGANIZATIONS" section above)
(800) 213-5821   www.epilepsyfoundation.org

This pamphlet describes drugs used to treat epilepsy. Includes foldout chart with pictures of the drugs and list of side effects. $1.05

Mother To Be: A Guide to Pregnancy and Birth for Women with Disabilities
by Judith Rogers and Molleen Matsumura
Demos Medical Publishing
386 Park Avenue South, Suite 201
New York, NY 10016
(800) 532-8663   (212) 683-0072
FAX (212) 683-0118   e-mail: info@demospub.com   www.demosmedpub.com

This book describes the pregnancy and childbirth experiences of 36 women with a wide variety of disabilities including epilepsy. Suggests practical solutions for the special concerns of women with disabilities during pregnancy and those of their spouses, families, and health care providers. Includes a glossary and a bibliography. $29.95 Orders made on the Demos web site receive a 15% discount.

Parenting and You: A Guide for Parents with Seizure Disorders
When Mom or Dad Has Seizures: A Guide for Young People
Epilepsy Foundation (see "ORGANIZATIONS" section above)
(800) 213-5821   www.epilepsyfoundation.org

"Parenting and You" discusses pregnancy, child care, and parenting issues. "When Mom or Dad Has Seizures" examines how children of various ages might feel about a parent's seizure disorder. $14.95 each.

Pregnancy and Epilepsy
Epilepsy Foundation (see "ORGANIZATIONS" section above)
(800) 213-5821   www.epilepsyfoundation.org

This booklet answers women's questions about birth control, seizures during pregnancy, antiepileptic medications, birth defects, complications of pregnancy for mother and infant, and breastfeeding. $1.10

Seizures and Epilepsy: Hope through Research
National Institute of Neurological Disorders and Stroke (NINDS)
PO Box 5801
Bethesda, MD 20824
(800) 352-9424   FAX (301) 402-2186
e-mail: braininfo@ninds.nh.gov   www.ninds.nih.gov

This booklet describes the disorder, diagnosis, and treatment as well as current research on the disease. Free

Surgery for Epilepsy
Office of Medical Applications of Research
National Institutes of Health Consensus Program
6100 Executive Boulevard
Rockville, MD 20852
(888) 644-2667   (301) 496-5641   FAX (301) 402-0420
www.consensus.nih.gov

Published in 1990, this consensus statement concludes that brain surgery is an alternative treatment when medication fails to control seizures. Free. Also available on the web site.

Surgery for Epilepsy
Epilepsy Foundation (see "ORGANIZATIONS" section above)
(800) 213-5821   www.epilepsyfoundation.org

This pamphlet describes current surgical procedures. $.75

Voices from the Workplace
Epilepsy Foundation (see "ORGANIZATIONS" section above)
(800) 213-5821   www.epilepsyfoundation.org

Individuals with epilepsy describe the coping strategies they use in the workplace in this videotape. 14 minutes. $19.95

When the Brain Goes Wrong
Fanlight Productions
4196 Washington Street, Suite 2
Boston, MA 02131
(800) 937-4113   (617) 469-4999   FAX (617) 469-3379
e-mail: fanlight@fanlight.com   www.fanlight.com

This videotape, which deals with seven types of brain dysfunctions, describes the experiences of an individual with epilepsy. 45 minutes. $199.00

Women and Epilepsy
by Michael R. Trimble (ed.)
John Wiley & Sons, Indianapolis, IN

Written by professionals who conduct research, counsel, and treat individuals with epilepsy, this book focuses on quality of life, reproductive health, pregnancy, sexual functioning, and independent living. Out of print.

Women and Epilepsy Initiative
Epilepsy Foundation (see "ORGANIZATIONS" section above)
(800) 213-5821   www.epilepsyfoundation.org

This kit provides information for women with epilepsy and their health care providers. Includes fact sheets on subjects such as hormones, birth control, pregnancy, parenting, sexuality, antiepileptic medications, and menopause. $4.95

The Workbook: A Self-Study Guide for Job-Seekers with Epilepsy
Epilepsy Foundation (see "ORGANIZATIONS" section above)
(800) 213-5821   www.epilepsyfoundation.org

This workbook guides individuals with epilepsy in job searches through the use of self-study exercises for finding and retaining employment. $9.95

Chapter 8

LUPUS

More than 1.4 million people in the United States have lupus (Office on Women' Health: 2000). Being female is the major risk factor for the development of lupus (Hochberg: 1992). Although the exact numbers are not known, various authorities have suggested that lupus affects eight or ten (Arthritis Foundation: 1993) or 10 to 15 (Lahita: 1992a) times as many women after puberty as men. The prevalence of lupus among women of childbearing age, mid-teens to mid-40s, is considerably higher than among any other population group. Although the disease may occur in men, children, and elders, it is far less prevalent among these groups. Researchers believe that the immune system is affected by female hormones, thereby putting women at greater risk to develop lupus. Hochberg (1992) reports that incidence, prevalence, and mortality rates for lupus are three times as high in African-American women as in Caucasian women.

Lupus is a chronic disease in which the immune system, which normally protects the body, produces abnormal antibodies that attack the body's connective tissues directly or cause synovitis, an inflammation of the membrane lining the joints (the synovium). The antibodies are produced by the immune system in response to the presence of antigens (foreign materials such as bacteria and viruses) forming antigen-antibody complexes. These "autoantibodies" interfere with blood clotting and cause a variety of symptoms, such as joint swelling and pain, fatigue, skin rashes, pleurisy, and anemia (Lupus Foundation of America: 1993). Lupus autoantibodies may also attack the kidneys, skin, lungs, membranes surrounding the heart, white and red blood cells, and, occasionally, the central nervous system. Lupus and rheumatoid arthritis are considered members of the same family of diseases since both affect the synovium. Nearly half of the individuals who have lupus have arthritis (Fries: 1995).

Diagnosing lupus is difficult, due to the variety of symptoms and their similarity to symptoms of other inflammatory diseases. Its symptoms often occur in flares, when the disease is active, and subside when the disease is in remission. Although there is no cure for lupus, improved diagnostic techniques and medications allow many individuals to continue to live comfortably throughout a normal lifespan.

The cause of lupus is unknown, but scientists suspect that environmental factors such as exposure to ultraviolet rays (sunburn), familial or ethnically determined genetic factors, drug reactions, or hormonal factors, may trigger its symptoms. The National Institute of Arthritis and Musculoskeletal and Skin Diseases has funded two projects that are searching for genetic markers that may be used to identify possible lupus genes. The Lupus Multiplex Registry and Repository in Oklahoma City is enrolling families in which two or more members have been diagnosed with lupus (see "ORGANI-ZATIONS" section below). In the United States, autoimmune diseases such as lupus, multiple sclerosis, and rheumatoid arthritis affect a disproportionate number of women, nearly 79% of the 8.5 million individuals affected (Whitacre et al.: 1999). Researchers believe that differences in women's immune responses; the effects of sex hormones such as estrogen, progesterone, and testosterone; and genetic influences may account for this gender gap. In 1999, the National Multiple Sclerosis Society established the Task Force on Gender, MS, and Autoimmunity; members included basic and clinical scientists, to review current data and make research recommendations (see Chapter 10, "Multiple Sclerosis").

Lupus is diagnosed primarily through patient history, physical exam, and laboratory tests. In addition, urinalysis is used to measure kidney function. Although blood tests may determine the presence of antinuclear antibodies (antibodies that attack cell nuclei) and anti-DNA antibodies (antibodies that attack DNA), often confirming a diagnosis of lupus when other symptoms are present, false positive or false negative results are not uncommon, requiring further monitoring. Individuals who have symptoms of lupus but who do not produce these antibodies may now have a blood test for anti-SR protein antibodies. If diagnosed and treated during the initial acute flare, women with lupus have a good prognosis. It is rare to experience flares after reaching menopause (Berkow: 1987).

TYPES OF LUPUS

Cutaneous lupus (or *discoid lupus*) and *systemic lupus erythematosus* (SLE) are the two major types of lupus. A rare condition that is similar to systemic lupus erythematosus may be caused by certain medications used to treat blood pressure or heart problems. This *drug-induced lupus* usually disappears when the medications are discontinued.

Cutaneous lupus affects the skin, appearing as red, scaly, raised patches usually found on the face, ears, scalp, arms, and chest. "Butterfly rash" appears most commonly on the cheeks and over the bridge of the nose. The inflammation may be triggered by skin injury or overexposure to sunlight, or it may appear spontaneously with no apparent precipitating cause. Only about ten percent of the individuals who have cutaneous lupus develop the systemic form (Berkow: 1987). Hair loss, scarring, or loss of skin pigmentation may occur. A diagnosis of cutaneous lupus is confirmed by skin biopsy. It is usually treated by topical application or injection of a corticosteroid medication or prescription of an antimalarial drug. To reduce further occurrences of cutaneous lesions, individuals are advised to reduce exposure to sunlight and to use sunscreens with high sun protection factors (SPF). Unlike systemic lupus erythematosus, cutaneous lupus is more common in men than women (Lahita: 1992b).

In *systemic lupus erythematosus* (SLE), the immune system malfunctions, producing antibodies that either attack healthy tissues directly or produce an inflammatory reaction, affecting the connective tissues that bind the muscles, joints, and skin together. The manifestations of lupus may vary in the same individual and appear and disappear unpredictably.

In 1982, the American Rheumatism Association (now the American College of Rheumatology) published updated and revised criteria to be considered by physicians when classifying patients with lupus (Tan et al.: 1982). Although the researchers who defined these criteria suggested that they be used mainly in classifying patients, physicians now use these criteria to confirm a diagnosis of systemic lupus erythematosus. If women exhibit four of the 11 criteria, they are considered to have SLE:

- a butterfly shaped rash across cheeks and nose
- discoid rash
- sensitivity to the sun resulting in skin rash
- ulcers or sores in the mouth or nose (usually painless)
- arthritis in two or more joints with swelling or tenderness
- excessive protein in the urine
- inflammation of the tissues around the lung (pleurisy) or heart (pericarditis)
- nervous system disorders such as seizures or psychosis
- immunologic abnormalities revealed through blood tests
- low platelet or white blood cell count or hemolytic anemia
- a positive antinuclear antibody test

About one-third of individuals with SLE develop heart or lung complications (Dibner and Colman: 1994). Heart problems include pericarditis, inflammation of the tissue around the heart; myocarditis, inflammation of the heart muscle; and coronary artery disease, due to high cholesterol levels that are linked to long term treatment with steroids, and high blood pressure, found in women who have kidney problems due to SLE. The lungs may be affected due to inflammation of the lining of the lung.

Some individuals with SLE develop a related condition known as Sjogren's syndrome, which affects the tear, salivary, and other moisture producing glands. The exact number of people with SLE who develop secondary Sjogren's syndrome is not known. While one observer states that the condition occurs in 10% of individuals with SLE (Wallace: 1995), others have estimated that it occurs in as many as 92% of these individuals (Skopouli et al.: 1995), Corneal erosions, conjunctivitis, and inflammation of the front of the eye are complications of the lack of tears. Sjogren's syndrome is ten times more frequent in women than in men (American College of Rheumatology: no date). Treatment options include artificial tears and ointments or pellets placed between the eyelid and eyeball that dissolve slowly, releasing moisture to the eye. Dry mouth (xerostomia), which may cause swallowing problems and tooth decay, may be treated with prescription medication. Its symptoms can be relieved by the use of artificial saliva and sugarless gum or candy.

Lupus nephritis is one of the most serious complications of SLE. Hughes (no date) believes that "the major factor influencing prognosis is the degree of kidney involvement at the time of diagnosis." Since lupus nephritis is often asymptomatic, urinalysis and blood tests are performed to detect this condition. If ultrasound and kidney biopsy confirm a diagnosis of lupus nephritis, immunosuppressive drugs and corticosteroids are prescribed. If renal failure occurs, dialysis is used to perform kidney function, or a kidney transplant may be performed.

About one-third of all individuals with SLE have antibodies to part of the cell membrane known as the phospholipid. These antiphospholipid antibodies lead to blood clotting abnormalities in about one-third of these individuals (Wallace: 1995). Possible complications caused by antiphospholipid antibodies include miscarriage, stroke, phlebitis (vein inflammation), and pulmonary emboli. Blood tests are used to screen individuals for the presence of antiphospholipid antibodies. Women may be advised to take a baby aspirin daily, or they are treated with an antimalarial drug such as Plaquenil. If a woman has had complications due to a blood clot, anticoagulants such as warfarin (Coumadin) are prescribed.

TREATMENT FOR LUPUS

Since SLE has varied manifestations and women may experience flares and remission, the medications used to treat it also vary. They include aspirin and other nonsteroidal anti-inflammatory medications (NSAIDS), corticosteroids, and antimalarial drugs. In severe cases, immunosuppressive medications (also known as cytotoxic drugs) such as cyclophosphamide (Cytoxan) and azathioprine (Imuran) may be prescribed. Each of these medications has potential side effects that must be balanced against benefits. The decision to take these drugs must be made with great caution, obtaining all possible information about the risk factors for experiencing the side effects. When SLE affects many body systems, gamma globulin may be administered intravenously to increase immunity, fight infection, and reduce bleeding.

Aspirin, an NSAID, relieves the inflammation responsible for joint discomfort and reduces fever. Women are also advised to take aspirin to prevent blood clots (Wahl et al.: 2000)_. However, aspirin may cause gastrointestinal distress, blood clotting problems, tinnitus (ringing in the ears), and impaired kidney function. Stomach distress may be minimized by choosing coated aspirin or taking the aspirin with milk or a meal. Antacids may be prescribed to counter gastrointestinal discomfort and protect the lining of the stomach. NSAIDS also relieve pain due to inflammation but must be taken with care due to potential gastrointestinal problems, such as diarrhea. The severe side effects of NSAIDS also include the possibility of impaired kidney function and damage to the liver.

Antimalarial drugs such as hydroxychloroquine (Plaquenil) are used to treat the skin rashes of SLE and reduce joint and muscle symptoms, but they also cause digestive system disorders. On rare

210

occasions, the toxicity of antimalarial drugs may cause retinal damage; however, the condition is reversible (Fries: 1995). Women should see an ophthalmologist for an eye examination before treatment with an antimalarial drug and receive follow-up examinations during the course of treatment. Wearing sunglasses with ultra-violet protection and a visor or broad-brimmed hat reduces exposure to sunlight, which may increase the risk of retinal damage (Fries: 1995). Hydroxychloroquine is prescribed most often in the United States, because it is less toxic to the eye.

Corticosteroids are naturally occurring hormones produced by the adrenal gland. They suppress inflammation dramatically and are often used to treat an active flare, then gradually reduced in periods of remission. "Booster" doses of corticosteroids may be required if the woman is undergoing physical or mental stress. Prednisone (Deltasone) is the corticosteroid most often prescribed to treat lupus; other corticosteroids include prednisolone (Prelone), and methylprednisone (Medrol). Corticosteroids in cream form may be used to treat skin rashes caused by SLE.

Because corticosteroids cause an increase in appetite, women may experience excessive weight gain that in turn affects weight-bearing joints. Corticosteroids may also hasten the development of osteoporosis, affect diabetes, cause mood swings, and increase blood pressure. The use of corticosteroids should never be stopped abruptly; a gradual reduction under medical supervision is advised. Dehydroepiandrosterone (DHEA), a naturally occurring male hormone, may offer some relief for the side effects of prednisone. Research is currently underway to try to determine if DHEA will diminish lupus flares or improve symptoms when prednisone dosages are reduced (van Vollenhoven: 1996). The Lupus Foundation of America (see "ORGANIZATIONS" section below) can provide information on these trials and enrollment criteria.

Rest, exercise, and diet are also important to women with SLE. During a flare, women often need more rest and should adjust their schedules at home and at work. Alternating rest and activity periods may help the individual maintain as close to normal a schedule as possible. When a flare subsides, it is important to exercise in order to avoid muscle weakness and joint stiffness. A physical therapist can design an exercise program, taking the individual's physical capacity and daily schedule into account. Exercise may also help women feel more fit and better about themselves.

SEXUAL FUNCTIONING

When SLE makes activities of daily living difficult, it may affect interpersonal relationships. These problems combined with mood changes due to medication and the need for the woman's partner to take on some of the roles she normally takes may also lead to sexual problems (Gerber: 1988). The woman with SLE may lose her sense of self-esteem, becoming self-conscious about body-image due to weight gain associated with use of corticosteroid drugs; skin rash; hair loss; and lack of energy. Regular exercise may help reduce weakness, contribute to weight control, and increase feelings of well-being.

Medications taken to reduce pain may also reduce libido. A woman may also fear pain during intimacy, while her partner may fear causing pain. Vaginal dryness may be reduced through the use of a commercial, water soluble lubricant. Fatigue and a diminished range of motion may also affect sexual function. Anti-inflammatory medication should be scheduled so that it will provide maximum relief during sexual relations without reducing arousal. A warm bath or shower may help to relax joints and muscles. Changing positions for intercourse may also reduce joint pain and improve sexual relations.

Communication between partners is key to living with a chronic disease as well as to maintaining sexual function. Relationships that were weak prior to the onset of SLE may be threatened by the adjustments needed in everyday life. Both partners may benefit from counseling.

FAMILY PLANNING, PREGNANCY, AND CHILDREARING

Couples must weigh the decision to have children carefully, as the flares of SLE usually occur during childbearing years. They must evaluate the risk to both mother and fetus, the effects of treatment for autoantibodies, and the effects on the family. Medications may affect fertility in the woman experiencing a flare. It is a good idea to seek obstetric care from a physician who not only has experience in the management of high risk pregnancies, but who is also willing to work with the rheumatologist to provide the best possible care.

Women who do not wish to become pregnant are advised to choose contraceptive methods with care. Women who have the antiphospholipid syndrome or other blood clotting problems, migraine headaches, high blood pressure, or a high cholesterol level are advised not to take birth control pills containing estrogen, due to an increased risk for stroke or other conditions caused by blood clots (Wallace: 1995). Diaphragms, used with contraceptive foam or gel, and condoms are better choices.

Couples should also consider the potential for stress on the partner due to the extra duties necessitated by pregnancy fatigue; concerns about passing on the disease to offspring; and the emotional stress caused by a greater chance of miscarriage due to abnormal antibodies in the mother's blood. Financial matters may be an issue if the couple is dependent on the wife's earnings. The physical tasks of baby care, such as lifting, bathing, and carrying the infant, must be planned in advance in the event the disease flares after delivery. Other children in the family, born before the mother was diagnosed with SLE, may need special attention to cope with the mother's new disabilities as well as a new sibling.

Hayslett (1992), in an analysis of the effects of SLE on pregnancy and pregnancy outcomes, reported that the best outcomes were experienced by women who were in remission at pregnancy onset. Pregnancy should be considered carefully in women with poor kidney function, since both mother and fetus may be affected (Rogers and Matsumura: 1991). A woman with lupus nephritis is more likely to have a flare during pregnancy. Immunosuppressive drugs should be discontinued before conception, but the use of prednisone does not cause birth defects, but there is growing concern that other drugs in this category may be harmful (Scott: 2002). Aspirin may help reduce the risk of toxemia of pregnancy (preeclampsia), a combination of increased blood pressure and protein in the urine that poses risks for both mother and baby. Hughes (no date) reports that although there is no increased risk of flares during pregnancy, the risk of flares increases after delivery. These flares are usually mild. Some physicians prescribe a steroid injection ten days to two weeks postpartum to avoid flares (Wallace: 1995).

The potential risks to the fetus include a greater than average risk of prematurity, retarded growth, and death. In the first trimester, there is a greater risk of fetal death due to placental damage (blood clotting) resulting in miscarriage. Ferris and Reece (1994) report rates of fetal loss of 5 to 15% in women with inactive SLE; 20 to 50% in women with active disease. Antibodies that interfere with the placenta are found in about a third of the women with SLE. Blood tests should be performed to determine the presence of these antibodies, since their presence indicates a high risk for fetal loss (Julkunen et al.: 1993). Blood clots may form in the placenta, interfering with fetal nourishment and retarding fetal growth (Lockshin: 1992). Women who have the lupus autoantibodies and a history of miscarriages are often advised to take baby aspirin or heparin, a blood thinner, throughout their pregnancies (National Institute of Arthritis and Musculoskeletal and Skin Diseases: 1997).

Problems later in pregnancy may be caused by kidney failure or high blood pressure in the mother. Ultrasound should be used to determine gestational age in order to determine whether there is growth retardation or risk of premature birth. There is also the risk of premature labor. Cesarean delivery is more common in mothers with SLE, due to prematurity or fetal distress. Transient skin rashes or low blood counts may be symptomatic of neonatal lupus; the only congenital defect resulting from maternal lupus is a slow heart rate. Steroid drug dosage is often increased prior to delivery but decreased subsequently, since steroids may interfere with breast milk production. Mothers may be advised not to breastfeed, since antimalarial and immunosuppressive drugs are passed through breast milk to the baby.

PSYCHOLOGICAL ASPECTS OF LUPUS

Women with chronic diseases such as SLE experience a wide range of emotions, such as depression, loss of self-esteem, and worry, which in turn make everyday life even more difficult. Denial, anger, and depression are classic responses, eventually leading to resolution. In rheumatic diseases such as SLE, this grieving cycle may be repeated as flares and remissions occur throughout the disease course (Partridge: 1988). Pain and fatigue are major manifestations of SLE, causing women to mourn the loss of their previous good health. They may find it difficult to learn how to adjust to the flares and remissions; to cope with the pain and possible changes in their appearance; and to undergo a medical treatment program. About half of all individuals with SLE develop neurological problems such as central nervous system disease and clinical depression. In some women, treatment with high dose of corticosteroids may lead to psychological distress and impaired cognitive functioning (Iverson: 1995).

It is important for the physician to explain these aspects of this chronic disease to the woman and her family and to suggest coping strategies. Family members must try to understand that symptoms may vary day-to-day. Overwhelming fatigue may occur without warning or outward symptoms, forcing changes in schedules. It may be necessary for family members to shoulder additional responsibilities in the home or to obtain household help. At times family members may be overprotective; at other times, they may want to disassociate themselves from the woman with SLE, resisting change and refusing to acknowledge her illness. It is crucial for the family and the woman with SLE to discuss their feelings of frustration, impatience, and resentment. Women with SLE must learn to ask for help rather than suffer in silence, while family members must become comfortable enough to suggest alternatives to old routines.

Strategies that may help the woman with SLE to continue working include education and environmental adaptations. She should explain the flares associated with SLE and how they may affect her work to her employer and ask about the possibility of a flexible schedule. Employees with SLE should avoid offices with windows and skylights to minimize sunlight exposure. It is also important to maintain a constant temperature in the office. If a job is physically demanding, it may be wise to consider a change.

The Arthritis Foundation recommends learning stress reduction or relaxation techniques and participating in recreational activities and social groups. A seven week Systemic Lupus Erythematosus Self-Help Course is offered by many local chapters of the Arthritis Foundation. The Lupus Foundation of America also serves individuals, their families, and health professionals (see "ORGANIZATIONS" section below).

PROFESSIONAL SERVICE PROVIDERS

Rheumatologists are physicians who specialize in the diagnosis and treatment of rheumatic diseases, which are inflammations and degenerations of connective tissues and joints. *Dermatologists* are physicians who specialize in the diagnosis and treatment of skin problems. Dermatologists may perform skin biopsies to confirm a diagnosis of cutaneous lupus. *Obstetricians* are physicians who provide primary care during pregnancy, labor and delivery, and postpartum. Some may be specialists in treating women with high risk pregnancies due to chronic disease; they should work with the woman's rheumatologist to provide multidisciplinary care during pregnancy.

Occupational therapists teach women with SLE new techniques to perform everyday activities, such as washing and dressing, homemaking, and recreation. Many assistive devices, such as reaching tools, built-up kitchen utensils, and writing aids, may be suggested.

Physical therapists design exercise programs with strengthening and range of motion exercises to keep women with SLE moving as easily as possible despite flares with joint pain and fatigue.

Social workers provide information about financial and medical benefits, housing, and community resources. They conduct individual, family, or group counseling and may refer individuals to self-help or peer counseling groups.

Rehabilitation counselors help individuals with lupus develop a plan that will enable them to continue functioning and working. Some individuals will need assistance in returning to their previous position or retraining to obtain a different type of position. Rehabilitation counselors help make the contacts and placements necessary to attain these goals.

WHERE TO FIND SERVICES

The health care professionals who provide services to women with SLE work in hospitals, rehabilitation centers, home health agencies, private and public agencies, independent living centers, and as private practitioners. Individual and group counseling may be available through a local hospital, community health center, or from mental health professionals in private practice. Members of self-help groups, often run under the auspices of voluntary associations, share emotional support and practical advice. Some women attend pain clinics which teach behavior modification techniques to limit the effect of pain.

Women who are severely disabled by SLE often require home health services. These services are provided by nurses or home health agencies; special homemaker services; Meals on Wheels programs; chore services such as housecleaning; and adult day activity programs. The services are often free to women with low income, or fees may be charged on a sliding scale.

The desire to remain independent provides strong motivation for rehabilitation. Patient education programs offered by hospitals, universities, and health organization chapters teach self-management skills to women with SLE in order to help them live as independently as possible. These courses often result in reduction in pain, dependency, and depression (National Resource Center on Health Promotion and Aging: 1989). Common topics in these courses are education about SLE, emotional support, and discussions of how women can advocate for themselves within the health care system and participate in choosing treatment options. Many women with SLE experience problems in obtaining or retaining medical insurance. Social Security Disability Insurance (SSDI) is often denied due to the patterns of flares and remissions. Group members, patient advocates in hospitals, and participants in courses can relate their experiences and offer strategies that have been effective in appealing these denials.

References

American College of Rheumatology
No date   Fact Sheet: Sjogren's Syndrome Atlanta, GA: American College of Rheumatology
Arthritis Foundation
1993   Systemic Lupus Erythematosus Atlanta, GA: Arthritis Foundation

Berkow, Robert
1987   "Discoid Lupus Erythematosus" pp. 1273-1274 in Robert Berkow (ed.) The Merck Manual of Diagnosis and Therapy Rahway, NJ: Merck & Co.

Dibner, Robin and Carol Colman
1994   The Lupus Handbook for Women New York, NY: Simon & Schuster

Ferris, Ann M. and E. Albert Reece
1994   "Nutritional Consequences of Chronic Maternal Conditions During Pregnancy and Lactation: Lupus and Diabetes" American Journal of Clinical Nutrition 59:February:2 Supplement:465S-4673S

Fries, James F.
1995   Arthritis: A Take Care of Yourself Health Guide Reading, MA: Addison-Wesley Publishing Company

Gerber, Lynn H.
1988   "Rehabilitative Therapies for Patients with Rheumatic Disease" pp. 301-307 in H. Ralph Schumacher, Jr. (ed.) Primer on the Rheumatic Diseases Atlanta, GA: Arthritis Foundation

Hayslett, J.P.
1992   "The Effect of Systemic Lupus Erythematosus on Pregnancy and Pregnancy Outcome" American Journal of Reproductive Immunology 28(3-4):199-204

Hochberg, Marc D.
1992   "Epidemiology of Systemic Lupus Erythematosus" pp. 103-117 in Robert C. Lahita (ed.) Systemic Lupus Erythematosus New York, NY: Churchill Livingstone

Hughes, Graham R.V.
No date Lupus: A Guide for Patients Torrance, CA: American Lupus Society

Iverson, Grant L.
1995   "The Need for Psychological Services for Persons with Systemic Lupus Erythematosus" Rehabilitation Psychology 40:1:39-49

Julkunen, H. et al.
1993   "Fetal Outcome in Lupus Pregnancy: A Retrospective Case-Control of 242 Pregnancies in 112 Patients" Lupus April:2(2):125-31

Lahita, Robert G.
1992a   "The Early Diagnosis of Systemic Lupus Erythematosus" Journal of Women's Health 1:2:117-121

1992b   Lupus in Men Rockville, MD: Lupus Foundation of America

Lockshin, Michael D.
1992   Pregnancy and Lupus Rockville, MD: Lupus Foundation of America

Lupus Foundation of America
1993   Lupus Rockville, MD: Lupus Foundation of America

National Institute of Arthritis and Musculoskeletal and Skin Diseases
1997   Systematic Lupus Erythematosus Washington, DC: National Institute of Arthritis and Musculoskeletal and Skin Diseases

National Resource Center on Health Promotion and Aging
1989   "Arthritis: Positive Approaches Offer New Hope" Perspectives in Health Promotion and Aging 4:(November-December)6

Office on Women's Health
2000   Lupus and Women Washington, DC: Office on Women's Health

Partridge, Alison J.
1988   "Psychosocial Aspects of the Rheumatic Diseases" pp. 307-309 in H. Ralph Schumacher, Jr. (ed.) Primer on the Rheumatic Diseases Atlanta, GA: Arthritis Foundation

Rogers, Judith and Molleen Matsumura

1991 <u>Mother To Be: A Guide to Pregnancy and Birth for Women with Disabilities</u> New York, NY: Demos Publications

Scott, J.R.

2002 "Risks to the Children Born to Mothers with Autoimmune Disease" <u>Lupus</u> 11:10:655-660

Skopouli, F.N. et al.

1995 "Sjogren's Syndrome and Systemic Lupus Erythematosus" <u>The Moisture Seekers</u> 13:1(January):1, 4

Tan, Eng M. et al.

1982 "The 1982 Revised Criteria for the Classification of Systemic Lupus Erythematosus" <u>Arthritis and Rheumatism</u> 25(November 1982):11:1271-77

van Vollenhoven, Ronald

1996 "Update on DHEA Research at Stanford University" <u>Bay Area Lupus Foundation Newsletter</u> 19:4:5

Wahl, Dennis G. et al.

2000 "Prophylactic Antithrombotic Therapy for Patients with Systemic Lupus Erythematosus with or without Anti phospholipid Antibodies" <u>Archives of Internal Medicine</u> 160:13(July 10):2042-2048

Wallace, Daniel J.

1995 <u>The Lupus Book: A Guide for Patients and Their Families</u> New York, NY: Oxford University Press

Whitacre, Caroline C. et al.

1999 "A Gender Gap in Autoimmunity" <u>Science</u> 283:5406(February 26):1277-1278

ORGANIZATIONS

Alliance for Lupus Research
28 West 44th Street, Suite 1217
New York, NY 10036
(800) 867-1743   (212) 218-2840
e-mail: info@lupusresearch.org   www.lupusresearch.org

Funds grants that study ways to prevent, treat, and cure lupus. Application information on the web site.

American Autoimmune Related Diseases Association (AARDA)
22100 Gratiot Avenue
East Detroit, MI 48021
(800) 598-4668   (586) 776-3900   e-mail: aarda@aol.com
www.aarda.org

Provides information on autoimmune diseases including lupus, type 1 diabetes, multiple sclerosis, Sjogren's syndrome, and rheumatoid arthritis. Web site offers brief explanations of conditions. Offers telephone support and referrals.

American College of Rheumatology
1800 Century Place, Suite 250
Atlanta, GA 30345
(404) 633-3777   FAX (404) 633-1870
e-mail: acr@rheumatology.org   www.rheumatology.org

A professional membership organization for rheumatologists who treat or study all forms of arthritis and associated diseases such as lupus. The web site provides a geographical listing of rheumatologists. Offers fact sheets on rheumatic diseases, including "Systemic Lupus Erythematosus." Free. Also available on the web site.

Arthritis Foundation
PO Box 7669
Atlanta, GA 30357-0669
(800) 283-7800   (404) 872-7100
FAX (404) 872-0457   www.arthritis.org

Supports research; offers referrals to physicians; provides public and professional education. Chapters throughout the U.S.; toll-free number connects to local chapter. Some chapters offer arthritis classes, clubs, and exercise programs. Membership, $20.00, includes the Arthritis Foundation's "Drug Guide," chapter newsletter, and magazine, "Arthritis Today." Also available by subscription, $12.95. Members receive discounts on purchases of publications. Many brochures are available on the web site. Several brochures are available in Spanish.

Lupus Foundation of America
2000 L Street, NW, Suite 710
Washington, DC 20036
(800) 558-0121   Spanish (800) 558-0231   (202) 349-1155
FAX (202) 349-1156   e-mail: info@lupus.org   www.lupus.org

Supports lupus research, provides public education about lupus, and assists more than 90 local chapters in serving individuals with lupus and their families. Web site has information on clinical trials that are recruiting patients and a physician locator. Publishes quarterly newsletter, "Lupus News," $25.00.

Lupus Information Network
230 Ranch Drive
Bridgeport, CT 06606-1747
(203) 372-5795   www.lupusinformationnetwork.org

Provides information about lupus through medical briefs, personal stories, book reviews, and articles about coping with lupus.

Lupus Multiplex Registry and Repository
Lupus Genetics Study
Oklahoma Medical Research Foundation
825 Northeast 13th Street
Oklahoma City, OK 73104
(888) 655-8787   (405) 271-7479
FAX (405) 271-3045   www.lupus.omrf.ouhsc.edu

Sponsored by the National Institute of Arthritis, Musculoskeletal and Skin Diseases, this center conducts genetic studies of families that have at least two members diagnosed with lupus. Currently recruiting study participants. Requires blood sample and medical history interview. Publishes annual newsletter, "The Lupus Linkage Newsletter," free.

Lupus Research Institute
149 Madison Avenue, Suite 205
New York, NY 10016
(212) 685-4118   FAX (212) 545-1843
e-mail: sberman@lupusny.org   www.lupusresearchinstitute.org

Funds innovative research projects to cure and prevent lupus. Application information on the web site.

MEDLINEplus: Lupus
www.nlm.nih.gov/medlineplus/lupus.html

This web site provides links to sites for general information about the condition, symptoms and diagnosis, treatment, nutrition, specific aspects of the condition, clinical trials, statistics, organizations, and research. Includes interactive tutorials on spinal cord injuries and myelograms. Some information is available in Spanish. Provides links to MEDLINE research articles and related MEDLINEplus pages.

National Institute of Arthritis and Musculoskeletal and Skin Diseases Information Clearinghouse
1 AMS Circle
Bethesda, MD 20892
(877) 226-4267   (301) 495-4484   (301) 565-2966 (TTY)
FAX (301) 718-6366   e-mail: niamsinfo@mail.nih.gov www.niams.nih.gov

Distributes bibliographies, fact sheets, catalogues, and directories to the public and professionals. Free. Many of the publications are available on the web site in English and Spanish. NIAMS supports clinical research, individual research, and specialized research centers, which conduct basic and clinical research; provide professional, public, and patient education; and sponsor community-related activities. Distributes a program planning kit, "What Black Women Should Know about Lupus: Ideas for Community Programs," free.

Sjogren's Syndrome Foundation
8120 Woodmont Avenue, Suite 530
Bethesda, MD 20814
(800) 475-6473   FAX (301) 718-0322
e-mail: ssf@idt.net   www.sjogrens.com

Provides information to individuals and professionals through support groups and conferences. Membership, $25.00, includes newsletter, "The Moisture Seekers," published 9 times per year, and discounts on publications.

Aspirin and Other NSAIDs
Arthritis Foundation (see "ORGANIZATIONS" above)
(800) 283-7800   www.arthritis.org

Using a question and answer format, this booklet discusses NSAIDs and possible side effects. Free

Coping with Lupus: A Practical Guide to Alleviating the Challenges of Systemic Lupus Erythematosus

by Robert H. Phillips
Penguin Putnam, Inc., Inside Sales
(800) 788-6262   FAX (607) 775-5586   www.penguinputnam.com

Written by a psychologist, this book provides information for everyday living with lupus for individuals with the condition and their families. $16.95

Facts About Lupus
Lupus Foundation of America
PO Box 932615
Atlanta, GA 31193-2615
(866) 484-3532   FAX (770) 442-9724   www.lupus.org

This series of 24 brochures discusses many aspects of lupus, including diagnostic tests, medications, lupus and pregnancy, joint and muscle pain, and central nervous system involvement. $10.00

The First Year: Lupus: An Essential Guide for the Newly Diagnosed
by Nancy C. Hanger
Distributed by Publishers Group West
1700 Fourth Street
Berkeley, CA 94710
(800) 788-3123   FAX (510) 528-3444   www.pgw.com

This book provides information to help individuals who are newly diagnosed with lupus come to terms with the conditions, adjust to lifestyle changes, and develop coping mechanisms. $15.98

Lupus
Arthritis Foundation (see "ORGANIZATIONS" above)
(800) 283-7800   www.arthritis.org

This booklet describes diagnosis and treatment of lupus and its relation to pregnancy and contraception; it also suggests coping strategies. Free

The Lupus Book: A Guide for Patients and Their Families
by Daniel J. Wallace
Oxford University Press
2001 Evans Road
Cary, NC 27513
(800) 451-7556   FAX (919) 677-1303
e-mail: custserv@oup-usa.org www.oup-usa.org

Written by a rheumatologist, this book describes the diagnosis and treatment of lupus. Includes discussions of the immune system and descriptions of the effects of the condition on other body systems. Also discusses, pregnancy, many newly approved drugs for treatment of lupus, genetics of the disease, and immunologic research. $27.50

Lupus: Living with It: Why You Don't Have to Be Healthy to Be Happy
by Suzy Szasz
Prometheus Books
59 John Glenn Drive
Amherst, NY 14228-2197
(800) 421-0351   FAX (716) 691-0137
e-mail: pbooks6205@aol.com www.prometheusbooks.com

Written by a woman who has lupus, this book describes her experiences from adolescence to adulthood in dealing with lupus flares, hospitalizations, and treatment, while pursuing an education and a professional career. $24.00

Lupus: My Search for a Diagnosis
by Eileen Radziunas
Hunter House, Alameda, CA

This book provides the personal account of the author's struggle to find a diagnosis, including her frustrations resulting from the lack of understanding in the medical community. Describes the effects of an unknown chronic disease on family relationships and friends. Discusses the need for a case management approach by health care professionals. Out of print.

Medications
Lupus Foundation of America (see "ORGANIZATIONS" section above)
(800) 558-0121   Spanish (800) 558-0231   www.lupus.org

This brochure discusses anti-inflammatory, antimalarial, and cytotoxic drugs and corticosteroids in the treatment of SLE. Includes information about drugs currently in clinical trials. Free. Also available on the web site.

Mother To Be: A Guide to Pregnancy and Birth for Women with Disabilities
by Judith Rogers and Molleen Matsumura
Demos Medical Publishing
386 Park Avenue South, Suite 201
New York, NY 10016
(800) 532-8663   (212) 683-0072
FAX (212) 683-0118   e-mail: info@demospub.com   www.demosmedpub.com

This book describes the pregnancy and childbirth experiences of 36 women with a wide variety of disabilities including systemic lupus erythematosus. Suggests practical solutions for the special concerns of individuals with disabilities during pregnancy and those of their partners, families, and health care providers. Includes a glossary and a bibliography. $29.95 Orders made on the Demos web site receive a 15% discount.

New Hope for People with Lupus
by Theresa diGeronimo
Prima Publishers
Random House, Order Department
400 Hahn Road, PO Box 100
Westminster, MD 21157
(800) 733-3000   www.randomhouse.com

This book covers the diagnosis, treatment, nutrition, and psychosocial issues. Includes information about complementary substances used in the treatment of lupus. $18.95

The New Sjogren's Syndrome Handbook
by Steven Carsons and Elaine K. Harris (eds.)
Sjogren's Syndrome Foundation
8120 Woodmont Avenue, Suite 530
Bethesda, MD 20814
(800) 475-6473   FAX (301) 718-0322
e-mail: ssf@idt.net   www.sjogrens.com

This book provides practical suggestions for living more comfortably with this chronic condition. $25.00.

Pregnancy and Lupus
Lupus Foundation of America (see "ORGANIZATIONS" section above)
(800) 558-0121   Spanish (800) 558-0231   www.lupus.org

This brochure discusses issues that arise when a woman with lupus is pregnant, including medication safety. Free. Also available on the web site.

Sexual Function in People with Disability and Chronic Illness: A Health Professional's Guide
by Marca Sipski and Craig Alexander
Aspen Publishers, Inc.
PO Box 990
Frederick, MD 21705-9782
(800) 234-1660   www.aspenpub.com

This book discusses many types of disability, their effects on sexuality, reproductive concerns, and treatment methods, as well as providing basic information on general sexual function and dysfunction. Includes spinal cord injury, diabetes, multiple sclerosis, arthritis and other connective tissue diseases, and heart disease. Offers a discussion of the issues faced by the partner of an individual with a disability. $59.00

Sjogren's Syndrome
Arthritis Foundation (see "ORGANIZATIONS" above)
(800) 283-7800   www.arthritis.org

This booklet explains the causes, symptoms, diagnosis, and treatment for this related condition. Free. Also available on the web site.

Systematic Lupus Erythematosus
National Institute of Arthritis and Musculoskeletal and Skin Diseases Information Clearinghouse
(see "ORGANIZATIONS" section above)
(877) 226-4267   www.niams.nih.gov

This booklet discusses lupus, its symptoms, diagnosis, and treatment. Includes pregnancy, health care, and quality of life issues. Free. Also available on the web site.

Taking Charge of Lupus: How to Manage the Disease and Make the Most of Your Life
by Maureen Pratt and David Hallegua
New American Library
Penguin Putnam, Inc., Inside Sales
(800) 788-6262   FAX (607) 775-5586   www.penguinputnam.com

This book, written by a woman who has lupus and a physician, is based on the woman's experiences managing the disease on a daily basis. $14.00

Travels with the Wolf: A Story of Chronic Illness
by Melissa Anne Goldstein
Ohio State University Press
c/o Chicago Distribution Center
11030 South Langley Avenue
Chicago, IL 60628
(800) 621-2736   FAX (800) 621-8476
e-mail: kh@press.uchicago.edu   www.press.chicago.edu

This autobiography, written by a woman who is both a teacher and a writer, describes her struggle to remain independent in spite of the debilitating nature of her disease, as well as her relationships with family and friends. Hardcover, $65.00; softcover, $22.00.-

We Are Not Alone: Learning to Live with Chronic Illness
by Sefra Kobrin Pitzele
Workman Publishing, New York, NY

Written by a woman with lupus, this book offers practical advice for coping with chronic diseases and maintaining relationships. It also provides practical suggestions for independent living.   Out of print.

What Black Women Should Know About Lupus
National Institute of Arthritis and Musculoskeletal and Skin Diseases Information Clearinghouse
(see "ORGANIZATIONS" section above)
(877) 226-4267   www.niams.nih.gov

This pamphlet describes types, symptoms, and treatment of lupus. Available in alternate formats.

When Mom Gets Sick
by Rebecca Samuels
Lupus Foundation of America (see "ORGANIZATIONS" section above)
(800) 558-0121   Spanish (800) 558-0231   www.lupus.org

This book was written by a young girl whose mother has lupus. $6.95

Xerostomia (Dry Mouth) Video
Sjogren's Syndrome Foundation
8120 Woodmont Avenue, Suite 530
Bethesda, MD 20814
(800) 475-6473   FAX (301) 718-0322
e-mail: ssf@idt.net   www.sjogrens.com

This videotape discusses the causes of dry mouth and current treatment options. 30 minutes. $35.00

Chapter 9

MULTIPLE SCLEROSIS

Multiple sclerosis (MS) is a chronic central nervous system condition in which the nerve fibers of the brain and spinal cord are damaged. A fatty substance called myelin protects the nerve fibers and enables the smooth transmission of neurological impulses between the central nervous system and the rest of the body. If inflammation damages or destroys the myelin, it may heal with no loss of function. Later, however, scar (or plaque) may form and interfere with the transmission of neurological impulses. Function may be diminished or lost. The disease is called multiple sclerosis because there are multiple areas of scarring or sclerosis (Minden and Frankel: 1989).

Multiple sclerosis affects twice as many women as men and twice as many whites as African-Americans (Scheinberg and Smith: 1989). The number of individuals with multiple sclerosis is estimated at about 400,000 (National Multiple Sclerosis Society: 2002a). Age of onset ranges from mid to late adolescence to middle age. Estimates of the number of individuals with multiple sclerosis vary from less than 200,000, based on hospital and physicians' records, to 500,000, based on public surveys and pathology records (National Institute of Neurological Disorders and Stroke: 1990).

Nearly 77% of individuals with multiple sclerosis have activity limitations (National Center for Health Statistics: 1988). The broad economic and social implications of multiple sclerosis include medical expenses, unemployment or underemployment, the cost of special services, and the emotional and physical effects on the individual and family members. Cognitive problems such as memory loss, forgetfulness, and the inability to maintain a train of thought have been reported by many individuals with multiple sclerosis (Sullivan et al.: 1990).

Each woman with multiple sclerosis has unique symptoms based on the location of the damage to the nervous system. These symptoms may include blurred or double vision, numbness in the extremities, balance or coordination problems, fatigue, muscle spasticity or stiffness, slurred speech, muscle weakness, or loss of bladder or bowel control.

The cause of multiple sclerosis is unknown. In the United States, autoimmune diseases such as multiple sclerosis, lupus, and rheumatoid arthritis (discussed in this book) affect a disproportionate number of women, nearly 79% of the 8.5 million individuals affected (Whitacre et al.: 1999). Researchers believe that differences in women's immune responses; the effects of sex hormones such as estrogen, progesterone, and testosterone; and genetic influences may account for this gender gap. In 1999, the National Multiple Sclerosis Society established the Task Force on Gender, MS, and Autoimmunity; members included basic and clinical scientists, to review current data and make research recommendations. The Task Force identified five research priorities:

- a comparative study of the immune responses of women and men
- investigation of the interaction of hormones and the immune systems of women and men
- clinical studies of fluctuating hormone levels, as experienced in menstruation, pregnancy, and menopause, and their effect on the development and course of autoimmune disease in women
- studies to determine genetic factors in gender-related autoimmune responses
- projects to determine whether gender affects the response to various therapies and whether sex hormones might be used in treating autoimmune diseases (National Multiple Sclerosis Society: 1999)

DIAGNOSIS OF MULTIPLE SCLEROSIS

In the past, positive diagnosis of multiple sclerosis often took months or years. Physicians would verify loss of function in more than one area of the central nervous system and confirm that these losses had occurred at least twice over an interval of at least a month. Individuals with multiple sclerosis were often frustrated by the length of time and the multiple procedures required to diagnose their symptoms.

The development of magnetic resonance imaging (MRI), which provides a recorded image of brain and central nervous system lesions, has led to changes in diagnostic criteria. The MRI is now considered an essential key in making an MS diagnosis. In July, 2000, in the first formal review since 1982, an International Panel on the Diagnosis of MS produced revised diagnostic criteria, integrating the use of MRIs with cerebrospinal fluid (CSF) studies and visual evoked potentials (VEP) (McDonald et al.: 2001). Cerebrospinal fluid studies may detect immune system antibodies that indicate the presence of MS. Visual evoked potentials studies assess the visual pathway to the optic nerve. The diagnostic result is either "MS," "possible MS" (for individuals who are at risk but whose evaluations may not be complete or meet all criteria), or "not MS."

TYPES OF MULTIPLE SCLEROSIS

In 1996, an international panel of physicians who treat individuals with multiple sclerosis recommended that the following terms be used to describe the types of multiple sclerosis (Reingold: 1996). *Relapsing-remitting* describes a pattern of multiple sclerosis in which exacerbations are followed by either full recovery or partial recovery and lasting disability. Individuals with the *primary progressive* form experience steady disease progression. The *secondary progressive* form has a clear pattern of relapses and recovery, becoming progressively worse between acute exacerbations. *Progressive relapsing* multiple sclerosis is progressive from onset with acute attacks.

These forms of multiple sclerosis are not exclusive; some individuals may experience progression from one form to another. Smith and Scheinberg (1985) report that there is a more favorable prognosis for individuals with early onset (before age 35); acute onset rather than gradual onset; complete remission after the first attack; and sensory rather than motor symptoms.

TREATMENT OF MULTIPLE SCLEROSIS

There is no cure for multiple sclerosis; however, physicians can treat the symptoms of multiple sclerosis and try to control its progress with anti-inflammatory medication.

Interferon beta-1b (Betaseron) is one of the medications used to treat ambulatory individuals ages 18 to 50 with relapsing-remitting multiple sclerosis. Clinical studies have shown that Betaseron reduces the frequency and severity of exacerbations. MRI studies have shown reduced number and size of brain lesions (Goodkin: 1994). Betaseron is injected by the individual subcutaneously every other day. The most common side effects reported are reactions at the injection site such as swelling, redness, and rashes and flu-like symptoms, including chills, fatigue, fever, and muscle aches. Individuals using Betaseron must learn to inject the drug and determine an injection schedule that works best for them, minimizing side effects. Betaseron is expensive, nearly $10,000 per year. The Betaseron Foundation aids underinsured individuals to obtain the medication (see "ORGANIZ-ATIONS" section below).

Interferon beta-1a (Avonex) has been shown to reduce disease activity in individuals with relapsing-remitting multiple sclerosis and to slow the progression of disability. Avonex is administered in a once-a-week intramuscular injection into the thigh, hip, or upper arm. Many individuals self-inject or receive treatments from a caregiver. Clinical trials found that initial side effects included flu-like symptoms, which diminished over the course of treatment. In March, 2003, Biogen and the FDA added new warning labels to Avonex, indicating that use of the drug can increase depression and psychotic diseases as well as autoimmune disorders. A "Patient Medication Guide" is included with the drug. Biogen, the manufacturer of Avonex, offers a toll-free support line and literature to individuals (see "ORGANIZATIONS" section below). Medicare provides coverage for Avonex treatments administered in a doctor's office or a hospital outpatient service.

In 2002, the FDA approved another form of interferon beta-1a, Rebif, for treatment of relapsing forms of multiple sclerosis. It is injected subcutaneously three times a week. Its major side effects are flu-like symptoms. Some individuals who used Rebif in clinical trials also had mild to moderate abnormalities in liver function tests, pain at the injection site, and decreases in white blood cell counts (National Multiple Sclerosis Society: 2002b).

Copolymer I or glatiramer acetate (Copaxone) also slows the rate of relapse in individuals with relapsing-remitting multiple sclerosis, but is not effective for primary progressive multiple sclerosis. It is injected subcutaneously on a daily basis. It does not produce the flu-like symptoms or depression associated with Betaseron and Avonex.

In 1998, the Medical Advisory Board of the National Multiple Sclerosis Society released a consensus statement on the use of interferon beta-1a, interferon beta-1b, and glatiramer acetate therapy in the treatment of multiple sclerosis. The Board recommends that:

- therapy be initiated as soon as possible following a definite diagnosis of multiple sclerosis and determination that the disease is the relapsing-remitting type
- access to therapy not be limited by age, level of disability, or frequency of relapses
- treatment should be continued unless there is a clear lack of benefit, intolerable side effects, new data which reveal other reasons for cessation, or better therapy is available
- these drugs be covered by third party payers
- the choice of drugs be decided upon jointly by the patient and physician
- movement from one drug to another should be permitted (National Multiple Sclerosis Society: 1998)

Although Avonex, Betaseron, and Copaxone have been shown to reduce MS exacerbations, users may still have symptoms, such as spasticity, fatigue, and bladder control problems. These continuing symptoms may lead individuals to discontinue taking the medications, believing that if they don't feel better, the drugs are not working.

Prednisone (Deltasone), adrenocorticotropic hormone (ACTH), prednisolone (Prelone), and other anti-inflammatory drugs have been effective in reducing the severity and duration of multiple sclerosis flare-ups. These medications are not recommended for long term use because of side effects such as nausea, drowsiness, changes in blood pressure and blood glucose levels, lowered resistance to infection, and thinning of bones (Lechtenberg: 1995). Medication may also be used to treat multiple sclerosis symptoms such as spasticity, dizziness, fatigue, bladder problems, tremors, depression, and sensory problems (a "pins and needles" feeling). The woman with multiple sclerosis and the physician must carefully consider each medication and its possible side effects, which may appear to be symptoms of the disease itself.

Mitoxantrone (Novantrone) belongs to a class of drugs called neoplastics. It is used for secondary progressive and progressive relapsing multiple sclerosis. Mitoxantrone suppresses the action of T cells, B cells, and microphages which are thought to attack the myelin sheathing. Because it decreases the white blood cells that provide protection against infection, it is important that a blood count and liver function test be administered prior to each dosage. A study (Hartung et al.: 2002) found that patients who received mitoxantrone fared better than a placebo group regarding number f treated relapses and neurological, ambulatory, and disability status. The treatment group experienced no serious adverse effects.

Fatigue is the most common symptom experienced by individuals with multiple sclerosis (Multiple Sclerosis Council: 1998). The lack of physical and/or mental energy interferes with activities of daily living, increasing individuals' feelings of powerlessness or lack of control over their lives. Since 1986 the Social Security Administration has recognized fatigue as a major determinant in evaluating individuals with multiple sclerosis for disability benefits (Taylor: 1998). The Multiple Sclerosis Council (1998) differentiates between chronic persistent fatigue, which is present for half the time for more than six weeks, and acute fatigue, new or significant increase of feelings of fatigue. The Council developed self-report tools for individuals with multiple sclerosis that measure sleep habits, fatigue symptoms, and the effects of fatigue on everyday living (see "PUBLICATIONS AND TAPES" section below). Occupational therapists may recommend energy conservation techniques that may help reduce fatigue, including moderate exercise, using assistive devices, and rest. Heat-induced fatigue may be treated with cooling devices such as ice packs and vests, air conditioning, and cool showers. Medications used to treat fatigue include amantadine (Symmetrel), an antiviral drug; stimulants; and antidepressants.

Optic neuritis, *double vision*, and *nystagmus* are common visual symptoms of multiple sclerosis. Inflammation of the optic nerve (neuritis) causes loss of vision. If the muscles of the eye are weakened by nerve demyelination, the woman cannot focus and experiences double vision (diplopia). Double vision may occur during an exacerbation and disappear during remission of multiple sclerosis symptoms. Cortisone is often used to treat optic neuritis and double vision. Nystagmus is an involuntary rapid eye movement; it interferes with focusing and may cause dizziness.

Some women with multiple sclerosis experience *problems with gait* including weakness, spasticity, and lack of coordination (ataxia). Antispastic medications, stretching exercises, and swimming may relieve the symptoms of stiff gait, foot drop, and toe dragging. Tizanidine (Zanaflex) was approved by the Food and Drug Administration (FDA) in 1997 for the treatment of spasticity (Kalb et al.: 1997). It may be used alone or in combination with baclofen, another antispastic drug. Orthoses are assistive devices used to support weakened areas, provide proper alignment, and improve function. An ankle foot orthosis worn inside the shoe may relieve the symptoms of spasticity. Ataxia is treated with a sequential exercise program in which the individual performs repetitive movements, often watching herself in a mirror, to increase sensory feedback and restore coordination.

About 80% of individuals with multiple sclerosis experience *urinary dysfunction* (Holland: 1996). Urinary tract infections, formation of bladder stones, and kidney damage may occur if the bladder is not completely emptied during voiding. Symptoms of urinary dysfunction include urgency, frequency, hesitancy, nocturia (waking up to urinate during the night), and incontinence. Symptoms of urinary tract infections may include discomfort when urinating, frequent urination, fever, and urine that smells unpleasant. Antibiotics are used to treat urinary tract infections. To avoid further problems, women, who are at greater risk for these infections (Schapiro: 1994), are advised to empty their bladders completely; wear cotton undergarments; drink six to eight glasses of fluid per day; take vitamin C; practice careful personal hygiene, wiping from front to back after voiding or bowel movements; and, for those who use catheters, keeping equipment clean. Although some women with occasional incontinence rely on absorbent undergarments, medications and catheterization are used when symptoms are more severe. Anticholinergic drugs may be used to control bladder dysfunction by regulating bladder contractions (Lechtenberg: 1995). Oxybutynin chloride (Ditropan XL), an antispasmodic, is often prescribed to decrease bladder muscle spasms and the urge to urinate. Taken once per day, the only major side effect is dry mouth. Tolterodine tartrate (Detrol) reduces contractions of the bladder muscle and increases the volume of urine voided. It, too, may cause dry mouth. In intermittent self-catheterization, a flexible catheter is inserted through the urethra into the bladder at planned intervals in order to empty it. Many individuals find that self-catheterization allows the bladder to regain normal function. (Holland: 1996).

Constipation is the most common bowel problem and may be caused by inadequate fluid and fiber consumption, medication, lack of physical activity, and decreased sensation in the rectal area. Eating high fiber foods, drinking eight to 12 cups of liquid daily, increasing physical activity, and using stool softeners or bulk formers (if necessary), are important in a bowel management program that will reduce symptoms and discomfort. To avoid constipation, women should develop a regular schedule for bowel movements, ideally about 30 minutes after eating. Holland and Frames (1996) also recommend changing the angle between the rectum and anus by using a footstool or altering the height of the toilet seat. Other bowel dysfunctions include diarrhea, caused by loss of sphincter control, medications, or viruses; fecal impaction, caused by weakened abdominal muscles; and flatulence.

Weakness of upper extremities and *speech problems* (dysarthria) are other disabling symptoms of multiple sclerosis. Women with severe multiple sclerosis may also have difficulty swallowing. Treatment options for these symptoms include medication, exercise, adaptations in everyday living, and counseling.

SEXUAL FUNCTIONING

Multiple sclerosis can have both neurological and psychological effects on a woman's sexual functioning. More than 70% of women with multiple sclerosis indicate that their sexuality has been affected (Schapiro: 1994). The neurological effects include reduced sensation in the vagina, decreased vaginal lubrication, and diminished orgasmic response. Spasticity may make some positions difficult or uncomfortable. Bowel or bladder incontinence may cause embarrassment and shame. Partners should know the effects of multiple sclerosis on sexual functioning so that they do not interpret responses as a loss of affection.

Some women are relieved when diagnosed with multiple sclerosis, because the diagnosis may help to explain sexual problems. However, the diagnosis may also affect their self-image severely. In some cases, both women with multiple sclerosis and their partners may reduce physical contact to avoid a possible failure in intimacy and the need to experiment with new positions. Health care professionals should ask routinely about sexual functioning to provide the opportunity for women and their partners to discuss any problems. Shuman and Schwartz (1988) report that some individuals feel as though they are sexual beginners when alternate methods of sexual functioning are suggested.

> A problem that sometimes gets ignored is the fact that MS causes such confusion about one's "identity," especially when cognitive and emotional symptoms are chronic. Then it's rather difficult to feel at all desirable. Self-esteem is sort of essential for a satisfactory sex life, and I don't mean just an orgasm. (Nichols: 1999, 138)

Women should discuss their medications with physicians to determine how they may affect sexual functioning. Some medications cause drowsiness and lethargy unconducive to sexual performance. Changes in the medications themselves or the schedule for taking the medications may solve sexual functioning problems. Mattson et al. (1995) report that patients who took corticosteroids prescribed for the alleviation of multiple sclerosis symptoms such as numbness, spasticity, fatigue, depression, and pain, experienced improvement in sexual function. Some women with multiple sclerosis find that they have more sexual energy during the morning. Others find that taking medication shortly before intercourse reduces the chance of muscle spasms and relieves their anxiety about having spasms.

Experimenting with different positions for intercourse may also reduce spasticity. Women who take drugs to combat fatigue should schedule them before sexual intercourse. Bladder and bowel incontinence may be avoided by reducing fluids and emptying the bladder and bowels prior to intercourse. An in-dwelling bladder catheter may be taped out of the way. Women with vaginal dryness are advised to use commercial, water soluble lubricants.

As is the case with many couples in which a partner develops a disability, communication patterns before onset of disability may be used to predict communication patterns after the onset of disability. Those who have a stable relationship and good communication patterns are often more willing to discuss their needs and experiment to solve sexual problems emanating from the disability. More than two-thirds of individuals with multiple sclerosis who discussed their sexual problems with their spouses and four of six who entered into formal counseling found these discussions helpful (Mattson et al.: 1995). Single women with multiple sclerosis face issues such as finding a partner and disclosing their illness prior to becoming intimate. Many avoid making a commitment for fear that the relationship will be affected by their condition.

Women with multiple sclerosis who are having difficulties with their sexual relationships should consider sexual therapy. If they find communicating with their partners difficult, a third party may help them understand how to continue a fulfilling sexual relationship. Talking with others, even on as sensitive a subject as sexual functioning, can help open the lines of communication, reduce feelings of isolation, and provide information about alternatives that have been helpful to others.

FAMILY PLANNING, PREGNANCY, AND CHILDREARING

Fertility is unaffected by multiple sclerosis, and women with multiple sclerosis may use the same birth control measures used by healthy women. Oral contraceptives do not affect the incidence of disease flares (Lechtenberg: 1995). The use of barrier methods of contraception such as diaphragms may be difficult if the woman experiences problems with spasticity.

In the past, some physicians routinely recommended that women with multiple sclerosis terminate pregnancies or undergo surgical sterilization (Segal: 1991). However, the long term course of multiple sclerosis seems to be unaffected by pregnancy. The number of relapses and exacerbations decreases during pregnancy, especially during the second and third trimesters. The reduction of relapses during pregnancy has led some observers to suggest that estriol, a pregnancy hormone, be used to treat women with multiple sclerosis. A study of oral estriol treatment of nonpregnant women found that relapses and certain lesions both decreased as a result of treatment (Sicotte et al.: 2002). When relapses do occur, it is safe to treat them with the steroid methylprednisolone (Adelson: 2003).

Mueller et al. (2002) found that, with the exception of maternal anemia, women with multiple sclerosis were no more likely to have pregnancy complications than healthy women. Their babies were no more likely to be preterm, low weight, or have malformations. The mothers with multiple sclerosis, however, were more likely to be rehospitalized three months following delivery than the healthy mothers, suggesting the need for close medical care during this period.

Both the Food and Drug Administration and the National Multiple Sclerosis Society recommend that women with multiple sclerosis who want to conceive a child should stop taking their medications a minimum of one month prior to conception. Potential damage to the fetus and miscarriages are the main reasons for this recommendation (Adelson: 2003). There is an increased risk of postpartum flares during the months after delivery. A flare of symptoms may require help from family, friends, or paid assistants in order to perform child care.

Couples should consider the woman's functional level prior to pregnancy. Since it is impossible to predict the course of the disease at the time of diagnosis, it may be prudent to delay childbearing for several years to see if significant disability develops. There is no reason that a woman with severe disease should not have children, but she should consider the physical demands that mothering will make on her. It is also important to assess the potential for stress on the partner due to the extra duties necessitated by the woman's fatigue during pregnancy. If the mother cannot continue to work during pregnancy, will the partner's income be sufficient? How will the couple handle the physical duties of child care, such as lifting, bathing, and carrying the infant? If the mother plans to return to work in about two months, she faces the increased risk of postpartum flares. She must determine if options such as part-time work, working at home, or a leave of absence are available.

In addition to standard obstetrical care, the obstetrician should consult with the woman's neurologist. The anesthesiologist should also be aware of the mother's multiple sclerosis and discuss anesthesia options with the woman. Some women may experience muscle spasms during labor, occasionally requiring a cesarean delivery. The erratic schedule of breastfeeding and infant care, coupled with an increased risk of postpartum flares, may significantly increase fatigue in women with multiple sclerosis. Child care assistance will reduce the stress on mother, father, and infant.

Women with visual impairment due to multiple sclerosis will find many books on child care topics available on "Talking Books," available from the National Library Service for the Blind and Physically Handicapped (see "PUBLICATIONS AND TAPES" section below).

Miller (1992) recommends that health care professionals be prepared to employ the following strategies for easing relations in the families of women with multiple sclerosis. Information about the disease should be provided to children who may be uneasy asking direct questions. Referrals for family therapy should be made if problems are observed. Many families find that support group participation strengthens family dynamics. The National Multiple Sclerosis Society publishes several booklets that provide support to family members (see "PUBLICATIONS AND TAPES" section below) and can make referrals to support programs.

PSYCHOLOGICAL ASPECTS OF MULTIPLE SCLEROSIS

From the onset of symptoms of multiple sclerosis, the course of the disease is fraught with uncertainty and unpredictability. The unpredictability of multiple sclerosis and the fact that individuals with the disease have a nearly normal life expectancy (Scheinberg: 1983) require continual adjustment and readjustment. The unpredictability of exacerbations is very frustrating.

Women must plan their daily living and work schedules to accommodate the effects of the condition. For example, exacerbations often cause fatigue, which interferes with normal activities, including employment. Women must find a balance between activity and rest periods. Not surprisingly, women who are experiencing exacerbations express higher levels of emotional disturbances than those who are in remission (Warren et al.: 1991).

Fears about the future are to be expected, given the unpredictable course of the disease and the serious consequences that may ensue. Family members may often find that they are taking on additional responsibilities for running the household and making important decisions, resulting in a role reversal between the woman and her partner. It may be difficult for the woman's partner to move back and forth between the roles of nurse and lover (Vermote and Peuskens: 1996). Women in strong relationships often find the relationship a source of strength and support to help them cope with the condition (Rodgers and Calder: 1990). At the same time, multiple sclerosis may add a strain to the relationship, including sexual problems. Counseling for both the woman with multiple sclerosis and other family members is often beneficial. Often ignored by health care professionals, the caregiving partner should receive advice on respite care and supportive counseling (White et al.: 1993). However, professional counselors themselves sometimes have fears about the disease that must be addressed in order to provide counseling that meets their clients' psychological needs (Segal: 1991).

231

In addition to the many physical adaptations required by multiple sclerosis, about half of all individuals with multiple sclerosis experience cognitive problems (Mahler: 1992; Rao et al.: 1991) and must take measures to overcome these difficulties. Among these difficulties are memory problems, concept formation, and depression. These intellectual losses, added to the physical symptoms of multiple sclerosis, may be devastating to the woman's self-esteem and affect social functioning as well as physical activities. Rao and colleagues (1991) found that individuals with multiple sclerosis who had cognitive problems were less likely to be employed and to engage in social activities than individuals without cognitive impairments, even though the severity of physical problems and the duration of the disease were similar for both groups. Cognitive rehabilitation techniques include retraining, in which exercises such as word drills are used to strengthen function, and compensatory training, which substitutes new approaches to specific functions. A study by Sullivan and colleagues (1990) found that most individuals who experienced memory loss and forgetfulness used simple aids such as notepads or daily agendas to keep abreast of their daily needs and schedules. If there are visual problems, large print or a tape recorder may be used to record information. Large print or speech software may be added to a computer system to enable continued use.

Symptoms such as stumbling, dropping items, incontinence, and slurred speech may lead to self-consciousness, anxiety, and depression. The woman's personal coping mechanisms and the support provided by family, friends, and the community are crucial to the active problem solving required in living with multiple sclerosis (Shuman and Schwartz: 1988). Women who exhibit these symptoms may also benefit from individual or group counseling.

Individuals with multiple sclerosis have a better than 50% chance of being depressed during their lifetime (Bakshi: 2001). Researchers are trying to determine whether these individuals become depressed due to physical or psychological conditions. Does the location of MS lesions affect the rate of depression? Can MRIs track changes in the brain that account for depression? Are symptoms usually associated with multiple sclerosis such as fatigue and cognitive problems, actually symptoms of depression? What is the relationship between these symptoms? Physicians should screen patients with multiple sclerosis for depression on a routine basis and recommend treatment.

PROFESSIONAL SERVICE PROVIDERS

The unique symptoms of each woman with multiple sclerosis require individualized treatment plans. The physical and emotional needs of each woman are best served through a team approach involving medical, allied health, and rehabilitation professionals.

Neurologists, who specialize in diseases and conditions of the brain and central nervous system, conduct neurological examinations and interpret the results of tests such as MRIs to diagnose multiple sclerosis and to rule out other possible conditions. *Physiatrists*, or rehabilitation physicians, design an individual treatment plan for patients with multiple sclerosis.

Physical therapists teach women with multiple sclerosis how to perform a range of exercises which help build endurance and strength. Physical therapists also prescribe therapeutic exercises to diminish or eliminate weakness, spasticity, and lack of coordination. Physical therapists provide training in the use of assistive devices such as canes, crutches, and orthoses. *Occupational therapists* assess functioning in activities of everyday living and teach simplified techniques of accomplishing them. They may recommend adaptations to the home and work environments. Occupational therapists also suggest adaptive recreation equipment and programs. They can suggest techniques for infant care that will help reduce the added fatigue caused by the physical duties of mothering.

Orthotists make and fit assistive devices (orthoses) for improving gait in women with multiple sclerosis. Orthotists, physical therapists, or occupational therapists provide instruction in the use of these devices, such as ankle or foot braces.

Social workers provide information about financial and medical benefits, housing, and community resources. They conduct individual, family, or group counseling and may refer individuals to self-help or peer counseling groups.

Rehabilitation counselors help individuals with multiple sclerosis develop a plan that will enable them to continue functioning and working. Some individuals will need assistance in returning to their previous position or retraining to obtain a different type of position.

Psychologists provide therapy for women and families living with multiple sclerosis. Depression and burnout, for example, may be reduced through marital therapy, helping the couple to balance each other's needs.

Low vision specialists may be ophthalmologists, optometrists, opticians, or other professionals trained to help individuals with vision loss use their remaining vision to the greatest extent possible with the assistance of optical and nonoptical aids.

WHERE TO FIND SERVICES

Neurologists work in private practices, acute care hospitals, and specialty clinics. Neurologists and other members of the multidisciplinary team may also work in transitional or independent living programs and in rehabilitation hospitals. In addition to medical services, MS Comprehensive Care Centers provide services such as physical and occupational therapy, counseling, and patient and family education. A list of these centers is available from the National Multiple Sclerosis Society (see "ORGANIZATIONS" section below). Women who have mobility problems and difficulty traveling to professional service providers' offices often may obtain services in their homes from physical and occupational therapists. Low vision services are often available in ophthalmologists' or optometrists' offices, in private or public agencies that serve individuals who are visually impaired or blind, or in independent practices.

ASSISTIVE DEVICES AND ENVIRONMENTAL ADAPTATIONS

Women with multiple sclerosis use a combination of environmental adaptations and assistive devices to make everyday routines easier. When making plans for living arrangements or for travel, they must consider a variety of alternatives in the event that their functional abilities deteriorate. For instance, in purchasing a home, it is wise to determine if there is room for a wheelchair ramp.

Some women with gait problems use a cane, crutches, walker, wheelchair, scooter, or a combination of these mobility aids. A woman who usually uses a cane or crutches may prefer to use a wheelchair or scooter when traveling long distances. Special controls installed on cars with automatic transmissions enable many women with multiple sclerosis to continue driving. The gas and brake pedals are operated by hand. These attachments do not interfere with the foot pedals used by other family members. Rehabilitation hospitals and centers offer driver evaluation services such as clinical testing and observation to determine an individual's need for adaptive equipment or training. Major automobile manufacturers offer reimbursement for adaptive equipment installed on new vehicles. (See Chapter 2, "TRAVEL AND TRANSPORTATION ORGANIZATIONS," for a listing of programs that offer adaptive equipment for automobiles.)

Heat and humidity affect many women with multiple sclerosis. Air conditioning helps to reduce fatigue and weakness. Physicians, rehabilitation counselors, or tax advisers may provide advice on whether the purchase of an air conditioner is a tax-deductible expense.

A referral to a low vision rehabilitation center offers women with vision problems the opportunity to improve visual function with low vision aids. An eye patch may reduce double vision. Prisms mounted on the eyeglasses lens will expand the visual field of the eye that is not patched. Sunglasses reduce glare and improve contrast for women with optic neuritis. Nonoptical aids such as large print, tape recorders, and high contrast markings are also useful.

Bathtub rails, elevated toilet seats, and grab bars are useful bathroom safety devices. A stall shower is safer and easier to use than a combination tub/shower. A shower chair or tub seat provides additional safety. A hand-held shower attachment is useful when seated.

Some women use assistive devices for dressing, including elastic shoelaces, velcro closures, and buttoning aids. Velcro, the hook and loop material, may be substituted for buttons or zippers for ease in dressing. National mail order companies offer clothes that open in front and have reinforced seams, elastic waistbands, and buttons sewn with elastic thread. Formerly these items were limited to leisure and hospital wear, but manufacturers are now designing suits, outerwear, and dressy items for working women who have disabilities. Loops of Velcro, attached to a brush or razor handle, slip around the hand, providing control for the user. Foam hair rollers, water pipe foam insulation, or layers of tape are used to build up the handles of items as varied as toothbrushes, pens, pencils, eating utensils, paint brushes, and crochet hooks. Weighted utensils, clamps, and suction cups assist individuals who experience impaired coordination or tremor. Dycem, a nonslip plastic, may be used as a pad under items such as mixing bowls, cups, or dinner plates to hold them in place. Remote controls turn on and off lights and televisions and open and close garage doors. Voice dialer telephones permit the storage of frequently called telephone numbers and automatic dialing. A speaker phone allows women with poor motor control or tremors to carry on a telephone conversation comfortably. Computer technology can enable women with multiple sclerosis to continue working and living independently. Screen readers or large print software, keyguards used to prevent unwanted keystrokes, and specially designed keyboards and word prediction software for individuals with limited dexterity are useful adaptations.

References

Adelson, Rachel
2003   "The Main Event" Inside MS April-June:21-25, 66-67
Bakshi, Rohit
2001   "Depression in Multiple Sclerosis: A Review" MSQR 20:4(Winter):6-9
Calvano, Margaret
1991   Facts & Issues New York, NY: National Multiple Sclerosis Society
1989   Facts & Issues New York, NY: National Multiple Sclerosis Society
Goodkin, Donald E.
1994   "Interferon Beta-Ib" The Lancet 344:8929:1057
Hartung, H.P. et al.
2002   "Mitoxantrone in Progressive Multiple Sclerosis: A Placebo-Controlled Double-Blind, Randomised, Multicenter Trial" Lancet 360:9350(December 21-28):2018-2025
Holland, Nancy and Robin Frames
1996   Understanding Bowel Problems in MS New York, NY: National Multiple Sclerosis Society
Kalb, Rosalind (ed.)
1996   Multiple Sclerosis: The Questions You Have, The Answers You Need New York, NY: Demos Vermande

Kalb, Rosalind et al.
1997   "Multiple Sclerosis: The Questions You Have, The Answers You Need, 1997 Update"
        Multiple Sclerosis Quarterly Report 16:3

Lechtenberg, Richard
1995   Multiple Sclerosis Fact Book Philadelphia, PA: F. A. Davis Company

Mahler, M.E.
1992   "Behavioral Manifestations Associated with Multiple Sclerosis" Psychiatric Clinics of North
        America 15(June)2:425-438

Mattson, David et al.
1995   "Multiple Sclerosis: Sexual Dysfunction and Its Response to Medications" Archives of
        Neurology 52:(September):862-868

McDonald, W. Ian et al.
2001   "Recommended Diagnostic Criteria for Multiple Sclerosis: Guidelines from the International
        Panel on the Diagnosis of Multiple Sclerosis" Annals of Neurology 50:1(July):121-127

Miller, Deborah
1992   "Some Effects of MS On Parenting and Children" pp. 9-24 in Rosalind C. Kalb and Labe
        C. Scheinberg (eds.) Multiple Sclerosis and the Family New York, NY: Demos Publications

Minden, Sarah L. and Debra Frankel
1989   PLAINTALK: A Booklet About Multiple Sclerosis For Family Members New York, NY:
        National Multiple Sclerosis Society

Mueller, B.A. et al.
2002   "Birth Outcomes and Need for Hospitalization after Delivery among Women with Multiple
        Sclerosis" American Journal of Obstetrics and Gynecology 186:3(March):446-452

Multiple Sclerosis Council for Clinical Practice Guidelines
1998   Fatigue and Multiple Sclerosis Washington, DC: Paralyzed Veterans of America

National Center for Health Statistics, Collins, John G.
1988   "Prevalence of Selected Chronic Conditions, United States, 1983-85" Advance Data From
        Vital and Health Statistics No. 155 DHHS Pub. No (PHS) 88-1250. Public Health Service
        Hyattsville, MD

National Institute of Neurological Disorders and Stroke
1990   Multiple Sclerosis: 1990 Research Program Bethesda, MD: National Institutes
        of Health

National Multiple Sclerosis Society
2002a   Just the Facts: 2001-2002 New York, NY: National Multiple Sclerosis Society
2002b   "FDA Approves Rebif for Relapsing Forms of MS - Updated Info" Research/Clinical Update
        March 19
1999   "Task Force Takes a Closer Look at the Gender Gap" Inside MS 17:4:52-57
1998   National Multiple Sclerosis Society Disease Management Consensus Statement New York,
        NY: National Multiple Sclerosis Society

Nichols, Judith Lynn
1999   Women Living with Multiple Sclerosis Alameda, CA: Hunter House Publishers

Rao, S.M. et al.
1991   "Cognitive Dysfunction in Multiple Sclerosis II. Impact on Employment and Social
        Functioning" Neurology 41(May)5:692-696

Reingold, Stephen C.
1996   "New Terms for MS Types" Inside MS Fall

Rodgers, Jennifer and Peter Calder
1990   "Marital Adjustment: A Valuable Resource for the Emotional Health of Individuals with Multiple Sclerosis" Rehabilitation Counseling Bulletin 34(September)1:24-32

Schapiro, Randall
1994   Symptom Management in Multiple Sclerosis New York, NY: Demos Publications, Inc.

Scheinberg, Labe
1983   "Signs, Symptoms, and Course of MS" pp. 35-43 in Labe C. Scheinberg (ed.) Multiple Sclerosis: A Guide for Patients and Their Families New York, NY: Raven Press

Scheinberg, Labe and Charles R. Smith
1989   Rehabilitation of Patients with Multiple Sclerosis New York, NY: National Multiple Sclerosis Society

Segal, Julia
1991   "Counselling People with Multiple Sclerosis and Their Families" pp. 147-160 in Hilton Davis and Lesley Fallowfield (eds.) Counselling and Communication in Health Care London: John Wiley and Sons

Shuman, Robert and Janice Schwartz
1988   Understanding Multiple Sclerosis Riverside, NJ: MacMillan Publishing Company

Sicotte, N.L. et al.
2002   "Treatment of Multiple Sclerosis with the Pregnancy Hormone Estriol" Annals of Neurology 52:4(October):421-428

Smith, Charles R. and Labe Scheinberg
1985   "Clinical Features of Multiple Sclerosis" Seminars in Neurology 5(June)2:85-93

Sullivan, Michael J., L. Krista Edgley, and Eric Dehoux
1990   "A Survey of Multiple Sclerosis Part 1: Perceived Cognitive Problems and Compensatory Strategy Use" Canadian Journal of Rehabilitation 4:2:99-105

Taylor, Ronald S.
1998   "Multiple Sclerosis Potpourri: Paroxysmal Symptoms, Seizures, Fatigue, Pregnancy, and More" pp. 551-559 in George H. Kraft and Ronald S. Taylor (eds.) Multiple Sclerosis: A Rehabilitative Approach Philadelphia, PA: W.B. Saunders Company

Vermote, R. and J. Peuskens
1996   "Sexual and Micturition Problems in Multiple Sclerosis Patients: Psychological Issues" Sexuality and Disability 14:1:73-82

Warren, S., K. G. Warren, and R. Cockrill
1991   "Emotional Stress and Coping in Multiple Sclerosis Exacerbations" Journal of Psychosomatic Research 35:1:37-47

Whitacre, Caroline C. et al.
1999   "A Gender Gap in Autoimmunity" Science 283:5406(26Feb99):1277-1278

White, David M., Marci L. Catanzaro, and George H. Kraft
1993   "An Approach to the Psychological Aspects of Multiple Sclerosis: A Coping Guide for Healthcare Providers and Families" Journal of Neurological Rehabilitation 7:2:43-52

ORGANIZATIONS

American Autoimmune Related Diseases Association (AARDA)
22100 Gratiot Avenue
East Detroit, MI 48021
(800) 598-4668   (586) 776-3900   e-mail: aarda@aol.com
www.aarda.org

Provides information on autoimmune diseases including multiple sclerosis, lupus, type 1 diabetes, Sjogren's syndrome, and rheumatoid arthritis. Web site offers brief explanations of conditions. Offers telephone support and referrals.

Amgen
(800) 466-8639   www.novantrone.com   www.amgen.com

This pharmaceutical company produces Novantrone, an immunosuppressive drug. The web site offers product information, information about multiple sclerosis, and an online journal. A 20 minute videotape and brochure, "Taking Novantrone for Worsening MS," is available. Free

Avonex Alliance
Avonex Start Assistance Program
(800) 456-2255   www.avonex.com

Provides information on Avonex, a drug used in treating relapsing forms of multiple sclerosis, distribution options, insurance reimbursement counseling, and training for self-administration of the drug. Phone lines open Monday through Friday, 8:30 a.m. to 8:00 p.m., E.S.T. Publishes quarterly newsletter, "The Alliance Exchange," free. Also available on the web site.

Betaseron Foundation
4828 Parkway Plaza Boulevard, Suite 220
Charlotte, NC 28217
(800) 948-5777   www.betaseronfoundation.org

Provides Betaseron to qualified underinsured patients. Requirements include a confirmed diagnosis of multiple sclerosis, prescription for Betaseron, inadequate medical insurance, and U.S. residence. Patient financial contribution is required (up to $25.00 a month). Uninsured patients will be referred to Berlex, the manufacturer of Betaseron, for assistance [(800) 788-1467].

Brain Resources and Information Network (BRAIN)
National Institute of Neurological Disorders and Stroke (NINDS)
PO Box 5801
Bethesda, MD 20824
(800) 352-9424   FAX (301) 402-2186
e-mail: braininfo@ninds.nh.gov   www.ninds.nih.gov

Supports clinical and basic research, maintains national specimen banks for the study of brain and other tissue, and publishes professional and public education materials. The web site has information about the disease and clinical studies. Many publications available on the web site and in print, free. Click on "Disorders," and then "Request Mailed Brochures." Some publications available in Spanish.

<u>Consortium of Multiple Sclerosis Centers/North American Research Committee on Multiple Sclerosis</u> (CMSC/NARCOMS)
Yale Neuroimmunology Program
PO Box 208018
New Haven, CT 06520-8018
(800) 253-7884   (203) 764-4285
e-mail: narcoms@mscare.org   www.mscare.org

Multidisciplinary organization of health care professionals who specialize in the care of individuals with multiple sclerosis. Participates in partnerships with Multiple Sclerosis Societies for education and outreach and with the Paralyzed Veterans Association (PVA) and Eastern Paralyzed Veterans Association (EPVA) to support research for veterans. Maintains the CMSC/NARCOMS Registry, which recruits individuals with multiple sclerosis for clinical trials and surveys MS patients. Individuals may enroll on the web site or by calling the telephone numbers listed above.

<u>Heuga Center</u>
27 Main Street, Suite 303
PO Box 491
Edwards, CO 81632
(800) 367-3101   (970) 926-1290   FAX (970) 926-1295
e-mail: rnorris@heuga.org   www.heuga.org

This center offers a five day "Can-Do" education program that stresses strategies for living with multiple sclerosis, such as self-management, exercise, nutrition, and social interaction. Scholarships are available.

<u>MEDLINEplus: Multiple Sclerosis</u>
www.nlm.nih.gov/medlineplus/multiplesclerosis.html

This web site provides links to sites for general information about multiple sclerosis, symptoms and diagnosis, treatment, alternative therapy, clinical trials, disease management, organizations, and research. Provides links to MEDLINE research articles and related MEDLINEplus pages.

<u>MSActiveSource</u>
(800) 456-2255   www.msactivesource.com

Sponsored by Biogen, maker of Avonex, this web site offers educational modules, information, "Ask the Expert," and real life stories. Those who do not have access to the Internet may call the toll-free number, Monday through Friday, 8:30 a.m. to 8 p.m., E.S.T.

<u>MS Lifelines</u>
(877) 447-3243   www.rebif.com

Sponsored by Serono Group, the pharmaceutical company that makes Rebif, an interferon beta-1a, this program offers injection training, reimbursement support, ongoing therapy support, and updates and information about the drug. A free injection device and a travel kit are available.

MS Pathways
www.mspathways.com   www.betaseron.com

Sponsored by Berlex, the manufacturer of Betaseron, this program provides information on Betaseron, a drug used in treating relapsing-remitting multiple sclerosis, self-administration training, insurance reimbursement, community support groups, and online services. Publishes quarterly newsletter, "MessageS," free. Also available on the web site.

MSWatch
www.mswatch.com   www.copaxone.com

Sponsored by Teva Neuroscience, the manufacturer of Copaxone, this site offers multiple sclerosis and health news, discussion boards and chat, journal, library, and "Ask An Expert."

MSWorld
www.msworld.org/communications.index.htm

Sponsored by Teva Neuroscience, this web site provides an official chat and message board site for the National Multiple Sclerosis Society. Includes e-mail support groups for individuals with multiple sclerosis and for caregivers.

Multiple Sclerosis Education Network
www.htinet.com/msen/resources.html

This web site provides links to service organizations; information about treatment, research, and clinical trials; and support organizations.

National Association for Continence (NAFC)
PO Box 8310
Spartanburg, SC 29305-8310
(800) 252-3337   (864) 579-7900
FAX (864) 579-7902   www.nafc.org

An information clearinghouse for consumers, family members, and medical professionals. Answers individual questions if self-addressed stamped envelope is enclosed with letter. Membership, $25.00, includes a quarterly newsletter, "Quality Care," a "Resource Guide: Products and Services for Continence" (nonmembers, $10.00), and a continence resource service. Free publications list. Also available on the web site.

National Multiple Sclerosis Society
733 Third Avenue
New York, NY 10017-3288
(212) 986-3240   FAX (212) 986-7981
(800) 344-4867 Information Resource Center and Library
e-mail: Nat@nationalmssociety.org   www.nationalmssociety.org

Provides professional and public education and information and referral; supports research. Offers counseling services, physician referrals, advocacy, discount prescription and health care products program, and assistance in obtaining adaptive equipment. Regional affiliates throughout the U.S. Information Resource Center and Library answers telephone inquiries from 11:00 a.m. to 5:00 p.m. E.S.T., Monday through Thursday. Membership, $20.00, includes large print magazine, "Inside MS," published three times a year. Individuals with multiple sclerosis may receive a courtesy membership if they are unable to pay. The text of past issues is available on the web site. The web site also has information about clinical studies that are recruiting patients.

Paralyzed Veterans of America (PVA)
801 18th Street, NW
Washington, DC 20006
(800) 424-8200   (800) 795-4327 (TTY)   (202) 872-1300
FAX (202) 785-4452   e-mail: info@pva.org   www.pva.org

A membership organization for veterans with spinal cord injury. Multiple sclerosis is a qualifying condition for membership. Advocates and lobbies for the rights of paralyzed veterans and sponsors research. Produces many publications to assist consumers. Some publications are available on the web site. Free. Membership fees are set by state chapters. The national office refers callers to the nearest chapter. The PVA Spinal Cord Injury Education and Training Foundation accepts applications to fund continuing education, post-professional specialty training, and patient/client and family education. The PVA Spinal Cord Research Foundation accepts applications to fund basic and clinical research, the design of assistive devices, and conferences that foster interaction among scientists and health care providers.

Shared Solutions
Teva Marion Partners
2800 Rock Creek Parkway
Kansas City, MO 64117-2551
(800) 887-8100   www.copaxone.com

This program, sponsored by Teva Neuroscience pharmaceutical company, provides information about Copaxone, a drug used to reduce the frequency of relapses in individuals with the relapsing-remitting form of multiple sclerosis, treatment reimbursement programs, and local resources. The web site provides a medication diary, discussion groups, chat rooms, and advice from professionals.

Simon Foundation for Continence
PO Box 835
Wilmette, IL 60091
(800) 237-4666   (847) 864-3913   FAX (847) 864-9758
e-mail: simoninfo@simonfoundation.org   www.simonfoundation.org

Provides information and assistance to people who are incontinent. Organizes self-help groups. Membership, individuals, $15.00; professionals, $35.00; includes quarterly newsletter, "The Informer." Also available on the web site.

ADA and People with MS
by Laura Cooper and Nancy Law with Jane Sarnoff
National Multiple Sclerosis Society (see "ORGANIZATIONS" above)
(800) 344-4867   www.nationalmssociety.org

This booklet explains how the Americans with Disabilities Act applies to individuals with multiple sclerosis. Large print. Free. Also available on the web site. Click on "Library," then "Brochures."

Aqua Exercise for Multiple Sclerosis
National Multiple Sclerosis Society (see "ORGANIZATIONS" above)
(800) 344-4867   www.nationalmssociety.org

This videotape presents exercises for building strength and endurance as well as reducing spasticity. Includes print reference card. 15 minutes. $15.00

At Home with MS: Adapting Your Environment
National Multiple Sclerosis Society (see "ORGANIZATIONS" above)
(800) 344-4867   www.nationalmssociety.org

This booklet suggests modifications that can be made to the home to compensate for mobility or visual impairment. Free. Also available on the web site. Click on "Library," then "Brochures."

Bowel Problems: The Basic Facts
by Nancy J. Holland and Robin Frames
Controlling Bladder Problems in Multiple Sclerosis
by Nancy J. Holland and Michele G. Madonna
National Multiple Sclerosis Society (see "ORGANIZATIONS" above)
(800) 344-4867   www.nationalmssociety.org

These booklets describe how multiple sclerosis affects the urinary and digestive tracts; how to control symptoms; and how to manage bladder and bowel dysfunction. Large print. Free. Also available on the web site. Click on "Library," then on "Brochures."

But You Look So Well
Aquarius Health Care Videos
266 Main Street, Suite 33B
Medfield, MA 02052
(888) 440-2963   FAX (508) 242-9854
e-mail: orders@aquariusproductions.com
www.aquariusproductions.com

This videotape portrays the effect of multiple sclerosis on four individuals and their families. Includes a neurologist discussing the disorder and daily activities. 59 minutes. $195.00

Depression and Multiple Sclerosis
National Multiple Sclerosis Society (see "ORGANIZATIONS" above)
(800) 344-4867   www.nationalmssociety.org

This brochure describes the symptoms of depression and whether it has a relationship to multiple sclerosis and side effects of treatment. Discusses the use of antidepressants and counseling. Free. Also available on the web site. Click on "Library," then "Brochures."

dirty details, the days and nights of a well spouse
by Marion Deutsche Cohen
Temple University Press
c/o Chicago Distribution Center
11030 South Langley Avenue
Chicago, IL 60628
(800) 621-2736   FAX (800) 621-8476
e-mail: kh@press.uchicago.edu   www.press.chicago.edu

A frank, personal account, written by a woman whose husband has multiple sclerosis, this book describes her caregiving experiences. Hardcover, $49.95; softcover, $20.95.

Employment Issues and Multiple Sclerosis
by Phillip D. Rumrill
Demos Medical Publishing
386 Park Avenue South, Suite 201
New York, NY 10016
(800) 532-8663   (212) 683-0072
FAX (212) 683-0118   e-mail: info@demospub.com   www.demosmedpub.com

This book provides information about vocational rehabilitation, job placement and retention, the Americans with Disabilities Act, and other legal issues. $29.95. Orders made on the Demos web site receive a 15% discount.

Enabling Romance: A Guide to Love, Sex, and Relationships for the Disabled
by Ken Kroll and Erica Levy Klein
No Limits Communications
PO Box 220
Horsham, PA 19044
(888) 850-0344   (215) 675-9133
FAX (215) 675-9376   e-mail: kim@leonardmedia.com
www.newmobility.com

Written by a man who has a disability and his wife who does not, this book provides examples of how people with a variety of disabilities have established fulfilling relationships. $15.95

Facts and Issues
National Multiple Sclerosis Society (see "ORGANIZATIONS" above)
(800) 344-4867   ww.nationalmssociety.org

A series of short reports on subjects such as pain, fatigue, and other issues of concern to individuals with multiple sclerosis. Large print. Free. Also available on the web site.

Family Challenges: Parenting with a Disability
Aquarius Health Care Videos
266 Main Street, Suite 33B
Medfield, MA 02052
(888) 440-2963   FAX (508) 242-9854
e-mail: orders@aquariusproductions.com
www.aquariusproductions.com

In this videotape, the children and spouses of individuals with disabilities describe their relationships and coping strategies. Includes a mother with multiple sclerosis. 25 minutes. $195.00

Fatigue and Multiple Sclerosis: Evidence-Based Management Strategies for Fatigue in Multiple Sclerosis
Multiple Sclerosis Council for Clinical Practice Guidelines
PVA Distribution Center
PO Box 753
Waldorf, MD 20604-0753
(888) 860-7244   (301) 932-7834   FAX (301) 843-0159
www.pva.org

This booklet presents guidelines for health care professionals who care for individuals with multiple sclerosis. Includes fatigue and sleep questionnaires and a daily activity diary that will assist individuals in reporting the effect of fatigue to their health care providers. Free

Fatigue: What You Should Know
PVA Distribution Center
PO Box 753
Waldorf, MD 20604-0753
(888) 860-7244   (301) 932-7834
FAX (301) 843-0159   www.pva.org

This consumer guide describes the types of fatigue associated with multiple sclerosis, their diagnosis, and treatment. Free

Gateway to Wellness
National Multiple Sclerosis Society (see "ORGANIZATIONS" above)
(800) 344-4867   www.nationalmssociety.org

This six week program provides education and skills training, including exercises and adaptations for everyday living. Offered by local chapters of the National Multiple Sclerosis Society. Free

Gentle Fitness
732 Lake Shore Drive
Rhinelander, WI 54501
(800) 566-7780   (715) 362-9260   FAX (715) 362-0304
www.gentlefitness.com

This videotape offers six exercise routines. Most may be done from a seated position. Includes "Guide to Exercise" booklet. $29.95 Orders placed online receive a 20% discount.

Hiring Help at Home
National Multiple Sclerosis Society (see "ORGANIZATIONS" above)
(800) 344-4867   www.nationalmssociety.org

This booklet describes various types of home care services and possible funding. It discusses the advantages and disadvantages of using agencies or hiring on your own. Provides sample needs assessment work sheet, job description, interview record, and employment contract. Free. Also available on the web site. Click on "Library," then "Brochures."

Knowledge is Power
National Multiple Sclerosis Society (see "ORGANIZATIONS" above)
(800) 344-4867   e-mail: KIP@nmss.org
www.nationalmssociety.org

This home study course provides information about multiple sclerosis including a medical overview, emotional aspects, legal issues, fatigue, sexuality, job accommodation under the Americans with Disabilities Act, family issues, and more. Once individuals are registered for the program, one article a week is mailed to them. Free

Life on Cripple Creek: Essays on Living with Multiple Sclerosis
by Dean Kramer
Demos Medical Publishing
386 Park Avenue South, Suite 201
New York, NY 10016
(800) 532-8663   (212) 683-0072
FAX (212) 683-0118   e-mail: info@demospub.com   www.demosmedpub.com

Written by a woman who has multiple sclerosis, this book reveals the emotional and practical aspects of living with a chronic disease. $18.95. Orders made on the Demos web site receive a 15% discount.

Living Beyond Multiple Sclerosis
by Judith Lynn Nichols
Demos Medical Publishing
386 Park Avenue South, Suite 201
New York, NY 10016
(800) 532-8663   (212) 683-0072
FAX (212) 683-0118   e-mail: info@demospub.com   www.demosmedpub.com

The author and other women from her online support group discuss their lives, adaptations, and treatments, as well as making inner peace. $14.95. Orders made on the Demos web site receive a 15% discount.

Living Well with MS: A Guide for Patient, Caregiver, and Family
by David L. Carroll and Jon Dudley Dorman
Harper Collins Publishers
PO Box 588
Scranton, PA 18512
(800) 331-3761   www.harpercollins.com

In addition to information on multiple sclerosis and its diagnosis, prognosis, and treatment, this book discusses emotional and sexual functioning. $13.00

Living with Low Vision: A Resource Guide for People with Sight Loss
Resources for Rehabilitation
22 Bonad Road
Winchester, MA 01890
(781) 368-9094   FAX (781) 368-9096   e-mail: info@rfr.org
www.rfr.org

This resource guide directs people who have experienced vision loss to services, products, and publications that enable them to keep reading, working, and enjoying life. Large print. $46.95 (See order form on last page of this book.)

Living with Multiple Sclerosis: A Handbook for Families
by Robert Shuman and Janice Schwartz
MacMillan Publishing Company, Indianapolis, IN

In this book, two psychologists discuss the role of the family with a member who has multiple sclerosis. Includes chapters on adolescents with multiple sclerosis, employment, and research. Uses real life experiences to suggest coping strategies and adaptations. Out of print

Living with Multiple Sclerosis: A Wellness Approach
by George H. Kraft and Marci Catanzaro
Demos Medical Publishing
386 Park Avenue South, Suite 201
New York, NY 10016
(800) 532-8663   (212) 683-0072
FAX (212) 683-0118   e-mail: info@demospub.com   www.demosmedpub.com

This book suggest strategies for everyday living with multiple sclerosis. Includes information on diet, nutrition, and exercise. $18.95. Orders made on the Demos web site receive a 15%

Managing Incontinence
by Cheryle B. Gartley (ed.)
Simon Foundation for Continence
PO Box 835
Wilmette, IL 60091
(800) 237-4666   (847) 864-3913
FAX (847) 864-9758   e-mail: simoninfo@simonfoundation.org
www.simonfoundation.org

This book provides medical advice, information on products, interviews with individuals who are incontinent, and advice on sexuality. $12.95

Mother To Be: A Guide to Pregnancy and Birth for Women with Disabilities
by Judith Rogers and Molleen Matsumura
Demos Medical Publishing
386 Park Avenue South, Suite 201
New York, NY 10016
(800) 532-8663   (212) 683-0072
FAX (212) 683-0118   e-mail: info@demospub.com
www.demosmedpub.com

This book describes the pregnancy and childbirth experiences of 36 women with a wide variety of disabilities including multiple sclerosis. Suggests practical solutions for the special concerns of women with disabilities during pregnancy and those of their partners, families, and health care providers. Includes a glossary and a bibliography. $29.95 Orders made on the Demos web site receive a 15% discount.

MS and Intimacy
by Tanya Radford
National Multiple Sclerosis Society (see "ORGANIZATIONS" above)
(800) 344-4867   www.nationalmssociety.org

This booklet discusses intimacy and sexuality, suggesting strategies for communicating with partners and physicians, managing male and female sexual problems, and treating the medical problems. Includes a resource list. Free. Also available on the web site. Click on "Library," then on "Brochures."

Multiple Sclerosis: A Guide for Families
by Rosalind C. Kalb
Demos Medical Publishing
386 Park Avenue South, Suite 201
New York, NY 10016
(800) 532-8663   (212) 683-0072
FAX (212) 683-0118   e-mail: info@demospub.com   www.demosmedpub.com

This book discusses issues such as caregiving, cognitive problems, financial planning, sexuality, and reproduction. Includes bibliography and resources. $24.95 Orders made on the Demos web site receive a 15% discount.

Multiple Sclerosis: A Guide for the Newly Diagnosed
by Nancy Holland, T. Jock Murray, and Stephen Reingold
Demos Medical Publishing
386 Park Avenue South, Suite 201
New York, NY 10016
(800) 532-8663   (212) 683-0072
FAX (212) 683-0118   e-mail: info@demospub.com   www.demosmedpub.com

This book provides information about multiple sclerosis and medical treatments as well as its effect on the individual and the family. $21.95. Orders made on the Demos web site receive a 15% discount.

Multiple Sclerosis and Intimacy
by Tanya Radford
National Multiple Sclerosis Society (see "ORGANIZATIONS" above)
(800) 344-4867   www.nationalmssociety.org

This publication discusses how multiple sclerosis affects sexuality and provides suggestions for solutions. Free. Also available on the web site. Click on "Library," then "Brochures."

Multiple Sclerosis and Pregnancy
National Multiple Sclerosis Society (see "ORGANIZATIONS" above)
(800) 344-4867   www.nationalmssociety.org

A special section reprinted form the April - June, 2003 issue of "Inside MS." Click on "Library."
Free

Multiple Sclerosis: A Self-Care Guide to Wellness
by Nancy Holland and June Halper
PVA Distribution Center
PO Box 753
Waldorf, MD 20604-0753
(888) 860-7244   (301) 932-7834   FAX (301) 843-0159
www.pva.org

This book discusses how MS affects the lives of both those with the disease and those who provide care, emphasizing strategies to promote independence, well-being, and productivity. $17.95

Multiple Sclerosis Quarterly Report (MSQR)
Eastern Paralyzed Veterans Association
PO Box 465
Hanover, PA17331
(717) 632-3535   FAX (717) 633-8920
e-mail: pubsuc@sheridan.com   www.unitedspine.org

This newsletter reports advances in the diagnosis and treatment of multiple sclerosis. Individuals, $65.00; institutions, $100.00.

Multiple Sclerosis: The Guide to Treatment and Management
by Chris H. Polman, Alan J. Thompson, T. Jock Murray, and W. Ian McDonald
Demos Medical Publishing
386 Park Avenue South, Suite 201
New York, NY 10016
(800) 532-8663   (212) 683-0072
FAX (212) 683-0118   e-mail: info@demospub.com   www.demosmedpub.com

This book describes current therapies. Includes sections on acute exacerbations, disease-modifying therapies, symptom management, and alternative therapies. $24.95. Orders made on the Demos web site receive a 15% discount.

Multiple Sclerosis: The Questions You Have, The Answers You Need
by Rosalind Kalb (ed.)
Demos Medical Publishing
386 Park Avenue South, Suite 201
New York, NY 10016
(800) 532-8663   (212) 683-0072
FAX (212) 683-0118   e-mail: info@demospub.com   www.demosmedpub.com

Written by professionals who care for individuals with multiple sclerosis, this book provides information about living with the condition and answers questions most commonly asked. Topics include neurology, treatment, employment, legal issues, physical and occupational therapy, psychosocial issues, sexuality, and reproductive health. $39.95. Orders made on the Demos web site receive a 15% discount.

Multiple Sclerosis: Your Legal Rights
by Lanny Perkins and Sara Perkins
Demos Medical Publishing
386 Park Avenue South, Suite 201
New York, NY 10016
(800) 532-8663   (212) 683-0072
FAX (212) 683-0118   e-mail: info@demospub.com   www.demosmedpub.com

This book discusses the legal problems that face individuals with multiple sclerosis, including disability benefits, insurance, taxes, family law, and working with physicians and attorneys. $21.95 Orders made on the Demos web site receive a 15% discount.

The Other Victim - Caregivers Share Their Coping Strategies
by Alan Drattell
Seven Locks Press
PO Box 25689
Santa Ana, CA 92799
(800) 354-5348   FAX (714) 545-1572

This book is a collection of personal accounts of nine caregivers of individuals with multiple sclerosis. $17.95

Pathways: An Exercise Video for People with Limited Mobility
Demos Medical Publishing
386 Park Avenue South, Suite 201
New York, NY 10016
(800) 532-8663   (212) 683-0072   FAX (212) 683-0118
e-mail: info@demospub.com   www.demosmedpub.com

This videotape demonstrates exercises, stretches, and breathing techniques, as well as a relaxation segment. 48 minutes. $29.50. Orders made on the Demos web site receive a 15% discount.

PLAINTALK: A Booklet about Multiple Sclerosis for Family Members
by Sarah L. Minden and Debra Frankel
National Multiple Sclerosis Society (see "ORGANIZATIONS" above)
(800) 344-4867   www.nationalmssociety.org

This booklet simulates a support group meeting for families of individuals with multiple sclerosis. Discusses diagnosis, everyday living, talking with children, and the well parent. Large print. Free. Also available on the web site. Click on "Library," then on "Brochures."

Providing Services for People with Vision Loss: A Multidisciplinary Perspective
by Susan L. Greenblatt (ed.)
Resources for Rehabilitation
22 Bonad Road
Winchester, MA 01890
(781) 368-9094   FAX (781) 368-9096   e-mail: info@rfr.org
www.rfr.org

This anthology discusses how health and rehabilitation professionals can work together to provide coordinated care for individuals who have experienced vision loss. Also available on audiocassette. $19.95 (See order form on last page of this book.)

Reproductive Issues for Persons with Physical Disabilities
by Florence P. Haseltine, Sandra S. Cole, and David B. Gray (eds.)
Brookes Publishing Company, Baltimore, MD

This book provides an overview of sexuality, disability, and reproductive issues across the lifespan for individuals with disabilities including multiple sclerosis. Includes academic articles as well as personal narratives written by individuals with disabilities. Out of print.

Sexual Problems Your Doctor Didn't Mention
National Multiple Sclerosis Society (see "ORGANIZATIONS" above)
(800) 344-4867   www.nationalmssociety.org

This magazine reprint discusses the effects of multiple sclerosis on sexuality. Free. Also available on the web site.

<u>Symptom Management in Multiple Sclerosis</u>
by Randall T. Shapiro
Demos Medical Publishing
386 Park Avenue South, Suite 201
New York, NY 10016
(800) 532-8663   (212) 683-0072
FAX (212) 683-0118   e-mail: info@demospub.com   www.demosmedpub.com

A multidisciplinary guide for health care professionals and individuals with multiple sclerosis which suggests management strategies for treating multiple sclerosis and minimizing and controlling its symptoms. $19.95. Orders made on the Demos web site receive a 15% discount.

<u>Talking Books for People with Physical Disabilities</u>
National Library Service for the Blind and Physically Handicapped (NLS)
1291 Taylor Street, NW
Washington, DC 20542
(800) 424-8567 or 8572 (Reference Section)
(800) 424-9100 (to receive application)
(202) 707-5100   (202) 707-0744 (TTY)
FAX (202) 707-0712   e-mail: nls@loc.gov   www.loc.gov/nls

This brochure describes a free program which provides books and magazines recorded on discs and audiocassettes for individuals with multiple sclerosis and other disabling conditions. Application forms are available from the NLS, public libraries, or local affiliates of the National Multiple Sclerosis Society. A health professional must certify that the individual is unable to hold a book or turn pages; has blurred or double vision; extreme weakness or excessive fatigue; or other physical limitations which prevent the individual from reading standard print.

<u>300 Tips for Making Life with Multiple Sclerosis Easier</u>
by Shelley Peterman Schwarz
Demos Medical Publishing
386 Park Avenue South, Suite 201
New York, NY 10016
(800) 532-8663   (212) 683-0072
FAX (212) 683-0118   e-mail: info@demospub.com   www.demosmedpub.com

Writing from personal experience, the author shares basic tips for conserving time and energy and provides practical information on everyday living. $16.95. Orders made on the Demos web site receive a 15% discount.

<u>Urinary Dysfunction and Multiple Sclerosis: Evidence-Based Management Strategies for Urinary Dysfunction in Multiple Sclerosis</u>
Multiple Sclerosis Council for Clinical Practice Guidelines
PVA Distribution Center
PO Box 753
Waldorf, MD 20604-0753
(888) 860-7244   (301) 932-7834   FAX (301) 843-0159
www.pva.org

This booklet presents guidelines for health care professionals who care for individuals with multiple sclerosis. Includes recommendations for bladder infection treatment, voiding dysfunction, and altered mobility treatment. Free

Waist-High in the World
by Nancy Mairs
Houghton Mifflin Company
PO Box 7050
Wilmington, MA 01887
(800) 225-3362   FAX (800) 634-7568   www.hmco.com

Written by a woman who has multiple sclerosis, this book examines her personal experiences as well as general issues for women with disabilities. $15.00

Wheelchairs: Your Options and Rights Guide to Obtaining Wheelchairs from the Department of Veterans Affairs
PVA Distribution Center
PO Box 753
Waldorf, MD 20604-0753
(888) 860-7244   (301) 932-7834   FAX (301) 843-0159
www.pva.org

This booklet provides information on eligibility criteria, lists the types of wheelchairs available, and describes DVA procedures. Available in English and Spanish. Free

Yes, You Can!
MS Awareness Foundation
PO Box 1193
Venice, FL 34284
(888) 336-6723   FAX (949) 733-3211
e-mail: info@msawareness.org   www.msawareness.org

This videotape demonstrates exercises for individuals living with multiple sclerosis. $19.95

You Are Not Your Illness
by Linda Noble Topf
Simon and Schuster
IBD
PO Box 218
Paramus, NJ 07653
(888) 866-6631   FAX (800) 943-9831   www.simonsays.com

In this book, the author, who has multiple sclerosis, shares her personal perspectives on living with chronic illness. She describes a step-by-step process for dealing with loss and maintaining feelings of self-worth. $12.00

Chapter 10

OSTEOPOROSIS

Osteoporosis is a skeletal disorder that involves compromised bone strength. In the United States, ten million people have osteoporosis, and 18 million more are at risk due to low bone mass. Osteoporosis is a major cause of fractures of the spine, hip, and wrist. Each year approximately 300,000 hip fractures, 700,000 vertebral fractures, and 300,000 wrist fractures occur due to osteoporosis. In addition, 300,000 fractures at other sites of the body occur. Many of these fractures cause disabling pain. Although men are also subject to osteoporosis, they generally develop it at a later age than women and comprise only about 20% of those with the disease (National Institute of Arthritis and Musculoskeletal and Skin Diseases: 2000).

Half of the individuals who experience a hip fracture caused by osteoporosis require some help with daily living, and 15 to 25% enter long term care institutions. The pain and disability associated with osteoporosis have economic consequences that are reflected in medical, nursing home, and social costs. In the United States, the annual costs are estimated at 17 billion dollars (National Osteoporosis Foundation: 2002a).

Although the causes of osteoporosis are not clear, it has been suggested that decreased levels of estrogen and calcium are responsible for weakened bones. Bone strength is also affected by exercise; women who exercise regularly lose less bone mass than those who remain sedentary. A study found that post-menopausal women who had previously been sedentary and who carried out supervised weight-lifting exercises twice a week for a year increased their bone mineral density, while a control group who continued in their sedentary lifestyle had a decrease (Nelson et al.: 1994).

The most susceptible individuals are fair skinned, white women who are thin, have small frames, have a family history of osteoporosis, or have had their ovaries removed at an early age (National Institute on Aging: 1983). A woman who has had her ovaries removed before menopause has severely reduced levels of estrogen; if she does not take estrogen, she is at greater risk for osteoporosis. Other factors associated with the development of osteoporosis are alcohol consumption and cigarette smoking; the use of anti-inflammatory drugs to treat arthritis and lupus, antiepileptic drugs, and blood thinners also increase the risk for osteoporosis. Women who have diabetes lose calcium through excessive urination; kidney dialysis contributes to calcium loss as well. A study reported that women over age 55 who were being treated with oral or inhaled corticosteroids had lower bone densities than men who received the same treatment (Marystone et al.: 1995).

Loss of height, which occurs when weakened bones in the spine compress, fracture, and collapse, is an early sign of osteoporosis, but the condition is most often confirmed only through the use of x-rays following a fracture. Conventional x-rays do not adequately measure loss of bone mass, but other procedures do. Single or dual-photon absorptiometry measures bone mineral content, exposing the individual to lower radiation levels than conventional x-rays. A bone mass measurement, also called a bone mineral density (BMD) test, measures bone density in the spine, hip, heel, hand and/or wrist. Bone density tests may be used to detect osteoporosis, predict future fractures, and determine bone loss rates or efficacy of treatment (when conducted at regular intervals). Medicare covers bone mass measurement testing for certain high risk beneficiaries.

Compression fractures of the spine may lead to the development of the "dowager's hump," caused by loss of height and rounded shoulders. This condition affects the woman's posture and may make her more susceptible to falls. It may also make the individual more prone to breathing problems, because the chest cavity is compressed. In women with osteoporosis, fractures can even be caused by a sneeze, cough, or hug.

To prevent osteoporosis, experts recommend that women exercise regularly, stop smoking, use caffeine and alcohol moderately, increase the amount of calcium in their daily diet, and consider estrogen replacement after menopause (see text below for recent data on estrogen or hormone replacement therapy).

In a recent study, Gehlbach and colleagues (2002) reported that primary care physicians diagnosed osteoporosis or vertebral fractures in less than 2% of older women and that, of those diagnosed, only a little more than a third were offered appropriate drug therapy. Therefore, it is important that older women initiate conversations with their physicians about their risks for osteoporosis and the need for screening and treatment.

Clinical trials supported by the National Institute on Aging are testing new approaches to maintain or increase bone strength in individuals over age 65. The causes of progressive bone loss in later life are also being studied.

TYPES OF OSTEOPOROSIS AND TREATMENTS

Bone tissue is formed, broken down, resorbed, and replaced throughout life in a process called bone remodeling. Cells called osteoclasts dissolve bone tissue, releasing calcium to be used in other parts of the body. The tissue is replaced by osteoblasts, cells that draw calcium and phosphorus from the bloodstream and deposit them on the bones as collagen. In several weeks the collagen hardens to form new bone. According to Lyon and Sutton (1993), the bone remodeling process replaces nearly one-third of an individual's bone tissue in a year.

Bone tissue grows during childhood, adolescence, and early adulthood, peaking between the age of 15 and 30; after age 35, bone loss overtakes bone replacement. *Post-menopausal osteoporosis*, also referred to as *estrogen-dependent osteoporosis* (Type I), is a phase of rapid bone loss accelerated by menopause; it occurs for a relatively brief period of time and increases the risk of spine and wrist fractures (Persky and Alexander: 1989). Both women and men are affected by *age-dependent osteoporosis* (Type II), which occurs in individuals over the age of 65 and makes them susceptible to hip fractures; bone loss occurs more slowly in this type of osteoporosis. *Secondary osteoporosis* is the term used to describe bone loss due to a known cause, such as the side effects of certain medications including steroids. Secondary osteoporosis is more likely to account for bone loss in men and in women before menopause (National Institutes of Health: 2000).

The following factors may help prevent the loss of bone mass, prevent the development of osteoporosis, and treat the symptoms of the disease:

The following factors may help prevent the loss of bone mass and development of osteoporosis:

• *Good nutrition* Calcium plays a major role in the development and maintenance of strong bones. Pregnant women and women who are breastfeeding should increase their intake of calcium, for their own health and their baby's health. The mother's calcium supply will be depleted by the baby's needs, so she should eat foods rich in calcium in order to replenish it. Most adults should consume calcium by eating dairy products and other foods rich in calcium, such as salmon, broccoli, soybeans, and almonds. It is recommended that daily calcium intake in post-menopausal women (age 50-64) who are taking estrogen should be 1000 milligrams; in post-menopausal women not taking estrogen and those age 65 and over, daily calcium intake should be 1,500 milligrams (National Osteoporosis Foundation: 1995). Vitamin D, formed in the body after exposure to sunlight, aids the body in absorbing calcium. Women who do not receive enough sunlight may need a vitamin supplement. A registered dietitian or nutritionist, physician, or pharmacist can advise women which calcium supplements have the best absorption rates, do not interfere with other prescription or over-the-counter medications, and will not lead to excessive calcium intake. Women who wish to lower their fat intake and those who have lactose intolerance may substitute skim and low fat milk and yogurt or products reduced in lactose in order to meet dietary guidelines for calcium intake. Fluoride therapy, which stimulates bone formation and density, is controversial because of undesirable side effects and doubts regarding its effectiveness in preventing hip fractures (Hahn: 1988).

- *Exercise* Walking, jogging, dancing, bicycling, and other forms of weight-bearing exercise are recommended to help decrease bone loss. Simple exercises which promote good posture and muscle strength will also help prevent injuries. Physical therapists caution women with osteoporosis to avoid bending forward during daily activities, which may lead to crush fractures in the spine.

- *Hormone therapy* Although estrogen/progestin hormone therapy has been shown to reduce the number of hip fractures in women, a large clinical study of the effects of this therapy in preventing heart disease, breast and colorectal cancer, and osteoporosis was halted due to evidence that the risks outweighed benefits. The Women's Health Initiative study (2002) showed a 26% increase in breast cancer, a 41% increase in stroke, and a 29% increase in heart attacks, as well as a doubling of blood clots in legs and lungs, in the women who used hormone (estrogen) therapy. Women are urged to weigh the benefits and their personal risks for these conditions and consider other options for prevention of osteoporosis.

- *Calcitonin therapy (Miacalcin)*, a hormone provided through injection or a nasal spray, has been found to be effective in women with Type I osteoporosis (Avioli: 1992). Although a runny nose is the only side effect reported for the nasal spray form of treatment, allergic reactions, nausea, frequent urination, flushing of the hands and face, and skin reactions are reported side effects of injectable calcitonin (National Osteoporosis Foundation: 1996). It is approved for treatment of osteoporosis only. Although a runny nose is the only side effect reported for the nasal spray form of treatment, allergic reactions, nausea, frequent urination, flushing of the hands and face, and skin reactions are reported side effects of injectable calcitonin (National Osteoporosis Foundation: 2002b).

- *Alendronate therapy* (Fosamax), a nonhormonal prescription medication, has been approved by the Food and Drug Administration for use by women after menopause for both the prevention and treatment of osteoporosis. In several large studies, individuals taking the drug showed a significant increase in bone mass in the hip and spine (Food and Drug Administration: 1995). Since nausea, heartburn, and irritation of the esophagus are possible side effects, it is recommended that a woman take the medication in the morning on an empty stomach, drinking six to eight ounces of water. She should avoid eating, drinking other beverages, or taking other medications, and she should sit or stand upright for at least 30 minutes to an hour after taking Fosamax, to reduce the risk of these side effects.

- *Raloxifene* (Evista) is a drug approved for the prevention and treatment of osteoporosis that appears to prevent bone loss at the spine, hip, and total body. It is an estrogen-like compound, called a selective estrogen receptor molecule or SERM, that does not cause uterine cell growth, may have no effect on breast tissue, and reduces LDL cholesterol while increasing HDL cholesterol.

- *Risedronate* (Actonel) is approved for use in the prevention and treatment of primary osteoporosis in women and glucocorticoid-induced osteoporosis in both women and men. It has been shown to benefit hip and spine bone mass and decrease spinal fractures. Like Fosamax, it must be taken on an empty stomach, with water, early in the morning, and the individual should remain upright and avoid eating and drinking and taking other medications for at least one half hour.

- *Teriparatide* (Forteo) is a parathyroid hormone that increases the rate of bone formation in post-menopausal women through daily injections. Side effects include nausea, leg cramps, and dizziness.
- *Vertebroplasty* stabilizes a fractured vertebra and reduce pain. The procedure involves injecting bone cement into the injured section (Eck et al.: 2002). An alternative procedure, percutaneous balloon kyphoplasty, involves inflating a balloon into the injured vertebral body in an attempt to restore height prior to injecting the body with bone cement (Theodorou et al.: 2002). A study of 70 kyphoplasty procedures concluded that the pain was reduced, function was restored, and height of the vertebral body was increased following the procedure (Lieberman et al.: 2001).

ACCIDENT PREVENTION

It has been estimated that a third of noninstitutionalized individuals age 65 or over fall each year; among elders in long term care facilities, the proportion is higher. In most cases, falls do not cause serious injuries, although more than 215,000 falls each year result in hip fractures (National Institute on Aging: 1991). Hip fractures, in turn, may lead to other health problems and a consequent loss of independence.

Risk factors for falls include the use of sedatives, cognitive impairment, alcohol consumption, and posture and gait problems. In addition to osteoporosis, other conditions found in elders, such as Parkinson's disease, stroke, and visual impairment, are predisposing factors for falls. Environmental hazards are also the source of a large proportion of falls. Many older women have multiple disabilities that are risk factors for falls, and often the exact cause or causes of a given fall are unknown.

Tinetti and her colleagues (1988) found that nearly one-third (32%) of individuals 75 years or older living in the community fell at least once during their one year study. Of those who fell, one-quarter (24%) sustained serious injuries.

Several investigators have suggested that the fear of falling itself results in the self-imposed limitation of activity by many elders (Duthie: 1989; Tinetti et al.: 1988). One study (Walker and Howland: 1991) found that fear of falling resulted in the curtailment of activities by 41% of the respondents.

Ironically, the fear of falling may actually result in additional falls, because inactivity may cause weakness and hinder joint mobility (Sattin: 1992; Walker and Howland: 1991). Research has confirmed that exercise may play a protective role in preventing fractures among elders (National Institute on Aging: 1991; Sorock et al.: 1988). Health care professionals, especially physical therapists, can help develop walking and exercise programs that build muscle strength and enable older women to continue to be active.

Since most falls in the older population occur in the home, environmental adaptations may reduce the occurrence of falls and provide reassurance to women who have fallen in the past and fear falling again. There are many obvious ways of making the home safer and preventing falls; these include using nonskid rugs, providing good lighting and reducing glare, installing grab bars in tubs and next to toilets, using bath chairs in the shower and tub, and eliminating elevated thresholds. Level, nonskid floors, uncluttered halls and aisles, night lights, and handrails along stairs may also help to prevent falls. The use of canes and other mobility aids may assist women who have trouble walking and bolster their confidence as well.

Personal response systems for emergencies may reduce the fear of falling, fostering self-confidence in older women with disabilities and enabling family members or other caregivers to feel comfortable when leaving the home. If a woman falls or experiences symptoms of a medical emergency, she activates the system, usually by pushing a device that is worn around the neck or kept nearby, that alerts a designated response network. Purchase and installation of equipment may be reimbursable by third-party payment, although the individual is usually responsible for monthly service fees.

Public health officials, recognizing that falls among elders pose a serious health problem, have suggested that prevention programs be implemented on a widespread basis. Using the risk factors associated with falling to determine the target population, occupational therapists, architects, and others trained in environmental adaptations could conduct assessments of the home environments of older women as well as places that they frequent, such as senior centers and churches. Checklists of home safety items are available from a number of organizations to facilitate this undertaking (see "PUBLICATIONS AND TAPES" section below).

Women who use exercise to maintain strong bones and muscles are less apt to be injured than those who are sedentary. With the following suggestions in mind, older women should perform a safety check of their homes to remove obstacles; they should make other changes to avoid falls and accidents which lead to fractures. Staff members at senior centers and other public areas where elders meet should also be aware of these suggestions:

- Sturdy, low-heeled, soft-soled shoes are safer than high heels with slick soles. Shoes that are too large and slip-on sandals and slippers are also dangerous. Long bathrobes or other full-length garments may result in falls.
- Scatter rugs, loose telephone and electric cords, and clutter should be removed. Nonskid mats should be used in bathtubs and showers, and grab bars should be installed.
- Night-lights should be used in bathrooms and halls, and bright bulbs should be used in stairs and halls.
- Handrails should be installed in stairways, and treads or carpeting used on stairs should be firmly fastened down.
- Caution should be used on wet, icy, uneven, or broken pavement. Curbs, slick floors, tile floors, and oil leaks present hazards to women with osteoporosis.
- Older women should ask their physicians about side effects of medications, such as dizziness, balance problems, or light-headedness. The use of alcohol may also affect balance and reflexes.
- Older women should have their vision and hearing checked regularly. Inadequate refraction for eyeglasses or the build-up of ear wax may cause balance problems.
- Older women should consult with a physical therapist for suggestions to help reduce their risk for fractures. Proper sitting and standing positions, correct pulling and pushing techniques, and reducing stress on the back and joints when sleeping or resting will enable them to live more comfortably with osteoporosis.

PSYCHOLOGICAL ASPECTS OF OSTEOPOROSIS

Older women with osteoporosis need to consider changes in their lifestyle to reduce the chance of injury. Such changes may include moving to a home or apartment with only one floor in order to avoid falls on stairs; giving up chores which involve heavy lifting; and learning to use assistive devices in everyday activities. Moving to a new environment, giving up normal routines, and finding new friends require psychological adjustments. Fear of falling often results in activity limitation and staying indoors. The social isolation that results may contribute to loneliness and depression. Older women who find themselves depressed by the multiple changes in their lives may wish to seek counseling from a social worker or psychologist or join a self-help group to learn from others in similar situations.

It is not unusual for older women to become depressed when hospitalized or placed in a long term care facility due to a fracture and to be anxious about their future. Daily living with osteoporosis may require that women use medication to cope with pain; receive physical therapy to maintain flexibility; and be very cautious in everyday activities. These factors may affect their motivation to participate in a rehabilitation program.

PROFESSIONAL SERVICE PROVIDERS

Gynecologists often serve as the primary care physicians for women in the age ranges most at risk for osteoporosis. Gynecologists may recommend estrogen replacement therapy for women at menopause, after carefully weighing the benefits and potential risks.

Orthopedic surgeons or *plastic surgeons* may perform surgery to repair or replace bones damaged by fractures caused by osteoporosis. Hip or knee replacement surgery may be recommended.

Physiatrists, physicians who specialize in rehabilitation medicine, will often first see the individual after a fracture and admission to a rehabilitation program. Physiatrists evaluate the fracture and develop the overall rehabilitation plan. Physiatrists act as case managers, coordinating medical and rehabilitation services, working with the primary care physician, and arranging for physical therapy, if necessary.

Physical therapists design individualized programs to improve posture and strengthen muscles. Physical therapists also teach how to move safely to avoid injury.

Occupational therapists may perform a home safety assessment, making suggestions for accident prevention, such as removing loose electrical cords and throw rugs, installing grab bars, and increasing lighting in stairways, halls, and bathrooms.

Registered dietitians or *nutritionists* recommend dietary measures to ensure that women eat the foods that supply important nutrients for the maintenance of their bones.

Social workers help patients with osteoporosis plan for discharge from a hospital or a rehabilitation center to an environment where they can function independently. This may include discharge to the individual's home with arrangements for home health care; to a relative's home; to a long term care facility; or to congregate housing.

WHERE TO FIND SERVICES

Women with osteoporosis will often be hospitalized for corrective surgery when a fracture occurs; when difficult diagnostic procedures are necessary; or for rehabilitation. They may enter a rehabilitation unit within a community hospital or a rehabilitation hospital. Most rehabilitation centers also offer outpatient services.

Women who have had a fracture may require home health services, including home treatment and maintenance care provided by nurses or home health aides; homemaker services such as meal preparation; Meals on Wheels; chore services such as housecleaning; and adult day activity programs. For some, these services may be needed on a short term basis. They are provided by public and private agencies.

Some of the transportation needs of individuals whose everyday functioning has been affected by osteoporosis may be met through the use of special van services or special parking placards for individuals with disabilities.

References

Avioli, Louis V.
1992   "Osteoporosis Syndromes: Patient Selection for Calcitonin Therapy" Geriatrics
        47(April)4:58-67

Duthie, Edmund H.

1989   "Falls" <u>Medical Clinics of North America</u> 73(November):6:1321-133

Eck, J.C. et al.

2002   "Vertebroplasty: A New Treatment Strategy for Osteoporotic Compression Fractures" <u>American Journal of Orthopedics</u> 31:3(March):123-127

Food and Drug Administration

1995   "FDA Approves New Drug for Bones Disorders" <u>FDA Talk Paper</u> October 2

Gehlbach, S.H., M. Fournier, and C. Bigelow

2002   "Recognition of Osteoporosis by Primary Care Physicians" <u>American Journal of Public Health</u> 92:2(February):271-273

Hahn, Bevra H.

1988   "Osteoporosis: Diagnosis and Management" <u>Bulletin on the Rheumatic Diseases</u> 38:1-9 Atlanta, GA: Arthritis Foundation

Lieberman, I.H. et al.

2001   "Initial Outcome and Efficacy of "Kyphoplasty" in the Treatment of Painful Osteoporotic Vertebral Compression Fractures" <u>Spine</u> 26:14(July 15):1631-1638

Lyon, Wanda S. and Cynthia E. Sutton

1993   <u>Osteoporosis: How to Make Your Bones Last a Lifetime</u> Orlando, FL: Tribune Publishing

Marystone, Jane F., Elizabeth L. Barrett-Connor, and Deborah J. Morton

1995   "Inhaled and Oral Corticosteroids: Their Effects on Bone Mineral Density in Older Adults" <u>American Journal of Public Health</u> 85:12:1693

National Institute of Arthritis and Musculoskeletal and Skin Diseases

2000   <u>Osteoporosis: Progress and Promise</u> August

National Institutes of Health

2000   <u>Osteoporosis Prevention, Diagnosis, and Therapy NIH Consensus Statement Online 2000</u> March 27-29 17(1):1-36

National Institute on Aging

1991   <u>Physical Frailty</u> Department of Health and Human Services, NIH Publication 91-397

1983   "Osteoporosis: The Bone Thinner" <u>Age Page</u> Washington, DC: National Institute on Aging

National Osteoporosis Foundation

2002a   <u>Prevalence of Low Bone Mass and Osteoporosis Affects Significant Percentage of Men and Women in U.S. 50 and Older</u> Washington, DC: National Osteoporosis Foundation

2002b   <u>Medications and Osteoporosis</u> Washington, DC: National Osteoporosis Foundation

1996   <u>Medications Used to Prevent and Treat Osteoporosis</u> Washington, DC: National Osteoporosis Foundation

1995   <u>Calcium: Important at Every Age</u> Washington, DC: National Osteoporosis Foundation

Nelson, M. et al.

1994   "Effects of High Intensity Strength On Multiple Risk Factors for Osteoporotic Fractures: A Randomized Controlled Trial" <u>Journal of the American Medical Association</u> 272(Dec 28):1909-1914

Persky, Neal and Neil Alexander

1989   "Issues of Aging in Preventive Medicine and the Example of Osteoporosis" <u>Primary Care</u> 16(March)1:231-243

Sattin, Richard W.

1992   "Falls among Older Persons: A Public Health Perspective" <u>Annual Review of Public Health</u> 13:489-508

Sorock, Gary S. et al.

1988 "Physical Activity and Fracture Risk in a Free-Living Elderly Cohort" <u>Journal of Gerontology Medical Sciences</u> 43:5:M134-139

Theodorou, D.J. et al.

2002 "Percutaneous Balloon Kyphoplasty for the Correction of Spinal Deformity in Vertebral Body Compression Fractures" <u>Clinical Imaging</u> 25:1(January-February):1-5

Tinetti, Mary E., Mark Speechley, and Sandra F. Ginter

1988 "Risk Factors for Falls among Elderly Persons Living in the Community" <u>New England Journal of Medicine</u> 349:26:1701-1707

Walker, J. Elizabeth and Jonathan Howland

1991 "Falls and Fear of Falling among Elderly Persons Living in the Community: Occupational Therapy Interventions" <u>American Journal of Occupational Therapy</u> 45(February):2:119-122

Women's Health Initiative

2002 "Risks and Benefits of Estrogen Plus Progestin in Healthy Postmenopausal Women" <u>JAMA</u> 288:3(July 17):321-333

ORGANIZATIONS

American Academy of Orthopaedic Surgeons
6300 North River Road
Rosemont, IL 60018
(800) 346-2267   (847) 823-7186   FAX (847) 823-8125
orthosinfo.aaos.org   www.aaos.org

Professional organization of physicians who specialize in treating the musculoskeletal system, including the bones, joints, muscles, ligaments, and tendons. Provides information to the public on arthritis, joint replacement, osteoporosis, and fracture prevention. Free. Also available on web site. Web site offers a "Find a Surgeon" link. Click on "Spine" for fact sheets. A quarterly e-mail newsletter, "Your Orthopaedic Connection," is available upon request.

American Chronic Pain Association (ACPA)
PO Box 850
Rocklin, CA 95677
(800) 533-3231   FAX (916) 632-3208   e-mail: acpa@pacbell.neet
www.theacpa.org

Organizes groups throughout the U.S. to provide support and activities for people who experience chronic pain. Membership, $30.00 first year, $15.00 thereafter; includes quarterly newsletter, "ACPA Chronicle."

American College of Obstetricians and Gynecologists (ACOG)
409 12th Street, SW, PO Box 96920
Washington, DC 20024-6920
(202) 638-5577   FAX (202) 484-1595
Resource Center: (202) 863-2518 www.acog.org

A professional society of obstetricians and gynecologists, this organization will send up to five publications at no charge.

American Dietetic Association (ADA)
216 West Jackson Boulevard
Chicago, IL 60606
(800) 877-1600   (312) 899-0040   FAX (312) 899-1758
e-mail: hotline@eatright.org   www.eatright.org

Consumers may receive a referral to a registered dietitian or receive information about nutrition on the telephone or on the web site. Available in English and Spanish.

American Pain Foundation (APF)
201 North Charles Street, Suite 710
Baltimore, MD 21201
(888) 615-7246   FAX (410) 385-1832
e-mail: info@painfoundation.org   www.painfoundation.org

This organization provides educational materials and advocates on behalf of people who are experiencing pain. Promotes research and advocates to remove barriers to treatment for pain. Distributes patient educational materials. Free. Information about the causes of pain and treatment as well as links to related sites is available on its web site.

MEDLINEplus: Osteoporosis
www.nlm.nih.gov/medlineplus/osteoporosis.html

This web sites provides links to sites for general information about osteoporosis, symptoms and diagnosis, treatment, prevention/screening, clinical trials, nutrition, research, and organizations. Includes an interactive tutorial. Some information is available in Spanish. Provides links to MEDLINE research articles and related MEDLINEplus pages.

National Aging Institute Information Center (NAIC)
330 Independence Avenue, SW, Room 4656
Washington, DC 20201
(202) 619-7501   FAX (202) 401-7620   www.aoa.gov/naic

Provides information and statistics related to research conducted by the National Institute on Aging. Free publications list. Many publications available on the web site.

National Alliance to Prevent Falls as We Age
National Safety Council
1121 Spring Lake Drive
Itasca, IL 60143
(630) 285-1121   FAX (630) 285-1315   e-mail: info@nsc.org
www.nsc.org

The members of the Alliance work to educate the public about fall prevention, home modification, and physical activity to promote balance and strength.

National Bone Health Campaign
www.cdc.gov/powerfulbones   (770) 488-5820

This web site, sponsored by the Centers for Disease Prevention and Control, targets girls 9 to 12 years old, in an effort to encourage healthy behaviors that lead to strong bones. Includes ideas for exercise, a dictionary, and a calendar of events.

National Institute of Arthritis and Musculoskeletal and Skin Diseases Information Clearinghouse
1 AMS Circle
Bethesda, MD 20892
(877) 226-4267   (301) 495-4484
(301) 565-2966 (TTY)   FAX (301) 718-6366
e-mail: niamsinfo@mail.nih.gov   www.niams.nih.gov

Distributes bibliographies, fact sheets, catalogues, and directories to the public and professionals. Free. Many of the publications are available on the web site in English and Spanish. The National Institute of Arthritis and Musculoskeletal and Skin Diseases supports clinical research, individual research, and specialized research centers, which conduct basic and clinical research; provide professional, public, and patient education; and sponsor community-related activities.

National Institutes of Health Osteoporosis and Related Bone Diseases National Resource Center

1232 22nd Street, NW
Washington, DC 20037

(800) 293-2356   (202) 223-0344   (202) 466-4315 (TTY)
FAX (202) 223-2237   e-mail: orbdnrc@nof.org   www.osteo.org

Provides public and professional education materials on metabolic bone diseases including osteoporosis. Operates a listserv, which sends information electronically to participants. Publications available both on the web site and in print in English, Spanish, and Asian languages. Free. Publishes quarterly newsletter, "NIH ORBD-NRC News." Free

National Osteoporosis Foundation (NOF)

1232 22nd Street, NW
Washington, DC 20037

(800) 223-9994   (202) 223-2226
FAX (202) 223-2237   www.nof.org

Provides public and professional education materials and supports research. Free. Membership, $15.00, includes quarterly newsletter, "The Osteoporosis Report," and discounts on educational materials. Web site offers links to an online video library of topics such as understanding osteoporosis, risk factors, bone density testing, and treatment.

North American Menopause Society (NAMS)

PO Box 94527
Cleveland, OH 44101

(440) 442-7550   FAX (440) 442-2660
e-mail: info@menopause.org   www.menopause.org

This scientific society studies perimenopause, early menopause, symptoms of menopause, and long term health effects. Provides referrals to clinicians and discussion groups. Many publications have information on osteoporosis and are available on the web site.

Women's Health Initiative (WHI)

National Heart, Lung and Blood Institute,
National Institutes of Health
6705 Rockledge Drive, Suite 300
Rockledge One, MSC 7966
Bethesda, MD 20892-7966

(301) 402-2900   FAX (301) 480-5158   e-mail: nmo9@nih.gov
www.nhlbi.nih.gov/whi/index.html   www.whi.org

This major women's health research project enrolled 162,000 women ages 50 to 79 to study the major causes of death, disability, and the quality of life in post-menopausal women. Osteoporosis is one of the conditions included in the study. The web sites include information about the findings of the study to date as well as references to articles that came out of the study.

After the Vertebral Fracture
National Institutes of Health Osteoporosis and Related Bone Diseases National Resource Center
(see "ORGANIZATIONS" section above)
(800) 624-2663   www.osteo.org

This fact sheet discusses vertebral fractures, treatment, and rehabilitation. Free. Also available on the web site.

Balancing Act: Your Fall Prevention Program
Terra Nova Films, Inc.
9848 South Winchester Avenue
Chicago, IL 60643
(800) 779-8491   (773) 881-8491   e-mail: tnf@terranova.org
www.terranova.org

This videotape reviews hazardous situations that can lead to falls in long term care facilities. Comes with presenter's guide. 24 minutes. $139.00

Be BoneWise - Exercise
National Osteoporosis Foundation (NOF)
PO Box 930299
Atlanta, GA 31193-0299
(877) 868-4520   FAX (770) 442-9742   FAX (202) 223-2237
e-mail: customerservice@nof.org   www.nof.org

This exercise videotape offers warm up, aerobic, wall, chair, and floor exercises. 40 minutes. $19.95

Better Bones and Balance: An Exercise Guide to Reduce the Risk of Osteoporosis and Falling
Bones and Balance, Inc.
301 SW 4th Street, Suite 160
Corvallis,OR 97333
(888) 431-9455   e-mail: info@bonesandbalance.com www.bonesandbalance.com

This exercise program, consisting of two videotapes and an exercise log, goes from beginner to advanced. Tape 1 includes an introduction to osteoporosis and demonstrates exercises (26 minutes). Tape 2 goes through a 45 minute exercise program. $69.95

Boning Up on Osteoporosis
National Osteoporosis Foundation (NOF
PO Box 930299
Atlanta, GA 31193-0299
(877) 868-4520   FAX (770) 442-9742   FAX (202) 223-2237
e-mail: customerservice@nof.org   www.nof.org)

This booklet includes information on the risk factors for osteoporosis, accident prevention, and posture and muscle strengthening exercises. $3.00.

Check for Safety: A Home Fall Prevention Checklist for Older Adults
National Center for Injury Prevention and Control
4770 Buford Highway, NE, Mailstop K65
Atlanta, GA 30341-3724
(770) 488-1506   FAX (770) 488-1667   e-mail: ohcinfo@cdc.gov
www.cdc.gov/ncipc/pub-res/pubs.htm

This checklist enables individuals to identify and remedy hazards in areas such as floors, stairs and steps, kitchen, bedrooms, and bathrooms. Available in English and Spanish. Large print. Free. Also available on the web site.

Exercise: A Video from the National Institute on Aging
Exercise Guide from the National Institute on Aging
National Aging Institute Information Center
Department W
PO Box 8057
Gaithersburg, MD 20898-8057
(800) 222-2225   (800) 222-4225 (TTY)   www.nia.nih.gov

The videotape (48 minutes) and book provide guidelines on how to start and stick with an exercise program. $7.00

Falls and Related Fractures
National Osteoporosis Foundation (NOF) (see "ORGANIZATIONS" section above)
(877) 868-4520   www.nof.org

This pamphlet discusses the relationship between osteoporosis, falls, and fractures and suggests risk reduction, exercises to improve balance, and osteoporosis prevention tips. Free. Also available on the web site.

Head over Heels: Falls and How to Prevent Them
Terra Nova Films
9848 South Winchester Avenue
Chicago, IL 60643
(800) 779-8491   (773) 881-8491
FAX (773) 881-3368   www.terranova.org

This videotape provides practical suggestions for preventing falls by elders. Comes with a 16 page presenter's guide. 14 minutes. $79.00

Home Safety Checklist for Older Consumers
U.S. Consumer Product Safety Commission
Washington, DC 20207-0001
(800) 638-2772   (301) 504-0580   FAX (301) 504-0281
e-mail: info@cpsc.gov   www.cpsc.gov

Provides information on simple, inexpensive repairs and safety recommendations. Available in English and Spanish. Free. Also available on the web site.

Living with Osteoporosis
National Osteoporosis Foundation (NOF)
PO Box 930299
Atlanta, GA 31193-0299
(877) 868-4520   FAX (770) 442-9742   FAX (202) 223-2237
e-mail: customerservice@nof.org   www.nof.org

This booklet provides tips for everyday living with osteoporosis. Includes recommendations for preventing falls and making every room in the home safe. $.35

Medications and Bone Loss
National Osteoporosis Foundation (NOF)
PO Box 930299
Atlanta, GA 31193-0299
(877) 868-4520   FAX (770) 442-9742   FAX (202) 223-2237
e-mail: customerservice@nof.org   www.nof.org
www.nof.org

This booklet discusses how medications such as steroids, taken for other medical conditions, may increase the risk of developing osteoporosis. $.75

Nutrition and the Skeleton
National Institutes of Health Osteoporosis and Related Bone Diseases National Resource Center (see "ORGANIZATIONS" section above)
(800) 624-2663   www.osteo.org

This fact sheet discusses the effects of calcium and other nutrients on bone health. Free. Also available on the web site.

Osteoporosis
Arthritis Foundation
1330 West Peachtree Street
Atlanta, GA 30309
(800) 283-7800   (404) 872-7100   FAX (404) 872-0457
www.arthritis.org

This booklet provides information about causes, symptoms, diagnosis, and treatment of osteoporosis. Includes home safety check list. Free. Also available on the web site.

Osteoporosis: A Woman's Guide
National Osteoporosis Foundation (NOF)
PO Box 930299
Atlanta, GA 31193-0299
(877) 868-4520   FAX (770) 442-9742   FAX (202) 223-2237
e-mail: customerservice@nof.org   www.nof.org

This brochure describes how women can assess their risk for the condition and prevent or slow its progress. Available in standard print and Large print. Free

The Osteoporosis Book: A Guide for Patients and Their Families
by Nancy E. Lane
Oxford University Press
2001 Evans Road
Cary, NC 27513
(800) 451-7556   FAX (919) 677-1303
e-mail: custservs@oup-usa.org   www.oup-usa.org

This book describes the condition, risk factors, diagnosis, and treatment. Also discusses falls and the prevention and treatment of secondary osteoporosis. Hardcover, $25.00; softcover, $13.95

Osteoporosis Overview
National Institutes of Health Osteoporosis and Related Bone Diseases National Resource Center
(see "ORGANIZATIONS" section above)
(800) 624-2663   www.osteo.org

This information packet contains medical articles, patient information, fact sheets, and a glossary. Free. Also available on the web site.

Pregnancy, Lactation and Bone Health
National Institute of Arthritis and Musculoskeletal and Skin Diseases Information Clearinghouse
(see "ORGANIZATIONS" section above)
(877) 226-4267   www.niams.nih.gov

This publication provides information for women who are breast feeding. Free. Also available on the web site.

Stand Tall: Every Woman's Guide to Preventing and Treating Osteoporosis
by Morris Notelovitz
Triad Publishing Company
PO Box 13355
Gainesville, FL 32604
(800) 525-6902   FAX (800) 525-4947   www.triadpublishing.com

This book provides basic information about osteoporosis and describes how nutrition and exercise help to prevent bone loss. Discusses drug treatments including hormone replacement therapy. $24.95

Stand UP to Osteoporosis
National Osteoporosis Foundation (NOF) (see "ORGANIZATIONS" section above)
(800) 223-9994   www.nof.org

This brochure describes the condition, risk factors, preventive measures, diagnosis, and treatment.
Free

Strategies for People with Osteoporosis
National Osteoporosis Foundation (NOF)
PO Box 930299
Atlanta, GA 31193-0299
(877) 868-4520   FAX (770) 442-9742   FAX (202) 223-2237
e-mail: customerservice@nof.org   www.nof.org

This packet of articles offers suggestions for coping with osteoporosis, including what to do after
diagnosis, recovery from fractures, and safety in the home. $15.00

Style Wise: A Fashion Guide for Women with Osteoporosis
National Osteoporosis Foundation (NOF)
PO Box 930299
Atlanta, GA 31193-0299
(877) 868-4520   FAX (770) 442-9742   FAX (202) 223-2237
e-mail: customerservice@nof.org   www.nof.org

This booklet discusses the body changes due to osteoporosis that make clothes difficult to fit. Provides
design and fashion tips for comfortable clothing. $1.75

Talking with Your Doctor about Osteoporosis
National Osteoporosis Foundation (NOF)
PO Box 930299
Atlanta, GA 31193-0299
(877) 868-4520   FAX (770) 442-9742   FAX (202) 223-2237
e-mail: customerservice@nof.org   www.nof.org

This booklet lists questions women of all ages should ask their physicians about preventing
osteoporosis, including topics such as exercise, diet, and lifestyle. $.30

Vertebroplasty: A New Interventional Radiology Treatment for the Pain of Spinal Fractures Caused
by Osteoporosis
Society for Interventional Radiology
10201 Lee Highway, Suite 500
Fairfax, VA 222030
(800) 488-7284   (703) 691-1805   FAX (703) 691-1855
e-mail: info@sirweb.org   www.sirweb.org

This brochure describes the procedure, its effects, and the recovery process. Free. Also available on
the web site.

Chapter 11

SPINAL CORD INJURY

Injury to the spinal cord is a traumatic physical injury as well as a serious psychological injury. Because the spinal cord is responsible for transmitting the brain's electrical impulses that control other organs of the body, an injury to the spinal cord affects many of the body's systems. Required modifications of life style may be extreme, depending upon the severity of the injury. When a spinal cord injury occurs in a woman who is expecting to have a family or who already has young children, her plans for the future may seem to go awry. Although the effects of the injury may be overwhelming at first, rehabilitation opportunities and the development of a wide variety of special assistive devices have enabled thousands of individuals with spinal cord injuries to live productive lives and to continue to participate in many recreational activities, albeit in modified forms.

It has been estimated that there are about 200,000 living Americans who have experienced spinal cord injuries, the majority of whom were injured during or after World War II. Prior to World War II and the development of penicillin and sulfa drugs that prevent death from urinary tract infections, it was unusual for those who had a spinal cord injury to survive (DeVivo et al.: 1987). Today, due to the development of these drugs and improved emergency medical care at the scene of accidents, the vast majority of individuals with spinal cord injuries live for many years.

Studies of patients admitted to the Model Spinal Cord Injury Care Systems have yielded demographic characteristics about the population. Less than one-fifth (18.4%) of individuals with spinal cord injuries are females. The average age at onset is 32.1 years. Automobile accidents account for 38.5% of spinal cord injuries. Violence as a cause of spinal cord injury has increased in recent years; it now accounts for 24.5% of all spinal cord injuries. Sports accidents (frequently diving accidents) account for 7.2% of all spinal cord injuries and are a major cause of spinal cord injuries among the younger population, while falls, which account for 21.8% of all spinal cord injuries, are a major cause among the older population (National Spinal Cord Injury Statistical Center: 2001).

A study of women with spinal cord injuries in one metropolitan area found that 28% had experienced violence that caused their injuries (White et al.: 1996). Sports accidents are a major cause of spinal cord injuries among the younger population, while falls are a major cause among the older population. Tumors and diseases such as poliomyelitis, arthritis, spina bifida, and multiple sclerosis may also cause spinal cord injuries.

A study (DeVivo et al.: 1992) investigated the characteristics of men and women who had received treatment for spinal cord injury at six federally supported model treatment centers between 1973 and 1986. The study found several significant differences between the population who had been injured in the period 1973-77 and those who had been injured in the period 1984-86; the mean age at the time of injury increased over time as did the proportion of individuals who were not white and the proportion with quadriplegia. Although the mean length of stays in hospitals for rehabilitation decreased, the cost of the rehabilitation increased. For those who entered the centers within the first 24 hours of injury, the probability of dying in the first two years following injury decreased by two-thirds. While virtually all of the subjects were discharged to live in the community during the entire study period, only a small percentage of the subjects were employed two years post-injury, ranging from a low of 12.5% in the 1978-80 period to a high of 14.7% for those who had been injured from 1984-86. While a substantial proportion were students and small proportions were either homemakers or retired two years post-injury, over half of the subjects were unemployed throughout the study period.

Women with spinal cord injuries comprise an underemployed group. Bonwich (1985) found that 31 of 36 respondents had worked prior to their injury, but at the time of her interviews only eight of the 36 were working full-time. This low rate of employment is consistent with other studies (for example, DeVivo et al.: 1992). Charlifue and colleagues (1992) found that level of impairment was significantly related to rates of employment; while 59% of women with incomplete paraplegia held jobs, only 18% of those with complete quadriplegia held jobs. Women with higher levels of education are more likely to be employed following spinal cord injury, because their work is usually sedentary and requires little physical activity.

THE SPINAL CORD

The spine has 33 bony, hollow, interlocking vertebrae including seven cervical or neck vertebrae, 12 thoracic or high back vertebrae, five lumbar or low back vertebrae, five sacral vertebrae near the base of the spine, and four coccygeal vertebrae fused to form the coccyx. The spinal cord, consisting of a narrow bundle of nerve cells and fibers, runs from the base of the brain through the hollow structure of the vertebrae. The brain's communication with the rest of the body is carried out through these nerve fibers.

Paralysis, the loss or impairment of motor function, occurs below the site of the injury or fracture. Not all injuries are complete, meaning that sometimes the individual may retain some sensation or movement below the site of the injury. *Paraplegia*, or paralysis of the legs and often the lower part of the body, occurs when the spinal cord is injured at the thoracic, lumbar, or sacral level of the spine. When injuries are complete, individuals also lose their sense of touch, pain, and temperature in the affected region.

Quadriplegia (or tetraplegia) is paralysis of all four limbs and the part of the body beneath the site of the spinal cord injury. Quadriplegia occurs when the injury to the spinal cord is at the level of the cervical vertebrae or the neck region. The lower the lesion within the cervical area, the greater amount of function that remains. Some individuals with cervical spinal cord injuries retain some function of the shoulders, biceps, upper arms, and the wrists. In general, the higher the site of the injury, the less function the individual retains. Individuals whose injuries are complete and at the chin level require respirators in order to breathe. These individuals require assistance with their everyday activities, although the use of mouthsticks and sip-and-puff mechanisms enables them to operate wheelchairs, computers, and other devices (Trieschmann: 1988).

According to Young and his associates (1982), there is a higher prevalence of quadriplegia (53%) than paraplegia (47%), but the injuries are more likely to be complete in paraplegia (60%) than quadriplegia (52%).

TREATMENT AND COMPLICATIONS OF SPINAL CORD INJURY

Acute medical care following an accident that has caused spinal cord injury includes x-rays, possible treatment for shock, and immobilization of the patient. Patients are often placed in a Stryker frame, which is used to immobilize the spine and prevent further injury. A catheter to control bladder function is inserted, and urine output is monitored. In some cases, surgery may be performed to stabilize or fuse the spine, free nerve roots, or remove bony fragments. Immediately following the injury, swelling and bruising near the site of the fracture may be present, preventing the determination of the extent of neurological damage (Trieschmann: 1988). Patients are positioned and turned frequently in an effort to prevent pressure sores (see below). Other injuries that often accompany spinal cord injuries, such as fractures and lung injuries, must also be treated. Pain may also be a major problem in the first weeks following injury.

Preliminary studies on the use of drugs immediately following spinal cord injury have found some positive benefits. Administration of methylprednisolone within eight hours following the injury resulted in the recovery of an average of 20% of the motor and sensory function lost (Hingley: 1993).

Although treatments have been developed for many of the complications of spinal cord injury, it is still necessary to constantly be aware of the development of these complications and to take measures to prevent them. *Pressure sores* or *decubitus ulcers* are lesions on the skin that usually occur over a bony surface and result from lack of motion. Because the individual may have no sensation at the site where the sores begin to develop, they may become deep before they are discovered. In an effort to prevent pressure sores, individuals who are confined to bed immediately following the injury should be moved frequently and great attention should be paid to cleansing the skin regularly. Special flotation pads and sheepskins are sometimes used to relieve pressure and distribute body weight. Because of their restricted mobility, individuals with spinal cord injuries must take precautions to prevent pressure sores for the rest of their lives.

Despite the loss of sensation to temperature and touch below the site of the lesion, *pain* and unusual sensations may be a problem for people with spinal cord injuries. According to Trieschmann (1988), until recently it was assumed that pain was not a problem, and little attention was paid to the subject. However, Trieschmann states that many individuals experience a tingling or pins and needles sensation as well as other types of pain, such as shooting or burning sensations.

Transcutaneous electric nerve stimulation (TENS) is a treatment method for pain in which low level electric impulses are delivered to nerve endings under the skin near the source of pain. It is not known why TENS should be effective in relieving pain or if it is really effective. Research is currently underway to gain a better understanding of the way in which this procedure works.

Loss of bladder and bowel control is another complication of spinal cord injury. Those individuals who have indwelling catheters are prone to develop bladder infections. When the extent of nerve damage permits, it is preferable to have the individual learn how to control her bladder through an individualized training program. Similarly, programs for bowel control enable the individual to empty the bowel on a regular schedule, thereby avoiding gastrointestinal complications such as distention and impaction. Attention to diet and the use of rectal suppositories may also contribute to control of bowel movements.

Spasticity (involuntary jerky motions) is common in individuals with spinal cord injuries. These spasms are caused by random stimulation of the nerves leading to the muscles. Severe spasms may interfere with some activity and in some cases may be strong enough to throw the individual from the bed or chair. Baclofen is a medication that is infused into the spinal cord through an implantable pump and has been shown to improve spasticity over a long period of time without causing drug tolerance or complications (Ochs: 1999).

Functional electrical stimulation (FES) is an experimental method that uses electrical stimulation to evoke skeletal muscle responses in areas that do not function normally because injury or disease has cut off the pathway for central nervous system communication from the brain. A functional electrical stimulation system consists of a control unit, a stimulator unit, and electrodes. In some instances, the goal of functional electrical stimulation is to restore movement or function and in other cases to strengthen muscles. A study by Petrofsky (1992) found that subjects with spinal cord injuries who participated in a two year experiment using functional electrical stimulation to exercise muscles had a reduction in the incidence of pressure sores and urinary tract infections. Another experiment (Granat et al.: 1992) that used functional electrical stimulation to restore movement in six subjects with incomplete spinal cord injury found that all subjects were able to stand and walk using an FES system, but half of the subjects found that the system was not practical for their lifestyles.

As more individuals with spinal cord injuries survive longer, they are also experiencing the normal physiological processes that accompany aging. There is little information on how these processes affect people with spinal cord injuries who have been disabled for many years. The effects of menopause on women with spinal cord injuries are unknown. However, preliminary indications are that physiological changes associated with aging have a greater impact on people with spinal cord injuries. Menter (1990) calls this phase "decline," noting that there is a decrease in muscle strength, range of motion, and respiratory and cardiovascular capacity and an increase in the breakdown of the skin.

The National Institute of Neurological Disorders and Stroke (see "ORGANIZATIONS" section below) is currently funding innovative research that may someday enable clinicians to restore function to those who have experienced spinal cord injury. Some promising innovations include treatment with steroids, promoting new growth in damaged nerves, and using electronic prostheses to carry out the functions previously achieved by the damaged nerves.

A recent technological advance, the Freehand System developed by NeuroControl Corporation (see "ORGANIZATIONS" section below), enables some individuals with quadriplegia to regain control over one hand. The system requires that the individual have some motion in the upper body, so that he or she can use the shoulder to control the system. The Freehand System is a neural prosthesis that involves the surgical implantation of electrodes that send signals to muscles in the hand. Individuals control the processor that sends the signals by moving the shoulder. Using the Freehand System, individuals may be able to carry out activities such as using dining utensils, grooming, and writing.

A number of research projects around the country are working on potential cures for spinal cord injury through nerve regeneration and drug therapy. Other projects have the goal of re-training individuals to walk (Huelskamp: 1998). Devices that use technology similar to the Freehand System are potential aids that will improve bowel and bladder control and enable individuals with paraplegia by a family member, friend, or a person specifically employed for this purpose.

SEXUAL FUNCTIONING

Spinal cord injury may affect sexual functioning in both men and women, although the effects are greater for men. Women often temporarily stop menstruating upon injury, but most will resume menstruating within six months and may conceive and bear children. Rehabilitation programs for people with spinal cord injuries should include counseling in the area of sexual functioning; however, a study found that only 37% of the women with spinal cord injuries had received information related to sexual functioning compared to 66% of the men with spinal cord injuries (White et al.: 1994). Many of the counseling programs that do exist are oriented toward male sexuality, and little research has been done on female sexuality following spinal cord injury. Counseling by trained professionals can help alleviate some of the fears and anxieties that women hold about their sexuality. Suggestions for alternative positions and techniques to use during sexual relations can be invaluable, especially if the woman's partner is included in the discussion.

The lack of mobility caused by spinal cord injury changes the role that women play in sexual relationships. Individuals who have spinal cord injuries lose sensation in the parts of their bodies that are below the lesion in their spinal cord; they may derive pleasure through stimulation of parts of the body above the injury. The ability to produce adequate lubrication and to feel sensation in the genital area varies, although little laboratory research exists on these subjects. Those women who do not produce adequate vaginal lubrication are advised to use commercial, water soluble lubricants.

Most women with spinal cord injuries are sexually active. Jackson and Wadley (1999) found that two-thirds of the women that they studied had sexual intercourse within one year of the injury, although 87% had had sexual intercourse prior to their injury. Subjects in this study and in a study by White et al.: 1994) expressed a number of concerns related to their sexual relationships, including urinary incontinence, positioning, not satisfying a partner, and feeling sexually unattractive.

Self-reports from women who have experienced spinal cord injuries suggest that many are able to achieve satisfying sexual relationships. One study of 25 women with spinal cord injuries reported that 44% were able to achieve orgasm (Sipski and Alexander: 1993). The same study found that the favorite sexual activities of women with spinal cord injuries were kissing, hugging, and touching, whereas intercourse was the favorite activity prior to their injury. Another study carried out by the same laboratory (Sipski et al.: 1995) found that over half of the women with spinal cord injuries (52%) achieved orgasm compared to all of the women without spinal cord injuries. The study was not able to identify any characteristics that could predict whether women with spinal cord injuries would achieve orgasm. A study by Charlifue and colleagues (1992) reported that 69% of the subjects were satisfied with their sex life following spinal cord injury, and about half said that they were capable of achieving orgasm. However, the women reported that sexual activity was not as important to them as it was before their injury. A study of 15 women with spinal cord injuries found that the use of fantasy resulted in increased sexual pleasure (Berard: 1989). Those women who did not fantasize and in fact had abandoned their sexuality were less likely to have accepted their disability.

Women who have recently experienced spinal cord injuries may find it difficult to resume a sexual relationship or to begin a relationship with a new partner. As in all sexual relationships, good communication facilitates the process. When women feel comfortable talking to their partners, they can discuss their preferences and ways to experiment with new positions and techniques that were not used prior to their injuries.

Fear of bladder and bowel incontinence during sexual relations may result in avoidance of sexual relations. It is not necessary for women with indwelling catheters to remove them during sex, although some may feel more comfortable doing so. Women who are on regular bowel programs are advised to empty their bowel prior to sexual activity to avoid the fear of bowel accidents.

In cases where attendant care is necessary (usually in cases of quadriplegia), the partner often becomes a caretaker by default when financial resources do not permit hiring an attendant. Yet some women have difficulty conceiving of a sexual relationship if their partners assist with their bladder and bowel control (Friedman Becker: 1978). For other women, their partner's role as personal attendant is viewed as normal and does not create problems in the area of sexual relationships. In those instances where a paid personal attendant helps the woman with her bodily functions, it is often necessary for the attendant to prepare and position the woman for sexual intercourse. Since being involved in another person's intimate affairs may cause embarrassment or tension, an open discussion between the attendant and the partners may prove useful.

FAMILY PLANNING, PREGNANCY, AND CHILDREARING

Spinal cord injury does not affect a woman's fertility, and in most instances women can deliver their babies vaginally. Recent medical literature suggests that most women with spinal cord injuries who do become pregnant have excellent outcomes for both themselves and their babies (Baker and Cardenas: 1996). One study found that over a third of women with spinal cord injuries decided not to have children, and most of these women attributed their decision to the injury (Charlifue et al.: 1992). Methods of contraception are somewhat limited for women with spinal cord injuries. Limited mobility often prevents the placement of a diaphragm. Birth control pills may increase the risk of blood clots, which are already a higher probability for women with spinal cord injuries because of their inactivity. A relatively new form of birth control, Norplant, prevents ovulation for up to five years through the implantation of synthetic progesterone. However, removal of the implant has caused both scarring and pain in some women. Some women who have definitely decided not to have children choose to have tubal ligation, a procedure that is sometimes reversible.

During pregnancy, women may be more likely to develop decubitus ulcers due to weight gain, and transfers become more difficult toward the latter part of the term. Most women with spinal cord injuries do develop urinary tract infections during pregnancy, in part due to indwelling catheters. Avoidance of indwelling catheters and the use of antibiotics may help to prevent this condition (Baker and Cardenas: 1996).

The ability of women to feel labor pains varies with the level of the lesion. It has been recommended that women with spinal cord injuries be hospitalized in preparation for labor as soon as they begin to dilate or at the thirty-second week of gestation (Patel: 1989). A condition called autonomic dysreflexia, in which drastic changes occur in body temperature, heart rate, and blood pressure, is a risk during labor for women with spinal cord injuries, especially when the lesion is at or above the sixth thoracic vertebra (Broderson: 1990; Patel: 1989). For this reason, women with spinal cord injuries should plan to deliver their babies in hospitals equipped to handle this type of condition.

Women with spinal cord injury experience more complications during pregnancy and in labor and delivery than they did prior to their injury (Jackson and Wadley: 1999). Urinary tract infections during pregnancy are more common, as are low birth weight babies.

The types of devices and adaptations that are necessary for child care vary with the woman's level of injury, her home environment, and the amount of assistance she receives from family members and paid help. Possible options include special trays that attach to wheelchairs and hold the baby (Through the Looking Glass: 1994). Some women with spinal cord injuries find that the most difficult stage of childrearing is when babies begin to crawl around the home; at this stage it is difficult for the mothers to control their child's actions and safety. However, as children learn to respond to verbal requests made by the mother, the mother's lack of mobility becomes less of an issue. Women with spinal cord injuries have noted that their children quickly learn to respond to verbal discipline, become involved in household activities, and develop independence at an early age. As children begin socializing with other children in the neighborhood and at school, they must learn to respond effectively to the taunts they may receive about their mother's condition. Some mothers may wish to visit their children's classrooms to explain their condition and to answer questions, so that classmates feel more comfortable and interested in visiting their home.

PSYCHOLOGICAL ASPECTS OF SPINAL CORD INJURY

Women who experience spinal cord injuries as a result of an accident have had no preparation for life with a disability. In an instant, they have changed from able-bodied women into women with severe physical limitations. The suddenness with which this change takes place and the wide ranging effects are likely to cause great anguish to the individuals as well as to their families and friends. The more severe the disability, the greater the loss of independence. For many women, these circumstances result in a loss of self-esteem and fear of re-entering the larger community. It is essential that women with spinal cord injuries receive help with their emotional adjustment, either in the form of individual or group counseling from professionals or through self-help groups and role models of other women who have adjusted successfully to spinal cord injuries.

Because most of the individuals who experience spinal cord injuries are males, women who have spinal cord injuries may feel isolated and without accessible peers or role models. They may need counseling about sexual functioning; the physical aspects of becoming pregnant; handling the responsibilities of motherhood; and other physical and emotional issues that affect women. Yet it is not unusual for a woman to be the only woman in a spinal cord injury unit or one of two or three women (Scheele: 1988). In a vulnerable position to start with, these women may feel uncomfortable asking the questions they have when health care and rehabilitation professionals have oriented their services to men. Obtaining support and counsel from other women who have successfully adjusted to spinal cord injuries may prove enormously beneficial to recently injured women.

Because the traditional role of women in society has been characterized by passivity and dependence, some observers have suggested that women will adjust better to spinal cord injuries than men, as spinal cord injuries result in dependence. The women's movement has expanded women's roles in society, with more women independent both financially and emotionally. Further, some women have experienced spinal cord injuries as a result of their physical activity, such as horseback riding or other athletic activities. These women must adjust to great modifications in everyday activities and loss of leisure activities that they valued.

A spinal cord injury often places a woman's self-esteem in jeopardy, as she questions her physical attractiveness and her ability to attract and satisfy a sexual partner. While men are judged based on power, wealth, career, and physical accomplishments, women are judged largely on their physical attractiveness.

In contrast to observers such as Trieschmann (1988) who contend that adjustment to spinal cord injury is more difficult for women than for men, Bonwich (1985) has noted that for some women with spinal cord injuries, self-esteem actually increases through what she refers to as "role gain." No longer tied down to traditional norms of what is expected of women, these women master a new role which is quite demanding and live up to their potential.

Some women may never lose the anger or guilt they feel about the circumstances surrounding the accident that caused the injury. In the period immediately following the accident, they may feel overpowered by the many professionals who have begun to make major decisions for them. In some cases, the accidents that caused spinal cord injuries involved the use of alcohol while driving. These factors, combined with inadequate counseling and the inability to cope with the effects of the injury, result in the abuse of alcohol or other drugs. Bozzacco (1990) suggests that all patients in rehabilitation units be assessed for their vulnerability to alcohol and drug abuse. She further suggests that patients become part of the decision-making process for their own treatment and rehabilitation plans as soon as possible and that alcohol and drug treatment programs be an integral part of rehabilitation.

The need to modify the activities of everyday living as well as the physical environment; the impairment of sexual functioning; and the financial aspects of living with spinal cord injury may place a great strain on marital and family relationships. In some instances, partners of women with spinal cord injuries deny that she has experienced an enormous change and that there will be a great impact on their relationship and roles (Friedman Becker: 1978). For this reason, it is helpful to include the partner in the rehabilitation and counseling program.

Although Young and his associates (1982) found that four years after spinal cord injury, nearly the same percentage of females (17%) and males (16%) were divorced, another study found that females were far more likely than males to be divorced. Brown and Giesy (1986) found that 40.6% of the females they studied were divorced/separated/widowed versus 15.9% for the general population. For males the corresponding figures were 18.1% and 9.3%. Similarly, they found that 26.1% of the females were married compared to 65.2% in the general population; 40.7% of the males were married compared to 62.6% in the general population. These findings suggest that spinal cord injuries are more difficult for women than for men in the area of marital relationships, despite the fact that women's sexual functioning is less impaired than men's.

Those women with severe injuries often require the help of a paid personal attendant to perform tasks related to bodily function and cleanliness. Although there is some government assistance to pay for these services, in most instances family members carry out these tasks. It is also common for family members in this role to feel both overburdened and guilty. Social workers should work with the family to arrange for respite care, financial assistance, and other services that can remediate the situation.

PROFESSIONAL SERVICE PROVIDERS

In most cases, the physician in charge serves as the case manager or coordinator for the person with spinal cord injury. The physician in charge may be a *physiatrist* (a specialist trained in rehabilitation medicine); an *orthopedist* (a specialist in treatment of the skeletal system); or a *neurologist* or *neurosurgeon* (a specialist in disorders of the nervous system). All of these physicians receive training in treatment of spinal cord injuries. Also on the multidisciplinary team are *urologists*, who specialize in treatment of kidneys, the bladder, the ureter, and the urethra. *Obstetricians/gynecologists* may also play an important role in helping women with spinal cord injuries to deliver their babies safely; these physicians should work in conjunction with others who specialize in the care and rehabilitation of women with spinal cord injuries.

Rehabilitation nurses receive special training available at schools throughout the country and may receive certification in this specialty after working two years in a rehabilitation setting (Livingston: 1991). They work closely with the physicians and in some instances may serve as case managers. In inpatient settings, rehabilitation nurses work with other health care and rehabilitation professionals to develop and implement medical and rehabilitation plans for patients. They may act as consultants in planning for discharge and may evaluate the individual's home to ensure that appropriate environmental modifications have been made. They are often the professionals in charge of following up on the individual's needs after discharge from the rehabilitation unit.

Orthotists specialize in the design of braces and other devices that help with mobility, support, and prevention of further injury. They also fit the devices and provide instruction in their use. *Rehabilitation engineers* specialize in the design of devices that enable people with disabilities to function at their maximum level of independence. Their research includes the development of robotic devices and other computer driven devices that serve as substitutes for the function that was lost as a result of injury or disease. In some instances, they may consult on individual cases to adapt wheelchairs or other devices for specific needs.

Physical therapists design exercise programs to maintain and strengthen residual motor function. They also teach transfer skills to and from the bed and how to use wheelchairs and orthotic devices, such as canes, braces, and walkers. They develop exercise programs to help individuals who are able to use crutches to build up muscles in their arms and shoulders.

Occupational therapists teach individuals with spinal cord injuries how to re-learn the activities of daily living. Included are eating, dressing, grooming, and the use of "high tech" devices that contribute to increased independence. After assessing a woman's home environment, family situation, and place of employment, the occupational therapist may recommend specially adapted equipment or environmental adaptations to enable her to continue with her activities.

Psychologists provide individual or group counseling to women with spinal cord injuries and to their family members. They may also provide special help in the area of sexual functioning. *Social workers* help to make the arrangements that enable individuals to return to the community. They also ensure that individuals with spinal cord injuries receive the financial assistance that they are entitled to. Social workers may also provide counseling for women and their families. In some instances, social workers or psychologists have developed group counseling or peer support groups especially for women with spinal cord injuries.

The federal government sponsors the "Model System of Spinal Cord Injury Care" in order to provide coordinated comprehensive care and to conduct research related to spinal cord injury. Administered by the National Institute on Disability and Rehabilitation Research (NIDRR) within the U.S. Department of Education, this model system encompasses treatment centers throughout the country that participate in research and data collection efforts. The major components of the model system include early access to care through rapid, effective transportation; an acute level one traumatology setting; a comprehensive acute rehabilitation program; psychosocial and vocational services that begin in the hospital and continue through discharge; and follow-up to ascertain that medical and psychosocial needs are met once patients have re-entered the community (Thomas: 1990).

Another federal system that offers special treatment for individuals with spinal cord injuries is the U.S. Department of Veteran Affairs (VA). Spinal cord units are located at a number of VA Medical Centers across the country. The National Institutes of Health also funds model research and treatment centers at several facilities.

Many rehabilitation hospitals have spinal cord injury units. The advantage of obtaining treatment in these settings is that other patients serve as role models. Some acute care hospitals also have rehabilitation units, and outpatient rehabilitation facilities offer services to people with spinal cord injuries. Many long term care facilities provide services to people with spinal cord injuries. The Commission on Accreditation of Rehabilitation Facilities (CARF) provides accreditation for these facilities (see "ORGANIZATIONS" section below). Independent living centers offer services and referrals to people with spinal cord injuries.

MODIFICATIONS IN EVERYDAY LIVING

In order to remain living in the community, many women with spinal cord injuries, especially those with quadriplegia, require personal attendant services (PAS). Personal attendant services may be provided by a family member, friend, or a person specifically employed for this purpose. Personal attendants perform tasks that enable the woman with a disability to carry out her activities of daily living. A variety of health care providers have observed that personal attendant services contribute not only to the improved physical well-being of individuals with spinal cord injuries and other disabilities, but also to their mental well-being (Nosek: 1993).

The major source of funding for the employment of personal attendants is Medicaid, although other state, local, and federal programs as well as private agencies often contribute. According to Nosek (1991), most individuals with disabilities rely on family members and have had no contacts with formal programs that provide personal attendants. Furthermore, those interested in hiring personal attendants often have difficulty locating qualified individuals. A number of consumer advocacy organizations, research organizations, and the federal government are paying increased attention to the issue of personal attendant services in an attempt to improve the provision of these services.

Most women with spinal cord injuries use wheelchairs for mobility. A wide variety of wheelchairs designed for different purposes and different types of impairments is available. Women whose injury prohibits them from using manually operated wheelchairs may use battery operated wheelchairs. Sip-and-puff controls, tubes that respond to changes in pressure caused by inhaling and exhaling, enable women with more severe impairments to control the movement of their wheelchairs. Wheelchairs are prescribed by physicians and must accommodate the individual's body size, disability, and functional criteria.

Women whose injury has resulted in paraplegia sometimes use braces as an alternative to wheelchairs. One study (Heinemann et al.: 1987) found that only about a quarter of those individuals who had braces continued to use them, while the remainder preferred using wheelchairs. Those who continued to use braces were less likely to have complete lesions than those who stopped using braces. Those who stopped using braces said that they preferred wheelchairs because they were safer, required less energy, and were less likely to fail.

Modification of the home environment requires the installation of ramps; wide doorways with doors that open easily; the removal of thresholds between rooms; and lifts for getting from one level of the home to the other. The kitchen should have accessible appliances, shelves, and working space, and pulls and knobs that are easy to use. The bathroom should be large enough to accommodate a wheelchair; the sink must be at an accessible level; showers should be the roll-in variety with grab bars; and toilets should have grab bars.

Many individuals with paraplegia learn to drive with special hand controls, locks, steering mechanisms, and wheelchair lifts. Major automobile manufacturers offer special programs to purchase adapted vehicles with special controls and wheelchair lifts (see Chapter 2, "TRAVEL AND TRANSPORTATION ORGANIZATIONS").

Special feeding devices are available for individuals with quadriplegia who do not have the use of their upper limbs. Devices may be installed that move people around a room. Use of these specialized devices increases the independence of individuals with quadriplegia.

References

Baker, Emily R. and Diana D. Cardenas
1996   "Pregnancy in Spinal Cord Injured Women" Archives of Physical Medicine and Rehabilitation 77(May):501-507

Berard, E.J. J.
1989   "The Sexuality of Spinal Cord Injured Women: Physiology and Pathophysiology. A Review" Paraplegia 27: 99-112

Bonwich, Emily
1985   "Sex Role Attitudes and Role Reorganization in Spinal Cord Injured Women" pp. 56-67 in Mary Jo Deegan and Nancy A. Brooks (eds.) Women and Disability: The Double Handicap New Brunswick, NJ: Transaction Inc.

Bozzacco, Victoria
1990   "Vulnerability and Alcohol and Substance Abuse in Spinal Cord Injury" Rehabilitation Nursing 15(Mar.-Apr.):2:70-72

Broderson, Linda C.
1990   "Motherhood, Pregnancy, and Spinal Cord Injury" Paraplegia News 44(October):110:50-53

Brown, Julia S. and Barbara Giesy
1986   "Marital Status of Persons with Spinal Cord Injury" Social Science and Medicine 23:3:313-322

Charlifue, S.W. et al.
1992   "Sexual Issues of Women With Spinal Cord Injuries" Paraplegia 30:192-199

DeVivo, Michael J. et al.
1992   "Trends in Spinal Cord Injury Demographics and Treatment Outcomes Between 1973 and 1986" Archives of Physical Medicine and Rehabilitation 73(May):424-430
1987   "Seven-Year Survival Following Spinal Cord Injury" Archives of Neurology 44(August):872-875

Finn, Robert
1998   "Neural Prosthetics Come of Age as Research Continues" FES Update 8:1(Summer):1-2

Friedman Becker, Elle
1978   Female Sexuality Following Spinal Cord Injury Bloomington, IL: Accent Special Publications

Granat, M. et al.
1992   "The Use of Functional Electrical Stimulation to Assist Gait in Patients with Incomplete Spinal Cord Injury" Disability and Rehabilitation 14(2):93-97

Heinemann, Allen W. et al.
1987   "Mobility for Persons with Spinal Cord Injury: An Evaluation of Two Systems" Archives of Physical Medicine and Rehabilitation 68(February):90-93

Hingley, Audrey T.
1993   "Spinal Cord Injuries: Science Meets Challenge" FDA Consumer July/August

Huelskamp, Scott
1998   "When Will We Cure Spinal Cord Injuries?" Advance for Occupational Therapy Practitioners 14:31(August 3):28-30

Jackson, Amie B. and Virginia Wadley
1999   "A Multicenter Study of Women's Self-Reported Reproductive Health after Spinal Cord Injury" Archives of Physical Medicine and Rehabilitation 80:11(November):1420-1428

Livingston, Carolyn
1991   "Opportunities in Rehabilitation Nursing" American Journal of Nursing 91 (Feb.):2:90-95

Menter, Robert R.
1990   "Aging and Spinal Cord Injury: Implications for Existing Model Systems and Future Federal, State, and Local Health Care Policy" pp. 72-80 in David F. Apple and Lesley M. Hudson (eds.) Spinal Cord Injury: The Model Atlanta, GA: Spinal Cord Injury Care System, Sheperd Center for the Treatment of Spinal Injuries

National Spinal Cord Injury Statistical Center
2001   Spinal Cord Injury: Facts and Figures at a Glance University of Alabama at Birmingham May

Nosek, Margaret A.
1993   "Personal Assistance: Its Effect on the Long-Term Health of a Rehabilitation Hospital Population" Archives of Physical Medicine and Rehabilitation 74(February):127-132
1991   "Personal Assistance Services: A Review of the Literature and Analysis of Policy Implications" Journal of Disability Policy Studies 2(2):1-17

Ochs, G.
1999   "Intrathecal Baclofen for Severe Spasticity in Spinal Cord Injury Patients: Pharmacokinetics, Indication and Results" Journal of Spinal Cord Medicine 22:Supplement(Fall):35

Patel, Madhura V.
1989   "Management of Pregnancy in Women with Spinal Cord Injury and

Petrofsky, Jerrold S.
1992   "Functional Electrical Stimulation, a Two-Year Study," Journal of Rehabilitation July/August/September 29-34

Rintala, Diana H. et al.
1992   "Social Support and the Well-Being of Persons with Spinal Cord Injury Living in the Community" Rehabilitation Psychology 37:3:155-163
Romeo, Allen J., Richard Wanlass, and Silverio Arenas
1993   "A Profile of Psychosexual Function in Males Following Spinal Cord Injury" Sexuality and Disability 11:4(Winter):269-276
Scheele, Chris
1988   "Women and SCI Part 1: Overview" Paraplegia News March 41-43
Sipski, Marca L. and Craig J. Alexander
1993   "Sexual Activities, Response and Satisfaction in Women Pre- and Post-Spinal Cord Injury" Archives of Physical Medicine and Rehabilitation 74(October):1025-1029
Sipski, Marca L., Craig J. Alexander, and Raymond C. Rosen
1995   "Orgasm in Women with Spinal Cord Injuries: A Laboratory-Based Assessment" Archives of Physical Medicine and Rehabilitation 76(December):1097-1102Thomas, J. Paul
1990   "Definition of the Model System of Spinal Cord Injury Care" pp. 7-9 in David F. Apple and Lesley M. Hudson (eds.) Spinal Cord Injury: The Model Atlanta, GA: Spinal Cord Injury Care System, Sheperd Center for the Treatment of Spinal Injuries
Through the Looking Glass
1994   "Adaptive Parenting Equipment" Parenting with a Disability 3(January)1:4
Trieschmann, Roberta B.
1988   Spinal Cord Injuries: Psychological, Social and Vocational Rehabilitation New York, NY: Demos Publications
White, Mary Joe et al.
1994   "A Comparison of the Sexual Concerns of Men and Women with Spinal Cord Injuries" Rehabilitation Nursing Research Summer
Young, John S. et al.
1982   Spinal Cord Injury Statistics Phoenix, AZ: Good Samaritan Medical Center

ORGANIZATIONS

American Association of Spinal Cord Injury Nurses (AASCIN)
75-20 Astoria Boulevard
Jackson Heights, NY 11370
(718) 803-3782   FAX (718) 803-0414   e-mail: info@epva.org
www.epva.org/AASCIN/aascin.html

A professional membership organization that encourages and improves nursing care of individuals with spinal cord injuries and sponsors research. Membership, $100.00, includes quarterly journal, "SCI Nursing."

American Paraplegia Society
75-20 Astoria Boulevard
Jackson Heights, NY 11370
(718) 803-3782   FAX (718) 803-0414
www.epva.org/APS.html

A professional membership organization for physicians, scientists, and allied health care professionals. Holds an annual meeting for the presentation of scientific research related to spinal cord injury. Membership, $100.00, includes quarterly journal, "Journal of Spinal Cord Medicine."

American Spinal Injury Association (ASIA)
2020 Peachtree Road, NW
Atlanta, GA 30309
(404) 355-9772   FAX (404) 355-1826
e-mail: patduncan@shepherd.org   www.asia-spinalinjury.org

A professional membership organization for health care providers dedicated to improving the care of individuals with spinal cord injury through research, education, and development of regional spinal cord injury care systems. Holds an annual meeting with presentation of scientific papers. Membership ranges from $100.00 to $350.00 depending on category; includes quarterly journal, "Journal of Spinal Cord Medicine" and online newsletter "ASIA Bulletin."

Center for Research on Women with Disabilities (CROWD)
Baylor College of Medicine
3440 Richmond Avenue, Suite B
Houston, TX 77046
(800) 442-7693   (713) 960-0505 (V/TTY)   FAX (713) 961-3555
e-mail: crowd@bcm.tmc.edu   www.bcm.tmc.edu/crowd

A federally funded center that conducts research and develops and distributes information on the health and independence of women with disabilities. Research areas include sexuality, relationships, general health, reproductive health, and abuse. Executive Summary of a four year "National Study on Women with Disabilities" is available on the web site in English and Spanish. Entire report available on the web site in English. Free

Christopher Reeve Paralysis Foundation (CRPF)
formerly the American Paralysis Association
500 Morris Avenue
Springfield, NJ 07081
(800) 225-0292   (800) 539-7309 (Spanish)   (973) 379-2690
FAX (973) 912-9433   www.christopherreeve.org

Supports research to find a cure for paralysis caused by spinal cord injury and other central nervous system disorders. Publishes "Walking Tomorrow," a newsletter about the organization's activities, and "Progress in Research," a newsletter about spinal cord injury research. Free. Also available on the web site. Operates the Christopher and Dana Reeve Resource Center, a federally funded center that enables consumers to obtain information on a wide variety of topics related to spinal cord injury. [636 Morris Turnpike, Suite 3A, Short Hills, NJ 07078; (800) 539-7309; (973) 467-8270; FAX (973) 467-9845; www.paralysis.org]

Commission on Accreditation of Rehabilitation Facilities (CARF)
4891 East Grant Road
Tucson, AZ 85712
(520) 325-1044 (V/TTy)   FAX (520) 318-1129
e-mail: webmaster@carf.org   www.carf.org

Conducts site evaluations and accredits organizations that provide rehabilitation, pain management, adult day services, and assisted living. Provides a free list of accredited organizations in a specific

Craig Hospital Aging with Spinal Cord Injury
Craig Hospital
3425 South Clarkson
Englewood, CO 80110
(303) 789-8202   FAX (303) 789-8441
www.craighospital.org (click on "Research")

Formerly a federally funded center that studied the physiological and psychological effects of changes brought about by aging on individuals with spinal cord injuries, the center has been following individuals with spinal cord injuries for 25 years. Produces consumer information brochures in English and Spanish. Many publications are available on the web site.

Foundation for Spinal Cord Injury Prevention, Care and Cure (FSCIPCC)
19223 Roscommon
Harper Woods, MI 48225
(800) 342-0330   FAX (313) 245-0812   e-mail: info@fscip.org
www.fscip.org

This organization supports research to find a cure for spinal cord injury, provides referrals to individuals and their families, and conducts a program to prevent spinal cord injury. The web site provides information about spinal cord injury as well as links to other resources.

Functional Electrical Stimulation Information Center
11000 Cedar Avenue, Suite 230
Cleveland, OH 44106-3052
(800) 666-2353   (216) 231-3257 (V/TTY)   FAX (216) 231-3258
e-mail: fesinfo@po.cwru.edu   feswww.fes.cwru.edu

Affiliated with the Rehabilitation Engineering Center at Case Western Reserve University, the center provides information to consumers and professionals about functional electrical stimulation. Publishes quarterly newsletter, "FES Update," in standard print and on audiocassette; free. Free publications list.

MEDLINEplus: Spinal Cord Injuries
www.nlm.nih.gov/medlineplus/spinalcordinjuries.html

This web site provides links to sites for general information about spinal cord injuries, symptoms and diagnosis, treatment, specific aspects of the condition, clinical trials, statistics, organizations, and research. Includes interactive tutorials on spinal cord injuries and myelograms. Some information is available in Spanish. Provides links to MEDLINE research articles and related MEDLINEplus pages.

Miami Project to Cure Paralysis
PO Box 016960 (R-48)
Miami, FL 33101-6960
(305) 243-6001   FAX (305) 243-6017
Automated Information Line: (800) 782-6387
e-mail: mpinfo@miamiproj.med.miami.edu
www.miamiproject.miami.edu

A research organization dedicated to finding a cure for spinal cord injury.

National Association for Continence (NAFC)
PO Box 8310
Spartanburg, SC 29305-8310
(800) 252-3337   (864) 579-7900   FAX (864) 579-7902
e-mail: lloudon@nafc.org   www.nafc.org

An information clearinghouse for consumers, family members, and medical professionals. Answers individual questions if self-addressed stamped envelope is enclosed with letter. Membership, $25.00, includes a quarterly newsletter, "Quality Care," a "Resource Guide: Products and Services for Continence" (nonmembers, $10.00), and a continence resource service. Free publications list. Also available on the web site.

National Institute on Disability and Rehabilitation Research (NIDRR)
U.S. Department of Education
400 Maryland Avenue, SW
Washington, DC 20202
(202) 205-8134   (202) 205-8198 (TTY)
FAX (202) 205-8515   www.ed.gov/offices/OSERS/NIDRR

A federal agency that supports research into various aspects of disability and rehabilitation, including demographic analyses, social science research, and the development of assistive devices. Supports a nationwide system of model spinal cord injury centers.

National Spinal Cord Injury Association (NSCIA)
6701 Democracy Boulevard, Suite 300-9
Bethesda, MD 20817
(800) 962-9629   (301) 588-6959   FAX (301) 588-9414
e-mail: nscia2@aol.com   www.spinalcord.org

A membership organization with chapters throughout the U.S. Disseminates information to people with spinal cord injuries and to their families; provides counseling; and advocates for the removal of barriers to independent living. Participates in the development of standards of care for regional spinal cord injury care. NSCIA will perform a customized database search; call for details. Holds annual meeting and educational seminars. Membership, individuals with a spinal cord injury or family members, free; professionals, $100.00; hospitals and other organizations, fees vary by size of budget; includes quarterly magazine, "SCI Life" (nonmember price, $30.00) and fact sheets.

Paralyzed Veterans of America (PVA)
801 18th Street, NW
Washington, DC 20006
(800) 424-8200   (800) 795-4327 (TTY)   (202) 872-1300
FAX (202) 785-4452   e-mail: info@pva.org   www.pva.org

A membership organization for veterans with spinal cord injury. Advocates and lobbies for the rights of paralyzed veterans and sponsors research. Membership fees are set by state chapters. The national office refers callers to the nearest chapter. The PVA Spinal Cord Injury Education and Training Foundation accepts applications to fund continuing education, post-professional specialty training, and patient/client and family education. The PVA Spinal Cord Research Foundation accepts applications to fund basic and clinical research, the design of assistive devices, and conferences that foster interaction among scientists and health care providers. Some publications are available on the web site.

Rehabilitation Research and Training Center on Secondary Complications of Spinal Cord Injury
Spain Rehabilitation Center
University of Alabama at Birmingham
619 19th Street South, SRC 529
Birmingham, AL 35249
(205) 934-3283   (205) 934-4642 (TTY)   FAX (205) 975-4691
e-mail: rtc@uab.edu   ww.spinalcord.uab.edu

A federally funded center that conducts research and holds educational conferences for people with spinal cord injuries, their families, and professionals. The National Spinal Cord Injury Statistical Center collects data from spinal cord injury centers throughout the country. Produces a variety of audio-visual materials and books for professional care providers and consumers, as well as a series of information sheets. A list of articles documenting some of the center's research findings is also available. Information sheets are available on the web site. Newsletter, "Pushin' On," is published twice a year; free. Also available on the web site. Also administers the Spinal Cord Injury Information Network, a database available on the web site.

284

Rolli-Moden Designs
12225 World Trade Drive, Suite T
San Diego, CA 92128
(800) 707-2395   (858) 676-1825   FAX (858) 676-0820
e-mail: rm@roli-moden.com   www.rolli-moden.com

Sells dress and casual clothing and accessories designed for wheelchair users. Free catalogue.

Simon Foundation for Continence
PO Box 815
Wilmette, IL 60091
(800) 237-4666   (847) 864-3913   FAX (847) 864-9758
www.simonfoundation.org

Provides information and assistance to people who are incontinent. Organizes self-help groups.
Membership, individuals, $15.00; professionals, $35.00; includes quarterly newsletter, "The
Informer." Also available on the web site.

Substance Abuse Resources & Disability Issues (SARDI)
Rehabilitation Research and Training Center on Drugs and Disability
School of Medicine, Wright State University
PO Box 927
Dayton, OH 45401-0927
(937) 775-1484   FAX (937) 775-1495
e-mail: feedback@sardi.wright.edu www.med.wright.edu/citar/sardi

A federally funded research center that investigates the relationship between drug use and disabilities.
Free newsletter.

Vocational Rehabilitation and Employment
Veterans Benefits Administration
U.S. Department of Veterans Affairs (VA)
(800) 827-1000 (connects with regional office)
www.vba.va.gov

Provides education and rehabilitation assistance and independent living services to veterans with service
related disabilities through offices located in every state as well as regional centers, medical centers,
and insurance centers. Medical services are provided at VA Medical Centers, Outpatient Clinics,
Domiciliaries, and Nursing Homes. VONAPP (VA Online Application) enables veterans to apply for
benefits on the Internet.

WheelchairNet
www.wheelchairnet.org e-mail: wheelchairnet@shrs.pitt.edu

This virtual community of wheelchair users enables participants to exchange information about
wheelchair technology. The web site includes resources, articles, and a discussion area.

PUBLICATIONS AND TAPES

Accessible Home Design: Architectural Solutions for the Wheelchair User
PVA Distribution Center
PO Box 753
Waldorf, MD 20604-0753
(888) 860-7244   (301) 932-7834
FAX (301) 843-0159   www.pva.org

Focusing on areas such as kitchens, bathrooms, and multiple levels, this book provides practical and economical designs to make homes accessible. $22.95

Adaptive Baby Care Equipment: Guidelines, Prototypes, and Resources (book)
Adaptive Baby Care Equipment (videotape)
Through the Looking Glass
2198 Sixth Street, Suite 100
Berkeley, CA 94710-2204
(800) 644-2666   (800) 804-1616 (TTY)   (510) 848-1112
FAX (510) 848-4445   e-mail: TLG@lookingglass.org
www.lookingglass.org

This combination of book and videotape describes products to help parents with disabilities diaper, bathe, dress, feed, and play with their babies. The 12 minute videotape demonstrates successful techniques used by parents with disabilities. $79.00

Aging with Spinal Cord Injury
by Gale G. Whiteneck et al. (eds.)
Demos Medical Publishing
386 Park Avenue South, Suite 201
New York, NY 10016
(800) 532-8663   (212) 683-0072   FAX (212) 683-0118
e-mail: info@demospub.com   www.demosmedpub.com

This book is an anthology of articles by a multidisciplinary group of experts in the field of spinal cord injury. Topics include research in the area of aging with a spinal cord injury, physiological and psychological aspects of the aging process, and societal perspectives. $99.95   Orders made on the Demos web site receive a 15% discount.

Alcohol, Disabilities, and Rehabilitation
by Susan A. Storti
Thomson Learning, Florence, KY

This book discusses alcohol abuse in individuals with disabilities and chronic conditions. Includes treatment and rehabilitation strategies. Out of print

The Body's Memory
by Jean Stewart
St. Martin's Press, New York, NY

A novel about a woman who must use a wheelchair as a result of surgery for removal of a tumor on her hip. Her story depicts relationships with colleagues, friends, and lovers, as well as her emotional upheaval and redefinition of her values. Out of print.

Brain and Spinal Cord Tumors: Hope through Research
National Institute of Neurological Disorders and Stroke (NINDS)
PO Box 5801
Bethesda, MD 20824
(800) 352-9424   FAX (301) 402-2186
e-mail: braininfo@ninds.nh.gov   www.ninds.nih.gov

This booklet describes the disorder, diagnosis and treatment as well as current research on the disease. Free

A Consumer's Guide to Home
Adaptive Environments Center
374 Congress Street, Suite 301
Boston, MA 02210
(800) 949-4232 (V/TTY)   (617) 695-1225 (V/TTY)   FAX (617) 482-8099
e-mail: adaptive@adaptenv.org www.adaptenv.org

A workbook that enables people with mobility impairments to plan the modifications necessary to adapt their homes. Includes descriptions of widening doorways, lowering countertops, etc. $12.00

Depression: What You Should Know
PVA Distribution Center
PO Box 753
Waldorf, MD 20604-0753
(888) 860-7244   (301) 932-7834
FAX (301) 843-0159   www.pva.org

This consumer guide discusses the signs of depression, its causes, and treatments. $9.95. Also available on the web site.

Enabling Romance: A Guide to Love, Sex, and Relationships for the Disabled
by Ken Kroll and Erica Levy Klein
No Limits Communications
PO Box 220
Horsham, PA 19044
(888) 850-0344   (215) 675-9133
FAX (215) 675-9376   e-mail: kim@leonardmedia.com
www.newmobility.com

Written by a man who has a disability and his wife who does not, this book provides examples of how people with a variety of disabilities have established fulfilling relationships. $15.95

Family Adjustment in Spinal Cord Injury
Spain Rehabilitation Center
University of Alabama at Birmingham
619 19th Street South, SRC 529
Birmingham, AL 35249
(205) 934-3283   (205) 934-4642 (TTY)   FAX (205) 975-4691
e-mail: rtc@uab.edu   www.spinalcord.uab.edu

This booklet provides support for family members, discussing their concerns and feelings. $2.00.
Also available on the web site.

Family Challenges: Parenting with a Disability
Aquarius Health Care Videos
266 Main Street, Suite 33B
Medfield, MA 02052
(888) 440-2963   FAX (508) 242-9854
e-mail: orders@aquariusproductions.com
www.aquariusproductions.com

In this videotape, the children and spouses of individuals with disabilities describe their relationships
and coping strategies. 25 minutes. $195.00

A Guide to Wheelchair Selection: How to Use the ANSI/RESNA Wheelchair Standards to Buy a
Wheelchair
PVA Distribution Center
PO Box 753
Waldorf, MD 20604-0753
(888) 860-7244   (301) 932-7834
FAX (301) 843-0159   www.pva.org

This book enables wheelchair users to make informed choices when purchasing a wheelchair. $19.95

The Impossible Takes a Little Longer
Instructional Support Services
Indiana University
601 East Kirkwood
Bloomington, IN 47405-1223
(800) 552-8620   (812) 855-2103   FAX (812) 855-8404
e-mail: issmedia@indiana.edu   www.indiana.edu/ ~ mediares

A videotape that profiles four women with disabilities, including one with paraplegia and one with
quadriplegia, who have been successful in demanding professions and in family life. Deals with how
they have handled insensitive reactions from the public. 46 minutes. Purchase, $170.00; rental,
$35.00.

Journal of Rehabilitation Research and Development (JRRD)
Scientific and Technical Publications Section
Rehabilitation Research and Development Service
103 South Gay Street, 5th Floor
Baltimore, MD 21202
(410) 962-1800   FAX (410) 962-9670   e-mail: pubs@vard.org
www.vard.org

A quarterly publication of scientific and engineering articles related to spinal cord injury, prosthetics and orthotics, sensory aids, and gerontology. Also available on the web site. Free

Journal of Spinal Cord Medicine
EPVA Subscription Services
PO Box 465
Hanover, PA 17331
(717) 633-3535   FAX (717) 633-8920
e-mail: pubsvc@tsp-sheridan.com

A quarterly journal that covers a wide range of topics related to treatment of the physical and psychological aspects of spinal cord injury. Free, with membership in the American Paraplegia Society or the American Spinal Cord Injury Association. Nonmembers, individuals, $120.00; institutions, $220.00.

Key Changes
Fanlight Productions
4196 Washington Street, Suite 2
Boston, MA 02131
(800) 937-4113   (617) 469-4999   FAX (617) 469-3379
e-mail: fanlight@fanlight.com   www.fanlight.com

This videotape portrays Lisa Thorson, a vocalist who experienced a spinal cord injury and continues performing in her chosen profession. 28 minutes. $149.00

Living with Spinal Cord Injury
by Barry Corbett
Fanlight Productions
4196 Washington Street, Suite 2
Boston, MA 02131
(800) 937-4113   (617) 469-4999   FAX (617) 469-3379
e-mail: fanlight@fanlight.com   www.fanlight.com

A series of three videotapes produced by an individual who has experienced spinal cord injury himself. "Changes" is about the consequences of spinal cord injury and the process of rehabilitation. "Outside" emphasizes the life-long aspect of rehabilitation for people with spinal cord injuries. "Survivors" interviews 23 men and women who have lived at least 24 years with spinal cord injuries. Single videotape, $99.00; series, $210.00.

Managing Incontinence
by Cheryle B. Gartley (ed.)
Simon Foundation for Continence
PO Box 835
Wilmette, IL 60091
(800) 237-4666   (847) 864-3913
FAX (847) 864-9758   e-mail: simoninfo@simonfoundation.org
www.simonfoundation.org

This book provides medical advice, information on products, interviews with individuals who are incontinent, and advice on sexuality. $12.95

Managing Personal Assistants: A Consumer Guide
PVA Distribution Center
PO Box 753
Waldorf, MD 20604-0753
(888) 860-7244   (301) 932-7834
FAX (301) 843-0159   www.pva.org

This book provides information on recruiting, hiring, training, retaining and firing personal care assistants. Describes funding sources and discusses tax issues. $15.95

Mother To Be: A Guide to Pregnancy and Birth for Women with Disabilities
by Judith Rogers and Molleen Matsumura
Demos Medical Publishing
386 Park Avenue South, Suite 201
New York, NY 10016
(800) 532-8663   (212) 683-0072
FAX (212) 683-0118   e-mail: info@demospub.com   www.demosmedpub.com

This book describes the pregnancy and childbirth experiences of 36 women with a wide variety of disabilities including spinal cord injury. Suggests practical solutions for the special concerns of women with disabilities during pregnancy and those of their partners, families, and health care providers. Includes a glossary and a bibliography. $29.95 Orders made on the Demos web site receive a 15% discount.

National Database of Educational Resources on Spinal Cord Injury
The Institute for Rehabilitation and Research (TIRR)
Division of Education, B 107
1333 Moursund
Houston, TX 77030
(800) 732-8124   FAX (713) 797-5982
e-mail: hullt@tirr.tmc.edu   www.tirr.org

This database of publications, audiocassettes, and videotapes covers topics such as environmental modifications and accessibility, adaptive equipment and aids, vocational management, and recreation and leisure. Available online at www.MSCISDisseminationCenter.org.   Entries that are specific to women or men are marked. Includes section on "Sexuality, Marriage, Pregnancy, and Fertility." For those without Internet access, TIRR will take phone requests for two searches at no charge.

New Mobility
Leonard and Associates
PO Box 220
Horsham, PA 19044
(888) 850-0344   (215) 675-9133   FAX (215) 675-9376
e-mail: kim@leonardmedia.com   www.newmobility.com

A monthly magazine with articles and resource information on spinal cord injury and other conditions that cause mobility impairments. $27.95

Nothing is Impossible: Reflections on a New Life
by Christopher Reeve
Random House, Order Department
400 Hahn Road
Westminster, MD 21157
(800) 733-3000   www.randomhouse.com

The author of this book, a well known actor who became quadriplegic after a horseback riding accident, writes about important decisions he made after his accident. These include choosing life over suicide, intensive physical rehabilitation, advocacy for himself and others, his faith, and establishing the Christopher and Dana Reeve Resource Center (see "ORGANIZATIONS" section above). Also includes a discussion of the stem cell research debate. $19.95

Not Just Surviving… Women Living a Full Life with a Spinal Cord Injury
Library Services
Magee Rehabilitation
6 Franklin Plaza
Philadelphia, PA 19102-1177
(800) 966-2433, ask for library   (215) 587-3423   FAX (215) 568-3533
e-mail: library@mageerehab.org   www.mageerehab.org

In this video, four women who have lived with a spinal cord injury for 15 to 30 years share their experiences and insights. They discuss such topics as rehabilitation, working, sexuality, menstruation, pregnancy, parenting, and menopause as well as advice on daily living. 40 minutes. Free

PN/Paraplegia News
2111 East Highland Avenue, Suite 180
Phoenix, AZ 85016
(888) 888-2201   (602) 224-0500, ext. 319   FAX (602) 224-0507
e-mail: pvapub@aol.com   www.pva.org

A monthly magazine sponsored by the Paralyzed Veterans of America. Features information for paralyzed veterans and civilians, articles about everyday living, new legislation, employment, and research. Twelve issues, $23.00

<u>Positive Images</u>
Women Make Movies
462 Broadway, Suite 500 WS
New York, NY 10013
(212) 925-0606, ext. 360   FAX (212) 925-2052   e-mail: info@wmm.com
www.wmm.com

In this videotape, three women with disabilities, including one with a spinal cord injury, discuss their lives at home, at work, and with family and friends. 58 minutes. Purchase, $295.00; rental for three days, $75.00.

<u>Pressure Ulcers: What You Should Know</u>
PVA Distribution Center
PO Box 753
Waldorf, MD 20604-0753
(888) 860-7244   (301) 932-7834
FAX (301) 843-0159   www.pva.org

This book describes various strategies to prevent pressure ulcers. $9.95

<u>Preventing Secondary Medical Complications: A Guide for Personal Assistants Working for People</u>
<u>with Spinal Cord Injuries</u>
Spain Rehabilitation Center
University of Alabama at Birmingham
619 19th Street South-SRC 529
Birmingham, AL 35249-7330
(205) 934-3283   (205) 934-4642 (TTY)
FAX (205) 975-4691   www.spinalcord.uab.edu

This booklet provides training in the proper health care for people with spinal cord injury with an emphasis on daily routines. $3.00 Also available on the web site at no charge.

<u>Reproductive Health for Women with Spinal Cord Injury</u>
<u>Part I: The Gynecological Exam</u>
<u>Part II: Pregnancy and Delivery</u>
Spain Rehabilitation Center
University of Alabama at Birmingham
619 19th Street South-SRC 529
Birmingham, AL 35249-7330
(205) 934-3283   (205) 934-4642 (TTY)
FAX (205) 975-4691   www.spinalcord.uab.edu

Part I of this videotape set discusses the issues women with spinal cord injuries must face when having a gynecological examination. 30 minutes. Part II discusses the experiences of women with spinal cord injury who have delivered babies as well as suggestions for medical management. 32 minutes. Single videotape, $15.00; both videotapes, $25.00.

Reproductive Issues for Persons with Physical Disabilities
by Florence P. Haseltie, Sandra S. Cole, and David B. Gray (eds.)
Brookes Publishing Company, Baltimore, MD

This book provides an overview of sexuality, disability, and reproductive issues across the lifespan for individuals with disabilities including spinal cord injuries. Includes academic articles as well as personal narratives written by individuals with disabilities. Out of print.

SCI Info Sheets
Spain Rehabilitation Center
University of Alabama at Birmingham
619 19th Street South-SRC 529
Birmingham, AL 35249-7330
(205) 934-3283   (205) 934-4642 (TTY)
FAX (205) 975-4691   www.spinalcord.uab.edu

This series of information sheets includes titles such as "Pregnancy & Women with SCI," which discusses planning for pregnancy, prenatal care, labor and delivery; "Pregnancy & Women with SCI," which discusses pregnancy, labor and delivery issues as they related to health professionals; and "Sexuality for Women with Spinal Cord Injury," which discusses women's sexual adjustment and issues with sexual partners. Also available by FAX and on the web site. Free

Sexual Function in People with Disability and Chronic Illness: A Health Professional's Guide
by Marca Sipski and Craig Alexander
Aspen Publishers, Inc.
PO Box 990
Frederick, MD 21705-9782
(800) 234-1660   www.aspenpub.com

This book discusses many types of disability, their effects on sexuality, reproductive concerns, and treatment methods, as well as providing basic information on general sexual function and dysfunction. Includes spinal cord injury, diabetes, multiple sclerosis, arthritis and other connective tissue diseases, and heart disease. Offers a discussion of the issues faced by the partner of an individual with a disability. $59.00

Sexuality After Spinal Cord Injury: Answers to Your Questions
by Stanley H. Ducharme and Kathleen M. Gill
Brookes Publishing Company
PO Box 10624
Baltimore, MD 21285-0624
(800) 638-3775   FAX (410) 337-8539
e-mail: custserv@pbrookespublishing.com
www.pbrookespublishing.com

This book discusses both physical and emotional aspects of sexuality, including anatomy, self-esteem, sexually transmitted diseases, fertility, and parenting after spinal cord injury. $24.95

<u>Sexuality Reborn</u>
New Jersey Spinal Cord Injury System
Kessler Institute for Rehabilitation
1199 Pleasant Valley Way
West Orange, NJ 07052
(800) 435-8866   FAX (973) 324-3527
e-mail: rehab@kessler-rehab.com   www.kessler-rehab.com

A videotape in which four couples discuss the physical and emotional aspects of spinal cord injury upon their sex lives, including dating, bowel and bladder control, sexual response, and sexual activity. 48 minutes. $47.95

<u>Spinal Cord Injury: A Guide for Living</u>
by Sara Palmer, Kay Harris Krieger, and Jeffrey Palmer
Johns Hopkins University Press
2715 North Charles Street
Baltimore, MD 21218
(800) 537-5487   (410) 516-6900   FAX (410) 516-6968
e-mail: all inside@jhupbooks.com   www.press.jhup.edu

This book, written for both survivors and their family members, describes the process from the time of injury through hospitalization, rehabilitation, and adjustment to life in the community. Hardcover, $49.95; softcover, $16.95.

<u>Spinal Cord Injury Desk Reference</u>
by Terry L. Blackwell et al.
Demos Medical Publishing
386 Park Avenue South, Suite 201
New York, NY 10016
(800) 532-8663   (212) 683-0072
FAX (212) 683-0118   e-mail: info@demospub.com   www.demosmedpub.com

This reference book provides basic concepts about spinal cord injury, including epidemiology, potential complications, long term management, and life care planning guidelines. $59.95. Orders made on the Demos web site receive a 15% discount.

<u>Spinal Network</u>
by Barry Corbet et al. (eds.)
No Limits Communications
PO Box 220
Horsham, PA 19044
(888) 850-0344   (215) 675-9133   FAX (215) 675-9376
e-mail: kim@leonardmedia.com   www.newmobility.com

This book describes the medical aspects of spinal cord injury and the wide variety of effects on functioning. Presents biographical accounts of people who have lived with spinal cord injuries. Discusses issues of everyday living, including sex, relationships, and parenting, recreation and sports, travel, and legal and financial concerns. $39.95

Sports 'N Spokes
2111 East Highland Avenue, Suite 180
Phoenix, AZ 85016-9611
(888) 888-2201   (602) 224-0500, ext. 319   FAX (602) 224-0507
e-mail: pvapub@aol.com   www.sportsnspokes.com

A bimonthly magazine that features articles about sports activities for people who use wheelchairs. Eight issues, $21.00.

Wheelchairs: Your Options and Rights Guide to Obtaining Wheelchairs from the Department of Veterans Affairs
PVA Distribution Center
PO Box 753
Waldorf, MD 20604-0753
(888) 860-7244   (301) 932-7834
FAX (301) 843-0159   www.pva.org

This booklet provides information on eligibility criteria, lists the types of wheelchairs available, and describes DVA procedures. Available in English and Spanish. Free

Yes, You Can! A Guide to Self-Care for Persons with Spinal Cord Injury
PVA Distribution Center
PO Box 753
Waldorf, MD 20604-0753
(888) 860-7244   (301) 932-7834
FAX (301) 843-0159   www.pva.org

This manual offers practical information and resources, including chapters on substance abuse, pain, exercise, alternative medicine, equipment, and staying healthy. $15.00

INDEX OF ORGANIZATIONS

This index contains only those organizations listed under sections titled "ORGANIZATIONS." These organizations may also be listed as vendors of publications, tapes, and other products.

A Woman's Guide to Coping with Disability

This <u>unique</u> book addresses the special needs of women with disabilities and chronic conditions, such as social relationships, sexual functioning, pregnancy, childrearing, caregiving, and employment. Special attention is paid to ways in which women can advocate for their rights with the health care and rehabilitation systems. Written for women in all age categories, the book has chapters on the disabilities that are most prevalent in women or likely to affect the roles and physical functions unique to women. Included are arthritis, coronary heart disease, diabetes, epilepsy, lupus, multiple sclerosis, osteoporosis, and spinal cord injury. Each chapter also includes information about the condition, professional service providers, and psychological aspects plus descriptions of organizations, publications and tapes, and special assistive devices. This new edition includes e-mail addresses and Internet resources. Fourth edition, 2003   ISBN 0-929718-33-x $46.95

"...this excellent, empowering resource belongs in all collections." Library Journal
"...crucial information women need to be informed, empowered, and in control of their lives. Excellent self-help information... Highly recommended for public and academic libraries." Choice
"...a marvelous publication...will help women feel more in control of their lives." A nurse who became disabled

A Man's Guide to Coping with Disability

Written to fill the void in the literature regarding the special needs of men with disabilities, this book includes information about men's responses to disability, with a special emphasis on the values men place on independence, occupational achievement, and physical activity. Information on finding local services, self-help groups, laws that affect men with disabilities, sports and recreation, and employment is applicable to men with any type of disability or chronic condition. The disabilities that are most prevalent in men or that affect men's special roles in society are included. Chapters on coronary heart disease, diabetes, HIV/AIDS, multiple sclerosis, prostate conditions, spinal cord injury, and stroke include information about the disease or condition, psychological aspects, sexual functioning, where to find services, environmental adaptations, and annotated entries of organizations, publications and tapes, and resources for assistive devices. Includes e-mail addresses and Internet resources. Third edition, 2003   ISBN 0-929718-32-1 $46.95

"a unique reference source." Library Journal
"a unique purchase for public libraries" Booklist/Reference Books Bulletin

The Mental Health Resource Guide

In a landmark report, the Surgeon General declared that mental illness is a public health problem of great magnitude. Both the public and professionals hold misconceptions about mental disorders. **The Mental Health Resource Guide** is designed to help individuals who are mentally ill, family members, and health professionals understand the issues surrounding mental2 illness and find services. The book provides information on treatments in current use, medications, laws that affect individuals who are mentally ill, employment, and the needs of children and elders. The effects of mental illness on the family and caregivers are also addressed. Chapters on anxiety disorders, eating disorders, depressive disorders, schizophrenia, and substance abuse include information about causes, diagnoses, and treatments as well as descriptions of helpful organizations, publications, and tapes. Includes Internet resources. 2001   ISBN 0-929718-27-5 $39.95

"...authoritative...will add value to professional health care collections and public libraries." Library Journal
"packed full of information...in crisp, clear prose."   American Reference Books Annual

Resources for Elders with Disabilities

This book meets the needs of elders, family members, and other caregivers. Published in LARGE PRINT, the book provides information about rehabilitation, laws that affect elders with disabilities, and self-help groups. Each chapter that deals with a specific disability or condition has information on the causes and treatments for the condition; psychological aspects; professional service providers; where to find services; environmental adaptations; and suggestions for making everyday living safer and easier. Chapters on hearing loss, vision loss, Parkinson's disease, stroke, arthritis, osteoporosis, and diabetes also provide information on organizations, publications and tapes, and assistive devices. Throughout the book are practical suggestions to prevent accidents and to facilitate interactions with family members, friends, and service providers. Plus information about aids for everyday living, older workers, falls, travel, and housing.

Fifth edition, 2002 ISBN 0-929718-31-3 $51.95

"...especially useful for older readers. Highly recommended." Library Journal
"...a valuable, well organized, easy-to-read reference source." American Reference Books Annual
"...a handy ready-reference..." Reference Books Bulletin/Booklist

Meeting the Needs of Employees with Disabilities

This resource guide provides the information people with disabilities need to retain or obtain employment. Includes information on government programs and laws such as the Americans with Disabilities Act, training programs, supported employment, transition from school to work, assistive technology, and environmental adaptations. Chapters on hearing and speech impairments, mobility impairments, and visual impairment and blindness describe organizations, adaptive equipment, and services plus suggestions for a safe and friendly workplace. Case vignettes describing accommodations for employees with disabilities are a new special feature.

Third edition, 1999 ISBN 0-929718-25-9 $44.95

"...solid and up-to-date." **Journal of Career Planning and Employment**
"...an excellent directory for those challenged with incorporating persons with disabilities in the workplace..."
AAOHN Journal
"...recommended for public libraries and for academic libraries..."
Choice
"...a timely resource." **American Reference Books Annual**

Making Wise Medical Decisions
How to Get the Information You Need

This book includes a **wealth** of information about where to go and what to read in order to make wise medical decisions. The book describes a plan for obtaining relevant health information and evaluating health facilities. Each chapter includes extensive resources to help the reader get started. Chapters include Getting the Information You Need to Make Wise Medical Decisions; Locating Appropriate Health Care; Asking the Right Questions about Medical Tests and Procedures; Protecting Yourself in the Hospital; Medical Benefits and Legal Rights; Drugs; Protecting the Health of Children Who Are Ill; Special Issues Facing Elders; People with Chronic Illnesses and Disabilities and the Health Care System; Making Decisions about Current Medical Controversies; Terminal Illness. Includes e-mail addresses and Internet resources.

Second edition, 2001 ISBN 0-929718-29-1 $42.95

"It is refreshing to find a source of practical information on how to proceed through the medical maze...this should become a popular resource in any public, hospital, or academic library's consumer health collection." **Library Journal**
"The book is very, very good. There's so much information, it's definitely worth buying." **A health care consumer**

Living with Low Vision
A Resource Guide for People with Sight Loss

This LARGE PRINT comprehensive guide helps people with sight loss locate the services, products, and publications that they need to keep reading, working, and enjoying life. Chapters for children and elders plus information on self-help groups, how to keep reading and working with vision loss, and making everyday living easier. Information on laws that affect people with vision loss, including the ADA, and high tech equipment that promotes independence and employment. Includes e-mail addresses and Internet resources.

Sixth edition, 2001   ISBN 0-929718-28-3 $46.95

*"No other complete resource guide exists..an **invaluable** tool for locating services.. for public and academic libraries."*
Library Journal
*"...a **good reference** for libraries serving visually handicapped individuals."*
American Reference Books Annual
*"...a **very useful resource** for patients experiencing vision loss."   Archives of Ophthalmology*
*"...a **superb resource**...should be made available in waiting rooms or patient education areas..."*
American Journal of Ophthalmology
*"This volume is a **treasure chest** of concise, useful information."   OT Week*

Resources for People with Disabilities and Chronic Conditions

This comprehensive resource guide has chapters on spinal cord injury, low back pain, diabetes, multiple sclerosis, hearing and speech impairments, vision impairment and blindness, and epilepsy. Each chapter includes information about the disease or condition; psychological aspects of the condition; professional service providers; environmental adaptations; assistive devices; and descriptions of organizations, publications, and products. Chapters on rehabilitation services, independent living, self-help, laws that affect people with disabilities (including the ADA), and making everyday living easier. Special information for children is also included. Includes e-mail addresses and Internet resources. Fifth edition 2002   ISBN 0-929718-30-5 $54.95

*"...**wide coverage** and **excellent** organization of this encyclopedic guide...recommended..."   Choice*
*"**Sensitive** to the tremendous variety of needs and circumstances of living with a disability."   American Libraries*
*"...an **excellent resource** for consumers and professionals..."   Journal of the American Paraplegia Society*
"...improves the chances of library patrons finding needed services..."   American Reference Books Annual

LARGE PRINT PUBLICATIONS

*Designed for distribution by professionals to people
with disabilities and chronic conditions*

These publications serve as self-help guides for people with disabilities and chronic conditions. They include information on the condition, rehabilitation services, products, and resources that contribute to independence. Titles include **After a Stroke, Living with Diabetes, Living with Low Vision,** and **How to Keep Reading with Vision Loss.**

8 1/2" by 11"   Printed in **18 point bold type** on ivory paper with black ink for maximum contrast.

*"These are **exciting products**. We look forward to doing business with you again."   A rehabilitation professional*

Providing Services for People with Vision Loss:
A Multidisciplinary Perspective

This book discusses how various professionals can work together to provide coordinated care. Chapters include Vision Loss: A Patient's Perspective; Vision Loss: An Ophthalmologist's Perspective; Operating a Low Vision Aids Service; The Need for Coordinated Care; Making Referrals for Rehabilitation Services; Mental Health Services: The Missing Link; Self-Help Groups for People with Sight Loss. Also available on cassette.

1989   ISBN 0-929718-02-X $19.95

"*...an excellent guide for professionals.*"   **Journal of Rehabilitation**

Meeting the Needs of People with Vision Loss:
A Multidisciplinary Perspective

This book discusses how to provide appropriate information and how to serve special populations. Chapters include What People with Vision Loss Need to Know; Information and Referral Services; The Role of the Family in the Adjustment to Blindness or Visual Impairment; Diabetes and Vision Loss; Special Needs of Children and Adolescents; Older Adults with Vision and Hearing Losses; Providing Services to Visually Impaired Elders in Long Term Care Facilities. Also available on cassette.

1991   ISBN 0-929718-07-0 $24.95

"*...of use to anyone concerned with improving service delivery to the growing population of people who are visually impaired.*"   **American Journal of Occupational Therapy**

RESOURCES for REHABILITATION

22 Bonad Road • Winchester, MA 01890
(781) 368-9094 • FAX (781) 368-9096 • e-mail: orders@rfr.org • www.rfr.org
Our Federal Employer Identification Number is 04-2975-007

NAME _____

ORGANIZATION _____

ADDRESS _____

PHONE _____

[ ] Check or signed institutional purchase order enclosed for full amount of order. Purchase orders accepted from government agencies, hospitals, and universities only.

[ ] Mastercard/VISA Card number: _____

Signature: _____Expiration date: _____

ALL ORDERS OF $100.00 OR LESS MUST BE PREPAID.

TITLE	QUANTITY	PRICE	TOTAL
A Woman's Guide to Coping with Disability	____ X	$46.95	____
A Man's Guide to Coping with Disability	____ X	46.95	____
The Mental Health Resource Guide	____ X	39.95	____
Meeting the Needs of Employees with Disabilities	____ X	44.95	____
Resources for People with Disabilities and Chronic Conditions	____ X	56.95	____
Resources for Elders with Disabilities	____ X	51.95	____
Making Wise Medical Decisions	____ X	42.95	____
Living with Low Vision: A Resource Guide	____ X	46.95	____
Providing Services for People with Vision Loss	____ X	19.95	____
Meeting the Needs of People with Vision Loss	____ X	24.95	____

MINIMUM PURCHASE OF 25 COPIES PER TITLE FOR THE FOLLOWING PUBLICATIONS

Call for discount on purchases of 100 or more copies of any single title.

Living with diabetes	____ X	1.50	____
Living with low vision	____ X	2.00	____
How to keep reading with vision loss	____ X	1.75	____
Living with age-related macular degeneration	____ X	1.25	____
Aids for everyday living with vision loss	____ X	1.25	____
Living with diabetic retinopathy	____ X	1.75	____
High tech aids for people with vision loss	____ X	1.75	____
	SUB-TOTAL		____

SHIPPING & HANDLING: $50.00 or less, add $5.00; $50.01 to 100.00, add $8.00;
add $4.00 for each additional $100.00 or fraction of $100.00. Alaska, Hawaii,
U.S. territories, and Canada, add $3.00 to shipping and handling charges
Foreign orders must be prepaid in U.S. currency. Please write for shipping charges.

SHIPPING/HANDLING _____

Prices are subject to change.   TOTAL $_____